REVERSED

RE VERSED

FROM CULTURALLY WOKE TO BIBLICALLY AWAKE

JAMES L. GARLOW

Assisted by FRANK KACER

WELL VERSED
PUBLISHING

Unless otherwise noted, all Scripture quotations are taken from the Holy Bible, New International Version®, NIV®. Copyright © 1973, 1978, 1984, 2011 by Biblica, Inc. TM Used by permission of Zondervan. All rights reserved worldwide. www.zondervan.com. The "NIV" and "New International Version" are trademarks registered in the United States Patent and Trademark Office by Biblica, Inc.™.

Scripture quotations marked (ESV) are from The Holy Bible, English Standard Version® (ESV®), Copyright © 2001 by Crossway, a publishing ministry of Good News Publishers. All rights reserved. ESV Text Edition: 2011

Scripture quotations marked (KJV) are from the King James Version of the Bible.

Scripture quotations taken from the New American Standard Bible®, Copyright © 1960, 1962, 1963, 1968, 1971, 1972, 1973, 1975, 1977, 1995 by The Lockman Foundation. Used by permission. (www.Lockman.org)

Scripture taken from the New King James Version®. Copyright © 1982 by Thomas Nelson. Used by permission. All rights reserved.

Library of Congress Control Number: 2024908858

First e-book edition, 2024: eISBN: 979-8-9906599-1-9
Originally published in paperback, 2024: ISBN 979-8-9906599-0-2

Published in the United States by Well Versed Publishing

Manufactured in the United States of America

CONTENTS

PART II: A BIBLICAL RESPONSE TO LAWLESSNESS

PART III: A BIBLICAL RESPONSE TO CONSTITUTIONAL
ISSUES AND THE LOSS OF FREEDOMS

PART IV: A BIBLICAL RESPONSE TO TECHNOLOGY

For more support materials on this book, go to

www.WellVersedWorld.org/ReVERSED-book

or

www.ReVERSED.org

to help in organizing and hosting small group Bible studies.

There is one short video for each chapter,
along with discussion questions.

In the back of this book, see information regarding the Well Versed
Children's Coloring Book,
with pages that match the chapter numbers of this book.

In addition, in the back of this book, see information regarding the Well
Versed Students book for Junior Highers, with pages that match the
chapter numbers of this book.

For general information on the ministry of
Dr. Jim Garlow,
Rosemary Schindler Garlow
and Well Versed,
go to

www.WellVersedWorld.org

Dedicated to

WINIFRED JANE MCHENRY GARLOW
My loving mother
May 27, 1921 – September 14, 2023

Who graduated to heaven while this book was being written;
who lived a life of 102 years, 3 months, 17 days, 22 hours and 28 minutes;
living by herself the last 25 years and taking care of herself till her final few days.

A lover of God and His Word, memorizing Scripture;
highly politically informed and savvy and articulate on the issues;
vocally/musically talented;
a strong and proud wife of a Kansas farmer;
skilled, even in old age, in tech, computers and typing.

Who had been not only a godly, loving, truly remarkable mother,
but who was the excellent proofreader of all I wrote for more than six decades,
from my years in high school (1961-1965) until her passing in 2023;
who would have proofread this, but is instead now enjoying heaven,
being with Jesus.

And to my godly father, James Burtis Garlow who has been there 25 years.

PART I

A BIBLICAL UNDERSTANDING OF THE SHAKING

How the erosion of Judeo-Christian values and the rise of relativism in the United States has ushered in a "brave new world" of cultural chaos, cancel culture, wokeism, and corrosive secularism.

*When the foundations are being destroyed,
what can the righteous do?*

PSALM 11:3

THE PRESUPPOSITIONS

This is an introduction to the "why" and the "what" of this book. However, I was concerned that if I called this chapter an Introduction, you might skip it. So, I chose to call it Chapter 1. It is a prerequisite in order to understand the rest of the book.

Some presuppositions of this book were covered in my previous book *Well Versed: Biblical Answers to Today's Tough Issues* (Regnery, 2016). In the time since its release, my goals for writing have not changed. In fact, my convictions have only deepened, and my reasons for writing are even more urgent: Bible-believing Christians admit that they do not speak out on political or cultural issues *because they do not know how to support their beliefs from a biblical basis.* Instead, they remain silent on critical issues like marriage, racism, and transgenderism because they feel uninformed and ill-equipped to defend their beliefs.

Of course, the title of this follow-up book plays off of the title *Well Versed*. Woke culture has taken our nation by force, and has even seeped into God's church. It's up to us, Bible-believing Christians, to apply the holy verses of Scripture to help us "*Reverse*" the corrosive and destructive trends we are now witnessing inside and outside the church.

In response, my goal is to offer a practical, biblical guide for the twenty-first century Christian that informs and prepares them to tackle the important issues of the day and engage with those around them in a loving, scripturally based manner. By tackling the five dozen topics in this book, my goal is to help us move from being culturally woke to biblically awake. That means examining the key cultural and social "hot buttons" in our nation in order to:

1. filter each of these critical, timely issues through the Word of God in order to reveal His truth; and then ...
2. separate the holy from the evil, and the good from the bad; so that ...
3. like the men of Issachar, we will be able to understand the times and know what we should do. (1 Chroinicles 12:32)

So, in that sense, this book is a follow-up companion to *Well Versed*. Also, space does not allow me to do an in-depth review of the key themes of the first book, even though they form the foundation, or the presuppositions, for this book. Instead, I am listing them briefly here to establish a plumb line from which the following chapters can be measured:

- There is a God, and you and I are not Him.
- God has inspired a book, called the Bible, that contains *the* answers to *all of life—including government.*
- God is the one who envisioned government.[1]

---

1 For more information, see James L. Garlow, *Well Versed: Biblical Answers to Today's Tough Issues*, Salem Books, an imprint of Regnery Publishing, 2016, page 6.

- The actual intended purpose of government is the focal point of this book.[2] The Bible has profound applications to present-day governmental issues.
- I have been involved in government, as much as I could, since I was nine years old.[3]
- My *ultimate* hope is not and has never been in a political party—Democrat, Republican or Independent—or in a political candidate. My hope is *ultimately* in the God of Abraham, Isaac, and Jacob, specifically in the Second Person of the Trinity, Jesus, who will someday arrive on planet earth to fully establish His government; that is, His kingdom (which is partially established now in the heart of his followers). In the meantime, temporal, earthly government is led by less-than-perfect political parties and elected officials. While I do recognize the lordship of Jesus as ultimate, I also, however, participate in the process of temporal government, desiring to help lift up and encourage biblical values. I do that by supporting parties or candidates that are as close to the scriptural standard as possible. Admittedly, that can be a challenging and complex process.

2 Ibid, pages 31-32.
3 https://www.wellversedworld.org/blog/search/Today%20is%20my%20birthday

- In the world in which much of the Old Testament[4] was written, Israel was a theocracy. America is not.[5] Although this book draws heavily from the Old Testament, this book does not call for a theocracy.[6]
- The book affirms the correct historical and biblical understanding of the separation of church and state.[7]
- This book follows standard hermeneutical (i.e., science of interpretation) principles when using Bible verses.[8]
- In that same vein, it is extremely important to note that some of the many Scripture references listed in this book may not necessarily mention the topic at hand, but rather that they contain principles, obviously biblical principles, which apply to the theme being discussed.
- The most often quoted, but totally misunderstood Bible verse is: "Judge not."[9] It is taken totally out of context. Most people who quote this—apparently the only Bible verse they know—are, in fact, *judging.* The verse means, in effect, "don't judge *unless* you are willing to be judged by the same—that is, biblical—standard." I am.

---

4 I so regret that our Bible is divided into an "Old" Testament, and a "New" Testament. "Old" usually refers to something that is of little value anymore, so we ignore it or discard it. Consequently, we focus only on that which is "new." The "old" and "new" adjectives are unfortunate. The 66 books of the Bible form one continuous narrative. While some of the covenants of the book of Genesis do have ending points (those made with Adam, Noah, and Moses), the Abrahamic Covenant, in contrast, continues through David, which continues through Jesus. It is one continuous "whole." Without the Old Testament, the New Testament makes no sense. Without the New Testament, the Old Testament lacks completion. Furthermore, the Old Testament, which I prefer to call the Tanakh as the Jews do, is filled beyond measure with applicable and profoundly relevant passages for today, if—and this is a big "if"—one understands the Hebrew idioms. The Tanakh is extremely important to understanding biblical governance and is relevant even in a Constitutional Republic.
5 Ibid, page X.
6 For further explanation, see Ibid, page 32.
7 For more, see Ibid, page 7.
8 Ibid, pages 12-14.
9 See explanation of this at Ibid, page 14.

- The notion that there is "your truth" vs. "my truth" is illogical. There can only be *one* Truth.[10]
- In that same vein, we hunger for truth. We long for truth. Conspiracy theories do exist and should be avoided. However, be extremely discerning. In recent years, much of what the Left has labeled "conspiracy theories" have proven to be true. Some of the people who have been defamed as "conspiracy theorists" have, in time, been proven to be truth tellers. In that same vein, beware of Big Tech's "fact checkers." They don't seem to know how or where to actually "check," thus they have no "facts."
- Evil exists.[11]
- Biblical anthropology reveals the accurate understanding of the nature of humankind.[12]

- The author is not an expert on all the many topics covered in this book. Therefore, a team of about fifteen people—please see the Acknowledgements page for the remarkable team who assisted in the writing of this book—was formed to help do research and writing. The author does not even pretend to be an expert on all these topics, or even fully understand them. Thus, he has relied on those who could help lay out the basic issues, and then Frank Kacer (assisting author) and the author attempted to understand the overarching biblical principles that are relevant.
- Finally, I long for revival, and the reformation that follows. I agree with the one who said, "It's all about Jesus. Spirit of God, move across the earth with revival. I think

10 See comments at Ibid, page 15.
11 Note Ibid, page 33-34.
12 See more thoughts on this at Ibid, page 34.

purity is where is starts, hunger is where it grows, and longing is how it stays."[13]

Assuming that one has read and understands these principles upon which this book is founded, let's proceed to see how to be biblically awake in an environment where culturally woke thinking has become normative, and even exalted.

---

13 https://www.thethirdheaventraveler.com/2023/02/ephesians-511-and-have-no-fellowship.html

CHAPTER 2

THE INSANITY OF BEING CULTURALLY WOKE

I n her response to Joe Biden's State of the Union address on February 7, 2023, Arkansas Republican Governor Sarah Huckabee Sanders clarified that "the dividing line in America is no longer between right and left—it's between normal or crazy."[1]

What you are about to read focuses on "normal" vs. "crazy," and sanity vs. insanity. As a result, the goal is to illuminate the difference between healthy and unhealthy.

What does crazy, insanity, or unhealthy look like? Here are just a few examples:

- Who would think that you could be fired for calling a man a man?
- Who would think that a top-rated female swimmer named Riley Gaines would tie with a man in a woman's

---

1 https://www.npr.org/2023/02/08/1155329293/sarah-huckabee-sanders-republican-response-state-of-the-union-2023

competition but not get a trophy? Riley tied with a man named Will Thomas, who had changed his name to "Lia," claiming to be a woman. The fifth-place trophy went to the man-who-called-himself-a-woman, rather than to a female—Riley Gaines—even though this was a woman's competition. Riley left with no trophy—she was told that they only had one award and that "Lia" came first in the alphabet.[2]

- Who would think that a state legislature would discuss not merely killing a baby in the womb but legalizing the killing of the baby up to 28 days after it was born?[3]

- Who would think that mentally ill and addicted people can put a tent on the sidewalk in front of your house, shoot up with drugs,[4] and leave human excrement there daily?[5]

- Who would have thought that young children would be exposed to books on pornography and homosexual activities in their school libraries?[6]

- Who would have thought we would have a president who has serious difficulties forming sentences,[7] or an elected US Senator who can't communicate effectively?[8]

- Who would have thought that when a garage attendant was attacked by a thief with a gun, and in the confrontation, the attendant was able to get the bad guy's gun,

2 https://nypost.com/2022/04/04/swimmer-who-tied-lia-thomas-taken-aback-in-trophy-handling/
3 https://www.lifenews.com/2022/03/24/california-bill-would-allow-killing-babies-in-infanticide-up-to-28-days-after-birth/
4 https://www.city-journal.org/article/san-francisco-hostage-to-the-homeless
5 https://www.msn.com/en-us/news/us/san-francisco-controller-report-finds-nearly-half-of-commercial-sidewalks-had-feces-in-2022/ar-AA1bEjML
6 https://www.washingtonpost.com/education/2023/05/23/lgbtq-book-ban-challengers/
7 https://www.youtube.com/watch?v=neCj_m2p4i0
8 https://townhall.com/tipsheet/saraharnold/2023/05/17/fetterman-struggles-to-speak-at-hearing-n2623388

who was shot in the struggle, that the good guy would be charged with a crime?[9]

- Who would have thought that if you shoplift items worth under $1,000, you will likely face no consequences?[10]

- Who would have thought that college campuses, once the champions of "free speech," would now stifle any voice that does not reflect the Marxist-leftist agenda?[11]

- Who would have ever thought that an American presidential administration would support the mutilation and chemical castration of children[12] and say that children do not belong to their parents?[13] But that's *exactly* what the Biden Administration has done.

- Who would have ever thought that a woman nominated to the Supreme Court of the United States would not be able to define what a woman is, even though she had been nominated to that position, in part because she is a woman?[14]

Tragically, examples such as these could fill this entire book. There is an irrationality that has been released on major segments of our culture.

---

9 https://nypost.com/2023/04/01/nyc-garage-worker-charged-with-attempted-murder-for-shooting-thief/

10 https://www.michaelsmithnews.com/2020/03/no-penalty-for-shoplifting-under-950-in-california-heres-the-brazen-result.html

11 https://www.nationalreview.com/2021/01/the-new-strategy-to-suppress-conservative-voices-on-campus/

12 https://pjmedia.com/news-and-politics/tyler-o-neil/2021/05/10/biden-hhs-lays-the-groundwork-for-the-chemical-castration-of-children-n1445710

13 https://news.yahoo.com/biden-claims-school-children-don-234147454.html?guccounter=1&guce_referrer=aHR0cHM6Ly9kdWNrZHVja2dvLmNvbS8&guce_referrer_sig=AQAAAK2VB4JQSRv2N4ERc7KW1hEbp4I26U7Njs9KCxZ1G4Chjm Nj4drjTofsOgYkiJXzzEKV4NCIkthwPdwM4KSwoASZBJlJl754XmC_qqm7MQBFp-bLy0oXp4J7MNiOMMFqBD7dwCNAno1p0xjgtC6yvljOTLwJR1iDqatxExTtM_-lk) (https://news.yahoo.com/biden-claims-school-children-don-234147454.html

14 https://nypost.com/2022/03/24/supreme-court-nominee-judge-ketanji-brown-wont-define-woman/

GASLIGHTING

In 1938 a play was written titled *Gas Light*, later remade into the 1940 British film *Gaslight*, and was remade in 1944 into an American film by the same name. The play portrays a manipulative husband who secretly brightens and dims the indoor gas-powered lighting. When the wife observes that the lighting is changing, the husband insists the light has not been altered, and thus she is losing her mind. His goal for "gaslighting"—although the term is not mentioned in the film—is to cause her to think she is going insane.

Thus, the term "gaslighting" was born, which means "to psychologically manipulate (a person) usually over an extended time so that the victim questions the validity of their own thoughts, perception of reality, or memories, and experiences confusion, loss of confidence and self-esteem, and doubts concerning their own emotional or mental stability."[15]

Having said that, let's cut to the chase: You are being gaslighted. If you call a man a man—who wants to be called something else (e.g., a woman)—you are condemned. If you say that only women can have babies, you are ridiculed. If you say that climate change is both unscientific and manipulative, you are scoffed at. If you say that looting laws should be enforced, you are called a racist. In fact, for almost any healthy view of how society should work, you are called either a homophobe, or transphobe, or Islamophobe, or xenophobe, or some "phobe." This is gaslighting. Withstand it. Resist. Push back. Do not fold. If you embrace the transcendent, eternal principles of the Bible, you are not the one who is insane. Those who oppose it are. You are sane. They are not.

GOOD VS. EVIL

The dividing line is no longer Republican vs. Democrat. It is no longer Right vs. Left. It is, however, Right vs. Wrong. It is light vs. darkness. It is good vs. evil. It is the ways of God vs. the ways of Satan.

15 https://www.merriam-webster.com/dictionary/gaslight

We are in a battle between biblical truth—which is transcendent, that is, above the shifting of culture, a timeless, eternal truth—and moral chaos and insanity. At its core, this is a battle between desperately needed holiness and the depravity of sin.

Conservative commentator Michael Savage stated that "liberalism is a mental disorder" and even wrote a book by that title. I don't agree because true "liberalism" is supposed to mean, in part, an open mind, and a willingness to consider other opinions (e.g., a Liberal Arts education). It's important to point out that leftism is different than liberalism. Whereas liberalism is supposed to be truly tolerant of other views, leftism is characterized by intolerance and totalitarianism. Leftism is most assuredly a sign of a mental disorder. Or perhaps we need to add it is evidence of sin.

Throughout the book I use the word totalitarianism, which *Merriam-Webster* defines as: "of or relating to centralized control by an autocratic leader or hierarchy: Authoritarian, Dictatorial; especially: Despotic." The secondary definition adds: "of or relating to a political regime based on subordination of the individual to the state and strict control of all aspects of the life and productive capacity of the nation especially by coercive measures (such as censorship and terrorism)."

When we hear the word totalitarianism, we may think of nations and regimes such as North Korea, Russia, or Venezuela. But I'd also challenge you to consider the danger of totalitarianism on our own shores. Leftism and totalitarianism go hand and hand. And like leftism, totalitarianism is evidence of sin.

SIN

What is sin? The Bible defines sin as a transgression of the law of God. It is rebellion against God. But the word "sin" is foreign to contemporary life. Why? Because few talk about sin today.

The trend to erase the word "sin" from the American vocabulary started in earnest during the 1960s with the sexual revolution. As evidence of this, in 1988 the world-famous psychiatrist Dr. Karl Menninger wrote a book titled, *Whatever Became of Sin?*[16] My concern now—some three-plus decades later—is not so much the fact that the word has become antiquated (at best) and offensive (at worst), but that sin's real and devastating impact can be witnessed so clearly firsthand.

What does sin do? Among other things, sin blinds. Sin makes people irrational. Sin makes people illogical. In the *New Century Version* of the Bible, which was written for young readers, Romans 1:28 says, "People did not think it was important to have a true knowledge of God. So, God left them and allowed them to have their own worthless thinking and to do things they should not do."

And that describes contemporary America and many nations of the world. No matter how secular our society becomes, and how hard people try to scrub the word "sin" from the books, its effects are more real than ever.

AMERICA'S SLIDE

If someone fell into a long sleep in 1960 and emerged from it today, he would not recognize the United States. What is worse, if someone had been in a coma for the last four years, that individual would be stunned at the radical—and very negative—changes in America.

Don't get me wrong. I am not discouraged. The very fact that I am writing this book and you are reading it is because we believe that God and His Word can make a difference. (See final chapter.) But sometimes, we need to stop and see how far we have gone in the wrong direction before we know how to turn and go in the right direction. In short, the collective thinking of our entire nation needs to be re-versed. We need to go from being culturally woke to being biblically awake.

---

16 https://www.amazon.com/Whatever-Became-Sin-Karl-Menninger/dp/055327368X

CHAPTER 3

"DON'T MESS WITH OUR KIDS"

I n 2017, a million and a half people marched in the streets of twenty-six cities in Peru with banners warning, "Don't Mess With Our Kids." (*Con Mis Hijos No Te Metas.*) The marches, originally proposed by a young man named Christian Rosas, were in opposition to the public gender development policies of the Peruvian government in education and other areas of public administration.[1] Nothing arouses the righteous anger of parents and grandparents more than when their children and grandchildren are attacked.

What occurred in Peru has been happening across the United States and around the world. Why? Because the institutions once committed to protecting people have now launched a frontal attack on families, marriages, and children. The government has become the family's enemy in much of the world.

Less than forty miles from Washington, DC, is Loudoun County, Virginia. Most Americans had never heard of it until it became the

---

1 https://en.wikipedia.org/wiki/Con_mis_hijos_no_te_metas

epicenter of a parental uprising that swept across the country. Parents objected to their children being indoctrinated with Critical Race Theory. They objected to COVID "vaccines," locked-down schools, coerced masking, pornography, homosexuality, and transgenderism.

The result? They were labeled "domestic terrorists" by the National School Board Association.[2] Not to be outdone, US Attorney General Merrick Garland bought into this pathetic narrative.[3] But abuse of our children is only one target of the radical Left—a cabal of Big Tech ("cancel culture"), Big Pharma (coerced "vaccines"), Hollywood, LGBTQ, Big Business, Academia, Main Stream Media, leftist pseudo-churches, and progressive politicians exercising unconstitutional governmental overreach.

RESIST: THE DEFENSIVE

Isaac Newton's Third Law of Motion states, "For every action, there is an equal and opposite reaction." That applies to anti-child, anti-parent, anti-biblical, anti-Christian actions from teachers' unions, school boards, and government officials. Parents have risen up, as they should.

In fact, an army of regular citizens is rising up. That is why this book came into being: to equip you to resist. To resist what? The totalitarian authoritarianism that is engulfing the USA and much of the world. In recent years, my wife and I have met government leaders in Israel, Egypt, Jordan, Kurdistan, Guatemala, Costa Rica, Panama, Bolivia, Brazil, England, Austria, Germany, Switzerland, Hungary, Finland, Norway, the Netherlands, Belgium, Albania, Macedonia, Romanian, Latvia, Liechtenstein, and Ukraine. We have also met with spiritual leaders in Singapore, New Zealand, Australia, and other

2 https://www.foxnews.com/us/letter-calling-parents-domestic-terrorists-has-thrown-gasoline-on-the-fire-parent-activist-says
3 https://nypost.com/2021/10/25/ag-merrick-garland-white-house-owe-americas-domes-tic-terrorist-parents-an-apology-and-an-explanation/

places. Our ministry, Well Versed (www.WellVersedWorld.org), has met privately with over ninety of the ambassadors of the 193 Member Nations of the United Nations in New York City. We have learned much. Simply stated, our broken world is in pain.

HOW EVIL AND SUFFERING BEGAN

God did not create a world in pain. He made a place so spectacular that it was called paradise. However, Lucifer, who was an impressive angel (Ezekiel 28:11-19), who was the "praise leader" of the heavenlies (Ezekiel 28:13), became envious (Isaiah 14:12-17).

Lucifer wanted what God had: to be worshipped. In his desire to elevate himself (Isaiah 14:13-14), he rebelled. He sinned, and in the process destroyed all that was perfect (Genesis 3:1-19). Paradise was lost.

The rest of Scripture is the story of God redeeming what was lost, first through Jesus' death (the Gospel, "good news," forgiveness from sin), then through the establishment of the invisible Kingdom of God (Luke 17:20; 1 Peter 2:9, "within the redeemed"). However—the *great* news is—the Kingdom of God will be fully manifested. Paradise will be regained as a "new heaven and a new earth" (Revelation 21:1).

Between "now" and "then," there are sin, suffering, death, and tears in this world. But that does not mean we sit idly by while evil prevails. We have a cultural mandate (Genesis 1:26) to take "dominion;" that is, to carefully *steward* what belongs to the Lord. In Luke 19:13, He said: "Occupy till I come." "Occupy" means to possess, to engage in service like a business leader, and to remain busy in daily affairs.

Critics of this assume that it means we are wanting to take "dominion" over others. That is not the case. The command is to be a good steward of this Earth for the One who created it.

Succinctly stated, if you are a follower of Jesus, you are a wholesome, healthy, and winsome force in culture until He returns. Sometimes, that means taking a stand against evil. That is defensive. Sometimes, that means spiritually invading evil spheres—through prayer, fasting, and declaring God's Word. That is being on the offensive.

THE OFFENSIVE

Here are several ways that you can be spiritually "on the offensive:"

1. Make sure your life is in conformity with God's ways. Make Jesus Savior AND Lord. "He's the boss." Do not expect God's blessings if you continue in known, willful sin. Ask the Holy Spirit to fill you and empower you to live in personal victory.

2. Fill your mind with the Word of God, the Bible. I care little whether you remember this book. My words will help you very little. God watches over *His Word* to perform it (Jeremiah 1:12) and accomplish His purposes (Isaiah 55:11). The value of this book is that it relies on His Book.

3. Be in fellowship with brothers and sisters. We are coming into some turbulent times. Rod Dreher's book, *Live Not by Lies,* may be one of the best manuals for how to survive and thrive during the days ahead. I don't say this pessimistically, but you need to be ready for what is coming. During the last ten years as a local church pastor, I would say to my congregation, "I am preparing you for what is to come. I don't know what 'that' is yet, but I am preparing you for 'that.'" Well, "that" is now here.

4. Know the truth. When I read renowned researcher and author George Barna's research that Christians do not speak out on the issues because they do not know what to say, something exploded in my heart, and motivated me to write *Well Versed: Biblical Answers to Today's*

Tough Issues, giving biblical foundations to 30 political topics. This book deals with twice that many.

5. Don't back down, capitulate, or compromise. Be kind and loving, but do not be bullied. Never surrender the truth. Don't get off Facebook, Twitter, or Instagram because somebody challenged the truth of God's Word. Facebook and other social media platforms are your "living room." You can invite people in or nicely escort them out whenever you want. And don't feel guilty about it. Have resolve. Having done all, stand (Ephesians 6:13).

GOD HAS ALL THE ANSWERS

Allow me to be candid: You need to know what to say and how. No excuses. Keep this book to look up an answer when you are confronted. The Table of Contents has been created in such a way as to make finding a specific subject easy and quick.

If you engage in a conversation that challenges the truth of Scripture or biblical morality, and you need time to seek out an answer, it's okay to say, "I am not sure, but I will check it out and get back to you." That is acceptable.

However, where can truth be found in an era of fake news and government-dispensed disinformation?

The answers are found in the Bible. He gave us His Word—it tells us how to live our personal life, how to order our family life, how to organize our church life, and—99% of Christians don't seem to understand this—how civil government is supposed to function. God designed communities and nations to have peace and to prosper.

BACK TO PERU

The "Don't Mess With Our Kids" movement in Peru was up against their own government and the United Nations (UNESCO) peddling transgenderism. But then President Pedro Pablo Kuczynski and UNESCO met their match with young activist Christian Rosas, his sister Dorcas Rosas Hernandez, the bold Catholic Cardinal Juan Luis Cipriani, and millions of moms and dads, organized as "Parents in Action," chanting "Don't Mess With Our Kids," helping to turn the nation.

MAMMA BEARS

Tina Descovich is a wife and mother who lives in Florida. Fed up with attacks on parental rights and educational failures, she launched Moms for Liberty in 2021. It has exploded to 120,000 members in 44 states. She is a "mamma bear" who decided to do something.

The Peruvian Cardinal and American parents could have run and hid. Evil would have prevailed. But they stood. They pushed back—defensively. Then they pressed forward—offensively. With truth. Truth has a way of exposing evil and eventually driving it back (1 Peter 5:8-9).

CHAPTER 4

A BIBLICAL WORLDVIEW

E veryone—every single person—from the philosophy professor to a homeless person on the street has some form of a worldview, whether they know it or not.

Some describe a worldview as a personal "lens" to interpret the world around them. Others think of it as a "grid" that prioritizes information and concepts to help them make sense of reality, or maybe like a "map" that helps make decisions. To a few people, a worldview is an overarching "story" that gives context and meaning to the complexities of life.

Many people, however, don't even realize they have a worldview because they bounce around from viewpoint to viewpoint and can radically change their values over time. This isn't unlike the Athenians in Paul's day, who were enamored with any new "teaching" that came along (Acts 17:16-21), but had no core of convictions.

WHERE DOES A WORLDVIEW COME FROM?

More often than not, your worldview is a complex mixture of experiences or ideas you've absorbed over your lifetime to understand and engage reality. Bits and pieces come from parents, teachers, siblings, peers, experts, celebrities, philosophers, movies, songs, books, social media, religious leaders, and key events in your life. All of these influences impact what you think about the big life questions: what's true? what's right or wrong? why are things the way they are? what happens after we die? does life even matter?

But what do you ultimately rely on to make serious value judgments about anything? The final authority for many people is staring at them in the mirror. But this begs the question: is it reasonable to make important judgments about the world, life, or relationships based only on how we feel each day, or the last podcast we listened to? If we rely totally on ourselves, are we a reliable, consistent determiner of what is right or wrong, what is sexually moral or perverse, or, for that matter, what truth is?

Here are some examples of shifting worldviews. The belief in the divine right of kings to wield absolute power held sway throughout much of history, until representative government began to be embraced by most of the world. In the US, our government has gone from being seen as a necessity to maintain order, execute justice, and approve (acknowledge) what is good, to becoming the equivalent of a parent meeting our every need, and deciding what we can or cannot do for our own good. And, no surprise to anyone, the public square has gone from fostering the influence of biblical values and acknowledgment of our accountability to an all-powerful God, to a sterile, secular atmosphere that is hostile to biblical truths.

LIMITS OF YOUR WORLDVIEW

When a worldview is a hodgepodge of ideas and beliefs that are loosely related, it can quickly change as life circumstances change, or when you find yourself doing things you know you shouldn't be doing—things that you would never have considered doing years before.

Unfortunately, left to our own devices we can justify almost any decision or behavior if we have no trusted, timeless standard to show us what's right and wrong. Our minds and our hearts are not neutral. We all have an agenda, but often, we're not even aware of our motives. We are like a ship with a broken compass, or a car with faulty steering. God's Word is clear about this. As fallen creatures, we will tend to live according to our selfish interests and preferences and not in a way that pleases Him (Romans 8:7).

THE SOLUTION: A BIBLICAL WORLDVIEW

When a person becomes a Christian, their heart, mind, soul, and spirit are forever transformed (Romans 12:2); they become a new creature in Christ (2 Corinthians 5:17, KJV). Their desire is to please God with their lives and their decisions, and their entire outlook on the world is forever changed. Believers are now capable of seeing God's handiwork in the creation around them in an entirely new light (Romans 1:18-20), and their conscience is now sensitized to God's will in their lives (Romans 2:13-16).

But there's far more. Because our interpretation and understanding of Creation and conscience can be imperfect, God has taken the initiative and graciously revealed the truth to us through His Word, the Bible (Psalm 18:30). Scripture now becomes a Christian's standard to see, evaluate, and understand the world around them. God's Word becomes the unchangeable, authoritative source, the foundation on which a believer bases their entire worldview concerning all of life.

Did you know there is true north and something called magnetic north? In fact, true north is the direction that points directly toward the geographic North Pole. This is a fixed point on the Earth's globe. Magnetic north is very different; it is the direction that a compass needle points to as it aligns with the Earth's magnetic field. What is interesting is that the magnetic North Pole shifts and changes over time in response to changes in the Earth's magnetic core. It is not a fixed point.[1]

This difference between true north and magnetic north is called magnetic declination—it is the "gap" between what is true and constant, and what is ever-changing. If you are navigating through the wilderness and don't adjust your compass to account for magnetic north, you will receive a false reading. It may only be a few degrees, but if you plot a course, say, over fifty miles and are a few degrees off, guess what? The reality of not accounting for magnetic declination will get you lost.

Magnetic north—which shifts over time—is like a worldview based on earthly things, whereas true north is constant and unchanging. Unless we adjust magnetic north—the beliefs, trends, and shifting values of the world—to line up with true north—the Word of God—we will lose our way.

IT IS WRITTEN

Jesus and God's Word are our true north. And just as Jesus and the Apostles repeatedly invoked the Bible as their final authority, we're to do the same. Jesus even prayed for His followers, asking the Father to "Sanctify them in the truth, your word is truth" (John 17:17).

In order to have a biblical worldview, we must have a new, spiritually alive mind rooted in the fear of God (Proverbs 9:10). This is the beginning of wisdom and insight into all of life; in other words, that is what produces a proper worldview.

This makes perfect sense. The God that created us in His image (Genesis 1:27) knows what's best for us, how our personal lives can be lived in a way that most pleases Him, and how we're to see and

---

1 https://www.rmg.co.uk/stories/topics/true-north-magnetic-north-whats-difference

understand the world around us without becoming captive to false and dangerous worldviews that can only destroy (Colossians 2:8; 1 John 2:15-17).

A biblical worldview also shows us how we're to interact with ungodly people and wicked government (Ephesians 5:11; Colossians 4:5-6), how we're to engage in politics (Matthew 5:13-16), what are the proper and improper roles of government (Romans 13:3-4; 1 Peter 2:13-15), and what we should look for in selecting leaders who are going to exercise authority over us (Exodus 18:21).

The more you read the Bible and the sharper your biblical glasses become, the more your biblical worldview toward all of life comes into greater focus. Using our navigation example, when we eliminate "magnetic declination" (that ever-shifting gap between the world's beliefs and the never-changing Word of God), we can follow God's true north. God's Word encapsulates this process well: "In your light do we see light" (Psalm 36:9, ESV).

If you don't develop and then draw on a biblical worldview, all you have to turn to is the pride and the speculations of human imagination. God has already judged human philosophy, secular worldviews, and man-centered religions. He shows us that all these other pursuits of "truth" are futile: "Where is the one who is wise? Where is the scribe? Where is the debater of this age? Has not God made foolish the wisdom of the world?" (1 Corinthians 1:20, NASB.)

MULTIPLE BIBLICAL WORLDVIEWS?

Some wrongly make the claim that there is not one single "biblical" worldview. They point out the great differences within Christianity, suggesting multiple worldviews exist. To make their point, they note that there are Catholics, Orthodox, and Protestants with many denominations. And they like to point out the cultural differences between Christians during different eras or in differing geographic regions.

However, the fundamental core of Christianity has remained a constant throughout time and across continents. Theologically, the Trinity is affirmed by almost all Christians, as is the atoning work of Jesus, who was both God and man. Furthermore, Christians historically have always valued life in the womb and one man-one woman marriage. The fact is, authentically biblical Christians, what I label the "ABCs," have a remarkably singular worldview.

BIBLICAL WORLDVIEW IN THE MIDST OF CULTURAL WOKENESS

Since a worldview is a set of values, principles, and truths that allow us to understand what's happening around us, it will inform and prepare us for our decisions and actions. And for a Christian, a biblical worldview will have God's interests in mind, and will focus on what pleases Him.

The Bible may not always have all the details you want, and applying God's Word to contemporary issues may be difficult at times, but I can guarantee you that Scripture will have an abundance of commands, principles, insights, or real-life examples that will apply no matter what the issue is. God's promise is that as we become adept at understanding and applying a biblical worldview, we will be able to "destroy arguments and every lofty opinion raised against the knowledge of God, and take every thought captive to obey Christ" (2 Corinthians 10:5, ESV). Thus, we can "See to it that no one takes you captive by philosophy and empty deceit, according to human tradition, according to the elemental spirits of the world, and not according to Christ" (Colossians 2:8, ESV).

Our duty in God's grand story is clear. Jesus told us to "occupy till I come" (Luke 19:13, KJV). Regardless of when we believe Jesus will return, when He does, He will expect to find each of us doing the practical work of Kingdom building by evangelizing the lost (Matthew 28:18-20) and applying God's truths to every social, cultural, political, and governmental issue of our day (Matthew 5:13-16).

Finally, in the most famous sermon in human history, the Sermon on the Mount, Jesus made this declaration: "Everyone then who hears these words of mine and does them will be like a wise man who built his house on the rock" (Matthew 7:24). God's Word is our foundation (our rock); it is authoritative, and it infuses us with a worldview that is trustworthy, never-changing, and a blessing for everyone who follows it.

CHAPTER 5

SOCIAL JUSTICE VS. BIBLICAL JUSTICE

T he US is still reeling from the events following the 2020 death of George Floyd, an unarmed Black man who died at the hands of the Minneapolis police. The massively destructive and deadly riots that followed were fueled by the "Black Lives Matter" (BLM) movement in the name of "social justice," whose leaders admit to being trained Marxists.

Besides being a powerful and noble-sounding political slogan, the term "social justice" has a very interesting history.

ORIGIN OF SOCIAL JUSTICE

The conservative who coined the term was Italian Jesuit priest Luigi Taparelli SJ (born Prospero Taparelli d'Azeglio), "the father of Catholic social teaching." He lived right after Napoleon and was staunchly committed to papal authority. The social justice d'Azeglio advocated was biblically sound. He said, "All individual human beings are naturally unequal among themselves in everything that pertains to their individuality, just as they are naturally equal in all that pertains to the species."[1] In other words, all are created equal, but every individual is unique in relative intelligence, ambition, strengths, accomplishments, etc.

According to d'Azeglio, governments are led by people who are naturally braver, more competent, more intelligent, wealthier, or better leaders than others. So, his version of "social justice" accepted the inequality of outcomes. Unfortunately, "social justice" is now applied to a radical economic equality that d'Azeglio never espoused.[2]

THE CONTEMPORARY "SOCIAL JUSTICE" MOVEMENT

Today, using the term "social justice" can instantly give a person the moral high ground. After all, no person wants to be an advocate of social *in*justice. To be a SJW—"social justice warrior"—is considered a noble calling among many young people. However, we must look deeper at the application of the phrase.

Social justice is also useful because it's a vague and malleable term that is "owned" by progressives/socialists/humanists who use it to promote an unbiblical ideal of equal redistribution.

When you peel back the wrapping on the current "social justice" movement, it's simply the ideology of godless humanists trying to create a utopia according to the failed social and economic theories of Karl Marx. In the name of love, everyone and everything must be equal; if you don't agree, you're the enemy of love.

Advocates believe unity and equity is the only way we can be happy. There can be no rich or poor, no male or female, and no families to pass your wealth onto. How can this be accomplished? Only by means of a totalitarian state controlling everything.

---

1 Taparelli d'Azeglio, 1845 par, 335, quoted in Burke, 2011, p. 37 The Concept of Justice: Is Social Justice Thomas Patrick Burke.

2 https://isi.org/intercollegiate-review/the-origins-of-social-justice-taparelli-dazeglio/

In their brave new world, you'll own nothing, and you'll be happy—or else.

Unfortunately, utopia will never happen. Recent history shows that when Marxist ideology is in control, its leaders live very well, while economic collapse destroys the initiative and innovation of the masses. As citizens of the former Soviet Union said, "They pretend to pay us, so we pretend to work." The equality they actually shared was that of being equally miserable, while leaders always seemed to find a way to prosper. For instance, when the brutal communist dictator of Cuba, Fidel Castro died, his net worth was an estimated $900 million.[3]

According to his friends, Marx's favorite slogan was: "Everything that exists deserves to perish." We must burn down the family, private property, and the church, and make the state into a god in the name of "social justice." Everything and everyone must conform to total collectivism or you're the enemy of the state. Using technology and reeducation, they believe they can remove the moral flaws of humanity and the human race can transcend itself. Any means can and must be used to achieve that end, including deception and deadly force, otherwise we won't survive as a species.

DEFINING BIBLICAL JUSTICE

Depending upon your definition, there's not necessarily a contradiction between "social justice" and biblical justice. Some well-intended Christians even argue the two terms are interchangeable.[4] But let's look a little closer.

One of the many great ministry aspects of Christ is that He came "to proclaim justice to the gentiles" (Isaiah 42:1; Matthew 12:18,

---

3 https://www.celebritynetworth.com/richest-politicians/presidents/fidel-castro-net-worth/
4 https://www.christianitytoday.com/better-samaritan/2021/october/social-justice-and-biblical-justice-are-actually-one-and-sa.html

ESV). When we read the Bible we find that the terms justice, salvation, faithfulness, and truth are used somewhat interchangeably:

> The Rock, his work is perfect, for all his ways are justice.
> A God of faithfulness and without iniquity, just and upright
> is he. (Deuteronomy 32:4, ESV.)

And in Psalm 99:4 we read: "The King in his might loves justice. You have established equity; you have executed justice and righteousness in Jacob."

God's justice is self-evident; it is written on our hearts (Romans 2:15-16), personified in Jesus (Luke 18:7-8), and confirmed by Scripture (Proverbs 21:15). If you start anywhere else, you're left with arbitrary, man-made opinions of justice that cannot be judged by a higher standard. When that happens, "might makes right," and those in power will inevitably enforce their idea of justice as the final authority. We call that tyranny.

Besides giving us the transcendent law—the standard—on which justice is based, God delegated the duty of exercising civic justice to governmental leaders (Romans 13:1-4). He even gave what their qualifications need to be:

> Moreover, look for able men from all the people, men who
> fear God, who are trustworthy and hate a bribe, and place
> such men over the people as chiefs of thousands, of hun-
> dreds, of fifties, and of tens.
> —*Exodus 18:21, ESV*

God also lays out the implications concerning adherence to His commandments and the upholding of justice:

> And if you faithfully obey the voice of the LORD your God,
> being careful to do all his commandments that I command

you today, the LORD your God will set you high above all the nations of the earth. And all these blessings shall come upon you and overtake you.
                    —*Deuteronomy 28:1-2, ESV*

Likewise, ignore His standards and there will be consequences:

But if you will not obey the voice of the LORD your God or be careful to do all his commandments and his statutes that I command you today, then all these curses shall come upon you and overtake you.
                    —*Deuteronomy 28:15, ESV*

Sadly, Old Testament Israel did not remain faithful in executing justice (national or social) and keeping God's Word. Their lack of repentance became so bad that God raised up foreign powers to discipline them. Israel in the north was captured and deported by Assyria, while Judah in the south was taken into captivity by the Babylonians. God will not overlook injustice forever, and He will judge the nations (Jeremiah 18:6-10). The only way we can see justice of any kind come to pass is when we conform our lives and our laws to God's standards and not our own.

Seek good, and not evil, that you may live; and so the LORD, the God of hosts, will be with you, as you have said. Hate evil, and love good, and establish justice in the gate.
                    —*Amos 5:14-15, ESV*

FINAL CAUTIONS

Terminology and definitions are important. When the term "social justice" is being used, make sure you know what is meant. Justice is a key biblical concept, but it is radically different than what Marxists and many culturally "woke" people mean when they use the term "social justice."

CHAPTER 6

WOKEISM DEFINED

Although "woke" may have been used as early as 1930, it first appeared in print in 1962 in a *New York Times* article about beatniks and pop culture absorbing jazz music and African American slang.[1]

The word took on new meaning in the 2010s, referring to racial disparities and discrimination. By the time of the Ferguson, Missouri riots, Black Lives Matter had appropriated the word to include grievances of Blacks with police. It became so widespread that by 2017 it was included in the *Oxford English Dictionary*.[2]

With the rise of politically correct "cancel culture," the term began to also mean that if cancelled, you had said something "not woke."[3] To understand how the word is used today, you need to understand some of the divisive issues that began in 2020.

---

1 https://www.foxnews.com/us/what-does-woke-mean
2 https://en.wikipedia.org/wiki/Woke
3 https://www.foxnews.com/us/what-does-woke-mean

ISSUE ONE: THE DAY THAT CHANGED AMERICA

March 17, 2020. On that day, America began COVID lockdowns, and thus began an enormous loss of personal freedoms.

At the start, most of us went along with it. At the "five-week mark," I sensed something was not right. At the "eight-week mark," I wrote, "The natives are getting restless," a popular line from the *New Zealand Parliamentary Debates: Third Session of the Fourth Parliament,*[4] describing rebellion by aboriginal inhabitants in British colonies. Soon, a large percentage of Americans felt they were being held hostage by "science" people, or in reality, pseudo-science. In summary, it was a tragic era of lost constitutional protections and freedoms.

THE REAL CASUALTY: TRUST

Over the next two years, new divisions emerged: "vaccine" vs. "no vaccine," lockdowns vs. freedom, masks vs. no masks. In time, many Americans no longer trusted the Centers for Disease Control (Anthony Fauci), the National Institute of Health, much of the medical community, Big Pharma, many teachers unions that cried, "close the schools" (as opposed to the teachers themselves—many of whom rose above and beyond to teach their students under arduous online conditions), the Main Street Media (MSM), along with well-known individuals like Bill Gates and Klaus Schwab (founder of the World Economic Forum). Censorship and cancel culture of anyone disagreeing with the prevailing "narrative" took center stage. Distrust mushroomed.

---

4 https://en.wiktionary.org/wiki/the_natives_are_restless New Zealand Parliamentary Debates: Third Session of the Fourth Parliament. Vol. 2, 1868, page 387.

ISSUE TWO: THE GEORGE FLOYD RIOTS

May 25, 2020, brought the death of George Floyd, followed by riots, burning, looting, and deaths. Estimates of property damage ranged from $1 billion to $2 billion, or even higher.[5]

Many of the destroyed businesses were owned by minorities. One of the most tragic and moving videos posted on social media was an older Black man pleading with rioters and looters, asking them why they were destroying his business. Repeatedly, he said, "I tried so hard to make it."[6]

More divisions: While President Trump offered federal help to end the burning, rioting, and looting, Democrat mayors and governors prevented him from doing so. Then presidential candidate Joe Biden didn't even comment on the rioting for nearly three months, while then vice-presidential candidate Kamala Harris helped raise bail funds for rioters.

VIRTUE SIGNALING

While some who questioned the rioting were called racists, another phrase entered the common language: "virtue signaling." This primarily referred to educated Whites trying to identify with Blacks by putting little black squares on their social media while ignoring the rioting and looting carnage. What emerged from elites: America is "systemically racist."

When some Blacks tried to stand against this, they were called an "Uncle Tom." When Blacks condemned virtue signaling and pointed

---

5 https://fee.org/articles/george-floyd-riots-caused-record-setting-2-billion-in-damage-new-report-says-here-s-why-the-true-cost-is-even-higher/
6 https://www.youtube.com/watch?v=aJorq3_F-hw

out that America was not systemically racist (that is, by law, racist), these same Blacks were called—get this—"*White* supremacists."

BLM, CRITICAL RACE THEORY, AND THE 1619 PROJECT

Added to the divisiveness was the rapid rise of BLM, which received untold millions of dollars with no accountability. Critical Race Theory (CRT) was forced onto school children, teaching them that all Whites are oppressors, especially if they are older, male, and Christian. According to CRT, Whites are the greatest oppressors of all and cause everything that's wrong with the nation and the world. (See Chapter 21 for a deeper analysis of CRT.)

Not to be outdone, the *New York Times* launched "The 1619 Project," claiming that the only way to understand America was based on the arrival of slaves to the New World, with everything that followed supporting "systemic" racism.

ISSUE THREE: THE COERCED "VACCINE"

With National Institute of Allergy and Infectious Diseases Director Anthony Fauci effectively crowned "healthcare king" of America, "medical freedom" became a new divisive issue as the government took draconian steps to coerce people to put vaccines into their bodies that they did not want. Added to the insult of the coercion of the so-called "vaccine" was the dishonesty of those who forced it to acknowledge the massive uptick in inexplicable deaths of people between the ages of 18 and 29, particularly among males.

ISSUE FOUR: ELECTION FRAUD OR INTEGRITY

Then came the election of 2020. In 2016, many Democrats claimed the election was stolen from them, and little was said. But in 2020 and 2021, when many Republicans made that same claim, the FBI, CIA, and DOJ began making arrests. Soon, it was as if Homeland Security viewed anyone raising questions about election integrity to be not just an election denier but a bad actor.

ISSUE FIVE: JANUARY 6

To some, January 6 was a full-blown "insurrection." To others, it was a peaceful rally of 120,000 people,[7] with 1,000 or so arrested for unlawful entry and damaging of property. Democrats, who had no interest in the twenty people killed in the 2020 riots,[8] suddenly had great interest in labeling everyone an insurrectionist, even though the crowd of 120,000 was unarmed. Even more bizarre: the only person shot was an unarmed White female veteran, killed by a Black policeman, which was an odd reversal of the standard woke narrative of "a White officer killed a Black person."

ISSUE SIX: HOMOSEXUALS AND TRANSGENDERS

A new phrase emerged among so-called evangelicals from normally biblically grounded institutions and denominations: "gay Christian." It was unclear if the term meant "Christians who practice homosexuality" or if it referred to people who experience same-sex attraction (SSA), but because of their commitment to Christ, had chosen celibacy. If the former, they should not call themselves "Christians." If the latter, they should not want to be defined by their previous practice of sin. No adjective—"gay," as an example—is needed before the noun Christian.

Paul wrote in 1 Corinthians 6:9-11, referring to several sins, including homosexuality, that "such were some of you," meaning they had

---

7 https://www.newsweek.com/exclusive-classified-documents-reveal-number-january-6-protestors-1661296
8 https://www.theguardian.com/world/2020/oct/31/americans-killed-protests-political-unrest-acled

left that sin behind. Paul does not say, "You can continue your sin and be a Christ follower." Nor did he say to wear your overcome sin as an adjective to describe you.

In this charged environment, a new movement emerged: drag queens reading to children. The Men's Gay Chorus of San Francisco recorded a music video, "We Are Coming for Your Children,"[9] which was confirmed by the chants of homosexuals and transgenders in the streets of New York City.[10] No amount of trying to walk this slogan back would or should calm the anger felt by parents nationally.

ISSUE SEVEN: DECONSTRUCTIONISM

In reality, deconstructionism may well be the basis or foundation for all of the six items listed above. They might well be considered simply symptoms of a much deeper philosophical issue called "deconstructionism." Frankly, the topic merits its own chapter or a whole book, but for our purposes, deconstructionism is the belief that language, even words themselves, have ideological biases implicit within them, applying to one's gender, race, economic views, political standing, and cultural issues.

At its core, deconstructionism is based on the notion that life is comprised of those who dominate and those who are dominated. The father of deconstructionist thinking was Jean Jacques Derrida, who lived from 1930 to 2004. What he wrote is very difficult to read or understand; and some suggested that is exactly how he wanted it.

If I am understanding him correctly, part of Derrida's belief was that we cannot know what anyone actually means by their speaking or writing, as words can mean very different things to the reader. As you are reading my words right now, assuming that you don't really know me well, you have no idea what I mean by these words. In

---

9 https://www.foxnews.com/us/san-francisco-gay-mens-chorus-your-children
10 https://www.foxnews.com/us/nyc-drag-marchers-chant-were-coming-your-children-during-pride-event

addition to that, you are reading into my words what the words mean to you, the reader, not as what I may have intended them to be as the writer. Therefore, language is ambiguous. There is, for example, no trustworthy "revelation from God" that is always truth. Instead, language, or the meaning of words, simply develops over time. Again, there is no hard, fast truth about anything.

Since there is no objective truth, then any supposed truth, such as "2 + 2 = 4," is too dogmatic and could even be considered racist or misogynistic. After all, who are you to tell me that "2 + 2 = 4." Maybe I want it to be 5 or 6.

But what Derrida intended—or didn't intend—is less important than how the word deconstructionism has evolved, or devolved, in contemporary evangelicalism. In popular language it has come to mean that one can deconstruct—that is, tear down—one's faith or abandon one's faith. In fact, one so-called Christian college, as will be noted again later, had "Deconstruction Week," for professors to remove from students everything their parents and pastor taught them, so they could "reconstruct" their faith. You can imagine how the "reconstruction" went.

The tragedy is that some evangelical young adults that want to seem chic are deconstructing their faith. When I was a young person, we had a name for that. It was called "backsliding."

THE SUMMATION OF ALL OF THIS

The list could be longer, but the seven issues listed above are some of the most conspicuous ones redefining the meaning of "woke" for many Americans, resulting in a profoundly deep divide.

The woke affirmed the BLM riots, as people were merely "venting." Looting was viewed as a form of "reparations." The "woke" marched lock step with government overreach, lockdowns, "vaccine" coercion, the forced use of masks, and the main stream media reporting on COVID. The "woke" want to teach young children how to have intercourse, anal and oral sex, and believe little boys and girls should be allowed to choose their "gender," while keeping it secret from their parents. The "woke" also support children being groomed by drag queens.

THE MUTIPLE MEANINGS OF "WOKE"

To informed historians, woke means Marxism. In the political realm, woke means big, crushing, overreaching governments. To family units, woke means ripping away childhood innocence where little boys are not called little boys. Woke is parental rights being destroyed by the teachers' unions and bureaucrats. It means redefining—and ultimately destroying—the sacred institution of one man-one woman marriage.

In the realm of health, woke means the baby is merely a glob of cells. "Reproductive rights" become the right to kill unborn babies. Sociologically and emotionally speaking, woke means playing the role of a victim for life. Economically, woke means envy; that is, wanting that which you did not earn, and demanding that those who did earn it, give it to you. To the scripturally grounded theologian, woke is, to put it succinctly, sin.

And being woke certainly does not help one's mental and emotional health. The *Scandinavian Journal of Psychology* announced in March 2024 that "(a) study from Finland found that those who adhere to 'woke' attitudes and beliefs are more likely to experience depression, anxiety, and an absence of happiness in life."[11]

---

11 https://catholicvote.org/study-finds-woke-beliefs-linked-to-depression-anxiety-and-unhappiness/?mkt_tok=NDI3LUxFUS0wNjYAAAGSBJE2_POeq5pXC7nTpL1Za-x8iEcjvzZq6PvNMWOXvNqdfFGWrhdy7nkRnapqtxC3Hw89ejaJJFm6TVT2y-6I0RopJwHXntCtRMWr5BnbZH

CULTURALLY WOKE VS. BIBLICALLY AWAKE

But the real issue is that the woke do not hold to a biblical view of a holy, righteous God who is Judge. They are content to "make god in their own image."

The non-woke—or rather the awakened—believe 1) there is a God, 2) we are not God, 3) God gives us all moral guardrails, and 4) we are to stay within those guardrails.

Bottom line: Will we adhere to God's ways or not? The woke say "no." In contrast, the awake say, "yes."

Culturally woke? Or biblically awake?

It's your choice.

CHAPTER 7

WOKE MILITARY

For the first time since the end stages of the Vietnam War, the viability of an all-volunteer American military is becoming questionable. Since the last draft was called in 1972, our military has become threatened on at least three fronts: cost, decay of warfighting superiority, and finding enough qualified volunteers. But even more serious, the military has become just another opportunity to showcase progressive ideals of inclusiveness, equity, and tolerance of aberrant societal behaviors that are antithetical to military cohesion and effectiveness.

A weakening of the pre-eminent military force in the world is exactly what Marxists want. That is where we are today. Is it any surprise that young "patriots" aren't signing up in droves to serve our nation?

THE ORIGINAL HOLY WAR

Old Testament Israel was ordered by the Lord to possess the Promised Land by conducting war on the pagan Canaanite nations. The Canaanite

sins were so vile (Deuteronomy 12:29-31) that God ordered their complete extermination (Deuteronomy 7:1-5). This was the first and only true "holy war" in human history. Following their conquest of Canaan, Israel continued to experience wars against their enemies but were restrained in how they were to be conducted (Deuteronomy 20:1-20).

With Christ's First Coming, the need for holy war was done away with. Until Christ returns, the Christian faith is advanced not by coercion or violence but by moral persuasion through spiritual means of prayer and proclamation.

THE MILITARY IN NEW TESTAMENT TIMES

In the New Testament, John the Baptist had soldiers coming to him: "…Soldiers also asked him, 'And we, what shall we do?' And he said to them, 'Do not extort money from anyone by threats or by false accusation, and be content with your wages'" (Luke 3:10-14). Was this a contradiction between "peace on earth and goodwill toward men" (Luke 2:14) and any military presence?

Historically, even some branches of Christianity have been expressly passivistic. To these believers, "turn the other cheek" means faithful followers of Christ must never defend themselves, and by extension, it is wrong to defend our nation. But wait, John the Baptist didn't condemn the military, he just said for them not to abuse their power. In fact, self-defense is a clear principle in Scripture (Numbers 22:2-3; Romans 13:4).

JESUS DID NOT CONDEMN THE MILITARY

Jesus met a Roman centurion who appealed to Jesus to heal his servant:

> Lord, I am not worthy to have you come under my roof, but only say the word and my servant will be healed. … When

Jesus heard this, he marveled and said to those who followed him, "Truly, I tell you, with no one in Israel have I found such faith."

—Matthew 8:8-10

One of the earliest and most profound affirmations of spiritual truth in the New Testament came from another Roman centurion who participated in the crucifixion of Christ:

When the centurion and those who were with him, keeping watch over Jesus, saw the earthquake and what took place, they were filled with awe and said, "Truly this was the Son of God!"

—Matthew 27:54, ESV

Even one of the most important converts to Christianity was a Roman centurion: Cornelius. He is the first non-Jew to receive the Holy Spirit and be baptized by the Apostle Peter (Acts 10:44-48).

The Apostle Paul was unjustly arrested and held in Rome under house arrest. As Paul's case wound through the courts, Paul's ministry impacted the Roman military. In his letter to the Philippians, Paul said:

I want you to know, brothers, that what has happened to me has really served to advance the gospel, so that it has become known throughout the whole imperial guard and to all the rest that my imprisonment is for Christ.

—Philippians 1:12-13, ESV

The examples of John the Baptist, Jesus, and the Apostles were very consistent. Those in the military were never told to resign their posts as a precondition of sincere repentance or conversion. That's because there is a biblical role for the military. The civil magistrate is God's minister of justice (Romans 13:4), with a duty to protect its citizenry and to maintain peace in the land (1 Timothy 2:2; 1 Peter 2:13-14).

JUST WAR THEORY

Beginning with the writings of Augustine, Christianity has settled on what is often called "just war theory." Using biblical principles and the right of self-defense, it clarifies the need for legitimate authority before military power can be used. When used, military power should only be exercised when there is a just cause (intention) and all other means of resolution have been exhausted.

But that's not all. Military force must be restrained to what is necessary to accomplish the intended goals while minimizing collateral damage. Unfortunately, Christianity has not always lived up to that standard.

ONE'S CONSCIENCE

Christians can serve in the military without concern over conscience issues as long as military might is exercised in a manner consistent with the limits God puts on the military. In fact, Jesus Himself cautioned His disciples to arm themselves for their own self-protection (Luke 22:36); how much more so a nation whose existence is being threatened.

Remember, though, military service means asserting deadly force as efficiently and effectively as possible against enemies, whether foreign or domestic.

WOKENESS THREATENS MILITARY READINESS

Because our military sons and daughters risk their lives for ours, we have an ethical responsibility to help ensure their ability to survive their service. They deserve our most qualified leaders and our best technologies. Social experiments don't accomplish that.

When radical racial, feminist, and queer ideologies are advanced by woke politicians and complicit military leaders, cohesion and morale are undermined at every level. Exaggeration? Consider what Thomas Spoehr, Director of the Center for National Defense, has cataloged concerning military wokeness.[1]

- A 2015 study concluded that gender-integrated combat formations did not move as quickly or shoot as accurately and that women were twice as likely as men to suffer combat injuries.
- All combat jobs are now open to women. "Gender-neutral standards" ensure females qualify for combat.
- The Pentagon has lifted the ban on transgender individuals in the military.
- Active-duty members can take time off for sex-change surgeries and receive hormones and drugs at taxpayer expense.
- The policy prohibiting individuals infected with HIV from serving in combat zones has been rescinded, necessitating the presence of HIV medications and increasing the danger of cross-infection by shared blood.
- The Army reduced its minimum standards for pushups to ten and increased its minimum two-mile run time from 19 to 23 minutes.
- The Navy has a training video on the proper use of pronouns and the need to create a "safe space for everybody" by using "inclusive language."
- Soldiers sit through indoctrination programs that differentiate service members along racial and gender lines; replacing hard-fought equality with equity, which undermines unit cohesion and loyalty.

---

1 https://www.heritage.org/defense/commentary/the-rise-wokeness-the-military

- One training slide at West Point read: "In order to understand racial inequality and slavery, it is first necessary to address whiteness," while another lecture includes, "Understanding Whiteness and White Rage."
- The Secretary of Defense ordered a one-day military-wide stand-down to address "extremism" despite the lack of any evidence. Commanding officers were required to discuss, "What is up with us White people?"
- All military organizations must have Diversity, Equity, and Inclusion (DEI) offices, strategic DEI plans, and a bureaucratic structure to report progress on DEI goals.
- The Pentagon devoted over $3 billion of its military budget to climate-related initiatives in 2023 alone.
- As if the above list of wokeness is not long enough, West Point announced in March 2024 that it would exclude the words "Duty, Honor, Country" from its mission statement.[2]

PROPER FOCUS

The military has a very limited, biblical role: reserve the God-given rights of its people and protect its citizens from enemies. The One World leftist idealogues, however, want to co-opt the US military for their own woke ends. Marxists are laughing as they deconstruct and criticize American values and demoralize our patriotic resolve in public schools.

Sadly, families that have honorably served in the US military are now discouraging their sons or daughters from enlisting because they do not trust the leadership, and they reject the military being used as a social laboratory for failed Marxist experiments. All too often,

2 https://www.msn.com/en-us/news/world/west-points-mission-statement-change-sparks-fury/ar-BB1jSEOW

what's left are those who lack the heart of a patriot who loves God, family, and country, or as C.S. Lewis aptly describes them, "Men without chests."

CHAPTER 8

WOKE CHURCHES

"I am not 'political' like you," he said. This pastor stood at least six inches taller than me, and I sensed he was looking down on me both physically and figuratively—that is, in a condescending way. Looking back up at him, I responded, "My problem with you is not that you aren't 'political,' but rather that you are not 'biblical.' Let me explain." And I did.

Continuing, I asked him, "If I were a slave in the South in 1850, would I want my slave owner to go to your church, Dave (not his real name), or to my church, that is, Jim's church? The answer is obvious: Jim's church. Why? Because I will preach on the evils of slavery and slave-owning because I regard it as a biblical issue. It is sin. It is evil. But you would not because it is—or certainly was—considered too 'political.'"

To drive the point home with a more contemporary topic, I continued, "If I was a baby in the womb of a scared 14-year-old girl who lived near Planned Parenthood, would I want the pregnant teenage mom to go to your church, Dave's church, or my church, Jim's church? The answer is again obvious because I would do everything I could to

53

save the life of the baby because that is the biblical response. But you, Dave, would not have preached on it because that is too 'political.'"

So as not to break from the theme, I said, "Dave, I am an ordained pastor in the Wesleyan denomination. Do you know how we were founded?" "No," he responded, aware that he was about to find out. "We were founded in 1843 when a group of Methodists (then called the Methodist Episcopal Church) were forced out or walked out of their denomination when they were told they could not discuss slavery anymore because it was too divisive."[1] After all, every good pastor knows you don't want people to leave and take their tithe checks with them.

"One of the early Wesleyans—Macajah McPherson—was hung for believing that slaves should be set free.[2] In fact, in one county in South Carolina, there was a saying, 'We need this rope to hang another Wesleyan.' Do you know why they wanted to hang them? Because they were accused of being 'political,' but they weren't. They were being biblical. So, once again, Dave, my problem with you is not that you aren't 'political.' It's that you are not biblical." (For the record, Dave and I are friends.)

One of my friends lost a lot of weight. People said, "You are too gaunt. You are too skinny." She finally retorted, "You have never seen healthy." May I make the obvious comparison? Many people have never seen "biblical," so they don't recognize it. If a preacher speaks on the evils of abortion, homosexuality or transgenderism, excessive national debt, or Israel-bashing (antisemitism), people say, "Oh no, he is political." However, the fact is, they just don't recognize "biblical."

"BUT I JUST PREACH JESUS"

Some pastors smugly say, "I just preach Jesus." That certainly sounds impressive. I preach Jesus, too. In fact, in almost every sermon

1 https://www.wesleyan.org/antislavery-roots
2 https://www.wesleyan.org/wp-content/uploads/2020/06/Micajah-MCPherson-en.pdf

I ever preached for many decades, I gave an opportunity to repent of sin, and make Jesus Savior and Lord of one's life. But I don't "just preach Jesus." I preach what Jesus preached. And what was that? Answer: the Kingdom. And what does a Kingdom have? Answer: a King. And who is the King? Jesus. Over what? Over everything. Does "everything" include the governmental or political? Yes. Everything is everything. Abraham Kuyper stated, "There is not a square inch in the whole domain of our human existence over which Christ, who is Sovereign over all, does not cry, Mine!"[3] Tragically, some Christian's version of the Great Commission is "go into all the world—except politics and government."

THE BIBLE AND CIVIL GOVERNANCE

Christians seem to understand that the Bible speaks to the personal issues. That is called self-governance. Christians understand that the Bible speaks to the issues of family life, which is called family governance. Most Christians understand that the Bible speaks to the issue of church or congregational life. That is called church governance. Unfortunately, very few Christians understand that the Bible speaks to the issue of civil governance: how a city, state, or nation is supposed to function.

There seems to be very little awareness that God is so loving and cares so much that He gives us clear guidance on the governmental or political issues we face. For the record, this is not "Christian nationalism" (which we will discuss in Chapter 12). It is not even—and I am making up this phrase—"Christian Internationalism." It simply means that Jesus is King. Over what? Over everything. Over all that is.

The reality is: 1) God loves us; 2) He cares for us so much that He arranged for a book to be available to help us navigate how to govern.

---

3 https://www.goodreads.com/quotes/99035-there-is-not-a-square-inch-in-the-whole-domain

God did not finish "the book" and go, "Oh wow, I forgot about the whole government thing!" God established government. He establishes nations. He cares about our communities. He desires us to have quiet and peaceful lives.

In fact, to the extent that a nation, long term, follows the biblical principles of governance, one can be assured that human pain, suffering, and poverty will be reduced. To the extent that a nation, long term, violates the biblical principles of governance, one can be assured that human pain, suffering, and poverty will be increased.

That is the reason that Scripture makes the bold claim: "Blessed is the nation whose God is the Lord" (Psalm 33:12). There is an entire chapter in Scripture that details the blessings that come to a nation that honors the Lord, but it also details the major catastrophes it will face if it turns away from the Lord (Deuteronomy 28:1-68).

PERCENTAGE OF CHURCHES AND PASTORS WITH A BIBLICAL WORLDVIEW

How many churches or pastors actually have a "biblical worldview?" George Barna believes that (before COVID) there were approximately 320,000 Protestant churches and approximately 20,000 Catholic churches in America. How many of those are Bible-believing? How many of America's pastors are Bible-believing? Or have what is called a "biblical worldview?"[4]

According to George Barna, 37% of America's pastors have a biblical worldview.[5] There are two reasons to be concerned with this reality. The first is obvious: Tragically, 63% of pastors do *not* have a biblical worldview. Shocking, to be sure.

---

4 Private phone call with George Barna, January 4, 2024.
5 George Barna, American Worldview Inventory 2022-23, Arizona Christian University Press: Glendale, AZ, 2023, pages 43-44.

But there is more difficult news. Of the 37% of those who do have a biblical worldview, how many of them actually preach what they internally, privately believe? That is, how many of them, to quote Barna, "intentionally and strategically develop others to have a biblical worldview"? Though the exact number might not be certain, the most educated guess I could secure for this was from, once again, George Barna. Based on his ongoing research regarding worldview in America, he believes that the answer is that no more than 10% of America's 340,000 churches have a pastor who is actually teaching, preaching, and discipling people in what would be labeled a "biblical worldview."[6] That would mean that 34,000 churches might actually be teaching how to respond scripturally to all the issues of life, including the governmental-political arena. The good news is that that is a "tithe" of America's churches. The bad news is that 90% of America's churches do not have consistent biblical worldview teaching.

The average-sized Christian church in the US is currently estimated to be about 150 adults, which means that perhaps 5 million of the nation's 336 million adults are associated with a church in which consistent biblical discipling of adults is occurring. This corresponds with Barna's other worldview research indicating that just 4% of adults have a biblical worldview and that approximately 3% of adults meet Jesus' criteria for being disciples, as described in six passages of Scripture (Luke 14:26; Luke 14:27; Luke 14:33; John 8:31; John 13:35; John 15:8).[7]

PERCENTAGE OF PASTORS WILLING TO SPEAK ON THE ISSUES

When George Barna surveyed pastors several years ago, approximately 90% of pastors agreed that the Bible speaks to the cultural

6 Private phone call with George Barna, January 4, 2024.
7 American Worldview Inventory—2023, Cultural Research Center at Arizona Christian University, www.CulturalResearchCenter.com; George Barna, Raising Spiritual Champions, Arizona Christian University Press: Glendale, AZ, 2023; private conversation with George Barna, January 4, 2024.

issues of our nation. However, when asked if *they* would speak out on what the Bible says about those issues (beyond marriage and abortion), approximately 90% said they would not.[8]

To be more precise regarding the research, Barna discovered that more than three out of four regular attenders of Christian churches want their pastor to teach them what the Bible says about the major social and political issues. A concurrent survey he conducted with a nationally representative sample of Christian pastors revealed that about half of them said they had or planned to preach about same-sex marriage and abortion. That is good. But the good news stops there.

From the remaining issues listed for pastors—such as immigration, environmental care, gun use, gambling, government spending, poverty solutions, and crime policy—less than 10% said they had or planned to speak about any of those issues.[9] To have a truly biblical worldview, the parishioners need their pastors to preach and teach about every current topic, *from the Scriptures.*

David Barton is a bestselling Christian author and historian, and the founder of Wallbuilders, an organization dedicated to presenting America's forgotten history and heroes, with an emphasis on our moral, religious, and constitutional heritage. Wallbuilders has a remarkable collection of some 160,000 primary documents of the Founding Fathers, written before 1812, located at the Wallbuilders Museum in Aledo, Texas.

When I was there, David showed me the manuscripts of the sermons of the early American preachers. What did the preachers preach about? Everything. They preached about every single current topic of the day, educating their church members about the biblical foundations to those issues.

---

8 Private meeting with George Barna in the fall of 2013, based on a national research study he had just completed at that time, later published on the website of the America and Culture Institute of United in Purpose.
9 "The Local Church and Political Engagement," presentation by George Barna, United in Purpose Election Forum, San Francisco, CA, based on surveys conducted by George Barna.

That is needed today. That is why this book exists.

THE PASTOR'S HIGHEST PRIORITIES

The responsibilities that a pastor shoulders are immense. Biblically, pastors are accountable to God to shepherd His flock (Hebrews 13:7). That means they preach, teach, and nurture the spiritual health of the sheep under their care. What does this mean? Well, they equip, exhort, correct, counsel, and yes, at times discipline members to train them in righteousness so they can be mature, attaining to the fullness of Christ (Ephesians 4:11-16). These are heavy duties and all-consuming.

So how does equipping sheep to be godly and influential citizens fit into a pastor's duties? The same as any other ministry: it needs to be shepherded so it will be biblical, Christ-centered, and relevant to the times we live in. Unfortunately, by allowing these types of ministries to be branded as "political" instead of "biblical," they have all too often become ignored. The result: too many Christians are now ill-equipped to engage contemporary issues biblically. That part of equipping that is now so rare has become an Achilles' Heel, coming back to destroy everything we stand for.

So, how bad is it really?

WORDS THAT GET LEFT OUT OF SERMONS

The good news is that there are many wonderful, compassionate, anointed, and bold pastors in America. The bad news is there are not enough of them. And it has become especially difficult to find ones who are truly bold and courageous, willing to stand on the whole counsel of God.

How many pastors are afraid to mention the "A word," abortion, or the "H word," homosexuality, or now the "T word," transgenderism? How many are afraid they will offend—and that is the big word, "offend"—someone in their congregation? Some are even afraid to mention the "M word," that is, that marriage is only defined as between a man and a woman. And some are afraid to mention the "S word," sex, making the case that biblically, sexual expression is to be saved for marriage between a husband and wife. Or how about the "C word," that is, cohabitation, living together outside of marriage?

There are times when pastors are hesitant to speak out and have the right motivation: not wanting to offend those whom they want to evangelize. That is understandable. However, how you bring them in is what you bring them to. In other words, if you are afraid to speak out on the major issues of the day as they come into the church, how will they learn of the lordship of Christ in all areas of life? You stand the risk of producing only "quasi-sorta-almost Christians" that cherry-pick what they accept—in reality, not becoming true followers of Jesus at all.

ACCEPTABLE ISSUES

There are some social issues that most pastors feel quite free to preach on. One would be the sin of racism (although, in reality, Genesis 1:27 implies we are all one "race"), and well, they should. Most pastors would be quite comfortable preaching about concern for the poor and disenfranchised (Matthew 22:39), and well, they should because God cares deeply about this. Most would preach openly, we would hope, on the sin of human trafficking (Psalm 82:4), and well, they should. But when it comes to certain issues—abortion, homosexuality, trans issues, Marxism/socialism, support for Israel, national debt—these same pastors suddenly grow silent.

HOW YOU WIN THEM IS HOW YOU KEEP THEM

A person was once talking to me, raving about a church in Las Vegas, Nevada. Knowing that it is nicknamed "Sin City," I asked, "Would a stripper be comfortable going to that church?" The man said, "Yes." Well, that fact, in and of itself, is not problematic. We would all want her to come and feel welcomed.

I then asked, "Would she feel comfortable, long term, to continue attending and also continuing the lifestyle of being a stripper?" He paused longer on this one and, after a slight pause, answered, "Yes."

Now, that *is* a problem. It is true that the good news is that God accepts us the way we are. However, the great news is He doesn't leave us that way. Yes, we would all want the stripper to feel comfortable in coming to church, but we would—assuming we are scriptural—want the conviction of the Holy Spirit to change her heart and then her actions and her occupation (Romans 12:2).

Some pastors live with the following naïve notion: "We can get them in, and then we can change them in our small groups or disciple groups, thus we don't have to address those topics from the pulpit." Don't be deceived. That is not happening in large measure. A simple examination of the sexual ethics of the youth, young adults, and even older adults within the contemporary American church indicates that this is not happening. How you win them is how you keep them.

THE TESTS

If your pastor will not preach on all the so-called "cultural issues" or "social issues"—which are, in reality, biblical issues—nicely ask him or her why those topics are not covered from the pulpit. You might consider even giving your pastor this book. (Warning: Pastors might see themselves in this chapter. That is good.)

Does your pastor bring up contemporary issues during sermons and do so in a way that helps equip you to engage with others biblically? If not, why not? How about Sunday School classes or special evenings of teaching on cultural issues, or making materials readily available to help educate you on what is going on in our nation and in our communities, and how we can stand for truth in private and public spheres (1 Peter 3:15-17)?

One of the many responsibilities of a pastor is to equip the sheep to identify evil (1 Thessalonians 5:21) and stand for righteousness (Ephesians 4:25) in this "woke world" we are now living in. Is that happening in your church? If not, why not? Are you being trained to confront—without being argumentative—(2 Timothy 2:14-15) the woke evils that you and your fellow church members are facing day by day, such as:

Being forced to use "preferred pronouns" that reject biological reality?

Being subjected to social pressure to "not judge" but instead affirm mutilations of adolescent bodies in the name of gender fluidity, or biological males competing in women's sports or using women's bathrooms, or a public school's "right" to hide gender identity issues from a student's parents, as well as allowing them to be "groomed" into a lifetime of pain (Matthew 18:5-6)?

Being identified as a racist because you are a White person, and being told—and here comes the tired rhetoric—that "our nation is *institutionally* and *systemically* racist?"

Is your pastor encouraging biblical, practical counseling and support (2 Timothy 2:2) to help families and children experiencing gender dysphoria issues?

Does your pastor warn you about so-called "family-friendly" events, parades, and theme parks that are now subtly (and not so subtly) desensitizing your children to sexual perversion and confusion?

If your pastor hasn't made it clear what Scripture says about the above issues (and so many other woke concerns), hasn't focused on training you to be that salt and light (Matthew 5:13-16) in standing for truth (Ephesians 6:14-15), or that the Lord expects you to be in this darkening world, then maybe there is a lukewarmness that needs to be gently confronted (Revelation 3:14-16).

So, if after respectful conversations with your pastor, he or she will not budge, I suggest you go into a time of prayer and fasting. Get a few others to fast and pray with you, not to be divisive, but to seek the Lord's will.

If, after fasting and prayer, your pastor does not change, may I humbly suggest that you find another church. No pastor—including me—approves of "church hopping." However, finding a place that preaches boldly on *all of Scripture* is vitally important to your soul and just might change the rest of your life!

CHAPTER 9

WOKE "CHRISTIAN" COLLEGES

T his was one speaking engagement that I did not want to accept. In fact, I tried to decline.

The topic was, "Why do Christian colleges lose their distinctives and cease being Christian?"

Three things made this engagement difficult to accept. First, it was to a sophisticated audience with five college presidents, their academic deans, and college board members. Second, attendees were given an exceptional book by the well-known scholar James Tunstead Burtchaell, titled *The Dying of the Light: The Disengagement of Colleges and Universities from Their Christian Churches*. The third was that I would have to speak right after a well-known scholar, George Marsden, who authored the classic work on the topic, *The Soul of the American University: From Protestant Establishment to Established Unbelief.*

The context of the conference was quite straightforward. There had been two "waves" of losing Christian colleges. The man who asked me to speak stated soberly that we were beginning to witness a "third wave" of Christian colleges losing their Christ-centeredness and biblical foundations.

The first wave was the loss of the Ivy League colleges. The second wave was in the mid to late 1800s. Examples included the University of Michigan (once a Catholic university),[1] and the now-named University of California at Berkeley (originally founded by a Congregational pastor).[2]

I prepared for the talk for six months. I can summarize the lecture in one sentence:

> *Any college, church, denomination, Christian organization, or even an individual will capitulate and compromise their fundamental beliefs once they value the accolades of other people more than they fear and reverence God.*

Period.

PASSION FOR CHRISTIAN EDUCATION

I grew up in a home where Christian education was highly valued. We were north-central Kansas farmers. When we took trips, Dad would go out of his way to drive through a Christian college campus. Once we arrived, my dad would pull the car over to the curb and strike up a conversation with some college student walking by. Within moments, Dad learned all about the college, and off we would drive.

My father and my Uncle Glen would help fund students to go to a Christian school near our farm. I inherited that passion. When I became a pastor, my father challenged me to "get the young people into a Christian college." So, I did. I jokingly say that I have talked to more students about Christian colleges than any other pastor in America.

---

1 https://en.wikipedia.org/wiki/History_of_the_University_of_Michigan#The_Catholepis-temiad_(1817%E2%80%931821

2 https://en.wikipedia.org/wiki/Henry_Durant

Even when I pastored a large congregation, I greeted people in the church atrium until the last person had left.

In the lines of people, I looked for high school or community college students or their parents. My goal was to encourage them to go to a Christian college. When I found a student open to going to a Christian college, I would phone a Christian university president or admission officer on the spot, tell them, "Get this kid into your college," and hand the phone to the student. It often worked. That's the good news. But there is bad news: much to my regret, my advice was often disregarded.

DECONSTRUCTION

In the 1990s, something became more apparent in Christian colleges. Some trustworthy evangelical colleges were becoming less faithful to their mission. I am not referring to the liberal denominational colleges of Methodists, Episcopalians, or Presbyterians. Those colleges drifted "far left" long before this time.

But many solidly evangelical colleges now had professors questioning what parents and pastors had taught. And as we touched on in Chapter 6, some Christian colleges even had what they called "Deconstruction Week," where they would say, "We are going to 'tear down' everything you learned from your parents and pastors, and then 'build your faith back up again.'" The problem: once "torn down," what was reconstructed was hardly recognizable to the shocked parents who were paying tens of thousands of dollars of tuition per semester.

While a college could have many godly professors, "a few bad apples" teaching a few requisite courses to impressible freshmen could yield catastrophic results.

CCCU

There are approximately 4,300 institutions of higher learning in the US, of which 2,600 are private colleges. About 140 of the 1,000 religiously affiliated colleges are considered theologically conservative and are affiliated with the Council for Christian Colleges and Universities,[3] the go-to organization for evangelical Christian colleges since 1976.

However, when two CCCU colleges affirmed the practice of homosexuality, the leadership of CCCU attempted to create a convenient "associate membership" for them. The leadership contended that since there is disagreement among member colleges on other issues (modes of baptism, speaking in tongues), why not allow member colleges to disagree on the practice of homosexuality? Obviously, there is an enormous difference between denominational practices (baptism or tongues) and a clear violation of scriptural sexual norms.

EXAMPLES

When a Christian college student at one well-known evangelical college sought help for his struggle with same-sex attraction, his professors encouraged him to celebrate his proclivity. Instead of experiencing the forgiveness of Jesus and the empowering of the Holy Spirit to walk free from sin, he is walking in his sin to this day.

When a professor was teaching pro-homosexual lessons (because "my daughter is gay"), she was promoted. When a professor taught that the book of Romans does not address homosexuality, he was simply moved to teach other classes. When an adjunct professor supported homosexuality, and the dean did not renew the contract, the other faculty rebelled against the dean's decision.

Although homosexuality is the epicenter of the devolution of Christian education, there are many other issues. Take abortion. Some Christian professors openly justify voting for pro-abortion candidates, saying pro-life people are not really pro-life but only "pro-birth," since they care little about the baby after it is born. Obviously, this is false and just an ungodly rationalization.

---

3 https://www.cccu.org/about/

Finally, when one college president and his board stood firm on biblical issues of sexuality, students and faculty voted and more than 70% gave a "no confidence" vote for the president. Bottom line: this is a failure to adhere to Scripture.

THE RESULT

A believing student goes off to college, but by the time they come home for Thanksgiving break of his or her freshman year, they are spouting views that are alien to the Christian values of their home.

Where are so many college students getting a positive view of socialism, communism and Marxism? Not from their parents! From college.[4]

If not Marxism itself, Christian colleges often advocate Marxist-based Critical Race Theory, ESGs (Environment, Social, Government), and DEI (Diversity, Equity, Inclusion). These concepts are based on the victimhood model of "the oppressor and the oppressed." The now all-wise, enlightened student might inform their parents that they, the parents, are, "White supremacists" (assuming they are White) with "White privilege" simply by being together and not divorced. Meanwhile the student was taught to wallow in shame for his "privilege." While writing this book, a brokenhearted mother told me about her son returning home from college, condemning his mother for owning a dishwasher because of her "carbon footprint."

WHEN SELECTING A COLLEGE

The good news: there are colleges that are standing strong. They are wonderful, Jesus-loving institutions led by godly presidents and filled with godly faculty. But how do you choose a Christian college?

---

4 https://intellectualtakeout.org/2020/10/half-of-gen-z-supports-marxism-socialism-heres-why/

1. *Use Caution*

    Do not believe the website or the belief system listed. Dig deep and find out where the institution really stands. Contact alumni; do online searches; ask friends.

2. *Ask Questions of the President and Select Faculty and Students*

    Ask the president straightforward questions, and expect non-equivocating answers. If the president won't meet with you, go to another college. Ask about the positions of professors in the religion department, the social sciences, and even the hard sciences. Meet with select faculty and ask, "How do you view Scripture?" and "Is the practice of homosexuality a sin?" "Can a person change their gender?" and "Does abortion kill a child?" How they answer these questions will tell you with 98% accuracy where they stand on other questions. The fun part: interview students and recent graduates. That should give you great insight into how *effective* the college is in preparing or confusing its students.

3. *Avoid the Dollar Trap*

    I cannot tell you the number of times a parent found out a school was questionable but then capitulated when they saw the amount of the scholarship or because it cost less. I do not know a nice way to say this, but that is putting a dollar price on the health of the soul of the student. The spiritual wellness of the soul of your child for the rest of their life is at stake.

4. *Don't be Deceived by "Christianese" Language*

    Do not automatically accept all the "Jesus talk." It can be deceiving. Don't go by websites. Read reviews of the school; and again, ask alumni and people you trust who are familiar with the school.

5. *Does Your Child Really Need College?*

I grew up thinking everyone needed to go to college. I was wrong. In fact, many should not. My late wife and I adopted four children. Three received college degrees. One did not. He went to an exceptional vocational tech training school. It fit him perfectly. He can get a job anytime and anywhere, with a strong salary to provide for his family, in a field he loves.

6. *Seek the Holy Spirit*

Ask God to show you truth. He will.

7. *Pray and Fast*

Pray as if your child's eternal destiny depends on it. Why? Because choosing the wrong college could unwittingly subject them to progressive or leftist ideologies at a very impressionable period in their life as a young adult. Barna estimates that approximately 70% of high school students who begin college as professing Christians will leave with little to no faith.[5]

8. *Relax*

Then, take a deep breath and trust God.

---

5 https://www.desiringgod.org/articles/will-you-lose-your-faith-in-college

CHAPTER 10

AMERICA'S FOUNDING: BIBLICAL OR SECULAR?

Running on treadmills side by side in the gym provided an opportunity to strike up a conversation with the stranger sweating next to me. In time, the conversation turned to politics. And then somehow to the issue of church involvement in politics. (Not surprisingly, many of my conversations move in this direction.)

SEPARATION OF CHURCH AND STATE

The runner next to me did not know that I was a pastor, nor did he know that I was governmentally active. (I prefer the word "governmentally" over the word "politically," as that is more biblical.) "But," he exclaimed, "we have separation of church and state." "Well," I responded, "that is not in our national 'birth certificate,' the Declaration of Independence."

"Okay," he continued, "it's in the Constitution."

"No, it's not."

"Yes, it is," he stated rather emphatically.

Knowing his error, I tried to drive the point home a little stronger, "The phrase 'separation of church and state' is not in either the Declaration of Independence or in the Constitution."

Undeterred, he stated with greater exasperation, "I *know* it is in there." Clearly, I had said all I could say. He was convinced he was right. But he was wrong.

The obvious question is: Then where does the phrase come from? From a letter written by Thomas Jefferson to the Danbury Baptists in Connecticut on January 1, 1802, when he assured them that the federal government would not intrude into church life (that is, forcing a certain denominational state church on the people) because of "a wall of separation."[1]

But nowhere did he—or any other Founder—try to distance the federal government from the basic tenets of Christianity. On the contrary, the Founders quoted Scriptures. Lots of them. In fact, it was the book they quoted the most.

Many people like to point out that Jefferson was not a Christian, that he was a Deist. Yet he got on his horse Sunday after Sunday and rode down Pennsylvania Avenue from the White House to the Capitol Building where weekly inter-denominational Christian worship services were held—complete with preaching by a pastor from the Bible.[2]

In fact, there were weekly worship services in the US Capitol Building from approximately 1800 to 1869.[3] The Founders affirmed this practice.[4] Weekly Christian worship services in our US Capitol? So much for them believing in the present-day understanding of "separation of church and state."[5]

---

1 Jefferson's Letter to the Danbury Baptists." The Library of Congress. https://www.loc.gov/loc/lcib/9806/danpre.html
2 Daniel Dreisbach, Thomas Jefferson and the Myth of Separation (New York: New York University Press, 2002), 29.
3 Ibid.
4 Ibid.
5 The above three paragraphs are from James L. Garlow, Well Versed: biblical Answers for Today's Tough Issues, Salem Books an imprint of Regnery Publishing, 2016, p. 7.

As noted above, the original use of "separation of church and state" meant exactly the opposite of the way it is used today. Thomas Jefferson was assuring the Danbury Baptists that the government could not come into the church; could not make decisions pertaining to the practice of one's faith.

However, Jefferson's own actions of supporting Christian worship services in the US Capitol Building, complete with the worship music being led by the Marine Corps Band, along with the writings of other Founding Fathers, make the case that religion or the "church," or certainly God or biblical teaching, *can* come into government.

THE REVERSAL

Not until the 1947 *Everson v. Ewing Township Board of Education*, and the 1948 *McCullum v. Board of Education* Supreme Court decisions was separation of church and state interpreted as it so often is today. Those decisions marked the beginning of turning Jefferson's words and intentions on their heads. Instead of the government not being allowed to regulate religion—allowing freedom of religion—as clearly stated in the First Amendment, now government could control religion, and disallow it in the public square. These late 1940s decisions were a profound departure from all previous government-religion understandings, and a clear violation of Jefferson's use—and twisting of—the phrase "wall of separation."

MONUMENTS AND BIBLE VERSES

Any visit to Washington, DC will reveal that Scripture was foundational to the thinking of our Founding Fathers. Fortunately, the biblical passages are in marble, which makes it difficult for the secular historical revisionists to easily erase. Cancel culture reactionaries might want to tear them down, but even that does not change the fact that our Founding Fathers—there are approximately 150 to 200 who are often assigned that title—overwhelmingly looked to Scriptures as the foundations of good government.[6]

GOD AND GOVERNMENT

Government was God's idea. He established government. In fact, He established four governments.

First, there is personal government; that is, exercising personal restraint, governing oneself.

Second, is family government. A successful family has order. It has "government."

Third, is church or congregational government. While the Scriptures might allow some latitude in congregational life, there is still a fundamental and basic pattern established by the Word of God.

Fourth and last, there is civil government. Cities and nations are to be ordered a certain way. The Torah ("teaching") provides profound wisdom for civil governance. That is why the scripture states aphoristically, "Blessed is the nation whose God is the Lord" (Psalm 33:12).

A CHRISTIAN NATION

"Is America a Christian nation?" some ask. Well, if you mean that everyone has to be Christian, no, it is not. If you mean that citizens are forced to be part of a particular church or religious persuasion, then no, America is not a Christian nation.

On the other hand, if by "Christian nation" you mean that the US was founded on Judeo-Christian—that is, biblical—principles, then the answer is an overwhelming "yes."

The nation was not formed on wokeness. Regardless of how you define "woke," that word cannot be used to define our Founders or their intentions.

---

6 https://wallbuilders.com/founding-fathers-jesus-christianity-bible/

In contrast, almost all of the 56 signers of the Declaration of Independence were Christians. Half of them had divinity (religion) degrees.[7]

On February 1, 2023, Tony Perkins of the Family Research Council and Congressman Mike Johnson (who later became Speaker of the House) hosted the first-ever National Gathering for Prayer and Repentance in Washington, DC, which continued the following year on January 31, 2024 (I will share more on this in Chapter 13.) At the solemn event, members of Congress, along with faith leaders, led prayers of repentance for personal sins, sin in the church, and America's sins, before a holy and just God. As I opened the event with co-emcee Tony Perkins, I shared the fact that 35 of the 45 presidents of the United States had issued calls for national prayer, days of humbling ourselves before an almighty God.

Certainly, not all Americans are Christian, but the nation was founded upon a distinctly Judeo-Christian foundation. The Founders were not culturally woke, a word that admittedly did not exist back then. They were, however, biblically awake, aware that our strength as a nation lies in the fact that we acknowledge our Creator and His Word. They also understood that individually, and as a nation, actions will be judged by a holy, righteous God. Obey Him, and blessings will certainly follow; reject Him, and God's wrath is inevitable.

7 https://historynewsnetwork.org/article/12089

CHAPTER 11

THE FINE LINE BETWEEN GOVERNMENTALLY WOKE AND AWAKE

The purpose of this chapter is to explain what I am labeling as the two "woke errors" that have emerged in Washington, DC as it pertains to the expression of the Christian faith. In order to do that, I need to give you background that leads up to two specific errors.

1950S AMERICA

For our purposes, let's pick up the story of American church life in the 1950s. Why do we pick up the story at that point? Because the ending of World War II was a time of great transition in America. And 1960 is now viewed as a bit of a watershed between the older, more inherently religious America and the new, considerably more secular America.

In the 1950s, discerning people sensed that after the great victory of World War II, and the national prosperity that followed, the nation was becoming increasingly secularized. Dwight Eisenhower, the highly loved Army general—"I like Ike" was the GOP campaign—who became president, felt lonely in the White House. Many presidents have felt that way.[1] His friendship with Senator Frank Carlson, a fellow Kansan, meant a great deal to Eisenhower. These two men would together address the nation's growing secularism in two legislative ways and one relational way.

UNDER GOD

On February 7, 1954, Pastor George MacPherson Docherty preached a message at the New York Avenue Presbyterian Church. Docherty, Scottish by birth, shared that he grew up pledging allegiance to the Queen. When his children came from school in America, the pastor expressed surprise that the Pledge of Allegiance did not include the words "under God." Sitting in the audience was President Eisenhower who was impacted by the pastor's words, called on his Congressional friends, and on Flag Day, June 14, 1954, the President signed into law the addition of "under God" to the pledge.

IN GOD WE TRUST

Although US coins included the phrase "In God We Trust" as far back as the Civil War, paper money did not include the phrase until 1957. On July 30, 1957, Eisenhower signed into law that "In God We Trust" was to be our official national motto.

THE NATIONAL PRAYER BREAKFAST

After his election in 1950, Dwight Eisenhower—who was named after Dwight Moody, the great evangelist of the 1800s—told a young evangelist named Billy Graham that the country needed spiritual renewal. Abraham Vereide had migrated from Norway to America in

---

1 https://abcnews.go.com/Politics/President44/story?id=6273508&page=1

1905, and became a Methodist minister in Seattle. He soon realized that to see the changes he longed for, he needed to reach government leaders.

By the 1940s, Vereide was discipling top government leaders in DC. He befriended Senator Carlson, who agreed with Graham that a "Presidential Prayer Breakfast" should begin. Graham convinced a hesitant Eisenhower, who was quite private about his now Presbyterian—originally "River Brethren" Mennonite—faith, to do so. Joined by Pastor Richard Halverson, the Presidential Prayer Breakfast was born in 1953, which had previously been known as the Senate Prayer Breakfast.[2] The name was changed in 1970 to the National Prayer Breakfast.[3] The National Prayer Breakfast has enjoyed enormous visibility, impact, and success, both nationally and internationally.

May I add a personal note? The first president I ever saw was Eisenhower, when I was five years old. The only funeral gathering of a president that I ever attended was that of President Eisenhower. And Senator Frank Carlson was a Kansas farmer, who lived only four miles from our farm. I am proud to say I knew him. Kansans were proud of them both.[4]

---

2 https://en.wikipedia.org/wiki/Frank Carlson
3 https://www.smithsonianmag.com/history/national-prayer-breakfast-what-does-its-history-reveal-180962017/
4 I grew up on a Kansas farm about 70 miles from Abilene, Kansas, the boyhood home of Dwight Eisenhower. The first president I ever saw in person was the 34th President when he returned to visit his boyhood home and library, when I was five years of age. Seventeen years later, in 1969, as a college senior, two buddies and I drove all night from Oklahoma City to Abilene, Kansas so we could stand along the streets of the town when the funeral cortege passed, carrying the body of the beloved President. 100,000 of us crowded into the town with a population of 5,000 that day. As Kansans, we were proud of our President.
Four miles from our farm was the farm of Senator Frank Carlson, near Concordia, Kansas. He was first a farmer, then a Kansas State legislator, followed by being a Member of the US House of Representatives, then Governor of Kansas, and finally US Senator. Then he happily returned to his farm, and could be seen out in the fields along State Highway No. 9 after he left Washington, DC.
When I was the Youth and Music Pastor in the summer of 1969 at his Baptist Church in Concordia, Kansas, I founded the "Greater North Central Kansas Crusade" which was a type of "Billy Graham Crusade," in our small town's football stadium. Knowing that ev-

BUT THERE ARE PROBLEMS

Certainly the 1950s seemed to be demonstrating a type of awakening. However, with all the rekindled manifestations of spiritual fervor—"under God" in the Pledge of Allegiance, "In God We Trust" on our coins, and a National Prayer Breakfast involving the highest elected officials in the nation, America did not become more inherently religious.

To the contrary, since the 1950s the Republic has become more apostate. Or should we even label it pagan?

And in the midst of all the wonderful things that have come through the prayer breakfasts—and they are many—there have emerged two serious problems that I am calling "woke errors." Why is this important to go over? Because the prayers of the leaders of a nation are very important to God, and they will have an impact on a nation. Hezekiah prayed for delivery from Assyria and it miraculously happened (2 Kings 19:19); Moses interceded when the Israelites sinned against God and deserved His wrath and the Lord was merciful (Exodus 32:11-14); David prayed for God's blessing upon Israel and his son Solomon and the Lord responded (1 Chronicles 29:10-22); and Solomon prayed for wisdom to govern a great nation so that it will continue to be blessed (1 Kings 3:3-14). The prayers of the "mighty" matter. Proverbs 29:2 captures this, when kings are righteous (and pray), the nation is blessed.

But when prayers of leaders attempt to manipulate God (like king Balak attempted to do through the pagan prophet Balaam), then God's judgment is deserved (Numbers 22-24).

---

eryone knew him, and many did not know me, I went to Senator Carlson and asked him if he would be the Honorary Co-chairman for the event, to which he graciously assented. Succinctly stated, we are proud of the spiritual leadership provided by two fellow Kansans: Dwight Eisenhower and Frank Carlson. (Later, a Kansas friend of our family would follow a similar pathway as Carlson as Member of the House of Representatives, Senator, Governor, and then Ambassador—Sam Brownback—all the time providing remarkable spiritual leadership in high places.)

God will not be mocked (Galatians 6:6-7); trifling with Him will not end well. Now, consider the two errors below, as we have finally arrived at the purpose for this chapter, to caution regarding these missteps.

WOKE ERROR #1: "JUST PRAY TOGETHER"

In recent years, a usual and dangerous concept has developed in Washington, DC. Here is the view: *So long as we—Democrat and Republican members of Congress—pray together, we can then go back out into our respective chambers and vote how we want.* That is a tragic error.

The ultimate purpose of prayer is not to convince God to do things. The ultimate purpose of prayer is to bring ourselves into alignment with His will. "Thy will be done," is a key phrase from the prayer Jesus taught His followers. *Thy will, not my will.*

When members of Congress pray together, it produces intimacy with God and conformity to His Word, His will, and His ways. Consequently, and this is key: *If people pray together, and come into agreement with His Word, they will not then go out on the legislative floor and one of them vote to support the mutilation of children by so-called gender-altering surgeries, or for the dismembering of babies in the womb, or for that for which God destroyed Sodom. Elected officials who pray together will—together—vote scripturally.*

TRANSFORMED LIVES

Let me ask a bizarre question: Can a prostitute be a Christian? The answer is yes, for about fifteen minutes (figuratively speaking). As a new creation in Christ, she will soon realize that she can no longer do the things she used to do. It is true that she is not saved by ceasing to practice prostitution. She is saved by what Jesus did for her on the cross. However, the evidence, or the "fruit" of her conversion will be her transformed life.

I will now make the application: Can a member of Congress truly be an *authentic* Christian and still vote to have penises cut off of little boys and breasts cut off of little girls in the name of so-called gender reassignment surgery? Yes, but only for the proverbial fifteen minutes. Conviction of the Holy Spirit will overtake them and, as a *true and serious* follower of Jesus Christ, they will repent and never vote that way again. Same with killing babies in the womb. Same with the violation of God's sacred definition of one man-one woman marriage. No true follower of our Lord and Savior would ever vote to violate those and other foundational biblical principles.

WOKE ERROR #2: "IN THE SPIRIT OF JESUS"

Another myth, or should we say heresy, that has emerged in Washington, DC is the notion that we all—Christians, Muslims, Hindus, Buddhists, Sikhs or even atheists—can gather and pray "in the spirit of Jesus." I have always loved the phrase "the Spirit of Jesus" from Acts 17:6—until I began hearing the phrase thrown around in conversations in Washington, DC.

I was quite puzzled by the way it was being used. What did they mean by "the spirit of Jesus?" Was it the Jesus of the Bible? Apparently not. The Jesus of the Bible was born of a virgin, lived a sinless life, was crucified for the sins of the world, died, was buried, resurrected on the third day, and is coming back someday as Judge. That is the *biblical, actual* historical Jesus.

Can a Muslim gather and pray in the name of that Jesus? Well, for starters, Muslims don't believe that Jesus is the Son of God, or that He died on the cross for their sins. So, the answer would be "no," unless it is the prayer of repentance to come to Jesus. Or any other religion? Likely not. Forming meaningful relationships with people who are of other religions is good and wise and Christ-honoring. Forming meaningful relationships with leftist woke progressives is a good thing. That is honoring to God. But thinking one can pray together "in the Spirit of Jesus," while continuing on in violation of biblical truths, is delusional at best and heresy at worst.

THE DANGER

Once again, the reason for this chapter is to help us all avoid the two "woke errors." They are serious:

- The first one regarding prayer tends to either equate Allah or other so-called gods of other religions with Yahweh of the Bible. Or it diminishes prayer to have no impact on how one votes, as if there is not a distinctly God-honoring, biblically grounded way to vote on issues.
- The second error regarding the phrase "the Spirit of Jesus," presents a nice, safe "interfaith," multi-religious "Jesus" without His virgin birth, sinless life, death (atonement for our sins), burial, resurrection, and soon-coming return to earth as King.

APPEAL

The prayer that God honors is the prayer from a broken and contrite heart, humbled before a holy and righteous God whose Name will not be shared with another. And when we pray, He changes us, and we conform to Him and His ways.

Let us obey Him. Let us bow before Him. In repentance. In humility. Seeking His Ways. Walking in His commandments. And may we all diligently pray for our leaders (1 Timothy 2:1-2), that they would faithfully and sincerely seek God's will in prayer, and that they would not compromise in the two "woke" areas mentioned above.

CHRISTIAN NATIONALISM OR BIBLICAL CITIZENSHIP?

C *hristianity Today*, a magazine that was once respected by most evangelicals, carried this headline on January 13, 2021: "Christian Nationalism Is Worse Than You Think."[1] The severely broad-brushed article, alluding to the events of January 6, 2021, continued in melodrama and panic that matched the headline: "In the aftermath of the Capitol attack, many saw a clear connection between the violence and Christian nationalism. As Tish Harrison Warren wrote for *Christianity Today*:

The responsibility of yesterday's violence must be in part laid at the feet of those evangelical leaders who ushered in and applauded Trump's presidency. It can also sadly be laid at the feet of the White American church more broadly.[2]

Notice a conspicuous string of words:

---

1 https://www.christianitytoday.com/ct/podcasts/quick-to-listen/christian-nationalism-capitol-riots-trump-podcast.html
2 https://www.christianitytoday.com/ct/2021/january-web-only/trump-capitol-mob-election-politics-magi-not-maga.html

- Christian nationalism
- Worse
- Violence
- Evangelical leaders
- White
- White American church

There you have it: the formula for the destruction of democracy, according to the naysayers.

If we can step away from the ginned-up hysteria for a moment, let's unpack this erroneous accusation and cut to the chase: the whole purpose of the accusatory phrasing is to delegitimize, intimidate, and bully conservatives in general, and evangelical Christians—that is, if they supported one particular candidate—into silence. After all, "you are dangerous," say the alarmists.

Like any phrase or term, "Christian nationalism" is bad or good, depending on who defines it and, thus, how one defines it. What are the characteristics of Christian nationalists according to their critics? Frankly, it is hard to say. It is complex. But allow me to try to make the complex simple.

ACCUSATION 1: EQUATING THE KINGDOM OF GOD WITH AMERICA

What is a Christian nationalist? Not surprisingly, most conservative people don't like the phrase.[3] The reason is obvious: It tends to overlap the notion of the Kingdom of God with the United States.

This accusation requires greater effort to unpack, but allow me to state at the outset: No serious, biblically grounded follower of Jesus equates the eternal Kingdom of God with the temporary—someday it will end—and temporal nation called the United States. To understand

---

3 https://townhall.com/columnists/michaelbrown/2022/08/13/is-christian-nationalism-dangerous-n2611672

this accusation, we need to explore some related terms: culture, religion, civil religion or culture religion, dominionism, reconstructionism, theocracy, the New Apostolic Reformation (NAR), the Seven Mountains, and MAGA pastors.

ACCUSATION 2: CIVIL RELIGION OR CULTURE RELIGION

While walking across the campus of Drew University in Madison, New Jersey one day, from which I would later receive my Doctorate in Philosophy in Historical Theology, I met the great Dr. Will Herberg, a renowned Jewish scholar. He was a legend on the campus and beyond. He was one of the few—if not the only professor—at the time at Drew University who was oft quoted in the *New York Times.*

As a graduate student, I was in awe of the professor who vaguely resembled—at least in my young and impressionable mind at the time—the famous founder of KFC, Colonel Sanders. Herberg was well known for having changed from a young communist to a champion of conservatism. But he was even better known for his classic work: *Protestant, Catholic, Jew: An Essay in American Religious Sociology.*

Part of Herberg's 1955 thesis, along with one stated in 1967 by sociologist Robert Bellah, was that there was a collective "American Way of Life" with an operative *religious* faith. The key word here is "religious." This was called civil religion, or sometimes culture religion. (On a personal side note, I almost went to Temple University for my doctoral program to study under the great Franklin Littell on this topic, but decided that due to the heavy crime on the Philadelphia campus, Drew University's peaceful New Jersey campus was a more logical choice for me.)

What does this phrase "civil religion" mean practically? It means that Americans, in general, have a type of shared "religious" belief, a type of *American national religious faith.* Simply stated, the nation adheres "to a nonsectarian 'civil religion,' which Herberg defined as a collection of beliefs, symbols, and rituals with respect to sacred things and institutionalized in a collectivity."[4]

At first glance, you might be saying, "So what?" Well, the implications in the 1950s were significant. It meant that the distinctions of truly biblical Christian orthodoxy—human sin and the cross of Jesus, for starters—were set aside for a type of Americana religion, complete with the flag, mother, and apple pie. The Fourth of July was a sacred holiday. America—not Jerusalem—was "the city set on a hill." Conservative Christians were accused of "wrapping the Bible in the flag." They were accused of weeping more at the National Anthem than at the sounds of "The Old Rugged Cross."

Simply stated, attacks on Jesus followers, who also happened to be patriots who were devoted to their country, are not new. At least one scholar has made the connection between the "Christian nationalism" of today with the "civil religion" label of the past.[5] What am I saying? These charges are hardly new. Anyone who loved their nation in the 1970s was castigated as well. The critics simply could not fathom that one could be fiercely committed to Jesus Christ as Lord and Savior and at the same time, have a profound respect and admiration for their nation. The two are not mutually exclusive, nor should a person be seen as suspect for doing so.

ACCUSATION 3: DOMINIONISM

On the failure of the "Civil religion" label to stick, critics seemed to migrate to a new pejorative characterization: "Dominionism." The implication is that Christians—as "dominionists"—are trying to take control of America's political structures. Hysteric articles and social media posts warn of this impending danger.

---

4 https://www.npr.org/2021/04/12/985036148/can-americas-civil-religion-still-unite-the-country
5 https://religion.ua.edu/blog/2021/02/08/civil-religion-or-christian-nationalism/

The term "dominion" comes from Genesis 1:26-28 which states, "Then God said, 'Let us make mankind in our image, in our likeness, so that they may rule...' So God created mankind in his own image, in the image of God he created them.... God ... said to them, '...fill the earth and subdue it. Rule....'" In the *King James Version*, the word is literally "dominion" (v. 26).

The word dominion comes from "rule" or "subdue." But what does this mean? Does this mean, as the leftist progressives claim, that Christians are trying to take over the government?

No, it's actually quite different and considerably more extensive than that. It means that as repentant and humble servants of a high and holy God who owns the entire cosmos, we are to carefully steward the Earth. To "steward" something means that it does not belong to us. It belongs to God. We only oversee it and take care of it for Him. We are accountable to Him for how we give leadership on this Earth. It is a call to serve. It is a call to be careful because everything belongs to God.

Leftists try to spin the argument and accuse Christians of wanting to "destroy" the Earth, which is ridiculous. They twist the phrase "rule over" (i.e., to steward) and claim that "those Christians" don't care about the forests, rivers, or seas. In fact, that's simply not biblical. What sane Christian wants the Earth to be destroyed? God calls us to steward, not destroy. Don't buy into this twisted view.

Secularists get profoundly nervous when Christians practice "spiritual warfare" praying. The uninitiated fail to understand that the "warfare" is spiritual—that is, praying and fasting, along with declaring the promises of God. But what really frightens the non-religious secularist or the religious left, and even the so-called "evangelical left" (assuming it actually exists) is when believers declare that they will rule and reign with Him. This, they assume, surely must mean that Christians are—well, here is that word—insurrectionists.

This popular leftist strategy demonstrates once again not only the lack of understanding of "Christianese" language, but also confuses the present-day world with the future spiritual Kingdom that Christ Himself will establish and reign over as predicted in Scripture (Daniel 7:27; 1 Corinthians 6:1-3; 2 Timothy 2:12; Revelation 5:10, 20:4-6).

ACCUSATION 4: CHRISTIAN RECONSTRUCTIONISM

Since this is viewed as a subset of dominionism, I will mention it only briefly. This view was promulgated by R.J. Rushdoony and his son-in-law Gary North. In his *Institutes of Biblical Law*, Rushdoony made the case that Old Testament law still had relevance for modern society and government. He is correct.

Many evangelicals, even if they have never heard the name of Rushdoony, are at least "partial reconstructionists," and they should not be ashamed for being such. At a most basic level, reconstructionism maintains that Jesus is king over all, a position that I (and most Christ-followers) share. His Kingship includes the government.

Full-fledged Christian reconstructionism believes that the Gospel is so potent, winsome, and compelling, that all of society will be "reconstructed" by the lordship of Jesus. Thus, it is closely allied with postmillennialism, meaning that society will increasingly conform to Christian values to the point that Christ will return after that (thus "post") and establish His reign for a millennium. (The opposing view is premillennialism, meaning Christ will come to earth before, or pre, His 1,000-year reign. Under this view things get worse and worse, at which time Jesus returns.)

ACCUSATION 5: THEOCRACY

Possibly because the dominionist label grew old, leftist progressives began accusing conservative Christians of attempting to set up a theocracy. (Note: I really do not recall if dominionism came before theocracy, or if they were in reverse order, or if these accusatory words were used at the same time, but the point is: more terms continued to arise as accusations.) "Theos" means "God." The "cracy" part of the word means "rule." Since "demos" means "people," democracy means people ruling. Theocracy is literally "God rule."

This charge of theocracy is most bizarre. As a Jesus follower, I don't even know what a theocracy might look like since Jesus is not yet here physically. Someday, He will come back, and He will rule. Until then, we reside in a constitutional (written laws) republic (elected people represent us) with democratic (each person one vote) voting.

What is the real goal of accusing someone of advocating a "theocracy?" The answer is simple: to intimidate and marginalize conservative Christians, to make them think they don't have a right to voice their views, and to accuse them of trying to "overthrow" the current government by a theocracy. That is bizarre. And inaccurate.

Also, interestingly enough, there are scant few theocracies in the world. Two that come to mind are Saudi Arabia, which is an Islamic theocratic monarchy, and Iran, which is an Islamic theocracy. Another is Afghanistan under the iron-fisted rule of the Taliban. But those are not Christian examples, though leftists like to blur the lines and make that comparison.

MARKETPLACE OF IDEAS—THE VOTING BOOTH

To those of us who are Bible-believing Christians, we are comfortable with a constitutional republic. We are not demanding or expecting a theocracy (until Jesus returns). Just as the atheist, the agnostic, the pagan, or the apostate can take their views into the voting booth, so can we. If Muslims or Hindus or Buddhists or Sikhs can take their view into the ballot box—which they can—so can we.

To advocate that candidates have biblical values is not to demand that we have a theocracy, nor does it mean that we are "dominionists" trying to overthrow the government. It simply means that in a constitutional republic where we vote democratically, Bible-believing

Christians can vote along with any other group. And yes, I hope we outvote any anti-biblical voters.

ACCUSATION 6: THE NEW APOSTOLIC REFORMATION (NAR)

More recently, critics of governmentally active Christian evangelicals or charismatics—assuming these Christians are politically conservative—have dredged up a phrase that was popular decades ago. C. Peter Wagner, who passed away in 2016, was formerly a professor of World Mission at Fuller Theological Seminary, and a specialist on church growth and spiritual warfare.

He studied the rapid growth of Christianity in South America, as well as Africa and Asia. He observed that local church pastors often had large networks of churches under their direction. He viewed their calling and function as being "apostolic."

Christians have not always agreed on what an apostle is. Some have contended it is one who physically saw Jesus. Others have observed that apostles are those whose ministry is manifested by miraculous signs. Wagner defined an apostle as:

A Christian leader, gifted, taught, commissioned, and sent by God with the authority to establish the foundational government of the church within an assigned sphere of ministry by hearing what the Spirit is saying to the churches and by setting things in order accordingly for the growth and maturity of the church and for the extension of the kingdom of God.[6]

By this definition, a pastor who has helped plant hundreds of churches (and gives oversight to them) is more than a pastor. He or she is an apostle.

6 C. Peter Wagner, Apostles Today: Biblical Governance for Biblical Power, page 27, Chosen Books, 2012.

Another mark of an apostle—according to Wagner and others—is that their ministry is trans-geographical, that is multi-locational.

Using Wagner's definition, contemporary apostles are to the church what C-level executives are to the business world: leaders of leaders.

These apostles were gifted at establishing new beachheads of ministry. It was this phenomenon that Wagner observed in South American Christianity's rapid growth, particularly in Argentina in the 1990s. He noted it was "new." He regarded it as a type of "reformation." At the core were "apostles," so he called it the "New Apostolic Reformation." He wrote about it. He had meetings about it. And that was it.

Dr. Wagner, writing in 2011, noted:

> The roots of the NAR go back to the beginning of the African Independent Church Movement in 1900, the Chinese House Church Movement beginning in 1976, the US Independent Charismatic Movement beginning in the 1970s and the Latin American Grassroots Church Movement beginning around the same time. I was neither the founder nor a member of any of these movements, I was simply a professor who observed that they were the fastest growing churches in their respective regions and that they had a number of common characteristics.[7]

However, in the last decade, critics of charismatics and evangelicals who are governmentally active—if they are politically conservative—have resurrected this term, using it in a negative way, asserting that such Christians are part of the NAR. And these critics define these believers as being part of a quasi-secret society, making it sound as if it's somewhat akin to the Masons, replete with secret handshakes, code words, and arcane rituals.

---

7 C. Peter Wagner (24 August 2011). "The New Apostolic Reformation Is Not a Cult". Charisma News. Retrieved 22 August 2018.

A number of years ago, I discovered that I too was accused of being an "apostle" in the "NAR." (The use of the term "apostle" is this context is meant to be a pejorative, or secretive term.) At the time, I could not recall what the NAR was. Thinking that they meant NRA, I thought to myself, "I have never been a part of the National Rifle Association." But of course, it was NAR, not NRA.

Even while writing this book, I have read some articles about "NAR apostles," and on a few occasions I have seen that I am listed among them. What is bizarre is of all the friends I have, and of the hundreds of conferences I have gone to, I do not remember once hearing the phrase "National Apostolic Reformation" ever used, publicly or privately, except when discussing one of the articles written against us. But those who use this label against us even use *that fact* against us, saying: "You see, they even deny knowing they are part of the NAR, and they deny using the term. That is one of their tactics." This is truly bizarre.

I do agree that Ephesians 4:11 refers to apostles, prophets, evangelists, pastors and teachers (or pastor-teachers). I do believe all of these offices or functions—including apostles and prophets to an important degree—still exist today. I don't believe those ended at the close of the New Testament time frame in 100 AD.

Admittedly, there are likely some who call themselves "apostles" who aren't. They should most assuredly not use that title. And there are some who call themselves "prophets" who likely are not. (Prophets should be held accountable for what they prophesy.)

And there is another irony. Some who are opposed to the title of "apostle" are so profoundly anointed, that they, in fact, are apostles themselves! The leaders of new theological movements most often have an "apostolic anointing" on their lives. John Wesley was an evangelist, but he was also an apostle in the 1700s. The same goes for Martin Luther 200 years prior to that.

If you look at the early founders of present-day denominations, they were almost always "apostolic." That is why people followed them. The irony is that there are apostles today who, because they object to the use of the term, refuse to use it, even though they (unknowingly) are apostles.

However, denominations tend to change sociologically. The founder of a new movement is usually a forceful, powerful, apostolic figure. Those raised up as the next generation of leaders tend to be strong, but somewhat less than the founder(s). But by the "third generation" of a movement, the apostolic leaders have been slowly replaced with "administrators." These leaders do not establish new beachheads of ministry. They play it safe. They do not or cannot adapt to the new cultural environment. The growth and vigor of the movement is gone.

Why have we talked about this in some detail? Because there are those who are profoundly adamant that labeling anyone an apostle today is not acceptable, that the office or function of an apostle ended with the close of the New Testament time frame. If one feels that way, fine. But there is no reason for those who object to the existence of apostles to become so hostile toward those who believe that apostles still exist. Christians should be able to differ on this, yet work together.

The office of prophet is an inherently more complex issue. Allow me to state it succinctly. There are those who call themselves prophets who likely are not. But time has a way of weeding them out. And God has raised up some contemporary leaders who, though they themselves affirm the calling of the prophet, are insisting on accountability for what prophets say or claim. That is good.

Deuteronomy 18:20-22 gives a strong warning about false prophets, and 1 John 4:1-6 provides us a test for prophets. Furthermore, beware of anyone claiming "new revelation" which goes beyond or in violation to biblical truth.

When I was a local church pastor, there were times when some stranger would show up after our services and announce that he was "a prophet." My standard response was, "Well, you are not a prophet *here*. You will only have that title here if the local elders of the fellow-ship here recognize and affirm that calling on you."

But the fact that some have abused the titles does not mean that there are not legitimate apostles and prophets today. There are true God-ordained apostles and prophets, who follow within the clear guidelines of Scripture. And they—these God-ordained ones—are needed today.

By way of illustration, a bad lawyer does not negate the legitimacy of the practice of law. Nor does a bad doctor negate the practice of medicine. In the same way, a person who calls himself an "apostle" or a "prophet," but who is not legitimately one, does not, in and of itself, negate the valid present-day function of an apostle or a prophet.

As a summation, apostles tend to lay good and solid foundations. Prophets tend to "call out" foundations that are not properly laid, and then correct them. At least that is one of the functions of a prophet. Other prophets are gifted for giving clear and specific words or coun-sel regarding a present-day situation in a person's life. Evangelists are anointed for making the Gospel understandable and compelling to unbelievers. Pastors nurture and disciple. Teachers take complex things and make them more simple and digestible. We need all five offices in Christianity today.

While this topic deserves an entire book to address, allow me to cut to the chase. There is no such movement, to the best of my knowl-edge, that identifies as the "New Apostolic Reformation." If there was, that would not be a bad thing. But in the US at least, I am not aware of any group that uses that phrase to describe itself. It was a phrase that had value in the 1990s, helping to explain South American church growth. There are, however, many critics of Pentecostals, charismatics, and some evangelicals—*particularly if they are active in governmental and/or political life*—as being part of—and here comes that dastardly phrase—the secretive and esoteric New Apostolic Reformation. It is the newest bogeyman of the leftists, as well as some accusatory evan-gelicals, to attempt to label, bully, and intimidate.

ACCUSATION 7: THE SEVEN MOUNTAINS

The "seven mountains" theory tends to be a subsection under the New Apostolic Reformation, so we mention it only briefly as well. In 1975, Bill Bright, founder of Campus Crusade (now CRU), and Loren Cunningham, founder of Youth With a Mission, independent of each other, were given a strategy by God for impacting culture. Since it covers seven areas, it is called the Seven Mountains, or Seven Pillars.[8] It refers to seven spheres of influence in culture and society. They are the family, the church, education, government, media, art/entertainment/sports, and business.

The seven mountains paradigm is simply a "tool" of evangelism, not unlike the way in which "The Four Spiritual Laws" booklet is a tool. Or the way Fellowship of Christian Athletes (FCA) focuses on those in sports. Tools or methods come and go. So it will be with the Seven Mountains. It is merely a "handle" on effective discipling.

However, for some reason, some Christians are highly put off by the strategy. And some non-Christians wrongly view the plan as being a diabolical plot to overthrow the government. It is not. It is merely a methodology which provides categories or "handles" for trying to influence culture for Christ and for biblical values. The seven mountains strategy is not some sinister plan. It is merely another way of defining what Christians have been attempting to do for the last 2,000 years: discipling nations. (See Matthew 28:19.)

ACCUSATION 8: MAGA PASTOR

Closely related is another new term, "MAGA pastor." Not mega, but MAGA. A *mega*church pastor is one who pastors a large church with an attendance of more than 2,000 (or maybe 5,000). But MAGA pastor is a brand-new accusatory phrase, meaning one who is a "Make America Great Again" pastor. Candidly, this phrase is so new (at the

---

8 https://www.the7mountains.com/history-of-the-7-mountains

time of this writing) that I can only assume it means a pastor who has supported one particular presidential candidate. But be assured, it is not intended to be a compliment, and it is meant to tarnish the reputation of the pastor. At its core, it is another attempt to intimidate the person from being governmentally active. (I do, however, want to see America become godly and righteous again. In this case, MAGA would mean "Make America Godly Again.")

ACCUSATION 9: CHRISTIAN NATIONALISM

Given the history of labels assigned to people of biblical values, what does the widely used buzz phrase Christian nationalism mean? I am not certain what the critics mean. But allow me to suggest some potential meanings, since I have, from time to time, been accused, by online "journalists" I have never met, that I am one.

First, I am a Christian. (Personally and theologically, I am an evangelical, one who believes in the authority of God's Word, in spiritual conversion and the new birth in Christ. Furthermore, I believe in the fullness of the Holy Spirit, in the baptism of the Holy Spirit, the sanctified life, and in all of the gifts of the Spirit. I am a Wesleyan by ordination and pastoral credentials, which is part of the Holiness Movement, which affirms the call to holy, righteous, and sanctified living. I believe Spirit-filled people should long to walk in holiness, reflecting the righteousness of Christ.) My ultimate desire is to please Jesus.

Second, I cherish my nation. I know its flaws. I know its national sins. But I care deeply for my nation. The military leader, the centurion, in Luke 7:5, was commended by the Jews for loving Israel, even though he was a foreigner in the land.

Furthermore, I care deeply about all other nations. I want a Hungarian Christian, for example, to cherish his country. I want a Brazilian Christian to cherish her country. Simply put, "Christian nationalism" might well mean that a person who has a deep passion and love of Jesus Christ might rightfully deeply value his or her nation.

The whole purpose of Paul's admonition to the Romans regarding how society is to function was so that evil is stopped and good is encouraged (Romans 13). This makes for good communities. If this is what is meant by "nationalism," then this would be a wonderful "biblical nationalism."

Some accuse people of being Christian nationalists if they believe that the nation was founded on Judeo-Christian values. On that charge I plead guilty. Why? Because America *was actually founded* on Judeo-Christian values. Only those ignorant of the writings of our Founding Fathers or those who are revisionists of history would deny that. As noted, our "national birth certificate"—the Declaration of Independence—states that our rights come from the Creator.

But be assured, the charge of Christian nationalism is merely a veiled—or not so veiled—attempt to muzzle and silence any biblical and political conservative. Simply stated, if you truly believe the Bible, and you are following your constitutional right to be active in the governmental or political arena, you will probably be labeled a Christian nationalist. However, a "Christian nationalist" as I see it, is one who is simply following Christ, and desiring biblical principles of governance for their respective country.

ULTIMATE CITIZENSHIP: THE HOLY NATION

My allegiance to my nation is, however, very secondary to the real "nation" to which I belong. I am a citizen of heaven (Phil 3:20), and I am part of a heavenly "nation" or "holy nation" (1 Peter 2:9).

At the same time, I do live here, on this earth, in a temporal nation. Jeremiah 29:7 teaches us to seek the good of the nation we find ourselves in. Jesus prayed for his nation, well, actually his city, Jerusalem (Matthew 23:37-39, quoted from Psalm 122:6).

Paul wrote to Timothy that we were to pray for our governmental leaders so "that we may live peaceful and quiet lives" (1 Timothy 2:1-2). The verse continues, "in all godliness and holiness." Now *that* should be the goal of all believers. And that, to me, would be the basis for so-called "Christian nationalism;" that is, desiring the best for one's nation.

Is patriotism—devotion to one's country—wrong? Is nationalism—identifying solely with one's own nation—wrong? I say "no" to both questions. Any follower of Jesus wants the best for their community and their nation. Any serious Christian would desire their nation to follow the biblical principles of governance and bring tranquility and prosperity to their community.

NATIONALISM—NEGATIVE

If the term "nationalist" is used as it was in Germany in the 1930s to say that one's group is the superior race, count me out. That is arrogance. Even more, it is a sin.

If "Christian nationalism" refers to an unscriptural Americentric obsession, that is, idolizing the United States, count me out.

Furthermore, based on the definition of "nationalism" that some advocate, one could not be both a Christ follower and a "nationalist" at the same time. In that case, those terms would be mutually exclusive.

NATIONALISM VS. GLOBALISM

On the other hand, if the term "nationalist" means each nation has its own sovereignty, as opposed to globalism (a globalist or "one world" government), then a person who is a nationalist would be a good thing. It simply means one cherishes or cares for one's country. The *Oxford English Dictionary* defines globalism as "the belief, theory, or practice of adopting or pursuing a political course, economic system, etc., based on global rather than national principles."

Make no mistake, globalism is a secular—and not biblical—worldview that downgrades the importance and role of individual nations and uplifts an anti-biblical agenda that is antithetical to God's Word: Abortion in the name of "population control;" euthanasia as a "safe, merciful alternative;" gay rights and transgenderism as "culturally correct and logical."

Scripture affirms nations. God establishes nations and their boundaries (Acts 17:26). He blesses the nations of the world (Genesis 26:4). Jesus died on the cross for all people of all nations (John 3:16). Furthermore, the Great Commission is a call to disciple the nations (Matthew 28:19).

Nowhere in Scripture is globalism exalted. In fact, globalism is most often associated with the Antichrist in the New Testament ("little horn" in Daniel 7; "the beast" in Revelation 13). The primary example of globalism in the Old Testament was the Tower of Babel in Genesis 11:1-9. It is never viewed in a positive light. God actually decimated their building efforts. The only one world government I want is when Messiah comes to rule the entire earth, and we "will study war no more" (Isaiah 2:4; Micah 4:3).

NOT CHRISTIAN NATIONALISM, BUT BIBLICAL CITIZENSHIP

If or when you are called a Christian nationalist, ask the accuser to define it. Most can't. But if they can define it, and if what they define is anti-biblical, then agree with them that Christian nationalism is a bad thing, and that you are not one.

If, on the other hand, you have the opportunity to define it as a Christ-follower who also has a healthy allegiance to his country, then should one embrace the term? One of my friends asked me, "Should we just accept the phrase 'Christian nationalism,' but redefine it, and give it a proper definition?" I am not sure. In the 1700s, the great evangelist and reformer John Wesley was able to change a negative term into a respectable label.

Wesley's followers were accused of being "methodical"—following a rigorous schedule of a certain number of hours per week of prayer, Bible reading, and caring for the poor—but he turned the pejorative catcall of "Methodists" into an honorable term. Should we attempt to do the same with the negative and false (as the critics define it) label of "Christian nationalism?"

I suspect that may be "a hill too steep to climb." I prefer using the more accurate phrase 'biblical citizenship,' which is the desire for one's community and nation to prosper (by God's definition of "prosper"), regardless of where one lives. Even while the Israelites were in exile, God had a clear admonition regarding this: "...seek the peace and prosperity of the city to which I have carried you into exile. Pray to the Lord for it, because if it prospers, you too will prosper" (Jeremiah 29:7). Given the fact that we, as citizens of heaven, are "exiles" on this earth, let us, like the exiled Israelites of Jeremiah's day, live out good biblical citizenship.

CHAPTER 13

AMERICA FIRST VS. BLAME AMERICA

One of the strongest manifestations of wokeness is the propensity to blame America for all the evils of the world. While we are fully aware of America's sins, at the same time, we know that America has been a most powerful global force for good.

AMERICA FIRST?

"How arrogant it is to say 'America first'" some exclaim. "That isn't even Christian! After all, doesn't the Bible say that 'the first shall be last.'" That raises the question: Is it wrong to put one's country first?

Columnist Robert Spencer asked precisely that: "What exactly is wrong with being America First? If the president of the United States doesn't put America first, which country *should* he put first? Or should he put some nebulous idea of 'global interests' first, with those interests being defined not by Americans but by the likes of China, the EU, and Iran?"[1]

---

1 https://pjmedia.com/columns/robert-spencer/2020/02/17/what-exactly-is-wrong-with-

President Trump made it clear in his inaugural address on January 20, 2017: "From this moment on, it's going to be America First.... We will seek friendship and goodwill with the nations of the world—but we do so with the understanding that it is the right of all nations to put their own interests first."[2]

How did people respond? Many thought, "Well, of course. The president of the US *should* put America first." But others, such as William Kristol tweeted: "I'll be unembarrassedly old-fashioned here: It is profoundly depressing and vulgar to hear an American president proclaim, 'America First.'"[3] Embarrassing? Vulgar?

HISTORY OF "AMERICA FIRST"

"America First" is hardly new. It was a phrase used as early as the 1880s as a Republican campaign slogan. President Woodrow Wilson made it a national catchphrase in 1915, hoping to keep America out of World War I. World-famous pilot Charles Lindbergh led the "America First Committee," with some 800,000 Americans, for the same reason: to keep the US out of the war.

But it was not merely a Democrat president and a popular aviator who used the term. When America began to rise as an economic world power during the post-World War I period, the phrase was even noted overseas. "The United States has achieved prosperity by the wise policy of America first," declared London's *Daily Express* in 1923. In 1927, the slogan got another boost when Chicago elected a headline-hungry mayor, William Hale Thompson, whose campaign anthem was "America First, Last and Always." He pledged to support the establishment of America First Associations around the country and

putting-america-first-n379905
2 https://pjmedia.com/columns/robert-spencer/2020/02/17/what-exactly-is-wrong-with-putting-america-first-n379905
3 https://pjmedia.com/columns/robert-spencer/2020/02/17/what-exactly-is-wrong-with-putting-america-first-n379905

said he would show English leaders who asked for economic help "where to get off."[4]

ACCUSATIONS AGAINST "AMERICA FIRST"

Those who dislike the "America First" phrase claimed that it was a slogan used not only by isolationists, but over the last century and a half by anti-immigrant groups, with some claiming the KKK, fascists, and nativists tried to co-opt the term. A "nativist" refers not only to indigenous people, such as Native Americans, but it can also apply to "established" residents, that is, those who are here, in juxtaposition to those who are trying to immigrate. Thus, those who disdain the phrase view it as xenophobic—that is, having a fear or hatred of immigrants or strangers.[5]

MEANING

What does "America First" *really* mean? According to popular (and sometimes questionable) Wikipedia, "America First" refers to a policy stance in the United States that generally emphasizes American exceptionalism and non-interventionism.[6]

Thus, a new phrase has been added to the equation: American exceptionalism. Understanding "American exceptionalism" is important for understanding "America First."

AMERICAN EXCEPTIONALISM

Like many phrases, "American exceptionalism" has many definitions. It is certainly not new terminology. The first reference was by

---

4 https://time.com/4273812/america-first-donald-trump-history/
5 https://www.vox.com/2018/10/22/17940964/america-first-trump-sarah-churchwell-american-dream
6 https://en.wikipedia.org/wiki/America First (policy)

the French writer Alexis de Tocqueville in his 1835 through 1840 work *Democracy in America.*[7]

Not only was the phrase used in America, but it is noteworthy that many foreign writers commented on American exceptionalism, including Karl Marx, H. G. Wells, G. K. Chesterton, and a host of others.[8]

What is more amazing is the fact that they used the phrase in a complimentary way, in contrast with the contemporary "blame America first" crowd.

Children were once widely exposed to the phrase "American exceptionalism:" "The theme became common, especially in textbooks such as the *McGuffey Readers*, a series of graded primers grade levels 1–6. From the 1840s to the late 19th century, the *McGuffey Readers* sold 120 million copies and were studied by most American students. The *Readers* "hailed American exceptionalism, manifest destiny, and America as God's country.... Furthermore, McGuffey saw America as having a future mission to bring liberty and democracy to the world."[9]

To some, the phrase American exceptionalism refers to ingenuity, given the creativity, number of inventions, patents, and copyrights. To some, the phrase refers to America's productivity, given the wealth of the nation. To some, it refers to America's resilience. To others, it might refer to the capacity to be a melting pot to the nations, that is, until "multiculturalism" began to be taught in the latter part of the twentieth century, which produced a generation of Marxists who are anti-American.

To others, American exceptionalism has to do with America's economic and military power. To some, it is the radical optimism that

---

7 https://en.wikipedia.org/wiki/American exceptionalism citing "Foreword: on American Exceptionalism; Symposium on Treaties, Enforcement, and US Sovereignty," Stanford Law Review, May 1, 2003, p. 1479.

8 https://en.wikipedia.org/wiki/American_exceptionalism citing Michael Kämmen and Stanley N. Katz. "Bernard Bailyn, Historian, and Teacher: An Appreciation." by James A. Henretta, Michael Kämmen, and Stanley N. Katz, eds. The Transformation of Early American History: Society, Authority, and Ideology (1991) p. 7.

9 https://en.wikipedia.org/wiki/American exceptionalism citing Quentin R. Skrabec (2009). William McGuffey: Mentor to American Industry. Algora Publishing. p. 223. ISBN 978-0-87586-728-1.

grips the national conscience, the "we can do it" mentality. To others, it is America's passion for freedom and liberty, a "give me liberty or give me death" mentality, or a Western US theme of "don't fence me in." To others, it is the fierce independence as demonstrated in the American Revolution-era flag, "Don't tread on me." All of these are important and play a part in the phrase American exceptionalism. But there is more. So much more.

DEFINING EXCEPTIONAL

"Exceptional" is defined as "the theory or belief that something, especially a nation, does not conform to a pattern or norm."[10] One could rightfully argue that every nation is unique or in some way exceptional. And every nation *is* exceptional. But what is truly exceptional about America—something that likely cannot be said about any other nation? It is the belief that *our rights are from God*.

The preamble of our national "birth certificate," the Declaration of Independence, states those memorable words:

> We hold these truths to be self-evident, that all men are created equal, that they are endowed *by their Creator* with certain unalienable Rights, that among these are Life, Liberty and the pursuit of Happiness. (Emphasis mine.)

By their Creator is the definitive phrase. Later it will speak of *Nature* (that is, natural law) and *Nature's God*. What other nation viewed inherent, inalienable human rights as being from God? How many of today's nearly 200 nations acknowledge in a founding document that all rights come from God?

---

10 https://duckduckgo.com/?q=exceptionalism+definition&t=chromentp&atb=v347-1&ia=definition

Americans believe rights come from God to "We the People," and then "We the People" loan those rights *temporarily* to elected officials. This recognition is unique. It is—and here is that word again—*exceptional*. *That* is the core of American exceptionalism.

The flag that most depicts this American exceptionalism is "An Appeal to Heaven," which was commissioned by George Washington, Commander-in-Chief of the Continental Army, in October 1775, to be used on a squadron of ships. This was, in effect, the flag of our earliest Navy.

The phrase "appeal to heaven" came from John Locke (1632-1704) in writings in which he refuted the previously presumed "divine right of kings:"

> And where the body of the people, or any single man, is deprived of their right, or is under the exercise of a power without right, and have no appeal on earth, then they have a liberty to appeal to heaven.... And ...they have, by a law antecedent and paramount to all ... laws of men, reserved that ultimate determination to themselves which belongs to all mankind, ... they have just cause to make their appeal to heaven.[11]

PRACTICALITY OF "AMERICA FIRST"

In all of life, we operate with that same mentality: family first, our loved ones and friends first, etc. The airlines, for example, instruct a mother to put her oxygen mask on first before her child and then help her child. Why? So she can stay alive to help her child. When you get paid, whose mortgage do you pay first? Yours. When you get paid, for whom do you buy groceries first? You and your family. You sustain

---

11 https://en.wikipedia.org/wiki/Pine_Tree_Flag citing John Locke. "Second Treatise on Civil Government"—Chapter 3 Sect. 20-21 & Chapter 14 Sect. 168.

yourself and yourselves, then you can help others. If you are not cared for, you cannot bless others.

I was raised on a farm. We would assist the sows (pregnant pigs) when they farrowed (gave birth to) piglets (baby pigs). Sometimes the ten or twelve or even more piglets—sometimes as high as sixteen—in their desire to get all the milk they could from the sow—would essentially "suck the life right out of her." We would have to keep the sow penned in a different area, separated for a while. We had to put her first. Why? If she was healthy, she could save the lives of a dozen piglets. If she died, so did all the piglets. She had to come first in order to save the lives of all.

A healthy America can bless other nations. If a president does what he is supposed to do, he will put his or her own country first, regardless of the nation. If a president puts America first, he is positioning our nation to be in a state of health which could, in turn and in time, bless many other nations.

NOT ARROGANCE, BUT HUMILITY

In Chapter 10, I wrote about a national call to repentance. Here is the fuller story. At 6:30 am on February 1, 2023, I organized and co-led with Tony Perkins the "National Gathering for Prayer and Repentance," which was held at the Museum of the Bible in Washington, DC. It was not a prayer breakfast, where there is often so much breakfast and too little prayer. It was prayer, with no breakfast. But not any prayer. It was prayers of repentance. No speeches or sermons were allowed, with the exception of some who were asked to give a seven-minute call to repentance.

Members of Congress and evangelical leaders were not even introduced, as we wanted to keep the focus on God and God alone. We did not allow applause, except at the very end, and then we applauded for God alone. No comments could be made "horizontally," that is, from a person to the crowd. All comments had to be vertical, that is, prayers of repentance from people to God. We began with repentance for personal sin. We then repented for sin in the church. And lastly, we repented for America's national sins. A standing-room-only crowd listened as seventy or so people cried out to God, repenting of sin. Some members of Congress wept openly as they asked a holy and just God to forgive us as a nation.

In the second year—on January 31, 2024—a total of 147 people prayed on the platform in the five-hour event. Members of Congress were joined by political leaders from around the world.

Why do I tell you this story? Because "America First" does not mean some arrogant, boastful, braggadocios nation. We have no right to do that. Given America's sins—slavery, violation of treaties with Native Americans, Jim Crow laws, abortion that has killed some 60 million Americans, endorsement of homosexuality, and now so-called transgenderism, along with antisemitic pro-Hamas terrorists' rallies, to name a few—America has plenty of sins for which to repent.

Thus, "America First" is not some showboating phrase. It is the humble recognition that God has truly blessed America. It is the recognition that "under God" was added to the Pledge of Allegiance on purpose. "In God We Trust" was made our national motto on purpose. We are dependent on Him.

Any "First" that America has is given by Him and can be taken away by Him. It is the recognition that "Blessed is the Nation whose God is the Lord" (Psalm 33:12). If that is true, and it is, the converse is true: cursed is the nation whose God is not the Lord. We are "America First," that is, blessed, only to the extent that we put God first.

The culturally woke do not understand this. They are obsessed with blaming America for the world's woes. They do not grasp the fact that the scriptural principle that applied to Israel— "You are blessed to be a blessing to others" (Genesis 12:1-3)—can apply to other nations as well, just as it does to individuals. It applies to America. In fact, it can apply to all nations. The principle is to "walk in obedience to God so that God can bless you so that you can bless others." That is the authentic, scripturally grounded view of "America First."

PART II

A BIBLICAL RESPONSE TO LAWLESSNESS

How God's people can arm themselves against the progressive and anti-biblical assaults on the pillars of our society: marriage, family, sexuality, and issues of race and identity.

And every man did what he thought was
right in his own eyes.

—JUDGES 21:25

CHAPTER 14

PARENTAL AUTHORITY

I n *Well Versed: Biblical Answers to Today's Tough Issues*, I told the story of a public school counselor who insisted on me—as the father—being absent from my elementary-age son's session.[1] I posed the question to the counselor, "To whom does the child belong? The parents or to the state (government or government schools)?" The counselor assumed I would say "the parents." But I did not. I explained that children do not belong to either the state (school) or the parents. The children belong to God. However, he assigns the children to the parents until the children arrive at responsible adulthood.

However, some state legislatures, thinking the government has all authority over children, want to be able to take children from their parents if the parents do not affirm that little Johnny wants to be considered a girl, or if little Susie wants to be viewed as a boy.[2]

---

1 James L. Garlow, Well Versed: Biblical Answers to Today's Tough Issues, Salem Books, an imprint of Regnery Publishing, 2016, pages 71-2.
2 https://www.californiafamily.org/2023/06/ca-senate-passes-bill-that-would-remove-custody-from-non-affirming-parents/

Other school officials want to take little Susie secretly to have a life-altering, baby-killing abortion without the parents even knowing. School boards discuss if teachers have to tell parents if students are in school acting out in a gender different from that in which they were born. This constitutes a massive loss of parental authority.

Simply stated, in many areas parents have lost authority over their children and their children's education. And parents have had it. If they can, they are leaving the public education system.[3] The nation's largest school district—New York City—"has lost some 50,000 students over the past two years. In Michigan, enrollment remains more than 50,000 below pre-pandemic levels…" In California, "more than a quarter-million public school students have dropped from California's rolls since 2019."[4]

Parents are fed up with being viewed in a condescending light. And for good reason. In an article titled "The Decline and Fall of Parental Authority," Ron Taffel underscored "parental dissatisfaction with the current childrearing situation: the tendency on the part of child experts, … to blame parents for what's going on. In fact, as I speak with child clinicians and educators across the country, the parent blame knocks me over. I can't help but think, *How can we help the very parents we seem to hold in such disdain?*"[5]

THE SOURCE OF PARENTAL AUTHORITY

All parental authority is limited authority, and the authority they have is delegated to them by God!

The Apostle Paul commanded fathers in the church not to abuse their children but to raise them to know and serve the Lord (Ephesians

---

3 https://www.publicschoolexit.com/
4 https://www.washingtontimes.com/news/2022/aug/8/more-parents-removing-their-children-from-public-e/
5 https://www.psychotherapynetworker.org/article/decline-and-fall-parental-authority/

6:4). The underlying assumption was that children belonged to God, and parents were His stewards in caring for them. Nowhere does God give the church or government the authority to educate children. In fact, it's parents, not the church or the government, that will be judged by how they disciple their children.

Deuteronomy 6 provides a wonderful illustration of the close nurturing, training, and equipping parents are responsible for doing with their children:

> And these words that I command you today shall be on your heart. You shall teach them diligently to your children, and shall talk of them when you sit in your house, and when you walk by the way, and when you lie down, and when you rise.... You shall write them on the doorposts of your house and on your gates.
>
> —*Deuteronomy 6:5-9*

Proverbs 22:6 (ESV) succinctly states the impact proper instruction will have on children: "Train up a child in the way he should go; even when he is old he will not depart from it."

These are not suggestions; they are imperatives from the Lord to parents who are entrusted with the care of children, all of whom are a gift from God (Psalm 127:3-5).

THE ROLE OF TEACHERS

That doesn't mean parents can't, in effect, "deputize" others to help educate their children when necessary, but they can never relinquish their own responsibility. In the founding era of America, it was the church that came to the aid of parents to help them disciple their children. When parents and churches worked together, America had the highest literacy rates in the world. But all that changed beginning in the late 1800s and early 1900s.

THE BEGINNING OF THE PROBLEM: JOHN DEWEY

One of the most influential educators in our country was John Dewey. A secular humanist, he became an atheist and one of the original authors of the Humanist Manifesto. Dewey is widely recognized as the founding father of America's "progressive" public education system.[6] An admirer of communist and socialist systems, his educational philosophy concentrated on the relationship between the individual student and society, and that school is a social institution through which social reform can, and should take place.[7]

Dewey's views concerning God and eternal truths have become the guideposts of modern, secular, public education: "There is no god and there is no soul. Hence, there is no need for the props of traditional religion. With dogma and creed excluded, the immutable truth is dead and buried. There is no room for fixed and natural law or permanent moral absolutes."[8] Not only has this philosophy dominated our public education system, but it was legitimized by devastating US Supreme Court decisions, including prayer removed from school (*Engel v. Vitale*, 1962); and posting of the 10 Commandments forbidden (*Stone v. Graham*, 1980).

Removing "religion" (read: Christianity) from school was just the start. Once biblical values were replaced by relativism, the door was opened for the explosion of all progressive influence in the classroom and school administration. The flood of setbacks included:

- the ability of school healthcare clinics to dispense contraceptives;
- transportation of young girls to abortion clinics without parental notification;

6 https://illinoisfamily.org/education/john-deweys-public-schools-replaced-christianity-with-collectivist-humanism/
7 https://en.wikipedia.org/wiki/John Dewey
8 https://www.allaboutphilosophy.org/absolute-truth.htm

- explicit sexual "education" without regard to age appropriateness;
- allowing biological males in girls' restrooms and shower facilities;
- promotion of LGBTQ awareness encouraging gender confusion;
- and yes, even hosting "drag queen hour" for the youngest and most vulnerable.

All of these destructive and erosive practices have become commonplace. And what is happening in the schools tracks with what is happening in many state legislatures: the removal of more and more parental rights in the raising of, and making decisions for, their own children. Such things as exercising discipline, not "affirming" their child's gender freedom, or disagreeing with having an abortion are now thought of as forms of child abuse, necessitating governmental intervention.

WHY IS THIS HAPPENING?

Because secularists don't believe in man's inherent sinfulness, and they don't see the need for spiritual regeneration. By continuing to subvert the family and control education, they hope to usher in their concept of a utopian, "liberated" world. Their worldview believes people are oppressed and need to be freed from social contracts, as well as arbitrary cultural and religious norms. But if history tells us anything, secularism leads to socialism, then Marxism (communism), which is total, tyrannical control. In a real sense, public schools in America are becoming the "churches" of the secular humanists.

Under Marxism, there are no God-given rights for anything, including children; the state is god. The totalitarian state can limit you to one child if they want, as we've seen in China's disastrous "one-child policy," or arbitrarily decide if you're competent to be a parent.

Everyone, especially parents (remember Proverbs 22:6!), must submit to government-identified "experts" in order to further the utopian humanist ideology. Love of God, love of parents, love of children, love of the household of faith; all must submit to this hegemony. No dissent is tolerated. God is dead, so liberty under God is their enemy.

JESUS' VIEW OF CHILDREN

In his earthly ministry, Jesus was enraged by the actions of His disciples toward children:

> And they were bringing children to him that he might touch them, and the disciples rebuked them. But when Jesus saw it, he was indignant and said to them, "Let the children come to me; do not hinder them, for to such belongs the kingdom of God. Truly, I say to you, whoever does not receive the kingdom of God like a child shall not enter it." And he took them in his arms and blessed them, laying his hands on them.
>
> —*Mark 10:13-16, ESV*

Not only did Jesus show his concern and appreciation for children, but He reserved some of his fiercest condemnations for those who would dare to harm them or lead them into sin: "It would be better for him if a millstone were hung around his neck and he were cast into the sea than that he should cause one of these little ones to sin" (Luke 17:2, ESV).

WHAT PARENTS CAN DO

It cannot be overstated how important a parent's involvement is in every aspect of their child's education. If their children are in public school out of necessity, parents need to be especially attentive to curriculum content, the teachers' values, and any inappropriate policies that put children at risk or expose them to ungodly material. When there is an issue, it must be brought to school authorities quickly and firmly, with a willingness to engage legal support if necessary. This has been successful in many instances across our nation as "mamma bears"— mothers who are incensed on what is happening in our nation's schools—have pushed back against the ungodly sexualizing of their children.

For those that can, charter schools, private schools, and home-schooling are far better options than the vast majority of public schools in our day and age. The movement to allow school vouchers is a critical development that needs to be supported so that our tax money can be used as we see fit and not unilaterally dictated by a non-responsive public education system.

Although this short chapter does not allow us to make the defense for this, homeschooling is, by far, the best option of all. Contrary to what some parents believe, almost all parents are thoroughly equipped, or can learn how to become equipped, to be homeschool teachers.

THE ROLE OF THE STATE

What role does the state have, biblically, concerning education? A minor role, but an important one: maintain the peace (Romans 13:4) so children can study and learn in a comfortable environment.

CHAPTER 15

SEXUAL CHAOS

W e used to laugh out loud when we saw a man wearing a dress. We laughed at it in movies and even Bugs Bunny cartoons. Now, if you laugh at a man in a dress, you're considered a bigoted transphobe who deserves to be "cancelled."

THE ORIGINAL SEXUAL REVOLUTION

When Christianity replaced the old, pagan Greco-Roman world with the Holy Roman Empire, the cruel, prevailing sexual ethic was mercifully displaced. In that culture, powerful men could indulge their sexual appetites at will on whomever they wanted. As historians have observed, "In so many ways, Roman sexual morality was abhorrent, and one of its most prominent features was the strong dominating the weak."[1]

---

1 https://www.challies.com/articles/sexual-morality-in-a-christless-world/

Christ transformed all that. Under the lordship of Jesus, all of life is to be sanctified and conformed to God's will. That includes the human sexual appetite. When the West adopted this sexual standard, it thrived. Where it was ignored, the inevitably destructive consequences followed.

THE ANTI-SEXUAL REVOLUTION

A shift in Western anthropology has been at work since the influential writings of Jean-Jacques Rousseau (1712-1778). Rosseau believed that man in a state of nature is a "noble savage" and should be able to express his natural sexual impulses at will. The problem is that this philosophy doesn't take into account mankind's sinful nature.

According to Rosseau and his disciples, sexual pleasure is considered the pinnacle of human happiness, no matter what religious and cultural taboos may have existed in the past. In our "modern" times, easy access to contraception and abortion and sex has been reduced to nothing more than mere "recreation."

Later, sexual anarchists argued that any limit on sexual expression is a limit on human flourishing and happiness. And, not content to keep their shameful acts to themselves, they're out and proud and literally "proclaim their sin like Sodom, they do not hide it" (Isaiah 3:9, ESV).

NO SEXUAL LIMITS OR BOUNDARIES

In our day, because sexual lust is insatiable (and satanic), people have to go to more perverse extremes in vain attempts to try to find pleasure and affirmation.

With the ubiquity of pornography and exposure to aberrant sexual themes and practices, children are being sexualized at earlier and earlier ages. The LGBTQ "Pride" agenda (including "drag queen" hour in public schools) is grooming children as young as elementary school to experiment in all manner of perverse sexual behaviors and to question what gender they are.

Even major companies are marketing lines of children's and babies' clothing that sport gay pride rainbows and slogans, sexual unity themes, and same-sex parenting. Swimsuits that are "tuck-friendly" cater to biological males trying to be transgender females. And "family-friendly" gay-pride parades and celebrations are anything but. Girls in junior high are taking pictures of their private parts and "sexting" them to boys in their classroom. Young women—following in the braggadocious pattern of males—boast of their "body count."

The campaigns to accept any and all forms of sexual deviancy, gender fluidity, and body mutilation to appear like the opposite gender have become political minefields and healthcare nightmares. Factor in the additional push to tolerate all of the above without regard to a person's age, consideration of the stability of their mental and emotional health, and without critical scientific inspection, and it is a recipe for sexual chaos and societal collapse.

Once "wokeness" establishes deep roots in governmental policy, public schools, competitive sports, and in sectors of the business world, anything that pushes back is immediately attacked as insensitive, bigoted, or hateful. Not only is this chaos contrary to reason, common sense, and scientific objectivity, but it irrationally breeds disgust for God's Word, the only true standard with which to judge all of these sexual practices.

BIBLICAL SEXUAL ETHICS

God created mankind as sexual beings, and our sexuality is His very good gift to us. We shouldn't be surprised that He alone knows what's best in the expression of that sexuality. However, when Adam and Eve disobeyed God, sin entered the world and affected everything, including our sexuality.

But God provided for the world. His perfect creation for the expression of our sexuality was through marriage. This was true before the Fall (Genesis 2:24), and it was true afterward. Jesus reaffirmed this as the pattern for all mankind in Mark 10:6-9 (ESV): "From the beginning of Creation, 'God made them male and female.' 'Therefore, a man shall leave his father and mother and hold fast to his wife, and they shall become one flesh.' So they are no longer two but one flesh. What therefore God has joined together, let not man separate."

Not only was sexual desire to be expressed within heterosexual marriage, but it was to be monogamous also. As Hebrews 13:4 (ESV) says: "Let marriage be held in honor among all, and let the marriage bed be undefiled, for God will judge the sexually immoral and adulterous."

Sexual sin is dispassionately recorded throughout the Bible because it was so prevalent and so destructive. The sexual perversions of Sodom and Gomorrah were so notorious that they became a biblical archetype of the final judgment (Jude 7). Israel, in the time of the Judges, was so backslidden that "Everyone did what was right in their own eyes." It was so bad that the tribe of Benjamin allowed the city of Gibeah to become as sexually perverse as Sodom and Gomorrah (Judges 19-21, ESV).

Paul also addressed in many of his letters the pervasive sexual sin of his day and pleaded for a return to God's moral standard (Romans 1:24-32; 1 Corinthians 6:9-11, 15-18; Galatians 5:19; Ephesians 5:3; 1 Thessalonians 4:3-5; 1 Timothy 1:8-11).

GOD'S CLEAR BOUNDARIES

Let's get a little more specific.

Outside of marriage, all other expressions of sexuality are forbidden in the strongest possible terms: incest (Leviticus 18:6), sodomy (Leviticus 18:22), bestiality (Exodus 22:19), rape (Deuteronomy 22:25-27), and adultery (Exodus 20:14).

Premarital sex (fornication) was also clearly condemned (1 Corinthians 6:18), as was dressing in the clothes of the opposite sex (Deuteronomy 22:5). For this last one, think clothes fetishes, "drag" queens, and ultimately transexuals who attempt to permanently change their physical appearance to that of the opposite sex.

The price for sexual deviations is high. Few seem to realize the inherent harm they are doing to themselves when they violate God's ways in wrongful sexual expression. Paul warned those living in Corinth on self-harm: "Flee from sexual immorality. Every other sin a person commits is outside the body, but the sexually immoral person sins against his own body" (1 Corinthians 6:18, ESV).

THE SOLUTION

Now that Rosseau's sexual anarchy has come to dominate the social fabric of the West, what has resulted? Sexual chaos. When God's Word is openly decried as hate speech, we as a civilization are doomed.

God prohibited the expression of deviant sexual proclivities and behaviors for the good of His people, but also for the common good of the rest of the world. However, our society has abandoned God in general and His moral standards specifically. We're now reaping the results as many in our society act according to base appetites like mere animals. For the most part, sexual sin (or inconvenience) has resulted in the "legal" killing of more than 64,000,000 children by abortion in the US alone (as of this writing—and counting).[2] Marriage is failing as an institution because it's no longer seen through the perspective of biblical sexual morals, while being "shacked up" ("living in sin") is considered wise.

We need to support biblical norms at every opportunity to secure the future of our own families, and to ensure that our society will

---

2 https://www.nrlc.org/communications/more-than-64-million-unborn-children-have-died-since-roe-v-wade/

thrive. Objective analysis can even convince non-believers of the benefits of returning to biblical moral standards. Oxford sociologist J. D. Unwin wrote a 600-page work in 1934 that summarized his analysis of 86 societies and civilizations to find any relationship between sexual freedom and the high energy of flourishing cultures. His conclusion? "Any human society is free to choose either to display great energy or to enjoy sexual freedom; the evidence is that it cannot do both for more than one generation."[3]

History and the Bible agree that repentance, turning back to God, and embracing His Word as our sexual standard are the only ways to prevent an otherwise inevitable cultural destruction. Policies strengthening "traditional" marriage need to be continually pushed for. And those trapped in destructive behaviors must be ministered to with compassion and understanding, with the prayer that the Lord would open their hearts and minds to God's truths.

---

3 J.D. Unwin, Sex and Culture, p.412.

CHAPTER 16

HOMOSEXUALITY

Paivi Rasanen is a medical doctor who has been a member of the Parliament of Finland for 28 years, who served as her nation's Minister of the Interior, and whose husband is the president of a Bible college. She was walking with her young grandson, perhaps around 6 or so years of age, when he looked up at a flag and expressed with profound concern, "Grandma, what flag is that? I know our flag. And I know the flag of Sweden, but that is neither one of those." In bewilderment, he asked his grandma, "Whose flag is that? Who has occupied our country?"

What was the strange flag that so disturbed this observant child? It was a flag promoting immorality and promiscuity. It was the homosexual flag, advocating LGBTQ. That child's question could be asked in many of the countries of the world: "Who has occupied our country?" The short answer is "sin."

THE ACCEPTANCE OF THE ABERRATION

When Gallup conducted their first poll in 1996 on the issue of same-sex marriage, 27% of Americans supported it. In 2008, one of the most liberal states in the nation, California, passed Proposition 8 by 52%, which defined marriage as only between a man and a woman (48% said "no").

In 2015, the same year the Supreme Court issued its historic *Obergefell v. Hodges* decision to legalize same-sex marriage, public support passed the 60% threshold. In 2023, Gallop found 71% of Americans believe same-sex marriage should be legal.[1] With the "normalization" of homosexuality and so-called gay "marriage," sexuality debates have moved on to transgenderism, children picking their own genders, and teachers being forced to use pronouns that don't match a child's biological sex.

Given how far our nation has fallen, is it too late to protect God's design for marriage? And does it really matter anymore? I know I'm being counter-cultural, but I believe that the case for marriage—between one man and one woman—has never been stronger, and the issue is even more important today.

From where does my optimism come? From the belief that God hasn't given up on mankind, and that He loves His children. Yes, things are dark. But with God, things are never hopeless. Ever.

THE BIBLE AND MARRIAGE

The key text on homosexuality and marriage is Genesis 2:24:

> Therefore shall a man leave his father and his mother, and shall cleave unto his wife: and they shall be one flesh. (KJV)

---

1 https://news.gallup.com/poll/506636/sex-marriage-support-holds-high.aspx
https://ballotpedia.org/California Proposition 8, Same-Sex Marriage Ban Initiative (2008)

Although this passage is crystal clear, some so-called biblical "scholars" not only claim the Bible doesn't prohibit homosexual relationships, but think this verse is not speaking to the *difference* between male and female, but instead to the *sameness* or *likeness* of male and female; a kind of "kinship" type of bond, or a union based on commonality, not differentiation.[2]

But wouldn't a more natural understanding be that both similarities and differences are in view?

Eve is human like Adam because she is made from his side (Genesis 2:21-23), but she is different from Adam because she is a female, not a male. This is clearly what Jesus has in mind in Matthew 19:4-6 when He says that in the beginning, God made them "male and female," quoting from Genesis 1:27, and then He quotes Genesis 2:24. Jesus deliberately notes that it is a "one flesh" union between two different sexes—male and female. There is no other biological, sexual, arbitrary choice of gender-marriage combination in view. Furthermore, this understanding aligns with thousands of years of church history and doctrine, and with the predominant world cultures throughout time.

HOMOSEXUALITY AND THE BIBLE

Biblical revisionists have applied any number of "interpretations" to biblical passages concerning homosexual behavior (Genesis 19:1-29; Leviticus 18:22, 20:13; Jude 1:7) to try to justify homosexuality. There are even attempts to show that the Apostle Paul was only describing the sin of excessive lust in Romans 1:26-27 and 1 Corinthians 6:9-11, and—according to these revisionists—that he was probably unfamiliar with consensual same-sex relationships of the time.

What is ignored is that Paul was well-traveled and would have certainly encountered people who had same-sex attraction, because

---

2 References: James V Brownson, New Testament Professor at Western Theological Seminary; book: "Bible, Gender, Sexuality"; "Scripture Ethics & The Possibility of Same-Sex Relationships" written by Karen R. Keen.

history tells us it was part of ancient culture. For example, Plato's *Symposium* (180-185, BC 385) includes lines about women who care for "female attachments" and men who "hang about men and embrace them." And Juvenal, a satirist of the day, even noted his contempt for marriages between two men (Satires, 2. 117-148, AD 127).[3]

The truth is, Paul writes in 1 Timothy 1:10 that homosexuality is against "sound doctrine." Those who practice it are doing the same as anyone else that exchanges the truth about God for a lie. Homosexuality rejects God's design for sex and marriage, as set forth from the very beginning in the Garden of Eden.[4]

HOMOSEXUALITY AND GENETICS

One of the most pervasive lies in our culture today can be summed up in the statement, "I was born this way." And when one believes that their sexual attraction is part of their genetic makeup, then it's easier for them to believe "*God* made me this way."

In his insightful video titled, "Is Being Gay Genetic?" Dr. Christopher Yuan explains that countless studies have been conducted to determine if there are any genetic components to one's sexual orientation, and the findings are far from being settled science.[5]

Dr. Christopher Yuan says this of genetics and homosexuality:

A predisposition is not equivalent to a predetermination. It's quite possible for a person to be born with a predisposition, but that predisposition does not predetermine their life experiences, nor can it predict their behaviors.[6]

3 https://www.catholic.com/magazine/print-edition/the-bible-on-homosexual-behavior
4 For a more extensive examination of the six major passages dealing with homosexuality, see James L. Garlow, Well Versed: Biblical Answers to Today's Tough Issues, Salem Books, an imprint of Regnery Publishing, 2016, pages 96-100.
5 https://www.youtube.com/watch?v=aagFTlK_XsI&t=108s
6 Is Being Gay Genetic?—What Would You Say. https://whatwouldyousay.org/is-being-gay-genetic/

One of the largest studies ever conducted on sexual behavior and genetics found that less than 1% of DNA markers (not DNA, just markers) could be linked to same-sex behavior. One of the researchers, Andrea Ganna, a biologist at the Institute of Molecular Medicine in Finland, stated, "We scanned the entire human genome and found a handful—five to be precise—of locations that are clearly associated with whether a person reports in engaging in same-sex sexual behavior."[7] Reuters News site put it this way: "This means that non-genetic factors—such as environment, upbringing, personality, and nurture—are far more significant in influencing a person's choice of sexual partner, just as with most other personality, behavioral, and physical human traits, the researchers said."[8]

The bottom line: people have chosen to make their sexual orientation and behavior part of their identity, wrongly believing that it's even part of their biological and genetic makeup. And, according to science, nothing could be further from the truth. As I mention in *Well Versed*, "In spite of the fact that we are created by God individually, we express the fullest image of God only when the two halves of humanity complement each other and become one."[9] This cannot happen with two males marrying together or two females marrying each other. (For the record, God—who first thought of marriage—defined it: a man and a woman.)

CHANGE CAN AND DOES OCCUR

Many people today fall into one of two camps, both using the oxymoronic phrase "Gay Christianity." One camp is "gay-affirming" and believes God blesses same-sex marriage. The other camp believes

7 No 'gay gene', but study finds genetic links to sexual behavior—Weekday Press. https://weekdaypress.com/no-gay-gene-but-study-finds-genetic-links-to-sexual-behavior/
8 https://www.reuters.com/article/us-science-sex/no-gay-gene-but-study-finds-genetic-links-to-sexual-behavior-idUSKCN1VJ2C3
9 James L. Garlow, Well Versed Biblical Answers to Today's Tough Issues, Salem Books, an imprint of Regnery Publishing, 2016, page 64.

same-sex relationships and marriage are sinful and, therefore, gays should live a life of celibacy, but one must maintain the "gay" identity. Both camps believe homosexual desires cannot change and are part of their actual identity.

Both camps wrongly diminish Jesus' death, resurrection, and the transforming power of the Gospel to change lives and make someone more like Christ. Romans 3:23 (ESV) says, "For all have sinned and fall short of the glory of God." The practice of homosexuality is a sin, but so is adultery, covetousness, jealousy, greed, and the list goes on. Believers don't identify their personhood by the sin that they struggle with. We don't have "Envious Christians," "Murderous Christians," "Alcoholic Christians," "Lustful Christians," "Gluttonous Christians," etc. Doing so is to reject our new identity, which is in Christ (2 Corinthians 5:17). No well-informed follower of Jesus would ever want the adjective "gay" to be in front of the label of "Christian."

Does a person lose same-sex attraction when coming to Christ? That depends. Some do. Some do not. It is similar to alcoholism. When alcoholics come to Christ, some no longer have a desire for a drink, finding even the thought of alcohol to be repulsive. Others, however, just as sincere, struggle daily not to touch the poison. Yet, they remain victorious in that struggle. Such it can be with same-sex attraction.

Dr. Christopher Yuan says very succinctly that "the opposite of every sin is holiness."[10] It is not to go from being gay to straight. The goal is holiness. It's not for us to abandon our sin patterns; it's to become more like Christ.[11] And this is exactly what Paul is talking about in 1 Corinthians 6:6-9 where he lists examples of sins (including practicing homosexuality) as being washed away by the blood sacrifice of Jesus Christ so that the new person in Christ is now sanctified and justified.

10 https://www.youtube.com/watch?v=EQF68WF-hWo
11 Ibid.

THE IMPORTANCE OF MARRIAGE BETWEEN ONE MAN AND ONE WOMAN

When God created males and females and put them together, he gave them a command: "Be fruitful and multiply" (Genesis 1:27-28). Both males and females are needed to fulfill this command, and sexual expression within the bond of marriage is the most beneficial one to raise children.

According to a 2015 study by Princeton University and the Brookings Institute, David Ribar from the University of Melbourne states,

> Reams of social science and medical research convincingly show that children who are raised by their married, biological parents enjoy better physical, cognitive, and emotional outcomes, on average, than children raised in other circumstances. ...[R]esearchers have been able to make a strong case that marriage has causal impacts on outcomes such as children's schooling, their social and emotional adjustment, and their employment, marriage, and mental health as adults.[12]

Can God provide for a child when a mother and or a father is not present? Yes, He can. But in God's original, perfect design, He intended for a child to have both a mother and a father.

THE CHRISTIAN RESPONSE TO THE PRACTICE OF HOMOSEXUALITY

Let me pose a question: Do you see people as being "loving, accepting, and affirming" of homosexuals if they believe the Bible does not condemn homosexuality? Or do you believe homosexuality is a sin

---

12 https://dailycitizen.focusonthefamily.com/kids-need-a-mom-and-a-dad-thats-what-the-research-shows/

and those that are in that bondage are beyond hope and need to be shunned? Both positions are ditches to avoid in finding the right road to travel. Biblically, you can fully love those who are in homosexual lifestyles because they are sinners just like everyone else, and just like everybody else, they are in need of the hope found only in the Gospel.

Sadly, many Christian leaders, and even entire denominations—taking the first compromising option above—are abandoning biblical truth in pursuit of culture's acceptance. When this happens, homosexuals are deprived of real, true, authentic love. A follower of Christ is to love them enough to share truth with them—biblical truth that can set them free from the bondage of their sin (John 8:32).

SALVAGABLE

Allow me to pose another question: Can marriage—as an institution—be saved? The answer is yes. Why? Because the culture has decayed to a point where people are desperate for someone to speak the truth to them. I encourage you to be loving, yet bold, and that your words will always be "seasoned with salt" (Colossians 4:5-6). The Gospel can set people free. It gives them a new identity in Christ and a calling bigger than any earthly desire—a calling to become more like Him.

CHAPTER 17

MARRIAGE

O ne of the marks of wokeness are its constant attacks on those institutions that have been honored for millennia. No creation of God is more sacred than marriage, and marriage is under severe attack by the woke crowd.

JUNE 28, 1969, THE DAY OF INFAMY

President Franklin Delano Roosevelt called December 7, 1941, "a day of infamy"—because of the bombing of Pearl Harbor at the hands of Japan. However, our nation faced the reality of that war and won it.

June 28, 1969, was also a day of infamy, a day of disgrace. It launched another war. And we have not won it. Truth has not prevailed. Yet.

On that day, the Stonewall Riots in New York City launched the homosexual revolution that we now refer to as LGBTQIA+ (and who knows how many other letters—sins—will be added?). Our nation is suffering for having decided to embrace that for which God destroyed Sodom.

Several years ago, we took a group of 26 intercessors on a tour of the Netherlands. The ladies in the group found out that the hotel where we were staying was once the official city hall of Amsterdam, complete with a wedding chapel. They excitedly asked to see it, so we were taken to the wedding chapel.

Unbeknownst to us, that room was presumably the place where the first-ever legal same-sex (so-called) "marriage" ceremony was performed on April 1, 2001. We were standing in the very place where God's sacred institution of marriage was first legally violated by a modern nation-state.

And then we discovered that we were there in that infamous room on a historically significant day: June 28, 2019. That was the 50th anniversary of the Stonewall Riots that launched the antibiblical movement known today as LGBT. This movement culminated in America with the tragic same-sex "marriage" Supreme Court case, *Obergefell v. Hodges*, announced on June 26, 2015.

However, this chapter is not primarily focused on homosexuals and the destruction of authentic marriage. Rather, I want to highlight God's definition of marriage from the Hebrew text in the first two chapters of Genesis.

As I noted in my previous book, *Well Versed: Biblical Answers to Today's Tough Issues*,[1] the Bible:

- opens in Genesis with a marriage—between a man and a woman;
- closes in Revelation with a wedding—between a groom and bride;

1 Much of the following is taken from pages 63—70 of James L. Garlow, Well Versed: biblical Answers for Today's Tough Issues, Salem Books, an imprint of Regnery Publishing, 2016. Ordinarily, I would not repeat sections from a previous book, but this topic is so critically important.

- and in between, one man-one woman marriage is extolled in both the Old and New Testaments, as well as by Jesus Himself.

Nowhere in the Bible is there any affirmation of homosexual "marriage" or of homosexual acts. In fact, quite the contrary: the entire focus of Scripture is *always* the one man-one woman covenant of marriage.

NEITHER MALE NOR FEMALE REPRESENTS THE FULL "IMAGE OF GOD"

God is neither male nor female. The Old Testament writers used metaphors to try to describe the indescribable. Sometimes, the words used to describe God are distinctly male in nature, most obvious by our use of "Father" or "He." At other times, the phrases used to depict God are female in nature—with terms like breastfeeding (Numbers 11:12), nursing mother (Psalms 131:2; Isaiah 49:15), giving birth (Deuteronomy 32:18), in labor (Isaiah 42:14), or a mother hen (Matthew 23:37).

The obvious conclusion: God is neither a "he" nor a "she." Nor is God some androgynous "middle ground." In Genesis 17:1, God's name is the Hebrew phrase *El Shaddai*. It is believed that *el* means mighty like a mountain, thus the strength of masculinity. *Shaddai* likely comes from the Hebrew word for breast, such as feeding a newborn baby, thus the feminine characteristic of nurture. In that single name for God is the full spectrum of masculinity and femininity.

We are made in His image. However, a male, by himself, is not fully representative of all the descriptors of the image of God. For example, a male, by himself, cannot manifest the full spectrum of God's features, historically associated with femininity (tenderness). Thus, no husband, for example, can fully represent the full image of God.

At the same time, a female, by herself, cannot do justice to the full spectrum of the image of God, due to an inability to depict classic masculine-type physical strength. Thus, no wife, for example, can fully represent the full image of God.

Although we are, as individuals, created by God, *the true, full spectrum of the entire continuum of the image of God is expressed only when the two halves of humanity complement each other and become one.*

"ADAM" THE MAN VS. *"ADAM"* AS HUMANKIND

The traditional view is that God created Adam, put him to sleep, took a rib, and created Eve. But the Old Testament was originally written not in English but in Hebrew. Is the Hebrew text saying that "God created Adam a male, and then Eve, a female, from Adam's rib?"

No.

Something much more profound is being said in the Hebrew Old Testament. In the beginning, God created not Adam the male, but *adam,* that is, humankind. Don't picture Adam, the male. The word *adam*—pronounced "awh-DAHM"—means humankind or personhood. It is later that Adam is attributed as the name of a male. But initially God created *adam*—small "a"—that is, humankind.

After creating humankind, God said, "it is not good that *adam*—small 'a,' that is, humankind—is alone" (see Genesis 2:18). This is the only time that God looked at what He had created and said that it was "not good." All the rest of Creation He labeled "good."

This was not a case of God creating a male and then saying, "It is not good that a male is alone, so I will make a female."

That is not what happened.

It is suggested that a more correct reading of the Hebrew would be, "It is not good for humankind—that is *adam* (again, not Adam the male, but *adam*, meaning humankind)—to be *as one* or "one"— or to live in solitude, alone.

It is at this point that we have the "splitting of the *adam*," so to speak. That is where *adam* or humankind gets split apart, and we now have male and female.

But what about the proverbial rib? The word "rib" does not appear in the ancient Hebrew text. The word that is there is *tsela, which* can be translated as "half" or "side." In fact, other places where *tsela* appears in the Hebrew Scriptures it is translated "half" or "side."

Instead of God creating Adam and taking his rib to create Eve, the text is saying that God created humankind, observed that it was not good for humankind to be "one" or alone, and then took a "side" or a "half" of humankind and created a female (Eve), and what remained was male (Adam).

In other words, the *whole* (humanity) that was created in the full image of God, with both the strength of masculinity and the tenderness of femininity, is now halved, and we have the two complementary halves of humanity: male and female.

One of the reasons for the strong sexual attraction between males and females is the desire for the two halves of humanity to come back together—undoing the "splitting of the *adam*"—thus reuniting males and females as "halves," now making a "whole," now depicting the full spectrum of the full image of God.

But there is more.

ISH AND *ISHAH: YOD* AND *HEY*

The Hebrew word for man is *ish*. (Perhaps Eve took one look at Adam and exclaimed, *ish!*)

The Hebrew language reads the opposite of English, from right to left. Thus, it is spelled, in Hebrew letters, as *aleph, yod,* and *sheen*. (See graphic on the previous page.)

The Hebrew word for woman is *ishah*, pronounced "i-SHAH." Reading from right to left, it is *aleph, sheen,* and *hey*.

Here is the difference between *ish* and *ishah:*

- In the Hebrew language, there is one Hebrew letter in *ish* (man) that is not in *ishah* (woman) and that is the Hebrew letter *"yod."*

- In the Hebrew word for *ishah* (woman) there is one Hebrew letter that is not in *ish* (man), and that is the Hebrew letter *"hey."*

What is the significance of these two letters?

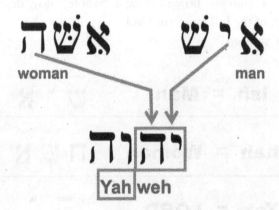

Yod Hey form the foundation or basis for the word *Yahweh* or YHWH, the name for God that is used 6,800 times in the Hebrew

Old Testament. In other words, when you put *ish* (man) and *ishah* (woman) together, then you have *yod hey*, or Yahweh or God. Therefore, the two together—*yod* and *hey*—provides the expression of *the full image of God*. Only the Hebrew words for man and woman depict this breathtaking construct.

Let's be clear: Two men do not express "the image of God." Two women do not bear "the image of God." Only a man and a woman—covenantally (permanently) and maritally joined—offer that spectacular reality and imagery. Thus, males and females form the two halves of humanity which, when coming back together, reflect the very name of God.

MALE AND FEMALE

When the two complementary halves of humanity unite—physically, spiritually, mentally, emotionally, and psychologically—the image of God, containing both tenderness and strength, is manifested. Male and female are made anatomically, emotionally, and spiritually for oneness. To be candid, they "fit" each other. Husband and wife, covenantally joined together, represent the full spectrum of the image of God.

In what way is the male-female union a depiction of God? One part of God's image is His creativity. In sexual union, husband and wife become co-creators, in a sense, with God. Children come into being as husband and wife unite, one more expression of the image of God; in this case, His creativity.

A sperm and an egg unite to form (miraculously) a human! A person! Male and female becoming one is what Genesis establishes as the components for this image. The breathtaking image of God! Science knows that an egg and a sperm unite to create a human. But science cannot explain *how* or *why* that happens.

This is one of the reasons that the Bible does not affirm homosexual marriage or the homosexual act. Nowhere. Not overtly. Not covertly.

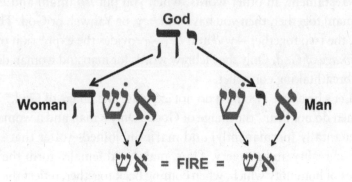

THE "FIRE" BETWEEN A HUSBAND AND WIFE IN COVENANTAL MARRIAGE

The Hebrew language, which some believe will be the language of heaven, is fraught with deep and profound meanings. If you remove the letter *yod* from *ish*, male (it is the middle letter of the three-letter word) and the *hay* from *ishah*, female (it is the last letter in the three-letter word; remember, Hebrew reads from right to left), you have only two letters in Hebrew, from the two words: *aleph* and *shin*. Those two letters form the Hebrew word *esh* (three letters in this English transliteration), meaning "fire."

אִשָּׁה Ishah = Woman

אִישׁ Ish = Man

יהוה Yahweh = God

אֵשׁ Esh = Fire

Is fire good or bad? That depends. If fire is properly contained, it cooks our meals, heats and air conditions our homes, powers our computers, recharges our cell phones, and propels our cars, trucks, boats, and planes. When not properly contained or parametered, it burns down cities, destroys property, and kills people. The fire of 2003 in San Diego where I live burned down 2,800 homes in four days. The Maui fires of 2023 destroyed the beautiful town of Lahaina and killed 100 people.

The "fire" or *esh* between a couple is the sexual attraction. Out of control and outside of the covenant of marriage, it is lust, and it harms everyone around it. However, if that same "fire," *esh* (or attraction) is harnessed within the boundaries of *brit,* it is covenantal (permanent) marital love, it is holy. Sexual intimacy between a husband and wife is a righteous act.

COVENANT

"covenant"

b'rit
(beh-REET)

The explanations of *ish* and *ishah* above were taught to me by trained Jewish teachers. What follows was also taught to me by a brilliant Jewish rabbi. The word for covenant in Hebrew is *brit.* It is made up of four Hebrew letters. *Brit* is the English transliteration for the four Hebrew letters in the graphic above.

If you take the word covenant, *brit*, and split it apart, with two letters on the right and two letters on the left, and then you place "fire" or *esh* within it, right in the middle of the word, you have the "fire" of attraction between male and female parametered by the *brit*, the covenant of marriage. The fire, *esh*, is occurring *within* the *brit*, covenant of marriage, not *outside* of marriage. Sexual relations between a husband and wife are a righteous and holy act. Sexual relations outside of that are not. Below is the word covenant, or *brit*, split apart, and the word fire, or *esh*, placed in the middle of covenant. This is a portrayal of the sacredness and holiness of the act of physical intimacy within covenantal marriage.

"beresheet"

ברית ← b'rit; "covenant"

בראשית

אש ← esh; "fire"

When you put these words together—the split word *brit* (covenant) with *esh* (fire) in the middle—as we have described above, the new word that is formed is *beresheet*. This is the first word of your Bible, in Genesis 1:1. It translates, "In the beginning." Jews don't call the first book of the Bible "Genesis." They call it *"Beresheet."* My Jewish rabbi friend said to me, "God so loved the distinct intimate and attractional relationship between a husband and a wife—the *esh*, or fire—within the *brit*, covenant of marriage, that He even used it to form the first word in the Bible." That's how important one man-one woman marriage is to God. Thus, it should be to us as well.

CHAPTER 18

NO-FAULT DIVORCE

Generally, the arguments in favor of no-fault divorce run something like this: if two people are unhappy together, they should be allowed to break up easily and without large attorneys' fees. Why prolong a relationship that is not working? Kids will be better off getting out of a high-stress environment with parents constantly fighting. We achieve good for everyone by allowing the marriage to dissolve as easily as possible. There is a superficial appeal to this kind of argument, but real harm if one buys into the premise behind it. Let's look more closely at the phenomenon.

THE GENESIS OF NO-FAULT DIVORCE

For most of our nation's history, a party seeking a divorce had to show some "fault" grounds (e.g., adultery, abuse). That changed in 1969 when California became the first state to adopt "no-fault divorce." Under the change, a single party to a marriage, unhappy for any reason, had a clear path to end the legal relationship.

Then-Governor Ronald Reagan signed the law into effect. He would later say his decision to do so was one of the greatest mistakes of his political life.[1]

Within five years, forty-five states had passed similar no-fault divorce laws. New York was the last hold-out, joining the ranks in 2010.

The 1960s and 1970s were a time of tumultuous social change, and no-fault divorce was a reflection of a changing national mood. Traditional values gave way to a growing focus on individual fulfillment. For example, the pursuit of pleasure brought the sexual revolution and drastic changes in generally accepted social norms. Drug use became a "personal choice." (People ask, "What harm does it do you if I use drugs?" The answer is a lot—in societal cost from overdoses, crime, children born addicted, and more.)

Similarly, abortion was deliberately reframed from a procedure that took an innocent life into an issue of one's personal rights. (As in, "Who are you to tell me what I can do with *my* body?") Sadly, even though the taking of an innocent life was widely viewed as a moral wrong, a person's *individual autonomy* became more important. Marriage was caught up in the same social arc of the era.

THE RELIGIOUS FRAMEWORK

Why did every state require a "fault" ground before this shift in public opinion? The answer is that, prior to the 1960s, marriage was viewed through a religious or faith framework that generally shaped our institutions. Fault grounds universally included adultery as a basis for divorce. (The adulterer had no such right, as the faithful spouse alone was considered the aggrieved party.) The moral basis of this is obvious; Jesus said this on the subject of adultery:

1 https://erlc.com/resource-library/articles/5-facts-about-no-fault-divorce/

It was also said, "Whoever divorces his wife, let him give her a certificate of divorce." But I say to you that everyone who divorces his wife, except on the ground of sexual immorality, makes her commit adultery, and whoever marries a divorced woman commits adultery.
—*Matthew 5:31-32*

This perspective defined most of the Christian world's view on the sacredness of marriage (as well as the conservative Jewish view of that time). As well, fault grounds usually included "cruel and inhumane treatment" and "abandonment" of a spouse (1 Corinthians 7:15), usually for a period such as six months or a year. Both of these circumstances were considered violations of the sacred marriage vow to (typically) love and honor, in sickness and in health, until death do you part. The words are familiar to many of us, but we forget they were conceived at a time when *the literal meaning of the words was taken seriously*—two parties were taking a vow *for life.*

We could initially point to how the Judeo-Christian revelation on marriage strongly favors faithful commitment and how much unjust divorce is disfavored. (See, for example, Malachi 2:16.) A person of faith would conclude that our Creator (the designer of marriage) knows best. Marriage under this model is about love and sacrifice and serving each other (Ephesians 5:22-33 has much to say about this). Steve Covey was right when he stated, "I am convinced that if we as a society work diligently in every other area of life and neglect the family, it would be analogous to straightening deck chairs on the Titanic."[2]

"IT'S ALL ABOUT ME"

But the premise behind no-fault divorce turns the idea of mutual love and service on its head and into a focus on individual autonomy, or even

2 https://libquotes.com/stephen-covey/quote/lbi6t7a

simply a preference when someone finds someone else more attractive. It transforms the idea of commitment into the self-focused spirit of an age that is about personal fulfillment. After all, it's all about me.

THE TRAGIC AND PAINFUL RESULTS

How has the relatively new view of marriage worked out? Has the no-fault concept brought good or bad results? The first and most obvious outcome is that we have many more divorces in the United States than before no-fault divorce. But is it proper to highlight the hypothetical of the children, who are suddenly supposedly "happier" because mom and dad are not fighting any longer?

The indisputable data tells us that children are worse off after a divorce. (Remember, we are talking about statistical averages and not any particular situation. There are always stories both ways.) First, children from divorced homes statistically suffer a significantly higher incidence of behavioral problems, drug abuse, poverty, alcohol abuse, and psychological distress.[3] The National Bureau of Economic Research has found clear evidence that making divorce "easier" has been bad for children.[4] And typically, women and children suffer more than men.

Since all this is indisputable—in other words, based on mountains of studies and research—it stands to reason that creating more divorces has resulted in more social and financial hardship for children.

A MORE EXCELLENT WAY

What is the Christian alternative to no-fault divorce? The answer is a default approach that works on relationships and provides resources

---

3 https://www.lifesitenews.com/blogs/no-fault-divorce-laws-are-devastating-thousands-of-children/

4 https://www.nber.org/digest/feb01/making-divorce-easier-bad-children

to improve marriages. The focus changes from personal fulfillment to a biblical model of committed mutual love and service. In other words, it is *not* about me.

This will sound naïve to some, and admittedly, all marriages won't be saved. But I am not advocating against obvious matters of concern. My advice to any woman suffering from physical abuse (for example) has always been to get out of the home quickly and call the police if necessary. We are not talking about extreme cases. What I am saying here is much different: the *default*—or standard—principle, where possible, should be to err on the side of working through issues in marriage and not breaking the marital bond over the pursuit of personal fulfillment.

As Ruth Graham once noted, "A happy marriage is the union of two good forgivers." For the record, a so-called 50/50 marriage never works. Much of the time, both spouses might actually feel like they are giving 90% of the time. But if they persevere, the results can be profoundly redemptive and fulfilling.

Some sources claim that harm to children is lessened when they no longer live in high-stress households from marital discord. But, what if, instead, society encouraged a God-inspired (or Bible-based) view of marriage, with a commitment to love and serve each other? Would it not be better to attempt to work on the sources of marital discord first rather than emphasizing the discord to argue that children need to get away from it? Some research has even found that divorce has a greater negative impact on children than the death of a parent.[5]

Again, this may sound naïve to some, but if people do not aspire to a larger and deeper understanding of marriage, it may be because it strikes them as unattainable, not undesirable.

---

5 https://www.demographic-research.org/volumes/vol46/20/46-20.pdf

SOMEONE IS ABOUT TO BE HURT

Even beyond divorce itself, other researchers have noted the effect of unequal bargaining power; that is, the availability of easy divorce allows one partner to extract demands on the other under the threat of leaving if the spouse does not comply. And it is generally the spouse with the greater leverage who makes the demand of the more vulnerable partner.[6]

Some people simply lack the tools to handle conflict well, but no-fault divorce discourages the incentive to try this approach. *New York Times* op-ed contributor Stephanie Coontz pointed out the paradox that people who went through the mediation process (which is often required as part of divorce) were more likely to express regret over a divorce compared with others who litigated instead (which accentuates the negatives and accusations). Sometimes, people just need to talk things through—often with a therapist or mediator who can help both sides regain trust and equilibrium.

Social change rarely comes without unanticipated consequences. The results of no-fault divorce have been largely negative for our nation and have devalued the institution that is the basis of our society.

---

6 https://papers.ssrn.com/sol3/papers.cfm?abstract_id=4081378

CHAPTER 19

TRANSGENDERISM

Suppose that 1,000 years from now, some archeologist comes across a collection of bodies in an ancient village that had a number of transgendered people in it. As the scientists examine the bodies, the determination of sex will be identified by the chromosomes as either XX (female) or XY (male). Whether the deceased had organs cut off or not makes no difference. They were—and still are—permanently either male or female and were so from the moment of their conception. In short, there is no such thing as "trans," that is, changing one's "gender." It is a fantasy. We use the term "transgender" here because that is the commonly used word. However, in reality, there is no such thing as "transgender." It cannot happen. We probably should use the word "trans-identify," as opposed to "transgender." In other words, one cannot switch biological genders.

And God has some views about that. Short and succinct, He declares in His Word, "A woman shall not wear a man's garment, nor shall a man put on a woman's cloak, for whoever does these things is an abomination to the Lord your God" (Deuteronomy 22:5, ESV).

HOW BAD HAS IT BECOME?

What is a woman? Just a decade or so ago, the answer was indisputable across all cultures, scientific communities, and religious sects. And yet, in 2022 in the confirmation hearings for Supreme Court Justice nominee Ketanji Brown Jackson, she could not define the word "woman." Why? She said simply, "I'm not a biologist." A Harvard graduate and Supreme Court Justice could not distinguish the difference between a man and a woman.[1]

Gender confusion, fueled by political correctness, has not only spread in our culture like a cancer, it is quite literally inflicting lifelong physical and mental harm on boys and girls.

In the following sections I am listing a few different studies and reports to give context to the transgender argument and provide *secular*—as opposed to biblical—definitions that many accept as "science." God's Word, of course, is our plumb line in all these issues.

GENDER DYSPHORIA

The American College of Pediatricians defines *gender* as "a term that refers to the psychological and cultural characteristics associated with biological sex."[2] They state, "It is a psychological concept and sociological term, not a biological one."[3] Even secularists acknowledge that there are only two "sexes"—male and female. How bizarre it is that with only two sexes, they try to claim there are 50 or 60 or more "genders." Once we start to deviate from God's definitions of "sex" and "gender," however, we begin to career off into sexual and gender chaos.

The American College of Pediatricians further states that *gender identity* "refers to an individual's awareness of being male or female

---

1 https://www.politico.com/news/2022/03/22/blackburn-jackson-define-the-word-woman-00019543
2 https://acpeds.org/position-statements/gender-dysphoria-in-children
3 Ibid.

and is sometimes referred to as an individual's 'experienced gender.'"
Gender dysphoria (GD), as defined by the American College of Pediatricians, "describes a psychological condition in which they experience
marked incongruence between their experienced gender and the gender
associated with their biological sex. They often express the belief that
they are the opposite sex."[4]

US TRANSGENDER STATISTICS

The Williams Institute, a think tank within UCLA's School of
Law, published a report in 2022 using data from the Behavioral Risk
Factor Surveillance System and the Youth Risk Behavior Surveillance
System, to examine the transgender population of youth and adults in
the United States. Key findings from this study stated, "Youth ages 13
to 17 comprise a larger share of the transgender-identified population
than we previously estimated, currently comprising of about 18% of
the transgender-identified population in the US, up from 10%
previously."[5]

The study also found, "Among US adults, 0.5% (about 1.3 million
adults) identify as transgender. Among youth ages 13 to 17 in the US,
1.4% (about 300,000 youth) identify as transgender."[6]

YOUNG GIRLS AND GENDER DYSPHORIA

Abigail Shrier, a Wall Street journalist who approaches issues from
a secular progressive point of view, wrote a compelling book called
*Irreversible Damage: The Transgender Craze Seducing Our Daugh-
ters.* She is supportive of beliefs that conflict with a biblical worldview,

---

4 Ibid.
5 Study: https://williamsinstitute.law.ucla.edu/publications/trans-adults-united-states/
New York Times Article that references the study: https://www.nytimes.com/2022/06/10/
science/transgender-teenagers-national-survey.html
6 Ibid.

such as supporting gay marriage and even transgenderism in adults, but she took a closer look at the statistics surrounding the surge of transgenderism in children, in particular, girls. She wrote:

> Gender dysphoria—formerly known as 'gender identity disorder'—is characterized by severe and persistent discomfort in one's biological sex. It typically begins in early childhood—ages two to four—though it may grow more severe in adolescence. But in most cases—nearly 70 percent—childhood gender dysphoria resolves. Historically, it afflicted a tiny sliver of the population (roughly .01 percent), and almost exclusively boys. Before 2012, in fact, there was no scientific literature on girls ages 11 to 21 ever having developed gender dysphoria at all.
>
> In the last decade, that has changed, and dramatically. The Western world has seen a sudden surge of adolescents claiming to have gender dysphoria and self-identifying as "transgender." For the first time in medical history, natal girls are not only present among those so identifying—they constitute the majority.[7]

TRANSGENDERISM'S ORIGIN

No one denies the fact that there have always been people who struggle with their identity and sexuality. But the enthusiasm fueling the transgender movement today *is* something relatively new. How did the modern phenomenon start?

R. Alfred C. Kinsey, an entomologist (not a physician) released two publications, *Sexual Behavior in the Human Male* (1948), and *Sexual Behavior in the Human Female* (1958). From these studies, Kinsey "devised a classification scheme to measure sexual orientation,

---

7 Irreversible Damage Page xxvii.

commonly known as the Kinsey Scale."[8] This Scale, as explained by Dr. Quentin Van Meter, president of the American College of Pediatricians, was an erotic sexual orientation scale with no fixed concept of male and female.[9]

Kinsey promoted extreme and reprehensible views of pushing sexual activity onto minors and eventually influenced culture and state laws across the nation. It wasn't until 1990 that his work was seriously challenged and deemed by many as fraudulent, unethical, and possibly criminal concerning children.

Dr. John Money is another voice that helped shape the transgender movement. He was a Harvard graduate and known for his work in psychoendocrinology and developmental sexology. He worked at Johns Hopkins University and is credited with pioneering the concepts of gender roles and identity.[10] In 1966, Dr. Money started the first gender-affirming surgery clinic in the United States. John Hopkins University continued to perform surgeries on minors until 1979, when the gender clinic was finally closed after studies revealed patients had worse mental outcomes from treatment and surgery.[11]

London's Tavistock Clinic became the world's largest gender clinic for minors, seeing just fourteen patients a year from 1989 to 1999. But as cultural pressure mounted surrounding LGBTQ issues, and as the work and unscientific ideologies of Kinsey and Money continued to be championed, London's Tavistock Clinic experienced rapid growth, seeing 3,585 patients in 2020-2021, with more than 5,000 patients on their waiting list.

8 https://kinseyinstitute.org/research/publications/historical-report-diversity-of-sexual-orientation.php.
9 Video: 13:35 https://www.youtube.com/watch?v=OGbz57wZ28A
10 https://kinseyinstitute.org/collections/archival/john-money.php
11 https://pubmed.ncbi.nlm.nih.gov/36191317/#:~:text=Johns%20Hopkins%20Hospital%20established%20the,claiming%20that%20GAS%20was%20ineffective

AUTHENTIC SCIENCE

The Society for Evidence-Based Gender Medicine states simply,

> First, there is insufficient evidence to justify the general clinical use of puberty suppression or cross-sex hormone use in youth experiencing gender dysphoria. Second, a treatment regimen that focuses exclusively on gender dysphoria, ignoring co-occurring mental health conditions, will not provide optimal care for young people. The shut-down of GIDS (Gender Identity Development Service) is not merely a restructuring move in response to the clinic's failed operations. It is a move away from the 'gender-affirming' intervention care model and toward whole-person-affirming care that is rooted in developmental psychology.[12]

THE TRUTH BEGINS TO EMERGE

Gender medical and surgical transitions didn't work back in 1966 when the first gender-affirming surgery clinic was founded, and they won't work today. In fact, they are already beginning to crumble despite the media and culture's praise of medical gender treatments and transitions.

In the spring of 2023, the world's largest pediatric gender clinic (London's Tavistock Clinic) closed its doors. The Society for Evidence-Based Gender Care said in part regarding the closing, "An independent review condemned the clinic as 'not a safe or viable long-term option' because its interventions are based on poor evidence and its model of care leaves young people at considerable risk of poor mental health."[13]

---

12 https://segm.org/UK_shuts-down-worlds-biggest-gender-clinic-for-kids
13 https://segm.org/UK_shuts-down-worlds-biggest-gender-clinic-for-kids

In a long-term follow-up of transsexual people undergoing sex reassignment surgery in Sweden between the years 1973-2003, a Swedish cohort study found "substantially higher rates of overall mortality, death from cardiovascular disease and suicide, suicide attempts, and psychiatric hospitalizations in sex-reassigned transsexual individuals compared to a healthy control population."[14]

SAFEGUARDING OUR CHILDREN

Here in the US, nineteen states have begun passing laws to protect children from this harm by passing some restrictions or outright bans.[15]

As more children, teenagers, and college students identify as a gender different from their biological sex, a fierce debate rages about protection of girls' and women's rights in the area of sports. In response, as of this writing, more than twenty states have passed some type of restriction on boys competing in girls' sports.[16]

Though great progress has been made to protect children's proper bodily development and girls' and women's rights, the culture war on this issue is far from over. It's critical that we continue to sound the alarm on the physical and psychological harm for someone of any age to go through a medical gender transition.

FORGIVENESS, NOT VICTIMHOOD

Can someone struggle with their sexual identity? Absolutely. But as Christians we have the God-given responsibility to share the truth that God made only two genders, male and female (Genesis 1:27). As

14 https://www.ncbi.nlm.nih.gov/pmc/articles/PMC3043071/#:~:text=This%20study%20found%20substantially%20higher,to%20a%20healthy%20control%20population
15 https://www.cnn.com/2023/06/06/politics/states-banned-medical-transitioning-for-transgender-youth-dg/index.html
16 https://www.nytimes.com/2023/04/20/us/politics/transgender-athlete-ban-bill.html

well, He makes no mistakes (Psalms 139:13-14; Ephesians 2:10; Deuteronomy 32:4), and He is not a God of confusion (1 Corinthians 14:33). Both males and females are made in the image of God and have equal value and worth, are complementary in nature, but they are not interchangeable physically. Rather than encouraging gender confusion that leads to psychological distress, we must point to the Lord and His lordship over every aspect of life.

Sadly, many Christians are buying into the lie that "affirmation" of one's gender fluidity or transition is "love" or that the use of pronouns that do not match one's biological sex is compassionate. But for a Christian to affirm what is not true is in no way loving.

Author and former gay activist Rosario Butterfield says these lies "which have entered the church and the Christian college, have one thing in common: They discourage repentance of sin and encourage the pride of victimhood." She continues, "The biblical truth is that homosexuality and transgenderism are found in the flesh, forbidden in the law, and overcome in the Savior."[17]

In other words, gender dysphoria is not an unforgivable sin, and there is hope for those who find themselves thinking they are trapped in the body of the opposite sex.

---

17 https://www.christianheadlines.com/contributors/milton-quintanilla/rosaria-butterfield-blames-revoice-cru-and-preston-sprinkle-for-spreading-lies-about-sexuality.html

CHAPTER 20

THE SOCIAL CONTAGION OF TRANSGENDERISM

W hereas the last chapter discussed transgenderism in general, this chapter demonstrates that so-called "transgenderism" is not an inherent reality but is rather "caught" or is considered a bit chic. Simply stated, this is a mental cancer, or rather, a social contagion.

JUST BE YOURSELF?

Kim was excited because she finally had come to grips with the dark cloud of fear, depression, and anxiety that had haunted her for the past few years, from about the time she entered junior high school. Just thinking about putting all that pain in the rearview mirror made her want to dance and sing. A glorious future now awaited her, a future where she could be the person that she was created—no, born—to be.

She had, of course, done the research and was making an informed decision. Her dozens of hours on TikTok, with the help of an AI algorithm, pointed her to many people who had improved their lives by coming out as transgender. Trans...that was the word that would make it all work for *her*...no, for him. He would now be joining two other trans friends who were as equally happy about their new identities.

SECRETLY "TRANSITIONING" WITHOUT PARENTS KNOWING

Of course, he—"she" is going by "he" now—knew his parents would freak out, but with a bit of stealth and misdirection, he might be able to hide it all until it was too late for them to do anything. His school had instituted a program that allowed him to change out of his "dead name"—the name a person is born with—and once on campus, go by his "new" name and switch into clothes that really represented who he now was. His school counselor—who went by the pronouns she/they— had taken him to a clinic which was really dope—a term meaning so good—because she/they never even questioned his decision and she/they never even talked about snitching to his parents. He had immediately been given hormone treatment. He had to see a therapist to sign off on the treatment plan, but that was so easy! The therapist was totally "down"—meaning, in agreement.

Jerri (his new name) was secretly just a little worried that he might someday regret this decision. He had heard whispers that there were people who later regretted their transition—but his doctor had assured him that all was reversible until surgery, which was a little ways away. The only problem left was church. He had grown up in the church and had liked it, but the Bible was so "transphobic," not to mention all of the church people who were "walking hate crimes." No, that was the past; he was bravely venturing into a new world where he could live freely and happily, embracing his true self, and no person or God could tell him he was wrong....

Does the above scenario seem far-fetched? It's not. This scene is playing out all over the US as I write this. And some parents have no clue that their under-age children are making life-altering decisions without them.

UNDERSTANDING THE CONTEXT

Before this past decade, the predominance of people suffering from gender dysphoria were boys. It was a rare disorder and usually surfaced in preschool. The number of boys presenting for treatment was .005-.014 percent of the population. Girls presented with a much lower rate of .002-.003 percent of the population.[1] This represents about one for every 10,000 people. In 2018, a British official ordered an inquiry into a 4,000 percent rise in children wanting "gender-affirming" care.[2]

From a purely medical perspective, this is a remarkable change!

If you were to see diabetes rates or cancer rates increase at even a few percentile points, there would be serious concern and then investigations to try and find causality. In the case of gender dysphoria, however, there are few questions asked. And there is a blanket acceptance that this is a legitimate medical phenomenon, which requires understanding and acceptance rather than concern and skepticism.

But wait, this phenomenon, though rare, has been seen before.

HISTORY'S LESSONS

In the 1980s a new scourge came upon teenage girls: bulimia and anorexia nervosa. It was known to practitioners and to the various

---

1 https://www.ncbi.nlm.nih.gov/pmc/articles/PMC6336471/
2 https://www.telegraph.co.uk/politics/2018/09/16/minister-orders-inquiry-4000-per-cent-rise-children-wanting/

iterations of the Diagnostics and Statistics Manual (DSM), but it was a rare occurrence. In the 1980s there were several celebrities who shared with the public their personal problems with body dysmorphia (having a distorted image about your own body image), anorexia, and specifically bulimia, manifesting in the form of food binging and then purging through self-induced vomiting. Beloved singing artist Karen Carpenter put anorexia in the spotlight when she succumbed to the eating disorder at just 32 years old in 1983.

A social contagion was forming and gaining speed. Bulimia, which was virtually unseen in the 1970s swept through high schools, colleges, sororities, and dorms to become the dominant female health problem in the 1980s, with reported cases in China of six million, and UK cases numbering seven million (one in 100 women!)

In the United States, the medical profession responded by opening treatment centers throughout the country. Many big cities had four or more treatment options. Interestingly, while there are still people presenting for treatment for eating disorders, the global crisis has abated. Thankfully, the number of girls suffering from bulimia is drastically lower, and most of the treatment programs around the world are not there anymore.

It seems obvious that this was a global social phenomenon that, for most, rectified itself as the social contagion burned itself out.

NOTHING NEW UNDER THE SUN

That's not to dismiss those who have legitimately struggled with these two terrible eating disorders. Many cases, of course, are legitimate—but certainly not on the scale reported in the 1980s. The fact that the number of cases—and the number of those seeking professional help—has plummeted in recent decades points to a compelling conclusion: As a social and psychological phenomenon, anorexia nervosa and bulimia as once reported in the 1980s seemed to more closely resemble mass hysteria than a medical manifestation.

It seems clear that the massively unexpected and unexplained rise in the number of adolescent girls seeking gender reassignment surgery also fits the same profile.

NOT TREATING THE PROBLEM

It is interesting that the predominant number of girls complaining of gender dysphoria disorder are upper middle class and White.[3] Girls coming from socially progressive families make up 70% of these girls. It is also interesting that most of the girls are part of friend groups that have several girls coming out as suffering from gender dysphoria. Not surprisingly, up to 86.7% of parents reported that their daughters had become deeply immersed in social media, with a particular focus on transgenderism, before deciding that they too, were suffering from this issue.[4]

An interesting anomaly in the epidemics, compared to prior social contagions, is the way in which the medical community is addressing the issue.

With the anorexia/bulimia crisis, a young woman would talk to her physician about her desire to be thinner and to cut her calorie intake. She would usually be defensive and protective of her dieting plans, knowing that the physicians and therapists that she would be seeing would be working at cross purposes to her own desires. Never during this crisis were healthcare workers encouraged to validate the desire to be grossly underweight. Also, they did not encourage restrictive diet planning, weight loss medications, or weight loss surgical options.

In regard to gender affirmative care, a completely opposite approach is being taken. Therapists, counselors, and physicians are encouraged to validate the wishes of the patient and to downplay the

---

3 https://journals.plos.org/plosone/article?id=10.1371/journal.pone.0202330
4 https://www.ncbi.nlm.nih.gov/pmc/articles/PMC6095578/

risks. This is the case even though they know that if left alone, these children would eventually see this problem resolve on its own, allowing them to live as their own gender with no medical consequences resulting from years of experimenting.

WHAT TO DO

Time will tell if this "social contagion" trend of gender dysphoria will begin to resolve itself naturally or not. In the meantime, be compassionate with those who are struggling with gender dysphoria while recognizing the sources of confusion that are messing with a child's concept of themselves and creating mental distress.

Fight any attempt by public schools or medical professionals to withhold medical or treatment information relating to your child, and be willing to seek legal recourse if necessary.

Everyone is made in the image of God (Genesis 1:27) and is due respect because of their intrinsic worth. But God has designed men and women with different chromosomes, body shapes, strengths, reproductive systems, and even brain types depending upon gender. There is no scientific proof that a person can be trapped in the wrong body.

Be patient with the person who is struggling; acknowledge their distress while gently focusing on the reality of what God has done physically for the person. Since God doesn't make mistakes, He can help a person as they work through their confusion.

CHAPTER 21

CRITICAL RACE THEORY

C ritical Race Theory (CRT) came to the US in the early 20th century. With the rise of Nazism and the persecution of intellectuals in Germany in the 1930s, professors Max Horkheimer, Theodor W. Adorno, Herbert Marcuse, and Erich Fromm sought refuge in the United States and settled at Columbia University to pursue intellectual and academic careers. Each of these German professors was Marxist and a critical theorist pioneer.

After starting the Frankfurt School at Columbia University, they pioneered ideologies around critical analysis of society, culture, and politics. Their social research culminated with Critical Legal Studies (legal theory), Critical Gender Theory, Post-Colonial Theory, Queer Theory, and yes—Critical Race Theory. While each of these academic fields is unabashedly Marxist and influential, it was Critical Race Theory that had the most corrosive effect on America.

THE "GENIUS" OF CRT

At its core, CRT provides an "academic" and intellectual justification to divide races. It does this by guilting and shaming "Whites" about their slaveholding past and their alleged, continuing discrimination and maltreatment of Blacks (or any minority for that matter). CRT clearly portrays the United States as being systemically racist and that racial oppression of Blacks, specifically, is ubiquitous. Why? Because CRT adherents firmly believe racism is knowingly or unknowingly ingrained in the hearts and minds of every White person. In fact, this is believed to be true for all time.

Once the CRT viewpoint is adopted, history must be reinterpreted from that perspective. That means our nation's belief in "life, liberty and the pursuit of happiness," and the fundamental principle that "all people are created equal," can only be understood if viewed from the perspective of slaves and other oppressed (victimized) peoples. CRT proponents also reject Dr. Martin Luther King Jr.'s societal warning and assertion to recognize one another based on their "content of character, not color of skin." Instead, CRT characterizes people in binary categories that are in conflict: one category labels Whites as "oppressors," and all other ethnicities are defined as the "oppressed" (victims of the oppressors).

CORE CRT BELIEFS

Some of the primary beliefs of CRT are that:

- All Whites are racists.
- All Whites are supremacists.
- All Whites are victimizers and oppressors of people of color.
- Racism is "normative" and systemic; that is, it's everywhere.

- "White privilege" enjoys the reality of White dominance.
- Subscribing to "color blindness" only keeps minorities in subordinate positions.
- All Blacks (or "voices of color") possess special insights into otherwise unknowable truths that Whites are incapable of truly understanding.
- All history, including the Bible, must be reinterpreted from a Black/minority perspective.
- All Whites are irredeemable.

Fundamentally, CRT adherents demonize everyone who is White and see them as irredeemable "oppressors" who enjoy supremacist "privilege." Because Whites cannot change their fundamental racist nature, CRT maintains that Whites must submit to being in a condition of never-ending penance toward those they are oppressing.

This never-ending (past, present, future) perspective is captured in the writings of author Ibram X. Kendi. Kendi states in his book, *How to Be an Antiracist*: "The only remedy to past discrimination is present discrimination. The only remedy to present discrimination is future discrimination." [1] Kendi is among the best-known and most celebrated proponents of CRT. He writes and speaks extensively to support CRT and Black Liberation Theology, so he skillfully crosses both the secular and religious spectrums while agitating race issues and then asserting how to combat them.

THE REAL RACISTS

But wait a minute, weren't we all taught that characterizing people's value or worth or competence based solely on immutable

---

1 Ibram X. Kendi, How to Be an Antiracist (One World; First Edition August 13, 2019), 287.

characteristics (like the amount of melanin in their skin, or their eth-nicity) is racist? Yes, we were. So, based on CRT's own clear pro-nouncements, it's (in and of itself) an undeniably racist ideology, since the key delineator is—you guessed it—the color of one's skin. That said, strident proponents of CRT are, by definition, racist.

How do they get around the charge that they are racist? Very simply, if you are the "oppressed," you cannot be, by definition, racist.

But wait, let me pose a scenario. Is an 89-year-old white, dis-abled, wheelchair-bound Pentecostal male, the son of sharecrop-pers, barely surviving on Social Security, living in a 40-year-old mobile home with a leaky roof and broken water heater, in a town of 3,000 population in the deep rural south an "oppressor" to a 40-year-old Black lesbian female tenured Muslim professor, the daughter of a medical doctor and an attorney, at Harvard Univer-sity in Cambridge Massachusetts? "Oh yes," they say. Why? How can this be? Because:

- He is male and she is female. That's one.
- He is White and she is Black. Now we have a second one.
- He is Christian, and she is Muslim. Now a third.
- He is old and she is young. And we have a fourth.
- He is heterosexual. She is homosexual. That is a fifth one.

Obviously, the CRT advocates say, she is profoundly oppressed by him.

And what about "privilege?" If your parents got married, then had babies, and stayed married, then you should be punished for being privileged because someone else's parents never married at all, or if they did, got divorced.

THE BIBLICAL RESPONSE

It's one thing to show compassion toward the plight of anyone who is unjustly suffering at the hands of someone else (Zechariah 7:9-10). It's something quite different to condemn an entire group of people as being racist with no hope of change.

To say someone is unredeemable is to accuse them of somehow committing the "unforgiveable sin" (Matthew 12:31). Not only that, but their "sin" is just being White! In other words, the tone of their skin determines their eternal destiny, not their relationship to a holy and just God! What about those with mixed race backgrounds, or albinos, or siblings with the same parents who have a wide range of skin tones?

God's Word is very clear: every human being has equal value and worth because everyone is created in the image of God (Genesis 1:27). Every person on earth is also descended from the same parents: Adam and Eve. So we're all related. And oh, by the way, the creation of "race" is an artificial human construct to differentiate between peoples; but truth be told, we are all part of the same human race.

Let's look even deeper. Everyone differs in physical characteristics such as mental aptitude, skills and abilities, and likes and dislikes; and we are all born with an inherent sinful nature (Jeremiah 17:9; Romans 3:10-11). It's from that sinful nature that racism comes (Romans 3:23), not from some physical attribute like the color of one's eyes. Because of the sinful nature, if it wasn't skin color, something else would be used to "justify" oppression or mistreatment or the harming of others. It's not the color of skin, or some genetic defect, it's the heart that's the source of sin (1 Samuel 16:6-7).

That's actually good news. Since it's a heart issue and not some immutable physical characteristic, there's hope that racial divisiveness can be tackled. But it needs to be on God's terms, and not based upon some academic ideology meant to confuse and stoke hatred (Ezekiel 36:26-27).

One other thing. Biblically, sin is an issue of personal account-ability (Ezekiel 18:19-20). If a person is racist, that sinful heart needs to be confronted appropriately. The generations following that person are not accountable for their ancestors' sins unless they do the same things. The Bible does mention the existence of "unintentional" sins (mistakes, ignorance, unrealized prejudice) of a people group or nation, and the need for them to be confessed and corrected (Numbers 15:22-26). So, where institutional prejudice does exist, it needs to be confronted and corrected to ensure everyone is treated fairly and justly (Proverbs 20:23).

TAKING ACTION

Let's call it for what it is: CRT is a destructive belief system intended to create hateful divisiveness to unjustifiably gain a morally superior position of power or influence. God's Word is clear, just as a divisive person (or ideology) is to be condemned (Proverbs 6:16-19; Romans 16:17-18; Titus 3:10) and rejected, so CRT is a divisive, racist philosophy, and it needs to be rejected.

Once CRT is recognized for what it is, a grievance industry that is never ending and feeds the sinful nature, then progress can be made to overcome real racial tensions and misunderstandings.

Are there racists? Of course there are. Is it limited only to "Whites?" Of course not. Any kind of racism, whether institutional-ized, overt, or covert must be recognized for what it is and dealt with. But in doing so we're to judge rightly, and not take unnecessary offense over slights or misunderstandings.

CRT is antithetical to the Gospel and how people of good will are to treat each other. The wider Body of Christ is at a critical pivotal point. It's time to decide whether to continue to embrace seductive "woke" ideologies and theories about genetic racism and guilt over the sin of prior generations, or focus on the golden rule (Matthew 7:12), loving our neighbor (Matthew 22:39), and exposing *true* racists (Ephesians 5:11).

On the negative side, Paul warned about those who cause division: "As for a person who stirs up division, after warning him once and then twice, have nothing more to do with him" (Titus 3:10, ESV). On the positive side, Paul provided us with a noble goal: "If possible, so far as it depends on you, live peaceably with all" (Romans 12:18).

PRAYERS FOR RACIAL RECONCILIATION

As Christians we are called by God to pray for our nation, and to "stand in the gap" and pray for present-day racial reconciliation. We can pray for the healing of past wounds and atrocities committed against the Host Peoples (Native American nations and tribes), Blacks, Latinos, Asians, and other minority peoples. As in all other circumstances, Jesus is our model. And the Word says that He sits at the right hand of the Father interceding on our behalf (Romans 8:34). Likewise, we are called to intercede on behalf of those who have been subjected to terrible injustice and racism.

Our clarion call to pray and intercede on behalf of racial healing is found in 2 Chronicles 7:14, which says,

> If my people, who are called by my name, will humble themselves and pray and seek my face and turn from their wicked ways, then I will hear from heaven, and I will forgive their sin and will heal their land.

Make no mistake, the devil does not want God's people to pray and act on behalf of healing between races and ethnicities—he wants us divided. And whereas CRT is not the biblical approach to truly biblical reconciliation, prayers prayed by the saints in a posture of humility are heard by our God in heaven. That is true biblical justice; that is the kind of racial reconciliation the Lord is calling us to. One based in humility, love, and genuine commitment to change where all are truly treated equal in the eyes of God and humanity.

CHAPTER 22

REPARATIONS

R eparations are a "hot" topic throughout the country. And by reparations, I am specifically talking about financial—or other material—payment for damages or injuries caused in the past. Panels, committees, and study groups are figuring out what the appropriate remedies should be to provide restitution for our nation's past racist evils.

A DIFFICULT PROBLEM PERSONALLY

The subject of reparations for past iniquities and abuses raises serious questions that demand objectivity and sensitivity. What type of financial response (if any) should be taken to heal the aftermath of the wicked treatment of people in our nation many years ago and the generational impacts that followed? That being said, I openly admit how difficult it is to walk in another man's shoes, much less answer for national sins from over 150 years ago.

Being White, I also acknowledge my perspectives growing up in the US will not be the same as those of Blacks, Latinos, or other minority groups. My ministry labors give me unique opportunities to work closely with the Black community at all levels of ministry, for example, but that doesn't make me an expert on the Black experience. Far from it!

Given those caveats, it is God's Word that must ultimately guide us, augmented by an objective treatment of history. Jesus said, "The truth will set you free" (John 8:31-32, ESV). That is my hope and prayer here.

SETTING THE STAGE

Excellent books have been written about the racial and cultural wounds of our nation. Obviously, one short chapter cannot provide a full account of the subject, thus I am primarily limiting my focus to a single facet of racism in America: the African American experience. By no means, however, does this diminish the importance of exploring issues of racial injustice among America's other minority groups.

Claims of unjust application of laws based on race and heart-wrenching instances of police brutality—such as George Floyd—have energized demands that some form of reparations be paid to Black Americans. The case is made that generational impacts of past US slavery continue to today in the unequal application of justice, disproportionate police brutality, and systemic institutional racism.

Historically, reparations have been made to victims (and survivors) of harmful treatment at the hands of evil people and governments. Some well-known instances include:[1]

- Germany compensated Holocaust victims, while West Germany agreed to give Israel billions. In total,

---

1 Vox article on Reparations—https://www.vox.com/2014/5/23/5741352/six-times-victims-have-received-reparations-including-four-in-the-us

Germany paid survivors of the holocaust approximately $86.8 billion.[2]

- South Africa compensated victims of apartheid over $85 billion.[3]
- The US government compensated Japanese-American citizens over $3 billion for being forced into internment camps during World War II.[4]
- The US government compensated victims of the Tuskegee experiments $10 million,[5] where 399 Black men were purposely infected with syphilis between 1932 and 1972, and intentionally left untreated to study and confirm the progression of the disease.
- The state of North Carolina compensated more than 200 victims of its forced sterilization programs $20,000 each, that took place from the 1930s to the 1970s to primarily poor Black women on welfare.[6]

Reparations are not new. It should be noted, however, that they were provided by the responsible entities that caused the harm and precipitated the evil acts.

Why is this important to note? Because the current reparations movement doesn't differentiate innocent from guilty parties, other than "America" is guilty of horrible sins toward Blacks.

---

2 https://www.state.gov/reports/just-act-report-to-congress/germany/
3 https://www.nytimes.com/2003/04/16/world/south-africa-to-pay-3900-to-each-family-of-apartheid-victims.html
4 https://en.wikipedia.org/wiki/Internment_of_Japanese_Americans#:~:text=In%20 1988%2C%20President%20Ronald%20Reagan,when%20the%20act%20was%20 passed
5 https://www.cdc.gov/tuskegee/timeline.htm#:~:text=Later%20in%201973%2C%20 a%20class,Presidential%20Apology%20for%20the%20study
6 https://www.tillis.senate.gov/2015/12/senate-passes-bipartisan-bill-to-assist-eugenics-victims-receiving-compensation-payments#:~:text=In%202013%2C%20North%20Carolina%20became,payment%20of%20approximately%20%2420%2C000%20each

THE REAL QUESTION

Basically, and again, focusing singularly on the issue of African Americans, the issue boils down to answering the question: Is America, as a nation, responsible for compensating Blacks for prior periods of slavery and the following times of discriminatory treatment or not? If America is not responsible, then who, if anyone, is?

BASIC BIBLICAL PRINCIPLES TO CONSIDER

Race relations, reparations, discrimination, and equal treatment under the law are all complex and difficult issues. (And again, fully deserving of further study beyond the purview of this single chapter.) Biblically, however, we are to treat each other with respect due to the fact that we are fellow bearers of God's image (Genesis 1:27), and recognize that God hates injustice (Proverbs 17:15).

Because we are still fallen creatures and sinful (Romans 3:23), the Bible does provide for restitution between the evil-doer and the victim (Exodus 22:1,3-6,14) when someone (or a family, or a group) is harmed. This principle is fundamental to our civil and criminal justice system, even though it is and always will be imperfect in practice.

Another biblical principle relates to personal accountability. Everyone is responsible for their own sin (Deuteronomy 24:16), but not the sin of others. There can be, however, generational "consequences" from sin (Exodus 20:5-6) that need to be confronted for what they are: ungodly attitudes, perceptions, judgmentalism, etc. When criminal harm occurs, restitution is appropriate between the evil-doer and the victim.

Finally, retribution is never justified—that is, taking revenge on someone (Romans 12:19). In a just world, just laws would mete out punishment in proportion to the harm done (Exodus 21:23-25), but not to be excessive or to punish those not causing the harm, or to reward schemes to use "guilt and shame" as a cudgel to encourage grift.

WHO, IF ANYONE, IS BIBLICALLY RESPONSIBLE?

Current demands for reparations in the form of government financial payouts, cancelled loans, free college, or other means, generalize responsibility onto the entire populace of America. This approach says all Americans today are somehow complicit with our nation's past slavery and its continuing racism.

Does that make sense? Let's look a little closer.

First, if those wholly responsible for historical injustices and institutions complicit with systemic racism could be identified, then why are all American taxpayers now liable?

Second, America endured a bloody Civil War that set enslaved Black people free. Some historians estimate that the loss of life on both the pro-slavery (South) and anti-slavery (North) sides was approximately 700,000 during the Civil War. On a personal note, my great-great-grandfather fought for the North, helping to free the slaves. Fortunately, he lived through the war. But is it reasonable for anti-slavery Northern families who already bore the loss of their grandfathers, fathers, brothers, and uncles to suffer loss again by their offspring paying reparations? Shouldn't surviving families of enslaved Black people owe some level of gratitude to those whose ancestors already paid the ultimate sacrifice to set them free?

Third, doesn't it make more sense to demand an accounting and possibly compensation from any identifiable groups that actually enslaved, maimed, lynched, and prolonged the suffering of enslaved Black people? But whom could that be?

In a recently released PBS documentary on Reconstruction following the Civil War,[7] historical records confirm there was one clearly identifiable demographic group responsible for promoting, then fighting to preserve and prolong slavery and its societal aftermath. So,

---

7 PBS Reconstruction: America After The Civil War"- https://www.pbs.org/weta/reconstruction/

fourth, if that group is still in existence today, wouldn't it be logical that they would carry the brunt of the responsibility, historically, for the various harms and associated evils they directed against enslaved Black people?

Fifth, since many Blacks also owned slaves—both Black and Native American slaves—wouldn't those Blacks have to join with the slave-owning Whites to pay reparations?

In summary, if Tom has abused Bill, and Tom and Bill are both still alive, then Tom can be held accountable for what he did to Bill. But if Tom and Bill have both been dead for—say—150 years, it is not possible to require Tom to pay Bill. They are dead. So, the big question: Is it then appropriate to locate someone who is a descendent of Tom, and then require that person to pay for sins committed by his great-great-great-grandfather?

A POLICITAL MINEFIELD

National progress toward the healing of racial wounds has been slow and difficult. And I want to be very clear: racism is wicked. There are racists in our nation, and it is clearly a heart issue that only the Gospel can fully heal (Romans 12:2). Racists must repent of sin. No excuses.

But we need a political reality check. What political group perpetuated slavery to the point of willingness to destroy our nation? What political group did everything conceivable to defeat the potential for legal and societal equality following the Civil War?

It's an historical fact that Southern Democrats perpetuated slavery and were complicit with its related evils. History confirms that Democrats used levers of power—legislation/laws, judges, schemes of partiality, and terror networks like the KKK—to harass, maim, and murder enslaved Black people. The resulting acts of racism and discrimination were broad and calculated, with the expressed intent to undermine Black life in America.

Since the historical progeny of this political faction is still around today, sincere people committed to having Blacks compensated for past evils should, at a minimum, objectively acknowledge their historical wickedness.

THE TOUGH QUESTIONS TO ASK

Reparations in the past have been specific about identifying responsible groups or governmental actions. Without clear accountability for racism, generalized demands for restitution only ring hollow and open current reparations efforts to the charge of being insincere, or worse yet, a generalized shakedown based on virtue signaling and political posturing.

Racism and racial discrimination are wicked schemes designed to permanently divide and undermine the inherent unity everyone made in God's image should strive for. In the end, people of faith should be sensitive to—and fully empathetic toward—the evil horrors that allowed and encouraged slavery in America, and any legacy racism that continues to exist.

Christians should also continue to demand the *just* enforcement of *just* laws to ensure equality of treatment of all peoples. Civil rights laws and anti-discrimination legislation have helped correct racial disparities that continue to linger in our nation. But to make even more progress, it's necessary to objectively identify what factors are still in play that foment racial conflict. To do this, consider the following questions. What political faction promotes:

- Victimhood instead of self-reliance and initiative?
- Dependence on government support instead of personal initiative?
- Autonomous school control instead of school choice?
- Protected categories of people instead of equal justice under the law?

- Abortions, disproportionately targeting low-income Black communities?
- The vile belief that all White people are racist and unredeemable?
- And ignores the generational catastrophe resulting from broken and fatherless Black families?

Once these questions are answered, and accountability identified, reparations discussions have some hope of being meaningful and also healing.

CHAPTER 23

DIVERSITY, EQUITY, AND INCLUSION (DEI)

Almost every government institution and private business has been impacted by a global whirlwind encouraging the immediate adoption of Diversity, Equity, and Inclusion (DEI) programs. Global organizations are already incorporating ESG (Environmental, Social, Governance) factors to determine their level of ethical consciousness by examining what are called "social credit scores," which are "report cards" (not unlike one's personal credit score) that score an organization's adherence to ESG factors. Indeed, DEI has become a preeminent factor supporting those global scoring schemes.

There is no argument that with globalist pressures, DEI adoption has been breathtaking. The United States adopted an "all of government" approach to implementing DEI through a Biden Presidential Executive Order. With this approach, DEI influenced every decision in every department and at every level of the government. With such intense focus and mandated adoption, it is vital that everyone fully understands where it comes from and what it is.

WORDS ARE IMPORTANT

Taking each term separately, DEI is defined as:

DIVERSITY

The condition of having or being composed of differing elements: VARIETY
especially: the inclusion of people of different races, cultures, etc. in a group or organization[1]

EQUITY

Justice according to natural law or right
specifically: freedom from bias or favoritism[2]

INCLUSION

The act of including the state of being included
Something that is included: such as the act or practice of including and accommodating people who have historically been excluded (because of their race, gender, sexuality, or ability)[3]

The terms sound relatively benign, and if they encompass passive indicators of the degree of opportunity existing within government, businesses, and education, or the degree that employees are treated equally (that is, without unmerited partiality), then they would be helpful management tools.

---

1 https://www.merriam-webster.com/dictionary/diversity
2 Ibid.
3 Ibid.

IMPLICATIONS ARE MORE IMPORTANT

Unfortunately, as DEI was aggressively adopted in workplaces, boardrooms, and across global enterprises, the outcomes resulting from DEI initiatives were not what the terms imply. Consider the following DEI-related headlines to gain a clearer understanding of the impact this "movement" is having as DEI-driven mandates are implemented:

"White people are not welcome in this space."[4]

"Coca-Cola diversity training tells employees, 'Be less White.'"[5]

"Being White" includes being "oppressive, arrogant, defensive, ignorant."[6]

"Democrat Chicago Mayor wants to eliminate homework and failing grades."[7]

"DEI director fired because colleagues complained her diversity project was 'unacceptable' because it... (didn't take steps toward) 'decentering whiteness.'"[8]

---

4 Whites not welcome- https://www.breitbart.com/europe/2023/05/21/white-people-told-they-are-not-welcome-at-performance-of-blm-inspired-play/
5 Coca Cola DEI Training; "be less white"- https://www.newsweek.com/coca-cola-facing-backlash-says-less-white-learning-plan-was-about-workplace-inclusion-1570875
6 Stossel- https://www.thenews-messenger.com/story/news/local/2023/03/25/stossel-diversity-training-disaster/70037005007/
7 Chicago Mayor video- https://rumble.com/v2h78qq-new-democrat-chicago-mayor-brandon-johnson-wants-to-eliminate-homework-fail.html
8 https://www.thecollegefix.com/fired-dei-whistleblower-details-attacks-she-faced-for-defending-jews-different-religions/

"Liberal College Professor Placed on Leave ... Suggesting it's OK to Murder Conservative Speakers."[9]

"New York City Teachers Union to Host Seminar on the 'Harmful Effects of Whiteness.'"

The above quotes are headlines from major news outlets. Do these headlines align with outcomes an objective person would expect from an effective and impartial program of diversity training and initiatives? There seems to be a significant disconnect between DEI being promoted as an altruistic and unifying tool to address alleged disparities in the workforce, and the reality of discriminatory abuse and disunity DEI appears to be creating.

ACTUAL MEANINGS IN TOO MANY CASES

In reality, given the present woke-ish political climate in America, DEI can and does devolve to the following:

Diversity: "We will affirm everyone, except 'old, White, Christian males,' in which case, we will blame you for everything that has ever gone wrong."

Equity: "Let's be Marxists and take from those who produce and give it to those who do not."

Inclusion: "Everyone who celebrates homosexuality and transgenderism is included, but people who do not affirm those perversions, especially Bible-believing Christians (*which is the only kind of Christian there actually is*), as well as all those heteronormative-affirming people, need to be embarrassed, shamed, doxed, ostracized, criminalized, cancelled, and fired."

---

9 "Ok to Kill Conservatives"- https://www.thegatewaypundit.com/2023/03/liberal-college-professor-placed-on-leave-for-suggesting-its-ok-to-murder-conservative-speakers/

In summary, Diversity is (reverse) racism, Equity is Marxism, and Inclusion is LGBTQ perversion. DEI has sometimes been summarized as "Didn't Earn It."

WHAT DEI SHOULD–OR COULD–BE

Ideally, DEI should create environments that leverage the life experience and background of each individual while promoting work unity and common respect. In theory, DEI types of programs could foster work environments reflecting the diverse nature of humanity and foster respect for each individual's unique ideas, perspectives, and backgrounds.

A principled approach to D and I (diversity and inclusion) could enhance an organization's reputation and brand image. Being perceived as honoring more inclusive environments helps confirm that the organization is socially sensitive and responsible. Improving brand image can also lead to increased customer loyalty and market share. As long as equal opportunity is encouraged instead of focusing on ensuring equal outcomes (the "E"—equity), organizations could anticipate improved morale and unity.

For followers of Jesus who know that the Kingdom of God is comprised of all ethnic groups, it's natural to desire input from all, especially given God's diversity in the world. For followers of Jesus, "inclusive" can be a good word, so long as it does not coerce Christians to affirm that which the Scripture labels sin.

Diversity is a gift from God! It takes focused intentionality to recognize this gift and to remember that everyone is created in the image of God and, as such, has equal worth (Genesis 1:27). Working in a diverse environment allows the opportunity for each person to be honored as unique and their participation valued as a necessary part of a mosaic representation of humanity. That is the beauty and purpose that a principled approach could deliver. However, environments that reflect a menagerie of diversity also require a rejection of "equity" and its ideological core: a Marxist worldview that does not elevate each individual's God-given uniqueness and gifts.

IT'S ALL ABOUT "E"

The core of DEI is focused on the equalizing of outcomes, as opposed to equality of opportunities and rewards based on merit. Proverbs 22:29 even promotes meritocracy as the natural order of things: a man skilled in his labor will serve before kings, not obscure men. In contrast, equality of outcomes is grounded in the collectivist ideas of Karl Marx. Marx's equity-based ideologies lead to racist-motivated retribution and social conditioning designed to collapse existing power structures and usher in the adoption of communism.

Not surprisingly, when organizations attempt to strengthen values of equality, trust, and commitment, they are quickly undermined when "equity" objectives arrive. Again, equity foments retribution and a "get even" attitude toward so-called "oppressors" or "victimizers." Who are those oppressors? In our nation, some claim it is all Whites.

It should be obvious that any schemes, ideologies, or programs that undermine the building of trust, competency, and merit-based rewards are destined to fail. Proverbs 12:11 reflects that truth: "Those who work their land will have abundant food, but those who chase fantasies have no sense." Hard work produces in abundance, but coercively implementing worthless pursuits is foolishness.

WHAT'S THE ALTERNATIVE?

Better outcomes can be achieved by modifying the DEI paradigm and shifting to a more principled diversity, *opportunity*, and inclusion mindset.

The most significant value diversity, opportunity, and inclusion provides is the encouragement of different viewpoints. In a non-hostile environment where the focus is on solving problems or accomplishing

goals, unity can take hold. Actively welcoming criticisms and assessments of different plausible solutions increases the diversity of ideas.

If all organizational contributors feel their input and perspective
are encouraged, honored, and respected, it can foster a rich, unifying
experience for employees. When corporate unity is increased, overall
corporate performance should also increase. A concerted effort encouraging equal opportunity for people with diversified skills, political
leanings, ethnicity, etc., is needed to produce a "melting pot" that will
support organizational successes.

WHAT CAN BE DONE PRACTICALLY?

Steps that help foster and leverage diverse work environments
include:

- clear and relevant communication;
- a willingness to adapt to change and to create based on
  diverse input;
- the ability to "freely think" out loud without fear or
  judgment;
- genuine interest in others and continual commitment to
  building relationships with them;
- honoring individual differences and valuing others;
- and giving full attention to seeking to understand others
  while accepting accountability for self and others.

It takes work, but when these relational aspects are reinforced and
incorporated organization-wide, it provides an environment of dignity
and value, which the current DEI push cannot do. In these organizations, employees can proudly proclaim, "Diversity is our strength!"

God endowed each person with special skills, talents, and abilities
according to His purposes. Since we don't possess the same level of
grace or circumstances with our God-given aptitudes (Ecclesiastes

9:11), this means "inequality" will always exist. Organizational attempts to coercively equate everyone based on an artificial scale of equal outcomes (i.e., equal compensation, promotion, and career advancement) while ignoring merit-based reality is not only foolish, it is destructive to human advancement and the God-given command to creatively have dominion over the Creation (Genesis 1:26).

Going forward, the best strategy to encourage inclusive and diverse environments is to move away from DEI (equity focus) and toward an opportunity focus! Then, no matter what skin color, ethnicity, race, or religious convictions differentiate people, everyone will be included in one growing mass of humanity. It's time to accept the beauty of one humanity flourishing together and completely reject broken world-views that create violence, hatred, and chaos.

During the time of the writing of this book, DEI began to fall out of favor with many. Some states have begun passing laws against DEI. As an example, Alabama's governor signed a new law on March 20, 2024, outlawing DEI at public schools and universities.[10] And other states are taking steps to do the same thing.[11]

It's time to reject fallacious and dishonest tropes that only serve to separate, not unify. It's time to reject theories that divide. As mature adults, we must now fully (and with intentionality) embrace the reality that we are one human family! This is obviously biblical, since we are all descended from the same parents, Adam and Eve, and are all part of one true race, the human race (Genesis 1:27).[12]

---

10 "Alabama Governor Signs Law Banning State Funding of DEI at Public Schools, Universities," by Katabella Roberts, The Epoch Times, March 20, 2024.

11 States Push Back Against 'Toxic Ideology' of DEI in Higher Education, as Focus Shifts To Closing Loopholes for Colleges," by Maggie Hroncich, nysun.com, 1/25/24.

12 Since Kevin McGary was a gracious contributor to some of the sections and some of the concepts in this chapter, by graciously allowing us to use those portions from his book-"DEI In 3D," Copyright © 2023, Kevin McGary, Published in Canada and the United States by Rational Free Press—
ISBN: 978-1-7772018-7-6 Rational Publishing.

CHAPTER 24

FATHERLESSNESS

n November 2023 I attended the "Alliance for Responsible Citizen-ship" in London, England, a brainchild of Jordan Peterson, featuring more than 90 speakers, with 1,500 invited delegates from 73 nations. One of the most tender and moving moments of the entire conference was when one speaker made an earnest appeal for the fathers of the world to stand up and do what was right. At this global conference, everyone knew we had a fatherlessness crisis.

FATHERLESSNESS: A SERIOUS GLOBAL EPIDEMIC

Fatherlessness is a major contributor to many of the crises we face globally. When fathers are not fulfilling their role as God designed, then significant individual, family, cultural, and even national troubles ensue.

Let's start by just listing a few of the disastrous consequences for the children that don't have a father (or father figure) in the home:

- Five times more likely to commit suicide
- Five times more likely to experience poverty
- Seven times more likely to get pregnant
- Nine times more likely to drop out of school
- Ten times more likely to abuse drugs
- Fourteen times more likely to commit rape
- Twenty times more likely to go to prison, and
- Thirty-two times more likely to run away from home.[1]

FATHERS ARE ESSENTIAL—BY DESIGN

By God's perfect design, fathers are pillars for the family and essential to serve with the mother in complementary and mutually supportive roles to raise, nurture, and equip children (Proverbs 1:8-9). The Lord is so adamant about the need to have fathers in the lives of children that He prescribes that others must help fill this vital role when providentially vacated. Consider just a few verses:

… for in You the fatherless find compassion.
—*Hosea 14:3*

Learn to do right! Seek justice, and encourage the oppressed. Defend the cause of the fatherless.
—*Isaiah 1:17*

Defend the cause of the weak and fatherless.
—*Psalm 82:3*

He defends the cause of the fatherless and widow.
—*Deuteronomy 10:18*

---

1 Sedlak, Andrea J. and Diane D. Broadhurst. The Third National Incidence Study of Child Abuse and Neglect: Final Report. US Department of Health and Human Services. National Center on Child Abuse and Neglect. Washington, DC, September 1996.

"FATHERS ARE EXPENDABLE"—ONLY BY CHOICE

Modern-day progressive societal and cultural trends are not just contrary to God's design but go out of their way to minimize the unique role a father has in a family, a role that cannot be fully compensated for by having a single parent.

Where is the biggest impact demographically?

We are told that fatherlessness is skyrocketing among White and Hispanic families. But for Black families, the numbers are heart-wrenching, with 67% of households now fatherless.[2] Is it any surprise that black and brown communities decimated by fatherlessness experience increased levels of crime and poverty compared to other groups? Studies show, and common sense informs, that fatherlessness is one of the most significant factors plaguing community progress and personal success.

WHAT FATHERS DO

When fathers participate in their children's lives according to God's design, many factors work together to positively impact the proper development of those children.

When children receive a sense of affirmation and belonging, acknowledgment, and encouragement, they emotionally, mentally, and spiritually mature and grow in a healthy way. When discipline and correction are meted out appropriately and consistently, children are provided with boundaries that will serve them for the rest of their lives (Proverbs 22:6; 29:17). When children are provided with a stable family structure, order, age-appropriate responsibilities, and shown how to set and achieve goals, they have a much greater opportunity to thrive in life.

Fathers are generally best suited for delivering these valuable life lessons (Ephesians 6:4), just like mothers are generally better

---

2 Percentage of Black Fatherless Homes in the US in 2024—EarthWeb

equipped to provide complementary skills and insights (Genesis 2:18). God's plan for the family includes both a father and a mother; each is essential. When one is missing, the fundamental health and proper human development of the child is far more difficult to bring about.

WHEN FATHERS ARE NOT THERE

When a father is absent from their children's lives, children are more likely to seek affirmation and a sense of belonging through some other source. Often, that source becomes street activities such as gangs or other criminal elements. Additionally, older kids or adults who often don't have the child's best interests at heart may give them false perceptions about what it means to grow up and be "mature." In effect, these other influences become the de facto role models for them.

Parenting is difficult, demanding, and designed by God for a man and a woman to pursue together in marriage. Mothers and fathers are not completely interchangeable. Circumstances may dictate the absence of a father, and in those difficult cases, the Lord will and does provide. Single parenting is not God's divine plan for the good of children, yet God Himself can step in and bring a certain level of "completion." In contrast, so-called same-sex (homosexual) "parenting" is a direct violation of God's plan. Any attempt to justify that for which God destroyed Sodom is an affront to God's holiness and righteousness.

Fathers provide a different set of life lessons and experiences (from mothers), and without their firm example, children will often escape appropriate discipline and correction. The result, responsibility, and accountability are too easily neglected. Inevitably, damaging consequences are then passed down from one generation to the next (Numbers 14:18).

WHAT MUST HAPPEN

An answer to help ease most of the issues plaguing today's cultural breakdown is relatively simple: active fatherhood. Engaged fathers committed to connecting with their children provide an antidote to the trajectory that would otherwise all too often lead to cultural decay.

WHY IT IS SO IMPORTANT

God gave fathers *authority* over their respective households. God's design for the "traditional" nuclear family is to allow it to reflect a microcosm of what it means to participate in the heavenly Father's Kingdom. When children grow up fatherless, they lack the perspective of what a real father is. It's not uncommon, therefore, that they have difficulty accepting a holy God as their Father.

When children grow up fatherless, they often think about "fatherhood" with some level of trepidation, as their experience often tells them "fathers can't be trusted." In fact, often, they will associate abandonment and distrust with fatherhood. This is yet another profound reason—if not *the* primary reason—why God emphasizes fatherhood; His divine institution of earthly fatherhood provides the foundation to more readily accept, understand, and fully appreciate having a relationship with Him as Father.

There's more. God's children learn that real success in life can only be achieved through having enough faith to "lean" on Father God as we endure (and overcome) all circumstances. When we enter God's house (His Kingdom), and come to know God as Father, we recognize and honor His authority. As we progress in our relationship with God and things don't quite go how we wanted, we learn to accept His discipline (Hebrews 12:9-11) and commit to aligning with His will.

As children learn respect for their imperfect, earthly fathers, children naturally learn to seek out and obey the heavenly Father who is perfect in all His ways. This pattern of a healthy father-child relationship can and will be repeated over and over again into the following generations.

THE CURRENT BATTLEGROUND

God wants fathers on the front lines of the global culture wars to engage faithfully and effectively. Unfortunately, fathers are all too often absent as wars are being waged against our children to desensitize them to sin, to confuse them concerning their sexual nature, to destroy their innocence as early as possible, and to turn them away from family and godly moral values. Ultimately, progressive goals aim to replace respect for God with obedience to those who reject God, ultimately to the destruction of their lives.

Based on the chaos precipitated by so many destructive cultural trends, it should be evident that secular humanists are motivated to come after the next generation through our children. But God has placed a demand on all fathers (every generation's "mighty men") to pick up their respective "battle gear"—"the whole armor of God" (Ephesians 6:10-17)—and to position themselves on the front lines of the cultural war all around us. As God has always done from the beginning of time, He seeks to use fathers as a protective shield against the rampant, ungodly influences that are targeting our children.

With God, we know the victory is already won. But we must do our part in this life, which includes encouraging fathers to take their rightful positions and to fight for the very lives of their children. God is calling fathers to the front lines; it's the battle of our lifetime ... it's the battle fathers must engage in to turn the tide of the current wicked global culture.

The question is, are fathers ready and willing to step up? The countless lives of innocent children hang in the balance as they await fathers to take their rightful position ... God awaits you!

What is your response?

CHAPTER 25

THE FEMINIZATION OF MEN

J ust look around. The world is going through very peculiar and unprecedented times. Besides the normalization of LGBTQ sexuality and gender dysphoria, there is another, more passive trend in play: to popularize and encourage the feminization of males in general. Specifically, a move to blur the lines between what is masculine and feminine, and negate the biblical—and long-standing cultural and societal—definitions of manhood and masculinity.

Is this a bad thing? Well, in two words—yes, very.

If God explicitly designed and then created men and women, male and female, as two different entities (Genesis 1:27), isn't it obvious then that men and women will be different from each other? And not just physically but in all kinds of ways?

This basic truth is obvious worldwide, throughout history, and with virtually every culture that ever existed. Men and women are different. They gravitate to complementary but different roles and have cultural appearances that distinguish between the two sexes. Scripture doesn't specify all of what the outward appearance differences must be, but they are to be recognizable.

Remember the old "unisex" trend? It came and went very fast, yet its roots of creating gender confusion, gender neutrality, or, in woke terms, gender inclusiveness, have never died out. So, what's going on with this "new" trend?

CLARIFYING MASCULINITY

Part of what is happening is an attempt to eliminate the traditional role of a man being the protector of the family. By "feminizing" men, this distinctive of men is reduced to no more than an option instead of a glorious calling. Scripture is clear: the dignity of a husband and father is in their sacrificial love (Ephesians 5:25, 28), provision (1 Timothy 5:8), and protective leadership (1 Corinthians 16:13-14) of those closest to them.

Being masculine is not wrong for a man. For clarification, what we are advocating is not "toxic" (today's favorite buzzword). Being masculine is not to be some renowned "sex machine" or aggressively rude to others or always wanting to be the "Alpha male" in the room. Biblical masculinity is not abusive, but it is lived out in a way that reflects a humble confidence, a sincere love for others, and a self-discipline that comes from wisdom (2 Timothy 1:7). Confusion over what God has designed a man to be only leads to gender identity issues, chaos in marriage and family relationships, and a reluctance, or unwillingness, to take responsibility for a family or be a powerful example and contributor to our society. A case in point is that the happiest wives in America have religiously conservative (traditionally masculine) husbands, according to a *New York Times* article by Brad Wilcox.[1] Furthermore, in her book *The Toxic War on Masculinity*, Nancy Pearcey

---

1 W. Bradford Wilcox, Jason S. Carroll and Laurie DeRose, "Religious Men Can be Devoted Dads, Too," New York Times, May18, 2018.

reports, "It is a dedicated, conservative Protestant family man who come closest to the ideal of the new fatherhood."[2]

Let's take some prominent examples. Several NBA players have been spotted wearing dresses, as have many hip-hop rappers (with purses). Even muscular and "studly" men like former pro wrestler John Cena have been seen wearing a dress! Hip-hop megastar Drake has been spotted wearing pink polished and manicured fingernails. What is happening? What we are witnessing is not simply feminine men. In contrast, these are masculine men pivoting to embrace a cultural trend of male-femininity. They're attempting to visually depict the message that to be "masculine," it is now desirable to appear to be "feminine."

When prominent actors, hip-hop artists, and athletes gladly help to undermine their own intrinsic masculinity, there's got to be something more to the story. Why has the attack on manhood become such a trend?

The reality is that the roots of this "re-invention" have been with us for a long time. And in the process, the human rights of boys and men are being violated.[3]

THE BIGGER AGENDA

Interestingly, world leaders and globalists applaud the antics of rappers and athletes who wear dresses and do all things effeminate. Having superstars act this way is fundamental to their misguided plans and aspirations for a "great reset" and "new world order."

Unfortunately, there are numerous globalist schemes to undermine God's natural order for humanity. Purposeful brainwashing of public school children through wretched curriculum depicting grotesque sex and confusing messages about "gender" is now commonplace. The result: the next generation will be saddled with deep confusion about

---

2 Pearcey, Nancy. The Toxic War on Masculinity, Baker Books, 2023, p 42.
3 https://endtodv.org/pr/why-did-human-rights-day-ignore-the-massive-human-rights-violations-against-boys-and-men/

what a "normal" family environment is and an unhealthy understanding of gender and sex.

Fatherless homes are no longer seen as problematic, no matter how pervasive and impactful the problem. Tropes are used to promote a negative view of manliness, such as saying someone has "toxic masculinity" if they don't conform to the new "woke" image of what a man is supposed to be.

We are not witnessing some assumed "normal progression" of humanity as it becomes more self-aware and introspective (although those things are not intrinsically bad of themselves). We are witnessing a basic deconstruction of the perfect design differences that God intended to be a blessing for both men and women. But why?

It is quite well known that one of the primary goals of globalists is to dramatically depopulate the planet. They foresee bringing the world population down from the current eight billion people to under 800 million (preferably around 500 million). This represents a 90% reduction in the world population.

DEPOPULATION STRATEGY

Realistically, the goal toward the feminization of men won't be brought about in a vacuum. There are related, larger factors at play. You may wonder, "So, what's the connection between this feminization trend and the push for other anti-biblical initiatives and paradigms such as abortion-on-demand, transgenderism, etc.?"

Go back to Chapter 17 where we discussed God's plan for covenantal marriage between one man and one woman. The opposite of this would be the curtailing of marriage, the blurring of the lines between the sexes, the acceleration of depopulation (read: increase in abortion rates), and the elimination of traditional, biblical roles by Marxist leftists and progressive globalists.

But again, you may ask, "But why would leftists push for the feminization of men in a larger push for sexual deconstruction and the smudging of the gender lines?" The goal is *equity*, remember? (And not *equality*, which means the recognition and freedom of the individual as God made each of us.) In other words, under the banner of Marxism, socio-economic lines are eliminated, gender traditions are obliterated, sexual mores are destroyed (remember Rousseau), and the boundaries of sexual propriety are smashed (see Kinsey).

The so-called "sexual revolution" that began in earnest in the 1960s is part of a larger push for societal revolution, and the elimination of what God created to be separate, healthy, and unique: male and female, the sanctity of marriage, and the beauty and uniqueness of individual nations.

Thus, male feminization is simply one of many tactics that elitist-globalists are using to achieve the same end: the elimination of all lines between the sexes, as well as the installation of anti-biblical initiatives. For example, they are encouraging subtle forms of eugenics, an immoral pseudo-science that focuses on the manipulation of genetics which was embraced by Hitler to develop a "super race" by eliminating "weak" humans (e.g., those with "impure" genes, the sick, the mentally challenged, etc.). They are also pushing for abortion-on-demand, lower birthrates, the experimentation of new uses of vaccines, new "pandemic" controls, implementation of digital currencies, encouraging AI (artificial intelligence) to control information, and welcoming various forms of social-cultural engineering.

China, the world's largest communist nation, has had negative population growth now for seven years running. Their "one child" policy of the 70s and 80s is now resulting in a population decline there.

Although these tactics are promoted as necessary to bring about a greater good (such as "saving the earth"), they ultimately culminate in undermining individual sovereignty (freedom), the traditional nuclear family, and the natural tendency for human procreation.

But there's more. When men are confused about their manhood and accept cultural narratives promoting homosexuality, they can easily turn away from God's design for "natural affection" (toward women) and instead turn toward other men (Romans 1:27). When men are confused about their role and reject the God-ordained purposes of one-man, one-woman marriage and family, they will not start families. When men are confused about their gender, they will not produce children. En masse, globalist and elitist encouragement of social and cultural confusion about the role of men will not just significantly impact birth rates, but that confusion will add to the spread of relationship chaos resulting in fatherlessness, divorce, family disunity, and ultimately, incalculable societal dysfunction and destruction.

The purposeful collapse of societal/cultural norms and traditions is on the horizon. This impending collapse will accelerate even more if men continue to deny their responsibility and ignore what God has called them to be. Men are to be men, but only as God has gifted and designed them.

Just as God uniquely creates each of us, so he uniquely creates men—there is no single stereotypical male. Some are feelers, others are thinkers. Others are highly emotional, while others rarely express emotion. Some are left-brained logicians while others are right-brained creatives. Some are night owls (yours truly; with tongue in cheek, I warn people that my sanctification does not turn on till 9 am), while others are wired to get up before dawn. And the list goes on. And that's the beauty of God's design: true biblical diversity.

Every war that has been fought and won has required men to be on the "front lines." Today, there is an aggressive cultural war being waged, but men are mostly missing in action. It's no wonder we see an acceleration and rapid embrace of cultural evils. Intense pressures within the woke culture have targeted men and rendered them mostly impotent. But God calls for "mighty men of valor" to position themselves on the front lines of culture and society to actively combat evils directed at our families and children!

THE "REAL" MAN

For Christians, the God-man, Jesus Christ, is the perfect example of what manhood is. One of the greatest influences in my life was the global men's movement pioneer Edwin Louis Cole.[4] He used to open auditorium rallies with his mantra, "Manhood and Christlikeness are synonymous." That one powerful phrase challenged and encouraged millions of men to emulate Jesus. He taught men to live consistent and godly lives, loving their wives and children.

Jesus was compassionate, merciful, and always had self-control. During those rare times that He was angry, His anger was always a righteous indignation against evil, and never in a sinful way (1 Peter 2:22). Yet, He was forgiving and tender at all the right times. One other thing: Jesus was always teaching and instructing, which is one of the fundamental responsibilities of a father in their family (Proverbs 1:8-9; Ephesians 6:4). These are the godly traits and characteristics that are to be instilled and taught to each generation of young men so that they will become mature, capable of being proper leaders in their community and in their own families.

It's time for the faith community to fully understand the implications of the woke trends that are tearing down the proper and noble roles God designed for both males and females. Instead of accommodating every whim of cultural deviancy in an attempt to be "sensitive" and "welcoming," it is time to acknowledge evil for what it

---

4 Edwin Louis Cole founded the Christian Men's Network, which spread to over 138 nations, training 8,000,000 men around the globe. The classic text was *Maximized Manhood*, which sold in the tens of millions. His son, Paul Louis Cole, now leads the Christian Men's Network as it continues to expand. (https://cmn.men/pages/about-us) Edwin Louis Cole was the 3rd greatest male influence in my life. He attended the church I then pastored in the heart of the Dallas-Ft. Worth area. I was profoundly humbled when he called me his "pastor," a title I never felt worthy of. Paul Cole, who carries the mantle of his father, was an advisor and close friend during my years in Texas. The Coles—father and son—are the epicenter of training men for godly living.

is—destructive and shameful (Ephesians 5:11). That does not mean believers are to be harsh, or name-callers. Rather, we must be compassionate and stand firmly against every whim of culture undermining God's authority.

Our secular culture wants to legitimatize and normalize every new wrinkle of human depravity in order to justify sinful actions. And those that are buying into the lie can't stand to be contradicted. In fact, Scripture says they think you are a bumpkin and ignorant if you don't plunge with them into these sinful passions (1 Peter 4:4). We hold out a better hope for everyone, and God will bless our faithfulness in not bowing to confusion, and in standing for what is right (Ephesians 6:10-11). In short, men, be men. Godly men.

CHAPTER 26

CHILD SEX TRAFFICKING

S ex trafficking is the illegal business of recruiting, harboring, transporting, obtaining, or providing a person, especially a minor, for the purpose of sex.[1] It is considered the fastest-growing crime worldwide, with the UN Office on Drugs and Crime reporting that 50% of all human trafficking victims were trafficked for sexual exploitation,[2] with this "business" taking in over $150 billion in 2020.[3] Drugs and weapons can be sold once; a child can be sold repeatedly. It is a low-risk, high-income crime.

THE NUMBERS ARE HORRENDOUS

In North America, sex trafficking is the most common form of human trafficking. The American Association of University Women

1 "Sex trafficking." Merriam-Webster.com Legal Dictionary, Merriam-Webster, https://www.merriam-webster.com/legal/sex%20trafficking. Accessed 2 Aug. 2023.
2 Human-Trafficking-Quick-Facts-Jan-2022.pdf (aauw.org)
3 Cracking The $150 Billion Business Of Human Trafficking (forbes.com)

(AAUW) reports that 72% of all victims are being trafficked for sexual exploitation.[4] AAUW adds, "Of sex trafficking cases reported in the US from 2007 to 2012, 85% of victims were women, with the US National Human Trafficking Hotline estimating there are hundreds of thousands of human trafficking victims in the United States alone."[5]

These numbers are heartbreaking, but even more heart-wrenching is that the average age of a child involved in sex trafficking is twelve, with many under the age of five being traded like commodities for the ever-expanding porn industry. It's literally hard to wrap one's head around, and as evil as the pagan rights of child sacrifice to the god Molech in the Old Testament (see Leviticus 18:21; 2 Kings 23:10). Does human action get any more evil than this?

ENTRAPMENT

Victims are often manipulated into believing they are being relocated to work in legitimate forms of employment. This was clearly depicted in the film *The Sound of Freedom,* where young children were targeted, and the father was led to believe his children were simply attending a modeling photo shoot.[6]

Once under a trafficker's control, children and adolescents are forced into creating sex videos for pornography websites, sold into child sex rings, forced into prostitution, and coerced into sex-related occupations such as nude dancing and modeling. We often think that boys are in the minority when it comes to sexual abuse and trafficking, but in Western and Southern Europe in 2020, more men and boys were victims than women and girls.[7]

4 Where We Stand: Human Trafficking—AAUW : Empowering Women Since 1881.
https://www.aauw.org/resources/policy/position-human-trafficking/
5 Ibid.
6 Monteverde, Alejandro. Sound of Freedom, Cartagena, Colombia, Santa Fe Films, 2023, 131 min.
7 GLOTiP_2022_web.pdf (unodc.org) pg 157.

TRAFFICKERS

Traffickers aren't just shadowy figures, pimps in a back alley targeting younger women or girls who are away from home. They can be a person willing to trade family members for sex in return for money, drugs, or anything of value. They can be a female friend who recruits online, in high school, or even while on the bus. The most dangerous type will use constant violence and threats to break down the will of a victim and bring the child or adolescent into total submission. This type of pimp often rapes, beats, and emotionally batters his victims in an effort to destroy hope.[8] Also, "Romeo boyfriends" will masquerade themselves as romantically interested, kind, and affectionate while grooming unsuspecting 'candidates' for pedophiles.

While men are the highest percentage of traffickers, the percentage that are women is rising worldwide, since they are more enticing than male traffickers, and victims will trust female traffickers more readily.

For example, my town of San Diego is one of the largest trafficking hubs in the US, so activity here is high. My friend's daughter, Hannah, who is 28, went to a restaurant to watch a friend's dad play with his band. While enjoying the music, Hannah struck up a conversation with a young woman in the next booth. It turns out they had a lot in common.

Unbeknownst to Hannah, however, the young woman slipped some sort of drug into her beverage when she was not looking. Soon Hannah found herself in the bathroom, feeling like she was going to pass out.

Thankfully, two "angels" in the form of total strangers noticed how out of it Hannah seemed, and helped her out of the bathroom. All the while the "friendly woman" and her two male companions followed behind. They even tried to say that Hannah was with them. The two women who were assisting Hannah, however, weren't buying

---

8 How Traffickers Exploit People for Sex—REST (iwantrest.com)

it. They were able to open Hannah's phone and re-dial the last active number—it was her friend, who quickly came outside to help Hannah. The strange woman and her male companions were none too pleased and quickly got into their car and sped away. Hannah was *that* close to being taken across the border into Mexico.

ONLINE DANGERS

Peer-to-peer victimization via the Internet has increased rapidly in the last decade.[9] Easy access pornography has been successful in reducing inhibitions and can easily trick children into seeing or participating in online encounters of a sexual nature. Children mimic what they observe and will sexually act out what they have seen. Unfortunately, a lack of parental supervision—particularly during the season of COVID-19—has left more and more children vulnerable to online predators.[10]

Predators online can trick a child simply by saying, "Let's do something silly." Sexting, or sharing nudes, has become common, where innocent young girls and boys are tricked into sending explicit pictures online.[11] Sending nudes is not only dangerous; the images cannot be retrieved. Thirty percent of teens have sexted, and 40% have received a sext. Of the 30% who have sexted, 46% of those are involved in sextortion.[12]

CONTRIBUTING FACTORS

Without the protection of a mother and father in the home, children are more likely to run away, go missing,[13] or spend time in the

---

9 Online Child Sexual Exploitation—Canada.ca
10 Lack of Digital Supervision is Leaving Kids Vulnerable to a Growing Group of Online Predators—Their Peers | FHSS (federationhss.ca)
11 FBI warns of explosion in sextortion cases targeting teenagers—BBC News
12 6388_OCSE_Infographic_EN_P6 (canada.ca)
13 How US Marshals Rescued 39 Missing Children in Georgia (dailysignal.com)

foster care system, making them easy targets for sexual exploitation. In a 2016 study, the National Center for Missing and Exploited Children revealed that more than 85% of sex-trafficked victims had been under the care of social services and in foster care when they disappeared.[14]

Sex trafficking, sexual exploitation, and prostitution all have common root causes: childhood sexual assault, incest, demand for paid sex, and pornography. Contributing factors include family disintegration, multiple parental partners, childhood sexual abuse, Adverse Childhood Experiences (ACE), unlimited access to social media, violent pornography, and socioeconomic vulnerabilities (e.g., poverty, homelessness, limited educational opportunities, racial disparities, and immigration issues).

PORNOGRAPHY

When Hugh Hefner produced the first *Playboy* magazine in the 1950s, it opened a very dangerous and destructive Pandora's box. Who would have known that we would now be inundated with a never-ending barrage of sexually explicit material coming not only in print but more often through our television and social media outlets via cell phones?

The Guardian reported that in 2021 alone, "A record 29.3 million items of child abuse imagery were found and removed across the internet."[15] The overwhelming majority of reports came from Facebook, where 22 million pieces of child abuse imagery were reported, followed by Instagram (3.3 million), and WhatsApp (1.3 million). Google made 875,783 reports, and Snapchat 512,522.[16]

Pornhub (owned by a company named MindGeek) is located in Montreal, Canada. It produces the majority of the world's

14 SexTraffickingReport3.pdf (cbcfinc.org) pg 8.
15 Sites reported record 29.3m child abuse images in 2021 | Internet | The Guardian
16 Sites reported record 29.3m child abuse images in 2021 | Internet | The Guardian

free-to-view porn and attracts 3.5 billion visits a month, more than Netflix, Yahoo, or Amazon. Pornhub rakes in money from almost three billion ad impressions a day. If you think porn is "for men only," a 2017 report showed that 17% of women describe themselves as addicted to pornography.[17]

GOD'S CHILDREN ARE NOT FOR SALE

The faith community is especially sensitive to this evil, knowing God is particularly protective of those who are weak and oppressed by others. Jesus specifically warned of severe punishment for anyone who leads children into sin (Matthew 18:6), so it is appropriate to lobby heavily for harsh punishment for anyone trafficking others, particularly when children are involved. The government doesn't hold the sword for no reason (Romans 13:4).

However, there is one encouraging note about traffickers. The Department of Justice in 2008[18] showed one-year reoffending rates fell by 40% after convicted sex buyers in San Francisco were forced to attend a *John school* (programs designed to teach buyers—the "Johns"—why their behavior is both exploitative and dangerous). In Seattle, the Organization for Prostitution Survivors, headed by Peter Qualliotine[19] reports that 95% of graduates say they don't think they'll ever buy sex again.[20]

Vigilance is also key. Look for signs that may indicate a child or adolescent is being trafficked and fulfill the imperative of Proverbs 24:11-12 to help save them. Reporter Katherine Hamilton lists the following concerns to look for:

---

17 http://www.telegraph.co.uk/news/science/11016874/Sex-Women-just-as-easily-hooked-on-online-porn-as-men.html
18 ojp.gov/pdffiles1/nij/grants/222451.pdf
19 Seattle "John School" Educates Men Who Pay For Sex (kuow.org)
20 John Schools: A practical, cost-effective way to reduce demand—Demand Abolition

- *Minors in unexplained possession of cash or extra cell phones*
- *Use of terminology such as "a night job," "do a date," "the life" or "for daddy"*
- *Drugs provided by a third party seemingly for free or in exchange for sexual activity*
- *Suspicious ads online or on social media for escorts, stripping parties, and other sexual activity*
- *Girls attempting to recruit other girls to become involved in suspicious activity*
- *Job opportunities involving modeling or the sex industry*
- *An unreasonable promise of money or fame from a third party*
- *Is the person accompanied by another person who seems controlling?*
- *Is the person rarely allowed in public except for work?*
- *Any signs of physical or psychological abuse?*
- *Does the person seem submissive or fearful?*
- *Does the person lack identification or documentation?*
- *Is someone else collecting the person's pay or holding their money for "safekeeping?"*
- *Does the person show signs of substance use or addiction?*[21]

Parents need to keep computers in common places to help prevent exposure to evil (Psalm 101:3a). There are also apps that will prevent your children from taking, sending, and uploading nude selfies and videos, most certainly a wise investment in your child's future. Restricting your child's cell phone and internet use is imperative, as well as

21 Hamilton, Katherine Here's how your porn habit could be helping human sex traffickers 2021—NBC2 https://archive.ph/Cnfgm#selection-2329.0-2331.18

warning them about the likelihood of peers viewing pornography online at school.

Better yet, how about keeping a child from having a cell phone until they are older? There are also phones you can buy that only allow phone calls and texting, with no access to the Internet. These may be difficult conversations to have with your child, but given the pandemic nature of human trafficking, it is necessary to help equip them for the rest of their life (Proverbs 22:6).

One final word. Most victims of child sex trafficking and prostitution end up drug addicted, severely traumatized, mentally ill, suicidal, and at greater risk of murder. The sad reality is that only far too few victims are able to escape the sex industry. Prevention is key.

CHAPTER 27

THE AGED AND EUTHANASIA

D eath is a universal truth. It can come as a result of an accident,
severe illness, or through natural causes as a person ages. Death is
the final enemy that we all face (1 Corinthians 15:26) as a result
of the Fall of our first parents, Adam and Eve, in the Garden (Romans
5:12). It can come tragically at a very early age, or after a full and
productive life. It is not a respecter of race, intelligence level, or the
amount of wealth a person has. Although it sounds contradictory,
death is a fact of life.

LIFE AND DEATH

Biblically, the giving and taking of life are the prerogative of God
alone (1 Samuel 2:6). Because of the sinfulness of humankind and our
propensity for violence, God instituted special protections to guard
against the unjust ending of life created in His image (Genesis 1:27;
9:6; Exodus 20:13). God also authorized government to wield the
sword against evil doers (Romans 13:3-4), and gave individuals the

right to use lethal force to protect themselves and their families (Exodus 22:2; Luke 22:36).

Satan, on the other hand, is the author of lies and has been a murderer from the beginning (John 8:44). It's not surprising he will use any means and rationale possible to cheapen and then destroy life. Why is Satan so jealous of human life in particular? Because human beings are the only part of Creation that is made—and can procreate—in God's image.

Therefore, Satan will do everything and anything he can to end human life—from the unborn to the elderly. This includes convincing people that their life no longer has value or meaning. One of the more insidious ways this is done is through euthanasia.

SUFFERING AND EUTHANASIA

You have no doubt heard of "mercy killings." Those extreme cases where someone "mercifully" takes the life of someone else to prevent them from suffering excruciating pain while waiting for certain death. In effect, euthanasia is the same thing as a so-called "mercy killing." It is promoted as a painless way to end a life that is suffering and believed to not be worth living any longer.

But, like any other slippery slope, without moral standards and a deep appreciation for life created in God's image, abuse will quickly start to develop. It happened with abortion. First legalized under restricted conditions, it quickly became legal to kill a child anytime during the pregnancy for any or no reason at all.

The same is happening with euthanasia.

What began with a morally questionable decision to end a life to prevent hours or days of "unnecessary" suffering, has developed into a variety of means to end life under the banner of "death with dignity," or some supposed "right to die." Euthanasia can either be active or passive in nature. Technically, both refer to the actions of usually a health care professional causing the death of someone wanting to die, either actively (lethal injection), or by withholding lifesaving treatment, that is, by "passive" means. Physician-assisted suicide differs in that lethal means are generally provided to someone that administers it to themselves to end their own life.

SUICIDE DOES NOT EXIST

It is important to note that, in reality, there is no such thing as actual "suicide," given the fact that "sui" means "self" or "oneself," and "cide" means "kill." No one can kill "one's self." It should be called "bio-cide." That is, one can end one's *physical* life, what I call biocide, but no one has the capability of extinguishing the permanent "self," or the spirit, one's *spiritual* self.

THE SECULAR RATIONALE FOR DEATH

How have we gotten to the point that as of April 2023, ten states and the District of Columbia had laws allowing assisted suicide?[1] Our nation has tragically gotten to this point by seeing life as only of value if we, as humans, give value to it. In contrast, life has value because *God says we have value.*

A wrong perspective states that if someone is experiencing pain, or severe depression, or extreme hardship of some kind, and "quality of life" doesn't meet expectations, then why continue to suffer? This false thinking says that if extraordinary efforts are being used to try to preserve a person's life, why not allow that life to end so that limited resources can be given to others who will have a greater benefit? This view of not valuing life asks, "Why continue to burden family members emotionally and financially?" The implication is that if a person doesn't choose to end one's life when things get tough, that person is being "selfish."

---

1 Assisted Suicide States [Updated April 2023] (worldpopulationreview.com)

But, like all secular, humanistic perspectives, once a moral standard is removed there is no rational basis to restrict the ending of life based on age, imminence of death, type of pain, amount of burden on others, mental state, or expected quality of life or circumstances, even if the person gives permission or not. Each of these criteria demonstrates a belief that the value of life is only dependent on the perceived quality of that life from a *human* perspective, and not from the perspective that it has intrinsic worth and value because it is from God and bears His image.

THE BIBILCAL PERSPECTIVE

Active or passive euthanasia have the same end goal: suicide. How does the Bible treat suicide? It turns out that every time it is mentioned in Scripture it is in a negative light, from Abimelech (Judges 9:50-56), to Saul (1 Samuel 31:1-13), to Ahithophel (2 Samuel 17:23), to Judas Iscariot (Matthew 27:3-6). Taking our own life breaks God's command to not murder (Exodus 20:13), in this case self-murder, and artificially shortens the opportunity for unforeseen circumstances to bring glory to God (2 Corinthians 5:1-9).

But what about those who are suffering unimaginable pain, with no apparent opportunity for recovery? Scripture is clear that we are to provide comfort and relief from pain as much as possible (Proverbs 31:6-7), without drugging them into permanent unconsciousness. This allows times of continued encouragement until death comes, and can be an especially sweet time for believers as eternity with the Lord is the focus (1 Corinthians 15:54-57).

I personally faced this twice, once as my wife of 42 years lay dying in 2013 and a second time, while working on this book, as my 102-year-old mother (who until that time had happily lived by herself and cared for herself) came to her final hours. Morphine had to be given to ease the pain. I was thankful there was something, as referred to in the Proverbs passage above, that could vastly reduce the suffering.

For unbelievers who are facing death, these extended moments can potentially give time in which the Gospel can be shared, which could change the person's heart, and grant eternal life (John 6:44; 14:6).

What about those who are elderly, tired, and suffering? The Lord reveals that we are to show special respect for those who are older (Deuteronomy 32:7; Job 12:12; 32:7), and value them. In their weakness (2 Samuel 19:34-35; Ecclesiastes 12:2-3) we are to protect them (Psalm 71:9), encourage them, and cherish them, and not see them as a burden as they approach the end of their earthly lives.

TRUE COMPASSION

All life is precious to God, but that doesn't mean that the end of life will be without difficulties. It may be awkward at first, but talking with parents, spouses, and family in general about medical care before the end is at hand will go a long way to minimizing decision uncertainty. Another critical step is to establish a health care directive that spells out your personal desires.

A few other things to keep in mind when the inevitable comes. Life is not to be treated as an idol. What I mean by that statement is that extraordinary measures to "postpone death" as long as possible may not be biblically justified. But, providing comfort, support, encouragement, and medication to manage pain until life comes to an end is biblical. By all means, when those times of decision do arrive, and they will, diligently seek the wisdom that the Lord promises to give to us if we just ask for it (James 1:5).

CHAPTER 28

THE YOUNG AND INFANTICIDE

The mere fact this chapter had to be written speaks volumes. In former and morally saner times, pro-life supporters approached many life issues with a somber warning: *this practice could justify infanticide someday.* Such warnings were laughed off as scare tactics and dismissed as the usual "slippery slope" bogeyman. Except for one thing: the warnings were correct.

LIVES WITH NO VALUE?

Perhaps the best-known advocate of something like infanticide is Peter Singer, a professor of bioethics at Princeton University and a known advocate for animal rights. Singer believes parents should have approximately one month *after birth* to decide whether the child should continue living. *After. Birth.*

To clarify this, Singer advocates this in the case of what he calls "serious disabilities." Of course, the killing of innocent children with disabilities is repulsive. But here is another problem. Someone has to define "serious," an issue he leaves mostly unexplored. But the key to understanding Singer's views is that some lives *are not worth living.*

Singer is not alone. Dominic James Wilkinson, writing in the *American Journal of Bioethics*, published a paper in 2011 with this description in the abstract:

> I conclude that it is justifiable in some circumstances for parents and doctors to decide to allow an infant to die even though the infant's life would be worth living. The (view presented in the paper) provides a justification for treatment decisions that is more consistent, more robust, and potentially more practical than the standard view.[1]

Note carefully the "even though the infant's life would be worth living" reference, similar to Singer's beliefs. Ponder these words for a moment. He's basically saying that even if that child has a chance at living, the parents and doctors should be able to end the life. (If that's not playing God, I don't know what is.)

Take Professor John Harris, a member of the British Medical Association's ethics committee and a professor of bioethics at the University of Manchester. (Harris was also a senior medical ethics adviser to the British government, the European Union, and the United Nations, so his views carry some weight.) During a House of Commons Science and Technology Committee debate, Harris made headlines when he noted that infanticide could be morally justified:

> I don't think infanticide is always unjustifiable … I don't think it is plausible to think there is any moral change that

---

1 https://philpapers.org/rec/WILALW

occurs during the journey down the birth canal. I don't think anything has happened during that time.[2]

Tragically, he clearly believes that some lives are not worth living.

HARD CASES DON'T JUSTIFY UNGODLY PRINCIPLES

Those advocating a "moral" case for infanticide typically portray the most dreadful situations imaginable, because it takes an extreme case to promote a *principle* that is so inhumane and dangerous, one that can easily then be applied to more than infants.

Case in point: the choice to withhold care under certain narrow circumstances is fully supportable under Christian ethics. Most likely, most of us would agree that if one's heartbeat is sustained only by a machine when one's body and brain are not functioning, we would want them to turn the machine off because all it is doing is prolonging one's death and my meeting the Lord. But the decision to withhold food and hydration to *cause* death is entirely different.

With infanticide, we are talking about an infant able to live but not meeting someone's standard on *whether the quality of life justifies keeping that child alive.* What could possibly justify that decision? Someone born without a limb? A cleft palate? Down Syndrome? Take it further. How about someone who is a disfavored race or sex? A baby girl born in China under the "One Child Policy" left to die because the parents needed a male to help work on the farm?

TWISTED LOGIC

Pro-life ethicists have long argued that there is no difference in humanity between a baby in the womb and a newly born child. Both

2 https://canadiancrc.com/Newspaper_Articles/Daily_Telegraph_Infanticide_is_ justifiable_25JAN04.aspx

are uniquely human life, though in different stages. The proponents of allowing infants to die essentially agree but reach an opposite conclusion. If abortion is morally justified (as it is in their eyes), then why not infanticide shortly after birth?

Peter Singer admits as much in an interview. Here are his own words:

> I don't draw a big distinction between abortion and infanticide. Those who think that it's O.K. for women to have an abortion need to show why there's such an important difference between the fetus before birth and the newborn infant after birth.[3]

How do those advocating for infanticide justify ending a life that would otherwise survive? A typical argument is an extension of their justification for abortion. The child in the womb is fully dependent on the mother and, therefore—they claim—not yet fully a person. Because of this, the mother is justified in opting for abortion for any (or no) reason. The same logic would apply to a newborn baby at three or six months of age. But that same egregious logic would also apply to an adult temporarily in a coma, needing feeding assistance, or a teenager fighting a severe illness.

Do you see where this is going?

The key point in the infanticide question is that someone is called to decide whether a baby is fit to live. Will there be times of heartbreaking situations and difficult decisions? Of course. But we must always remember that God is the author of life, and the decision should be His and not ours. This belief will challenge us in heart and soul. But it will be in the way that all humanity has experienced such challenges

---

3 April 25, 2021 at https://www.newyorker.com/culture/the-new-yorker-interview/peter-singer-is-committed-to-controversial-ideas

throughout Creation. There is no physical or mental perfection in this life, but there is hope for every life to embrace God's redemptive work through Jesus Christ.

GOD CREATES EACH PERSON

When Moses, the towering figure of the Jewish faith, received his call from God to confront Pharaoh, he immediately objected. He was insufficient for the task and not able to speak well. God replied to Moses this way:

> Then the Lord said to him, "Who has made man's mouth? Who makes him mute, or deaf, or seeing, or blind? Is it not I, the Lord?"
> —*Exodus 4:11*

This is a difficult verse to understand. As Christians, we tend to think that things gone wrong in this world are the result of sin and the fall of man. That is most certainly often the case, yet at the same time, God sets the limits of how far that goes and how we will enter this world. The whole of Creation ultimately answers to His will, even in its fallen state. The person born with disabilities is no less an image-bearer of God (Genesis 1:27) than an Olympic athlete. If God has created someone with less than human "perfection," who is fit to tell God He has erred?

Once humankind opens that Pandora's box of judging who decides to live and who doesn't—a task that should wholly rest in God's hands—the chaos of "death culture" ensues. Abortion was the beginning. Now we are grappling with the horrors of eugenics, euthanasia, and "mercy killing."

And yes, again, there will always be difficult cases. To parents who face the news of a child with significant disabilities, we should offer our prayers and loving support. This is exactly how God intended relationships to work in a fallen world. As the Apostle Paul notes in 2 Corinthians 1:3-4 (ESV):

> Blessed be the God and Father of our Lord Jesus Christ, the Father of mercies and God of all comfort, who comforts us in all our affliction, so that we may be able to comfort those who are in any affliction, with the comfort with which we ourselves are comforted by God.

Those with disabilities and special needs will always be with us. In the world's eyes, they are the "least" among us. Those like Peter Singer would argue they are disposable when not up to our standards of what constitutes "worthy" life. But to the follower of Christ, "whatsoever you have done for the least of these, you have done for me" (Matthew 25:40).

PERSONAL EXPERIENCE

My nephew has Down Syndrome. There have been times he can communicate with a few words. At times, he has been silent for years. Yet, in family gatherings, he is often the epicenter of love and entertainment. He knows he is loved. And sometimes he can actually say, "I love you."

And he knows what he wants. Once, while our family was visiting my brother, they moved my nephew out of his room so we could sleep there. After breakfast, I came back upstairs and found that all our suitcases had been drug out of the room into the hallway. I slowly opened the door of the room I had been staying in—his room—to see him sitting proudly on his bed with a big smile that said without words, "This is my turf, and I am now, once again, 'king' of my room."

I am so glad Peter Singer and others could not determine his value at birth. He is priceless to God. And to us. And to me.

CHAPTER 29

HOMELESSNESS

I love the beach. It's a place where I would go—not nearly as often as I would like—to rest, write, reflect, and basically escape the pressures of life. In my memory, at least, the beach was clean and relaxed, people were friendly, and I could safely take my family there.

TIMES HAVE CHANGED

Today, the beach that my family and I frequented is still available, but like many places in California, it has been inundated with a flood of humanity that sleeps on sidewalks, has set up tent homes, or aggressively demands money. In many areas of California, especially in urban centers, drug deals are commonplace, with people openly injecting their veins with needles provided by the local government. In California, not only is common decency becoming rare, but law and order is collapsing. Psalm 11:3 (ESV) asks a haunting question: "If the foundations are destroyed, what can the righteous do?"

But the problem extends far beyond California. Homelessness is a national problem. New York and Texas host about 27,000 homeless people each. But that pales in significance to the 38% (or about 161,000) of America's homeless that "live" in California (US Department of Housing and Urban Development). And indicators are that the next release of figures will be much higher. This isn't just because of California's mild, year-round climate! California has intentionally crafted laws that not only accommodate the presence of the homeless but provide benefits that serve as a siren song to attract more from all over the country and the world.

And what is the result of this mishandling of the crisis? Hardly a day passes that we don't hear on the news of some innocent person being threatened, assaulted, attacked or even killed by a homeless person. It does not have to be this way. The mayor of my city in California is Bill Wells. He helped me write this chapter. He is a specialist in homelessness. He has worked in emergency rooms for years. He has a nursing degree and a doctorate in psychology. He owns and operates a clinic. He knows the root factors and causes of homelessness. He could fix it. But California laws won't allow him to do that. And your state might not be much better.

THE BOTTOM LINE

No person—anyone, anywhere—has the right to simply pitch a tent on private or public property and permanently live there, complete with trash, disease, urine, and feces. One would think that everyone would understand this, that it would be a "given." But it is not. And many politicians, and apparently a lot of voters, do not understand this simple axiom: You cannot arbitrarily take up residence anywhere you want on property that is not yours.

RE-DEFINING CRIME

California provides the perfect model for how to handle homelessness incorrectly. In the name of equity and addressing racism,

California passed Assembly Bill 109 (2011) to adopt a policy of "realignment." Proponents claimed prisons were unsafe and over-crowded due to "inherent" racist policies of past generations. The solution: redefine more than seventy crimes as "less serious" or "non-violent." The result? Because of Assembly Bill 109, the California Department of Corrections and Rehabilitation reports that two prisons have been closed in the past two years, with 60,000 felony parole violators transferred from state prison to county control each year.[1]

In 2014, California Proposition 47 was approved to convert a series of felony crimes to misdemeanors. Besides keeping more people out of prison, it had many unintended consequences. One was making shop-lifting of items less than $950 a misdemeanor. The result: a criminal can steal what they want, the store owners can't effectively protect their property, and police can only write a ticket if they actually catch the perpetrator. Not surprisingly, the Public Policy Institute of California reported that property crime rose in twenty-four counties in 2021. In thirteen counties it rose by at least 10%, with the largest increase recorded in San Francisco with 16.9%. Stores are closing all over the nation, in our largest cities, punishing many law-abiding minorities who live there. California's Proposition 47 also made personal use of most drugs a minor offense and at most, subject to a ticket.

In 2017, the California State Legislature passed Senate Bill 180, limiting law enforcement's ability to send chronic drug abusers back to prison. From a biblical perspective, all of the severe consequences of these new laws should have been anticipated. Ecclesiastes 8:11 (ESV) tells us: "Because the sentence against an evil deed is not executed speedily, the heart of the children of man is fully set to do evil." If justice delayed opens the door to more criminality, what do we expect if laws are not enforced at all or criminal acts are no longer of concern?

---

1 Fox News: https://www.foxnews.com/us/did-california-prison-reform-lead-to-an-increase-in-crime

And this is just in California—and I'm acutely aware of these events because I live here. What about your state? Are you seeing similar trends?

A GOVERNMENT SOLUTION

It's common to hear people, even elected officials and experts, say that homelessness is about people being down on their luck and unable to afford housing.

Seizing on the affordability issue, the Housing First model has become a preferred solution to tackle homelessness. The idea is that once basic housing is provided, other issues the homeless grapple with can then be addressed. It sounds logical and simple, but it has been a disaster. More than $10 billion has been spent on the Housing First model. In San Francisco, a housing unit can cost up to $750,000. In Los Angeles, voters passed a bond issue for homeless housing at a cost of $140,000 each. Instead, the cost tripled, with some costing more than $700,000. Homeless advocate and author Michele Steeb writes,

> In many cities, landlords receive massive rents or use third-party for-profit maintenance companies to earn millions on properties for the homeless. In California, the only state to fully adopt the Housing First model, there has been, at great public cost, a 33% increase in permanent homeless housing units. But California's homeless population rose by 33.8% overall, and by 47.1% in the unsheltered portion of that population.[2]

Thinking that money will solve the problem, the California Comeback Plan of 2021 spent $22 billion.[3] Not addressing the root causes,

---

2 Taken from https://wng.org/articles/hotel-california-1674280451 and
https://www.michelesteeb.com/september-2022-affordable-housing-charge-testimony/
3 https://www.gov.ca.gov/2021/09/28/governor-newsom-signs-legislation-to-increase-affordable-housing-supply-and-strengthen-accountability-highlights-comprehensive-strategy-to-tackle-housing-crisis/

not surprisingly, homelessness, along with violence, has skyrocketed in Gavin Newsom's California.

THE REAL ISSUES

The Bible identifies three general categories of people who are in need of help. In 1 Thessalonians 5:14 (ESV), we read: "And we urge you, brothers, admonish the idle, encourage the fainthearted, help the weak." It seems that these groups can be loosely associated with:

1. criminals and others for not taking responsibility for their lives ("the idle");
2. those who are crushed by life's circumstances or who have turned to addictive substances ("the fainthearted");
3. those who are mentally incapacitated, or unable to function normally for some reason ("the weak").

It takes wisdom to discern the real needs of each person, and the government by its nature is incapable of judging—much less addressing—the root causes of the issues that each individual person is facing.

MENTAL ILLNESS

Mental illness is not addressed very much in Scripture, but it did exist, of course, in biblical times (1 Samuel 21:12-15). Scripture does say that when a society crumbles, "The LORD will strike you with madness and blindness and confusion of mind" (Deuteronomy 28:28, ESV). So, it's not surprising that mental illness is so prevalent in our day, whether a result of a real medical condition, or brought on by chemical abuse of the body, or—and this one is so evident today—people who choose to walk long term in vile sin.

The compassionate solution is to provide treatment options for those with mental health issues who would accept the opportunity for help. But for those sad individuals who insist on continuing to live this way, they must be removed from their hell and taken to a state hospital for proper care.

ADDICTION

Most government and homeless advocacy groups say that about 20%-30% of the people on the streets struggle with addiction. However, if you ask any police officer, ER doctor, paramedic, or social worker, they'll tell you that the prevalence of drug and alcohol use by homeless people is more likely in the 90% range. Drug addiction takes treatment to resolve, but without addressing the spiritual problems that created the situation to begin with, the cycle of addiction, more often than not, will continue to repeat itself.

The world says the compassionate thing to do is to respect their right to live in the manner they choose. However, in reality, the least compassionate thing is to allow people to rot in their addiction on the side of the road, living in constant fear of violence and predation.

CRIMINALITY

For those homeless who are addicted to criminality, applying law and order is biblical, with punishment proportional to the crime essential for a just system to be effective (Exodus 21:23-25). In Colossians 3:25 (ESV) we read: "For the wrongdoer will be paid back for the wrong he has done, and there is no partiality." Punishing crime creates the incentive to not continue on in criminality; as Deuteronomy 13:11 says, when one is punished appropriately, others will "hear and fear." When law is taken seriously, deterrence occurs; when it is ignored or not enforced, the opposite happens.

America once took these problems seriously and dealt with them. Deinstitutionalization was the new magic solution. It failed.[4] Now, the streets of many cities are filled with the mentally ill, along with urine, feces, and needles. The streets are dangerous.

Our streets could be free from the drug-addicted and mentally ill. Governor Gavin Newsom cleaned the streets for China's Communist dictator Xi Jinping's visit.[5] But he will not clean them for the citizens who live and pay taxes there. Instead, California spends the equivalent of $42K per year for each of its homeless people (including illegal immigrants).[6]

SEVERE REVERSALS IN LIFE

Another category of homelessness is those who are "down on their luck," or so goes the expression. When you see black and white pictures of a destitute family during the Great Depression or the Dust Bowl days, you know these are not people who are mentally ill, addicted, or criminal. Rather, life dealt them some serious blows.

It is true that people resent being taken advantage of by homeless people who want everything provided for them—who will not work or will not seek help for their personal problems. However, I have never met anyone who does not want to help people who have suddenly encountered a catastrophic circumstance—job loss, illness, divorce, health challenge—to help them get up and get going once again. That being said, in America, we don't really have a "homeless" problem. We have problems with mental illness, addiction, and repeat criminals who have been released.

---

4 https://1md.org/article/why-mental-health-crisis

5 https://townhall.com/tipsheet/leahbarkoukis/2023/11/13/san-francisco-cleaned-up-ahead-of-xi-visit-n2631138

6 https://www.ocregister.com/?G2I_ActionId=123580&returnUrl=https%3A%2F%2Fwww.ocregister.com%2F2023%2F07%2F18%2Fsomething-is-clearly-off-with-californias-homelessness-spending%2F%3FclearUserState%3Dtrue

CHAPTER 30

PORNOGRAPHY

T he roots of pornography can be traced back to ancient civilizations
such as Mesopotamia, Greece, and Rome. These early forms of
erotica served various purposes, including religious rituals, fertility
rites, and entertainment.

ANCIENT PORNOGRAPHY

Pornography has existed throughout recorded history, transforming with the introduction of each new medium. For example, hundreds
of sexually explicit frescoes and sculptures were found in the Mount
Vesuvius ruins of Pompeii.[1]

With the rise of Christianity in Europe, attitudes toward sexuality
and pornography shifted dramatically as the Church condemned
explicit depictions of sexual acts as sinful and immoral. The Renais-
sance period, however, witnessed a renewed interest in human

---

1 Source: https://neurosciencenews.com/neuroscience-pornography-brain-15354/

sexuality and art, leading to the creation of explicit paintings and sculptures.

The availability of printed materials with the invention of the printing press in the 15th century allowed for the mass production of erotic literature and explicit images. During the Enlightenment, philosophical thinkers challenged societal norms and advocated for sexual liberation. While still considered taboo, erotic literature and pornographic materials began to gain popularity among the aristocracy and upper classes.

The advent of photography in the 19th century presented new possibilities for the porn industry, with the creation of explicit images with greater realism. Mass-produced erotic photographs, known as "French postcards" (small pocket-sized cards with a risqué photograph), were the pornography of the late 1800s and early 1900s.[2]

MODERN COMMERCIAL PORNOGRAPHIC INDUSTRY

The 20th century witnessed the emergence of a more organized and commercialized pornographic industry. Hugh Hefner launched *Playboy*, giving birth to porn magazines.[3] His friend Alfred Kinsey promoted a lascivious sexuality that took root in the 1960s and led to a habitual and progressive cultural desensitization toward pornography. Motion pictures allowed the creation of explicit adult content, while the sexual revolution of the 1960s and '70s fueled the growth of adult theaters, magazines, and home videos.

The advent of the Internet in the late 20th century revolutionized the industry yet again. With the rise of online platforms, explicit content became far more accessible, affordable, and anonymous. The proliferation of free and paid adult websites, streaming services, and

2 Erotic French postcards from the early 1900s (NSFW) | Dangerous Minds
3 Gillies (2017). Closing the Floodgates: Setting the Record Straight on Gender and Sexuality. Word Alive Press: Manitoba. Closing the Floodgates | Restoring the Mosaic

social media platforms led to an exponential growth in both the production and consumption of pornography.

WHAT'S WRONG WITH PORNOGRAPHY?

Even from a secular standpoint, there has been increasing concern about the impact of pornography, not only on individuals but on society as a whole. The exploitation of performers, the non-consensual distribution of content, the effects of excessive consumption, and the limits of personal freedom have all raised profound ethical and legal questions.

However, the primary concern about pornography is its distortion of perceptions of sexuality. The explicit and often exaggerated portrayal of sexual acts creates unrealistic expectations about sexual experiences, which in turn leads to sexual dissatisfaction,[4] body image issues, and difficulty establishing healthy intimate relationships based on genuine emotional connection.

Researchers have found that the earlier a person starts using porn, the more likely they will turn to bestiality or child porn in the future.[5] Higher exposure to pornography and sexual imagery is also associated with earlier initiation of sexual activity, greater sexual risk-taking behavior, and increased acceptance of sexual promiscuity.[6]

So, what about children? A 2020 report[7] on people, pornography, and age provides some of the most conclusive research concerning children. Some of the findings:

4 The Role of Discrepancies Between Online Pornography Created Ideals and Actual Sexual Relationships in Heterosexual Men's Sexual Satisfaction and Well-Being—Hio Tong Kuan, Charlene Y. Senn, Donna M. Garcia, 2022 (sagepub.com)
5 Seigfried Spellar, C.C. and Rogers, M.K (2013) "Does Deviant Pornography Use Follow a Guttman Like Progression?" Computers in Human Behavior 29, no. 5 (2013): 1997–2003.
6 Wingood,G.M., DeClemente, D.J., Harrington, K., Davies, S., Hook, E.W. & M. Oh, K. (2001) "Exposure to X-Rated Movies and Adolescents' Sexual and Contraceptive-Related Attitudes and Behaviors," Pediatrics 107, no 5 (1116-19).
7 BBFC-Young-people-and-pornography-Final-report-2401.pdf (revealingreality.co.uk)

1. Young people who had seen pornography at an early age, often under the age of 11, reflected that they had been "too young" to understand what was happening.[8]

2. Approximately 63% of children ages 11 to 13 have viewed pornography, often unintentionally.[9]

3. For boys, the use of pornography usually increased as they got older, often between the ages of 14 and 16.

4. The amount of pornography boys watched peaked at three to five times a day, with most boys reporting having watched pornography daily for some period of time in their lives.[10]

5. A full 75% of parents didn't think their child[ren] had accessed porn. Of the parents that thought that, 53% of their children said they had.[11]

ADDICTION, VIOLENCE, AND MENTAL HEALTH

Not only is pornography highly addictive, but research indicates that consumers are more likely to sexually objectify and dehumanize others,[12] more likely to express an intent to rape,[13] less likely to inter-vene during a sexual assault,[14] more likely to victim-blame survivors

---

8 BBFC-Young-people-and-pornography-Final-report-2401.pdf (revealingreality.co.uk) pg 40.
9 Ibid, pg 6.
10 Ibid, pg 20.
11 Ibid, pg 27.
12 Zhou, Y., Liu, T., Yan, Y., & Paul, B. (2021). Pornography use, two forms of dehu-manization, and sexual aggression: Attitudes vs. behaviors. Null, 1-20. https://doi.org/10.1080/0092623X.2021.1923598
13 Foubert, J. D., Brosi, M. W., & Bannon, R. S. (2011). Pornography viewing among fraternity men: Effects on bystander intervention, rape myth acceptance and behavioral intent to commit sexual assault.18(4), 212-231. doi:10.1080/10720162.2011.625552
14 Foubert, J. D., & Bridges, A. J. (2017). What Is the Attraction? Pornography Use Motives in Relation to Bystander Intervention. Journal of Adolescent Research, 32(20), 213–243. https://doi.org/10.1177/0743558414547097

of sexual assault,[15] more likely to support violence against women,[16] more likely to forward sexts (texts with sexual content) without consent,[26] and more likely to commit actual acts of sexual violence.[17]

Brain scans have even shown that viewing pornography stimulates the brain's reward circuitry in the same way as alcohol and addictive drugs by releasing dopamine.

In a 2021 study,[18] between 13.5% and 20% of students reported severe or extremely severe levels of depression, anxiety, and stress, respectively, with compulsive pornography use significantly affecting all three mental health parameters in both sexes.

You may think this is the outside world's problem, but Christians are not off the hook. A 2020 survey by the Barna Group revealed that 68% of Christian men and 50% of pastors view pornography regularly, and that 11- to 17-year-old boys reported being its greatest users.[19]

Even secular research has to admit that something beyond just warnings is needed to help curb the growing destructiveness of pornography. Specifically, faith, morals, and personal motivation were the primary variables reported to help reduce pornography use.[20]

PORNOGRAPHY AND THE BIBLE

Biblically, there is no responsible consumption of pornography.

15 Ibid.

16 Seabrook, R.C., Ward, L.M., & Giaccardi, S. (2019). Less than human? media use, objectification of women, and men's acceptance of sexual aggression. Psychology of Violence, 9(5), 536-545. doi:10.1037/vio0000198

17 Goodson, A., Franklin, C.A., & Bouffard, L.A. (2021). Male peer support and sexual assault: The relation between high-profile, high school sports participation and sexually predatory behaviour. 27(1), 64-80. doi:10.1080/13552600.2020.1733111

18 Compulsive Internet Pornography Use and Mental Health: A Cross-Sectional Study in a Sample of University Students in the United States—PubMed (nih.gov)

19 The Porn Phenomenon—Barna Group

20 Ibid.

From the earliest days, there has been a battle between indulging sexual appetites and exercising modesty toward sexual matters. The different responses of Noah's sons toward his drunken nakedness are a case in point (Genesis 9:20-27). But Scripture is very clear, whether it is our thoughts (Matthew 5:28), or the desires of our flesh (and specifically our eyes) (1 John 2:16), we are not to be captive to sinful passions. Sexual relations are a gift from God reserved for marriage between one man and one woman; it is Satan who wants to pervert what God has intended for our good (natural sexual desires) into something that is destructive and enslaving, as is pornography (1 Corinthians 6:12; 2 Peter 2:18-19).

The insidiousness of porn, like so many sins, is that it is addictive (Romans 6:19) and can lead to more and more sinful behavior. At its core, it is a heart issue that rapidly becomes an obsession as we look at things that we should not. The warnings in Scripture about sin entering our souls through our "eye gate" are very common and show we are to be proactive to not put ourselves in those tempting situations (Job 31:1; Psalm 119:37; Proverbs 6:25-28).

THE PURITY OF MARITAL SEX

In contrast, sexual expression between a husband and wife is a righteous, holy act. The best way to ensure satisfying and fulfilling sexual relations in marriage is to follow God's pattern of celibacy until marriage, regardless of how "Neanderthal" that may sound to you.

Our sexuality is at the core of our being. That is why a molested child has such difficulty overcoming the pain and betrayal. His or her "spiritual self" has been violated. That is why it is so hard for a person to stop homosexual activity. That is why one rarely hears of a pedophile being set free. *There is something about our sexual selves and our spiritual selves that is all wrapped up as one.*

Simply stated, sexual expression between covenant (married) partners is holy. All other sexual deviations—fornication (sex before marriage), cohabitation before marriage, adultery (sex after marriage to someone other than one's spouse), homosexuality, so-called "transgenderism," pedophilia, bestiality, and the list continues—do massive harm to one's chance of ever knowing and experiencing *ultimate* sexual satisfaction.

God is the one who thought of sex. It was His idea. It was one of His best ideas. But sexual expression will eventually bring great pain and a lack of genuine intimacy and warmth when expressed outside that which God designed. When you buy a product, whether a refrigerator or an automobile, you follow the "manual" that was prepared by those who created the item.

That is also true of our bodies. God made us. He has a "manual" for us. *The sooner one uses the "owner's manual," the Bible, on proper sexual expression, the more delight, satisfaction, and even ecstatic joy one will experience in intimacy with one's spouse.* Tragically, due to pornography, millions will never know the fulfillment that could have been theirs. They are empty or will eventually become empty. Searching. And don't even know it.

STRATEGY

So, what are we to do in a pornographically addicted world? First and foremost, Scripture says in order for us to keep our lives pure before the Lord that, we are to immerse ourselves in His Word (Psalm 119:9), and recognize the destructiveness of pursuing and exposing ourselves to impure things. Ask God to fill our minds with thoughts that are honorable, pure, and lovely (Philippians 4:8) as we strive to walk in the Spirit (Galatians 5:16,19).

On the practical level, install filters that block pornography on your computer and cell phone, limit carefully what you watch on TV, and if necessary, install accountability software on your devices that will keep you accountable to someone else.

One final piece of advice: be careful about handing your child a cell phone. Contrary to popular opinion, your child will survive without one. Or if you must get them one (for logistical reasons for pick up after school, emergencies, etc.), look into what is called a "dumb phone"—they will be able to make calls and text, but not access the Internet.

CHAPTER 31

ABORTION

Seven years ago, I wrote *Well Versed: Biblical Answers to Today's Tough Issues*. Although this book covers many more topics, there are two times that I am choosing to repeat sections from that 2016 book. One is the chapter on marriage. The other is this chapter on abortion.[1]

I go on Facebook from time to time. I posted a story once that produced over 18,000 "shares" and more than 71,000 "likes." Why? The story touched a nerve. Allow me to explain.

RAPED AT 14 YEARS OLD

Angela (not her real name) grew up in the Midwest. After turning fourteen, she was flattered that two high school seniors wanted to take her to a movie. However, instead of going to a movie, they drove the

---

1 Much of this chapter comes from James L. Garlow, *Well Versed: Biblical Answers to Today's Tough Issues*, Salem Books, an imprint of Regnery Publishing, 2016, pp. 79-88.

truck into a field in the darkness of night, and there they raped her. Several months later, a doctor confirmed her pregnancy, and the decision was made to place the baby for adoption.

Angela's pregnancy was difficult due to health factors and the closest hospital that could assist such a complicated pregnancy was sixty miles away. Her alcoholic father and mother were raising four other children, including two toddlers, and could not come to see her. For several months, the fourteen-year-old lay flat on her back, by herself, in a large city a long way from her small town. Finally, the baby was born—a girl. My late wife and I adopted her. We named that baby girl Janie.

Thirty-six years later, my wife Carol died of cancer. We buried her in California in a cemetery near our home, but we also had a memorial service for her in Kansas, in the cemetery on the beautiful hill overlooking the farm on which I had grown up. As the service ended for my wife, we attended a reception for family and friends hosted by my cousin at his farmhouse. It was there that our daughter Janie was able to talk with the doctor who had, thirty-six years earlier, cared for Janie's birth mother. As a result of that conversation, Janie began a process that resulted in her talking with her birth mother by phone and eventually meeting her face-to-face.

It was as they talked that Janie learned her birth mother had been raped. In the thirty-six years of Janie's life, we had always felt such gratitude toward this woman whom we'd never met but who had made such a great sacrifice. Becoming aware of the component of rape and her young age caused our already immense gratitude toward her to skyrocket.

My Facebook post—shared with the permission of Janie—contained only portions of the information I just shared with you. But it resonated with tens of thousands of people.

Why? The pathos of the story. A baby was saved. A scared fourteen-year-old was remarkably brave and sacrificial. A baby grew up to become a truly amazing woman of God. What the enemy meant for evil, God has turned for good (Genesis 50:20). And birth mother

Angela is our hero. We honor her. We praise God for her. And just for the record, the horrors of rape, a most vile act, do not merit the taking of an innocent life. Had Angela made that decision, I would have been robbed of the joy of my adopted daughter.

GOD'S VIEW

What does God say about when life begins? This is one of those political or social issues about which the Bible is crystal clear. God's Word clearly reveals how He values pre-born life:

> For you created my inmost being; you knit me together in my mother's womb. I praise you because I am fearfully and wonderfully made; your works are wonderful; I know that full well. My frame was not hidden from you when I was made in the secret place. When I was woven together in the depths of the earth, your eyes saw my unformed body. All the days ordained for me were written in your book before one of them came to be.
> —*Psalms 139:13–16*

> The word of the Lord came to me, saying, "Before I formed you in the womb I knew you, before you were born I set you apart; I appointed you as a prophet to the nations."
> —*Jeremiah 1:4–5*

> The children struggled together within her, and she said, "If it is thus, why is this happening to me?' So she went to inquire of the Lord. And the Lord said to her, 'Two nations are in your womb, and two peoples from within you shall be divided; the one shall be stronger than the other, the older shall serve the younger."
> —*Genesis 25:22–23, ESV*

From birth I was cast on you; from my mother's womb you
have been my God.

—*Psalms 22:10*

As soon as the sound of your greeting reached my ears, the
baby in my womb leaped for joy.

—*Luke 1:44*

There is no Bible verse saying an embryo only becomes a living
soul in the second or third trimester.

Old Testament Scripture actually places a greater emphasis on the
protection of life for a pregnant woman than for others in society.
Exodus 21:22–23 states, "If people are fighting and hit a pregnant
woman and she gives birth prematurely, but there is no serious injury,
the offender must be fined whatever the woman's husband demands
and the court allows. But if there is serious injury, you are to take life
for life." This was the law God established through Moses. Why was
it so serious to place a pregnant woman in harm? Because it was not
just one life but two at risk.

The same people who say *it is merely a blob of tissue* are quick to
condemn and sue a car company for killing a *baby* when a woman
and her pre-born child are killed in a car crash. If a man shoots and
kills a pregnant woman, he can be charged with killing the mother
and the baby. When a doctor diagnoses a woman as pregnant, he
doesn't say, "You're going to have a fetus." He says, "You're going to
have a baby."

In all these scenarios, the truth remains constant: from the moment
of conception, life exists.

Abortion kills a human being. Watching the daily news and the
brutal executions that were carried out by Hamas in 2023 on innocent
Israeli citizens, even burning babies in ovens, we are reminded of the
capabilities of humans to so harm each other. Equally horrific are the
murderous actions happening to the unborn in our communities. Every

single day in America, innocent blood runs under the streets of our cities. And what does God say about this?

> Rescue those being led away to death; hold back those staggering toward slaughter. If you say, 'But we knew nothing about this,' does not he who weighs the heart perceive it? Does not he who guards your life know it? Will he not repay each person according to what he has done?
> —*Proverbs 24:11–12*

THE GLOBAL GENOCIDE

The World Health Organization states that there are 73,000,000 abortions globally per year. This means a stunning 200,000 are killed daily.[2] That is more than 8,300 an hour, or 138 a minute, more than two babies every second. In the length of time it has taken you to read this sentence, 10 babies have been dismembered, torn apart, with no anesthesia.

Approximately 1.5 million abortions occur annually in the US, one of the highest rates of any developed country. That means that 4,100 babies are murdered daily in the US, 171 every hour, and nearly three every minute.

We have to wonder—with each life given a purpose from God—what might they have accomplished that could have made this world a better place?

UNWANTED PREGNANCY?

Here's the bottom line: There may be unwanted pregnancies, but there are no unwanted babies. Even in those rare cases when the birth

---

2 https://www.worldometers.info/abortions/

mother and father do not want babies, there are many couples willing to adopt the baby.

IS A FETUS REALLY A HUMAN BEING?

To answer that question, consider these realities:

Eighteen days after conception, a baby's heart begins to beat with its own blood.

Twenty-eight days from conception a baby has eyes and ears.

At forty-two days, the baby has brain waves.

At ten weeks, babies can feel pain and even have developed tiny fingernails.

Babies have been born and have survived at only twelve weeks.[3]

INVITING GOD'S JUDGMENT

Despite incredible scientific advancement in monitoring the growth of a baby in the womb, the killing of unborn babies continues as our culture becomes more and more hardened to the reality of the life inside its mother. Look at America's calloused condition:

When we discovered the so-called fetus had a heartbeat—we did not stop killing.

When sonograms were developed, allowing us to physically see the form of a baby—we did not stop killing.

When Jane Roe from the Supreme Court case *Roe v. Wade*, which legalized abortion through the third trimester, came out explaining she never actually had an abortion and admitted the case was the "biggest mistake of her life"—we still did not stop killing. Roe said in a television ad, "You read about me in history books, but now I am

---

3 "Baby Developmental Facts," ProLife Across America, no date, https://prolifeacrossamerica.org/bhttps://prolifeacrossamerica.org/learn/?gad_source=1&gclid=Cj0KCQiAy9m-sBhD0ARIsANbk0A8w5dmjfadhQoMdJqtonemjOEtjal36FqphF4hIn8sDs1d33JHXl4YaApzhEALw_wcB

dedicated to spreading the truth about preserving the dignity of all human life from natural conception to natural death."[4] When she came out against abortion—we did not stop killing.

When abortion was exposed through the "Silent Scream" documentary in 1984—we did not stop killing.

When Planned Parenthood began dismembering post-aborted babies' body parts and selling them for profit—we did not stop killing.

Pro-life advocates rejoiced when the Supreme Court overturned Roe v. Wade in June 2022, but abortions continue in the majority of states.

EVER WATCH AN ABORTION?

What will it take to completely end the killing? Are we as numb as Nazi Germany when six million—some say eight million—Jews of every age were marched off to gas chambers? As a nation, we have ignored every ounce of science and turned our backs on millions of dying people.

Hitler killed six million Jews (or more) in the death camps of Europe in the 1940s. The abortuaries of America have killed more than 60 million in the last half of the 20th century and first part of the 21st century. According to a British documentary by Tracy Borman titled "Private Lives," Season 3, Episode 4, Hitler wanted no contact with the process. "While atrocities were being carried out in his name, he never visited an extermination camp," Borman said in the program. "When a train carrying Jews to the camps stopped on an adjacent platform to his Fuhrer train, he pulled down the blinds. ... Hitler never wanted to be confronted with the brutal reality of what was going on. He just wanted to know that it was being done."[5] Since Hitler

---

4 Steven Ertelt, "Woman Behind Roe v. Wade: 'I'm Dedicating My Life to Overturning It,'" LifeNews.com, January 22, 2013, http://www.lifenews.com/2013/01/22/woman-behind-roe-v-wade-im-dedicating-my-life-to-overturning-it/

5 https://www.timesofisrael.com/uk-documentary-claims-hitler-was-very-hands-off-in-

supported the starvation, gassing and killing of the Jews, he should have gone and seen what he supported. He should have been made to face the horrors he created. Ordinarily, top-level US governmental leaders have tried to distance themselves from actually going to a place where babies are intentionally killed. That is, until March 14, 2024. As Kamala Harris became the first vice president to visit an abortion facility, the vice president denounced pro-life laws as "plain old immoral," said she wanted to "uplift" abortion, and praised an abortionist as an "extraordinary health care provider."[6]

Imagine this: A sitting US vice president praised the killing of innocent babies, and called the saving of life "immoral." Can God's judgement be far behind? Kamala Harris—and all elected officials who support abortion—should have to watch a sonogram of a developing baby, and then watch the barbaric dismemberment of that child, with no anesthesia. Better yet, they should watch a partial birth abortion—watching the murderer cut the spinal cord and suck out the brains of a baby who is about to be born.

I have often asked those who are running for office who are in support of abortion if they have ever witnessed an abortion. Most have not. I have actually invited candidates to my office, with my computer open, and said, "Since you support abortion, and have not ever seen one, let's have you watch one now."

IS ABORTION OKAY IN THE CASES OF RAPE AND INCEST?

Killing a child because of the circumstances of its conception is not biblical.

Deuteronomy 24:16 states, "Fathers are not to be put to death for their children, nor children put to death for their fathers; each will die for their own sin." Killing the child because of someone else's crime is

implementing-final-solution/
6 https://washingtonstand.com/news/kamala-harris-calls-prolife-laws-immoral-on-1st-vp-visit-to-abortion-facility

wrong and can never be justified. What is the crime that the child has committed that deserves death? Taking the innocent life of a child because of the sin of a parent is committing an even worse sin, one that can never be rectified. We also need to realize that abortions due to rape and incest make up only about 1 percent of all abortions.[7] Ninety-nine percent of abortions have nothing to do with these extreme or severe situations.[8]

MORAL STANDARDS VIOLATED

Two key moral standards must be recognized in order to protect human life. We are all familiar with the first—the Sixth Commandment in Exodus 20:13, "You shall not murder." The second moral standard is found in Psalms 139:13: "You knit me together in my mother's womb." Human life begins at conception and, therefore, has all rights to life. Simply stated, human rights begin at conception.

At Mount Sinai Hospital in New York, a nurse was forced to aid in a non-emergency abortion procedure even though the hospital knew it violated her religious beliefs.[9] The irony: the hospital that forced the nurse to perform the abortion is called Mount Sinai, which is the location where the Lord God commanded, "Thou shalt not murder!"

America, stop the murder.

7 A. Torres and J. Forest, "Why Do Women Have Abortions?" Family Planning Perspectives 20, no.4 (July-August, 1988): 169-76.
8 A. Bankole et al., "Reasons Why Women Have Induced Abortions: Evidence from 27 Countries," Family Planning Perspectives 24, no. 3 (August 1998): 117-25, 152.
9 "Faith and Justice Details Fault Lines," Faith and Justice 3 no. 2, http://www.adflegal.org/detailspages/faith-and-justice-details/fault-lines

CHAPTER 32

ANTISEMITISM, ANTI-ZIONISM, THE JEWISH PEOPLE, AND ISRAEL

W hy are the Jewish people the most consistently persecuted people group in all of human history? Why? Why is that?

The answer is simple: they remind people of God. And if there is a God, we are not God, but He is. And if there is a God, there is a moral law of right vs. wrong. And if there is a moral law of right vs. wrong, people should obey what is right. But people don't want to obey it, so they take it out on the Jews. Ludicrous? No. That is reality.

How do the Jews remind us of God? They gave us the Law. They gave us the Torah (teaching). They gave us the prophets. They gave us Jerusalem. They gave us the prophecies on the Messiah. And they gave us the Messiah, Jesus.

ANTISEMITISM AND ANTI-ZIONISM

Antisemitism has been debated, with definitions changing from time to time,[1] so let me cut to the chase and say that antisemitism is Jew-hatred. There is no way to sugarcoat this.

Some say, "Well, I am not an antisemite (hating the Jews), but I am an anti-Zionist." What is "anti-Zionism?" First, let's examine, what is "Zionism." Let's go for the simplest definition. Zionism is the belief that: 1) the Jews have a right to exist; 2) have a right to have a homeland; (3) have a right to gather there; 4) and have a right to defend themselves.

Don't let anyone fool you. Anyone who is an anti-Zionist is an antisemite. What good is it to affirm a certain people group (the Jews) but not believe they have a right to exist somewhere on the planet in their own land?

THE LAND

Jews are "married" to the land.[2] When pop star Pat Boone—who has recorded 2,600 songs, more than any other singer—wrote down the words to "Exodus" on the back of a Christmas card on Christmas Eve, December 1959, he might not have fully understood in that inspired moment exactly how true the words are for the Jewish people: "This land is mine, God gave this land to me.... If I must fight, I'll fight to make this land our own, Until I die this land is mine."

Simply stated: *The Jews don't "occupy" the land. They own it.*

In the present culture, we are dealing with more than antisemitism or anti-Zionism. There is such a thing as being anti-Torah as well. The Torah, which means "teaching," comprises the first five books of the

---

1 https://en.wikipedia.org/wiki/Antisemitism
2 This actually happened when the Children of Israel entered the promise land at Mount Gerizim and Mt. Ebal, foretold by Moses in Deuteronomy 11:26, 29; 27: 9-26, and experienced under the leadership of Joshua, in Joshua 8:30-35; Also consider https://www.jta.org/2019/05/21/ny/married-to-the-land

Bible. It is quite shocking that Christians sometimes ignorantly treat the Old Testament as if it is something "old." What do you do with old things? You throw them away. Some Christians seem to think the "real" Bible begins with Matthew.

How wrong that is.

For millennia, much of the church has fallen into the sin of Replacement Theology, the misguided and arrogant notion that we Christians have somehow replaced the State of Israel or the Jewish people. Where there is the heresy of Replacement Theology, it is followed by another subtle "anti," which is a strain of anti-Hebraic Scripture. Time does not permit us here to unpack the truth of this next statement, but it still needs to be made: *To the extent that we follow the Greek and Roman thinking, we are that much off course from biblical truth. In contrast, to the extent that we embrace the Hebraistic way of thinking, we are touching the heart of God.*

BUT IT'S NOT THE LAND

Since the Muslim Arabs have demanded that Israel surrender its land, some have mistakenly believed the issue is about the land. It is not. The Jews possess only approximately 1/6th of 1% of all the land in the Middle East.[3] The issue is not about the land. The Muslims surround the Jewish people so much more than the land. Many Muslims want to drive them "from the (Jordan) river to the sea," as the current anti-Jewish saying goes.[4] The charter of the Palestinian Liberation Organization openly states that the establishment of Israel is "illegal."[5]

3 https://carleton.ca/studyisrael/israel-fun-facts/
4 https://www.algemeiner.com/2014/02/20/did-arab-states-really-promise-to-push-jews-into-the-sea-yes/
5 https://www.algemeiner.com/2013/08/21/the-plo-charter-still-calls-for-israels-destruc-tion/

WHIRLWIND HISTORICAL TOUR

In Genesis, God called a man named Abraham (approximately 1800 BC).[6] He responded affirmatively. He was married to Sarah. The Jews are the physical descendants of Abraham and Sarah through Isaac. The Muslims are the physical descendants of Abraham and Sarah's servant girl, Hagar, through Ishmael. Little did Abraham know what his cohabitation with Hagar would cost.

Abraham became:

a family,

then a tribe,

then a confederation of tribes (1200 BC),

then a kingdom, Israel (1020 BC), which split north and south and had 39 kings and one queen. It is at this point that Israel's painful story of oppression begins.

The story I am about to tell you may be one you know, but it is worth hearing again. If you are one who does not know the story, you need to hear it and see that the word antisemitism is very real.

ASSYRIA, BABYLON, PERSIA, GREECE, AND ROME

In case you like things summarized and would like to skip the next few paragraphs (which I hope you won't) covering 2,700 years, here is what happened: Israel was controlled and/or pummeled by the ...

- Assyrians
- Babylonians
- Greeks
- Romans
- Umayyads (Muslim)
- Abbasids (Muslim)
- Seljuk Turks (Muslim)

---

6 I use "BC," "before Christ," as there is no such thing as a "common era."

- Fatimids (Muslim)
- Seljuks (Muslim) a second time
- "Christian" Crusaders
- Mamluks (Muslim)
- Ottoman Turks
- British (during Germany's slaughter of 6,000,000 Jews by Hitler)

All this before the Jews finally declared their independence on May 14, 1948 as the State of Israel. *No people group has ever continuously suffered more than the Jewish people.* I recognize that you will never be able to remember this long list of nations that have controlled and savaged Israel and the Jewish people who were there. But I wanted to provide the long list of what Israel has had to withstand. There is a name for it. It is called Jew-hatred. To see more detail on the travesties surrounding the list above, read on.

ASSYRIA, BABYLON

The Northern Kingdom was overrun by the Assyrians (what is today northern Iraq and southeastern Turkey) in 722 BC, more than 2,700 years ago. The Southern Kingdom was overrun by Babylon (modern-day Iraq) in 586 BC, almost 2,600 years ago. That would be the last time that Israel would be free from oppression. Israel would be oppressed from 586 BC until 1948 AD, a period of more than 2,500 years!

PERSIA, GREECE, THEN THE MACCABEES

When the Babylonian Empire ended (539 BC), the Persians (modern-day Iran) controlled Israel and the Jews from 538 BC to 332 BC when they were defeated by the Greeks. The defeat of Persia did not mean that Israel was free, but rather that they simply had another oppressor, the Greeks. A powerful revolt (166 BC-160 BC) led by Judah Maccabees and his four brothers provided Israel with a partial (Judea) and short-lived season free from oppression. The descendants of the remarkable Maccabees family established the Hasmonean Kingdom, which lasted only 66 years, from 129 BC to 63 BC. The books of 1st and 2nd Maccabees, though not included in Protestant Bibles, cover the great revolt and show us how to walk in God's truth under hostile oppression—highly relevant for Christians today.

The Jews' semi-independence was short-lived when, in 63 BC, the Romans conquered Israel and ruled in one form or another until roughly 614 AD, when the Muslim Sassanids defeated the last remnants of the Eastern Roman Empire.[7] Roman control was particularly onerous to the Jews. They chafed under it, rebelling in 66 AD over the next couple of years. The Romans crushed the nation, slaughtering so many that the Sea of Galilee turned red from the blood of the Jewish men, women, and children.[8] Even those who fled up the steep hillsides to caves were not spared. Roman soldiers found them and slaughtered them all.

THE TWO TEMPLES

The First Temple, the most sacred site of Jewish worship, was built in 960 BC and destroyed in 586 BC. The Second Temple was built by Zerubbabel in 515 BC. The Second Temple was originally built quite small by Zerubbabel in 515 BC (Ezra 5-6), and was later dismantled and rebuilt much larger by Herod in 20 BC. To add insult to injury, the Romans destroyed Jerusalem and the Second Temple in 70 AD, like the Babylonians had done centuries earlier.

In 73 AD, a small group of Jews at Masada unsuccessfully made a "last stand" against the massive Roman armies. By 130 AD, the

---

7 https://embassies.gov.il/UnGeneva/AboutIsrael/history/Pages/History-Israel-Timeline.aspx
8 https://touringisrael.com/the-story-of-magdala-in-the-galilee/

Romans further insulted the Jews by naming Jerusalem "Aelia Capi-tolina." In the revolt (132 AD-135 AD) that followed, 580,000 Jews were slaughtered.[9] Although the name "Palestine" likely already existed, some suggest the renaming of Israel by the Romans, calling it Palestine, was most likely a derivation of the word Philistines, the archenemy of Israel, and was done to further humiliate the Jews.[10]

As noted above, when Rome fell, Israel was controlled by more enemies of the Jewish people,[11] one after another (we will add the years to the list that present above):

- Umayyads (Muslim)—beginning 636 AD
- Abbasids (Muslim)—beginning approximately 750 AD
- Seljuk Turks (Muslim) –beginning approximately 935 AD
- Fatimids (Muslim)—beginning in the 970s AD
- Seljuks—again—1071-1098 AD
- "Christian" Crusaders—approximately 1100 to around 1250 or 1300 AD
- Mamluks (Muslim)—approximately 1291 to 1916
- Ottoman Turks—1517 to 1917, 400 years
- British—1917 to 1948

The British season of control was punctuated by Muslim Arab uprisings in which Jews were killed in mass.[12] The Brits were initially very supportive of the Jews having a homeland. However, when oil was discovered on Arab lands, the British violated their commitment to a Jewish homeland so they could curry the favor of the Arab

---

9 https://en.wikipedia.org/wiki/Historical_Jewish_population_comparisons
10 Scholars are not united on this issue.
11 https://www.britannica.com/place/Palestine/World-War-I-and-after
12 James L. Garlow and David Barton, This Precarious Moment, Salem Books, an imprint of Regnery Publishing, 2018, pp. 106-112.

Muslims.[13] In addition, more than 75% of what had been promised to the Jews was carved off, and Jordan was created.

A CONCENTRATION CAMP FOR JEWS—IN THEIR HOMELAND

As if the above was not wounding enough to the Jews, Britain built a concentration camp to house Jewish people *in* Israel (called Palestine at the time). Those who survived Hitler's death camps and were able to get back to their Promised Land, despite British gunboats attacking their old ships, could be incarcerated.[14] We are not speaking about the 44,000 killing centers run by Hitler[15] across Europe. The camp in Atlit, in present-day Israel, was operational from 1946—that is, *after* World War II—and continued to be used to confine Jews until Israel became an independent nation in 1948.

Imagine if you were a 25-year-old Jewish man in Germany who had somehow miraculously survived one of the concentration camps, and you made it onto an overcrowded, antiquated boat back to Israel, surviving the assault of a British gunboat trying to drive you back out to sea. And then when you finally make it to the land promised to your forefathers, the British put you in a concentration camp—on that very land. When has a people group ever been subjected to so much abuse?

MUSLIM CLAIM

There are approximately 50 Muslim-majority countries in the world. Muslims have plenty of places to go. But many of them want that one tiny land mass called "Israel." They say it is their land. But consider the facts. Islam came:

---

13 Ibid, p. 111.
14 https://en.wikipedia.org/wiki/Atlit_detainee_camp
15 https://encyclopedia.ushmm.org/content/en/article/nazi-camps

- 2,600 years after Abraham, the Father of the Jewish people
- 2,000 years after Joshua, who led the Israelites into the land now called Israel
- 1,600 years after David, the one who established Jerusalem as his capital
- 600 years after Jesus, the epicenter of the Christian faith
- The Temple Mount is where the First Temple was built in 960 BC, and it wasn't until 687 AD—more than 1600 years later—that Islam's Al Aqsa Mosque was built. If you visit the Temple Mount today, you can walk to the far southeastern corner and peer down the outer wall several hundred feet into the Kidron Valley. Some say this is where Satan took Jesus to tempt Him in Matthew 4:5 (i.e., "the highest point of the temple"). The Dome of the Rock, located near Al Aqsa Mosque, was built by the Muslims over the revered spot where it is said that Abraham laid Isaac on the altar before the Lord—an event that took place some 2,600 years before the Muslim mosque and dome were erected.

This most holy Jewish place on Mount Moriah (the present-day Temple Mount) is the site of epochal events in the biblical and cultural history of Judaism, and stretches back two millennia before the prophet Muhammed walked the earth.

And yet, Muslims *claim the land is theirs*. It is not.

BALFOUR, SAN REMO, LEAGUE OF NATIONS, UNITED NATIONS

In the late 1800s, the British, Germans, and French suddenly became very interested in what was then called Palestine. The latter half of the 1800s marked the beginning of Zionism, the belief that the

Jews could actually have their own land once again. Theodor Herzl became the epicenter of the movement.

British support for Israel was marked by the 1917 Balfour Declaration. Several nations signed the San Remo Agreement in 1920, assuring the Jews of their own country. The League of Nations—a precursor to the United Nations—agreed that the Jews must have a home. And the United Nations, formed to keep another world war and a holocaust from ever happening again, voted on November 29, 1947 to reestablish the modern State of Israel. The final vote was 33 yes, 13 no, with 10 abstentions and 1 absent.

This was the moment for which the Jews had waited for over two and a half millennia.[16]

MAY 14, 1948, MIDNIGHT—THE MOMENT

On midnight of May 14, 1948, David Ben Gurion declared the independence and sovereignty of Israel. Israel did not know what other nations might do to them. Eleven minutes later, at 6:11 PM Eastern Time in America, US President Harry Truman, against the advice of all his advisors, announced the US support for the new State of Israel. That "sealed the deal." The next day, Egypt, Jordan, Iraq, Syria, and other nations attacked Israel. Supernaturally, the one-day-old nation stood.

In 1967, Israel would again be at war with nations that surrounded her: Syria from the northeast, Egypt from the south, and Jordan on the east. Supernaturally she stood again and won in only six days.

In fact, between 1947 and now, there have been approximately 14 seasons of attacks on Israel. Still, she stands.

And she is still surrounded by what has been called a "ring of fire:" Hamas to the southwest with rockets (although Israel has been forced to rout out Hamas), Hezbollah to the north with its estimated 150,000

---

16 It was actually far more complicated than this. Please see: James L. Garlow and David Barton, This Precarious Moment, Salem Books, an imprint of Regnery Publishing, 2018, pp. 105-118.

to 200,000 missiles, Syria to the northeast, Iraq to the east, and the big one, Iran further east.

Do Israel's enemies want land? Israel offered "land for peace" in 1937, 1947, 1967, 2000, and 2008. All the offers were declined. They don't want land. They want the Jews dead. They want them eliminated from the Jordan River to the Mediterranean Sea. Perhaps the same gods (read: demonic beings) of Egypt—Isis and Osiris, among others—that preoccupied Hitler's mind and bent the Nazis toward the Jews' destruction, are the same forces that want to bring death upon modern-day Israel.

Israel only possesses about 23% of the land promised by the various agreements in the early 1900s. What does God say about this? God promised that Israel would have the land from the Euphrates to the Nile (Genesis 15:18). That amounts to approximately 300,000 square miles. During the time of King David, Israel, at its zenith, owned 200,000 square miles.

How much land does Israel have now? 8,100 square miles. That's just 2% of what God promised them. Put in context, Texas is approximately 268,000 square miles, or just a bit smaller than the amount of land the Lord promised the Israelites. Comparatively, one single county in my state of California—Riverside County at 7,300 square miles—is nearly the size of current-day Israel.

MOVING THE EMBASSY—MAY 14, 2018

When President Donald Trump considered moving the US Embassy from Tel Aviv (which is not Israel's capital) to the city the Israelis know is their capital, Jerusalem, every one of his advisors in the room said, "Don't do it, you will start World War III." That is, except for three advisors: Vice President Mike Pence, US Secretary of State Mike Pompeo, and US Ambassador to Israel David Friedman. Trump moved the embassy, affirming Israel. There was no World War III. My wife and I were present for this glorious event. It was amazing.

Jerusalem is called an international city as a way to say "the Jews can't call it their capital." No, it is not an international city. It is a Jewish city. It belongs to Israel, to the Jews, and not the world. It is their capital.

OCTOBER 7, 2023

Certain days forever remain days of infamy, such as December 7, 1941 (attack on Pearl Harbor), November 22, 1963 (assassination of President Kennedy), and September 11, 2001. Everyone who was a child or older remembers where they were and what they were doing when they heard the word on those days.

Add to those historic days of infamy October 7, 2023.

In what has been characterized as the most vile and violent attack ever launched against civilians, Hamas committed atrocities that shocked and stunned the world. But apparently not all the world. Much of the Muslim world celebrated the atrocities. Most shocking were the rallies in most of the Western World, rallying in favor of the demonically filled Jihadists. Even more horrific were American university students demanding support for Hamas. But most jolting were the three presidents of prestigious universities—Harvard, MIT, and the University of Pennsylvania—testifying before Congress, saying that they were unable to affirm that "calling for genocide against the Jews" was unacceptable on their campuses.[17] (Fortunately, Harvard's president later resigned, when charges of plagiarism erupted. She should have been forced out for anti-semitism.) How is it possible that the world, but more specifically, America, could have fallen to such moral depravity? Is there no end to the suffering of the Jews?

---

17 https://www.insidehighered.com/news/quick-takes/2023/12/08/house-members-call-harvard-mit-and-penn-fire-presidents

SUFFERING

The purpose of this chapter was for us to review the horrific journey of pain that has been inflicted on the Jewish people. Biblically grounded people stand with Israel and stand in solidarity with the Jewish people. To be pro-Israel is not to say the nation, its leaders or its people are perfect. They are not. Nor is any nation.

To stand with the Jewish people is not to be anti-Palestinian. To presume so is a binary fallacy. The Palestinian people have suffered. A lot. No sane person celebrates or condones the deaths of civilians in war zones—whether it's Gaza, Syria, or Ukraine. As I write, the Israel-Hamas War rages on. Innocents are dying—some because they are being used as human shields by Hamas.[18]

As people of faith, we pray for an end to the conflict. Unlike the Hamas Jihadists on October 7, however, the IDF is not purposefully killing civilians. Nor are they hunting down women, children, and babies to torture and slaughter in unimaginably evil ways, only to then celebrate such ghoulish acts.

Yes, the Palestinians are suffering. However, the root of the problem does not lie at the feet of the Jews. Rather, those in Gaza and elsewhere suffer because of their own leaders in Hamas, the Palestine Liberation Organization, and the Palestinian Authority. Who is in charge in the West Bank and Gaza? That is a complex question that would take an entire book to tackle. Hamas, a militant group born out of the Intifada Uprising in the 90s—which the EU, the US, and many other Western nations see as a terrorist organization—has run Gaza since 2006. Hamas does not want co-existence with Israel—they want its eradication. That is why they slaughtered more than 1,400 innocent Israelis on October 7, 2023.

I want to quickly add, however, that it would be both inaccurate and inappropriate to lump all Palestinian Arabs into the Hamas camp. There are many Palestinian Arabs who want peace with their Jewish

---

18 https://www.washingtonpost.com/opinions/2023/11/14/hamas-human-shields-tactic/

WELL VERSED

neighbors. There are many wonderful Christian Palestinians as well. As people of faith, we pray for an end to the violence and a meaningful, long-lasting resolution.

However, when it comes to the land, the Jews don't "occupy" the land. There are no "occupied territories." They own the land. Join together to stand against the antisemitism and anti-Zionism that circles the globe.

PART III

A BIBLICAL RESPONSE TO CONSTITUTIONAL ISSUES AND THE LOSS OF FREEDOMS

How biblically aligned citizens can prepare for and respond to the negative cultural and societal effects of leftist and progressive ideologies in the public square.

The Israelites groaned in their slavery and cried out, and their cry for help because of their slavery went up to God.

—EXODUS 2:23

CHAPTER 33

THE EFFORT TO MAKE CHRISTIANITY ILLEGAL

W e are a religious people whose institutions presuppose a Supreme
Being. We guarantee the freedom to worship as one chooses. ...
When the state encourages religious instruction or cooperates
with religious authorities ... it follows the best of our traditions.[1]

The above words come from a United States Supreme Court decision. Who wrote them? A recent appointment by a Republican president pushing religious rights? Hardly. The author was liberal icon
Justice William O. Douglas, appointed to the Supreme Court by President Franklin D. Roosevelt. When those words appeared in the 1952
decision of *Zorach v. Clauson,* Douglas accurately stated what everyone knew then: Americans are a religious people, and the values of the
Christian faith are baked into our governing institutions. Douglas even
warned about the dangers of "preferring those who believe in no religion over those who do believe."

---

1 https://supreme.justia.com/cases/federal/us/343/306/

Douglas was a liberal judge appointed by a Democratic president—advocating for religious vigor at every level of American society. How radically things have changed in just 70 years.

AMERICA'S CHRISTIAN FOUNDATION

The influence of Christianity in our nation's founding cannot be doubted by any fair-minded reader of history. Supreme Court Justice Joseph Story noted the following:

> Probably at the time of the adoption of the Constitution, and of the (First Amendment), the general, if not the universal, sentiment in America was that Christianity ought to receive encouragement from the state, so far as it is not incompatible with the private rights of conscience, and the freedom of religious worship.
>
> Indeed, in a republic, there would seem to be a peculiar propriety in viewing the Christian religion as the great basis on which it must rest for its support and permanence, if it is, what it has ever been deemed by its truest friends to be, the religion of liberty.[2]

Our nation was not created as a theocracy. All faiths, including atheism, were protected against government compulsion. But as the quotes above show, the *accommodation* of religion—especially Christianity—was considered essential to our freedoms.

WHY RELIGIOUS FREEDOM IS ESSENTIAL

Totalitarian regimes hate religious freedom for a simple reason: religion introduces a higher authority than the state in the form of

---

2 Joseph Story, Commentary on the Constitution (1833).

conscience before God. The notorious despots of the 20th Century created atheistic regimes, like Stalinist Russia and Maoist China. Dictators who were not officially atheistic allowed only token churches that never contradicted the state's dictates –like Hitler's Germany and Mussolini's Italy. Totalitarianism and the freedom of religious conscience cannot co-exist. Allow me to summarize this reality: *To believe in the lordship of Christ automatically implies a limited earthly government.*

That is why some people would like to make the Christian faith (and others) illegal. Admittedly, this sounds like an audacious claim, so I will try to make the case for you.

We have all heard the expression "the separation of church and state." As noted in a previous chapter, Thomas Jefferson used it in a letter to one Danbury Baptist Church. The church wrote to Jefferson, expressing fear that it would be persecuted by a hostile government. He responded this way:

> Believing with you that religion is a matter which lies solely between Man & his God, that he owes account to none other for his faith or his worship, that the legitimate powers of government reach actions only, & not opinions, I contemplate with sovereign reverence that act of the whole American people which declared that their legislature should 'make no law respecting an establishment of religion, or prohibiting the free exercise thereof,' *thus building a wall of separation between Church & State"*[3] (emphasis mine).

Jefferson saw the "wall" as a *defense* for churches against government intrusion into matters of faith—not a defense of secular society from churches. But the wall of separation is no longer seen primarily as a shield protecting churches from government coercion. Rather, it

---

3 Jefferson's Letter to the Danbury Baptists (June 1998)—Library of Congress Information Bulletin. https://loc.gov/loc/lcib/9806/danpre.html

is viewed as a sword for excluding religion from public discourse. That transformation was not accidental and came from a good deal of judicial sleight of hand.

THE DECAY TAKES ROOT

Historically, religious neutrality concerns focused on the danger of sectarian preference (hence the term "non-sectarian"). The Congregationalists were strong in New England, while Baptists migrated to Rhode Island and Quakers to Pennsylvania (which was open to all faiths). Catholics found a home in Maryland, and on it went. And these sects often did not play well together.

Building on sectarian concerns, proponents of "separation of church and state" began lumping Christians together in one monolithic block. In doing so, the lawsuits subtly shifted to ask whether Christianity (of any variety) was being preferred over a non-Christian faith or even *non-religion*.

Framing the argument at this level was a set-up because there were (and still are) more Christians than any other faith in the United States. According to a Pew Research study, religions in the US in order of size are: 70.6% Christian faiths; 5.9% non-Christian (including 1.9% Jewish, 0.9% Muslim, 0.7% Buddhist, 0.7% Hindu); 22.8% unaffiliated (including 3.1% atheist, 4% agnostic); the rest "don't know."[4]

Over a seven-decade period, school prayer was found to violate the Constitution—by 1962 it was banned in public schools; then in 1992 high school graduation prayers were banned; religious symbols were banned on public property; religious perspectives on the Genesis account of Creation could not be considered next to secular alternatives; public funds were restricted for religious education, and more.

In the last twenty years, however, that trend has slowed, with some significant religious freedom wins at the Supreme Court. But those

---

4 https://www.pewresearch.org/religion/religious-landscape-study/

trying to eradicate religious influence (especially Christianity) have not let up. The accommodation of religion envisioned by the founders has been rejected by many who view religion somewhere between misguided and evil. Some of these individuals would even make religious expression and conscience illegal if they could. The totalitarian worldview of Stalin or Mao is present, but (happily) not the mechanism to enforce it. Yet.

THE VERY SLIPPERY SLOPE

Given the Judeo-Christian foundations of America, Christian expression naturally had a preference over atheism. (Think "In God We Trust," or "Under God.") However, secularist attacks gradually reduced the presence of Christianity in the public square, inevitably lessening its overall influence on the culture. This set the stage for the next attacks to destroy Christian influence.

And again, while there have been notable court victories, the efforts to make Christianity illegal (or irrelevant) have not ceased. The hostile view argues something like this: "Believe whatever you like, but you cannot refuse any government demands on how to act (or not act) or shield your children from what we teach in public education. If your Christian conscience is offended by some government requirement, too bad."

A few examples show how far this mindset has progressed. A Supreme Court decision involved a Christian website designer. Ignoring public misinformation, the court record shows the designer served everyone and did not discriminate against any group. However, the designer would not use her artistic talents to create *all* messages. Her faith-informed view of marriage did not allow her to create a unique website for a same-sex wedding.

The state of Colorado said she could be prosecuted for that refusal, with fines *and mandatory reeducation programs*, which should terrify a sane reader. The state was saying *you are free to believe but must violate your beliefs and do what we say.* The website designer prevailed in a 6-3 vote because of her speech rights, but what would the outcome have been if the 2016 presidential election had gone the other way and a president with radically different views had filled the three Supreme Court vacancies?

In some places, efforts are underway to make "misgendering" a crime. New York City passed a law (and later repealed it) that an adult with unwanted same-sex attraction could not receive professional religious counseling. However, counseling to encourage same-sex attraction or to explore gender identity was just fine. Laws have attacked Christian education and homeschooling (mostly unsuccessfully). Diversity requirements are infiltrating professional associations and licensing authorities, in some cases requiring a person to affirm a belief that violates their religious convictions at the risk of losing their professional license.

All these incidents show a growing, intolerant political presence clashing with faith. Its impulse is to suppress religious beliefs that conflict with their "ideal" society. Religious beliefs that conflict with those aims must be rendered irrelevant or (if necessary) destroyed.

Remember our definition of "totalitarianism" from Chapter 2 (via *Merriam-Webster*): "of or relating to a political regime based on subordination of the individual to the state and strict control of all aspects of the life and productive capacity of the nation especially by coercive measures (such as censorship and terrorism)."

Could totalitarianism be at our doorstep? Or has it already entered the "house?"

THE IRONY OF IT ALL

There is a supreme irony to this battle. Those against Christianity enjoy freedoms (right to advocate) that are built on religious conscience accommodations. Protecting religious freedom nurtures all of our other freedoms. Jefferson, Story, and Douglas saw it. Secularists destroying this foundation don't realize that without that foundation, everything else collapses.

.Not only did these great Americans see it. So did Joshua in the Bible, about 1,400 years before Christ. In a remarkable awareness of individual conscience, he declared: "But if serving the LORD seems undesirable to you, then choose for yourselves this day whom you will serve, whether the gods your ancestors served beyond the Euphrates or the gods of the Amorites, in whose land you are living. But as for me and my household, we will serve the LORD" (Joshua 24:15).

Want to be an atheist? You can. Want to serve God? You can. And that right is rooted in the religious conscience accommodations that came from Christianity itself.

CHAPTER 34

GLOBALISM

lobalism has become a popular buzzword in recent decades as politicians around the world call for cooperation to address our world's biggest challenges. In Chapter 12 we offered a definition of globalism as a system that elevates global rather than national principles. It is a decidedly secular—and not biblical—worldview that downgrades the importance and role of individual nations and uplifts an anti-biblical agenda that is antithetical to God's Word: Abortion in the name of "population control;" euthanasia as a "safe, merciful alternative;" gay rights and transgenderism as "culturally correct and logical."

But globalism is not new. Its origins date all the way back to the first chapters of Genesis when the serpent deceived Adam and Eve into wanting to be "like God" (Genesis 3:5). After the Fall, mankind organized into groupings of peoples, with Cain being the first mentioned city builder (Genesis 4:17).

THE ORIGIN OF GLOBALISM

A few chapters after the flood, the earth began to form recognizable, independent nations: "according to their genealogies, by their nations, and from these nations spread over the earth" (Genesis 10:32). Then, in Genesis 11:1-9 we see man's desire to be like God again as people banded together to build a city (Babylon) "whose top is in the heavens" to "make a name" for themselves by erecting the tallest structure the world had yet seen—the Tower of Babel.

Fallen man was determined to be like God, so God confused their single language and scattered them over the earth, dividing nations for millennia, according to their new languages and cultures, no matter how powerful an empire became (Acts 17:24-27). God does not like homogenization—He prefers diversity of the biblical type!

GLOBALISM DEFINED

As mentioned previously, Oxford Languages defines globalism as "the operation of planning of economic and foreign policy on a global basis." By definition, globalism attempts to unite or align nations around money and power. Do you see the Babel-type pattern here? Globalism has always been about control and being autonomous from God.

But is everything about globalism bad? Not necessarily. Trade among nations promotes prosperity (1 Kings 10:14-29; Ecclesiastes 11:1-2). Also, promoting mutual peace, encouraging the preservation of human rights, and providing help in times of crisis is how responsible nations should conduct themselves. But globalism today is an ideology that goes far beyond independent nations cooperating with other nations for their own individual benefit. Globalism inherently promotes an anthropocentric (man-centered) view, as opposed to a theocentric (God-centered) view. Much worse, globalism, or a "one world government," tends to identify biblically with what would be labeled as the spirit of the Antichrist.

THE WORLD ECONOMIC FORUM

One of the most powerful organizations promoting today's globalism is the World Economic Forum (WEF), a not-for-profit founded by Klaus Schwab in 1971. It has become widely recognized for bringing together the most influential government, business, and cultural leaders from around the world to "shape global, regional and industry agendas" as an "international organization for public-private cooperation."[1]

Some of the most recognizable names in the world attend their annual Davos, Switzerland meetings. In 2023, over 100 countries were represented, with at least 40 national heads-of-state and over 600 CEOs.[2]

The WEF gained notoriety during the COVID-19 pandemic when Schwab and now King Charles III of the United Kingdom announced the "Great Reset Initiative" to reconstruct the world's economic system. Later, Schwab co-authored a book with French economist Thierry Malleret titled, *COVID-19: The Great Reset*, with the goal of leveraging the COVID-19 crises to advance global agendas in the name of environmentalism and health.[3]

In essence, Schwab wants to capitalize on opportunities to shift power to more global governance. Another WEF voice, Yuval Noah Harari, referring to artificial intelligence, said, "We are almost like gods. We can create new life forms and destroy much of life on earth,

1 Source: World Economic Forum Website "About" Page: https://www.weforum.org/about/world-economic-forum/

2 https://qz.com/davos-2023-world-economic-forum-attendees-1849990706

3 https://capitalresearch.org/article/the-great-reset-and-its-critics-part-1/?utm_source=Google&utm_medium=cpc&gclid=CjwKCAjwkeqkBhAnEiwA5U-uM0EobQHEl11pLEu-xxz2hhaLOeB6hJaZFQANiN8rr78uzy9JQVE_LxoC6LAQAvD_BwE

including ourselves." Does Harari's tone sound similar to those building the Tower of Babel?[4]

WORLD HEALTH ORGANIZATION

Another powerful globalist organization is the World Health Organization (WHO), often cited as *the* global authority during the COVID pandemic. We will only mention it here briefly because it will be discussed in more detail in another chapter. Governments are encouraged to cede their authority to the WHO during a health crisis or under the threat of a crisis.

In 2023, the governing body of WHO, the World Health Assembly, discussed revising a public health "treaty" with 194 nations. The WHO director-general said the treaty was necessary to "urgently strengthen WHO as the leading and directing authority on global health, at the center of the global health architecture."[5] He also said: "We all want a world in which science triumphs over misinformation; solidarity triumphs over division."[6] He concluded his speech with what could be a mantra for the globalist agenda, "We are one world, we have one health, we are one WHO."[7]

THE PANDEMIC

If WHO gets its way—and it is dangerously close to accomplishing it—they will preempt the sovereignty of the world's almost 200 nations. (Once again, more on that later.) When would this occur? When there

---

4 https://cne.news/article/3207-ai-can-write-a-new-bible
5 WHO Director Speech Quotes: https://www.who.int/director-general/speeches/detail/who-director-general-s-opening-remarks-at-the-150th-session-of-the-executive-board-24-january-2022
6 Ibid.
7 Ibid,

is a pandemic. But who defines when we have a pandemic? WHO does. And what is a pandemic? Whatever WHO says is a pandemic.

John Kerry announced at the World Health Assembly in Geneva in June 2023 that disease is caused by climate change. Thus "climate change" is a pandemic. But there is more. Guns are a pandemic. In fact, "infodemic" is a pandemic. What is "infodemic?" It is either misinformation or disinformation. But who defines "misinformation" or "disinformation?" You guessed the answer. WHO. This is totalitarianism at its worst.

THE DANGERS AND DECEPTIONS OF GLOBALISM

Adherents say globalism will create a more equitable, fair, and just world; that it will bring unity and connectivity, create a sustainable world, and lift people from poverty. These sound like biblical values, and one could easily think this ideology is compassionate and Christlike. But there are two critical truths being overlooked:

- Human nature
- The role of government

Rather than believing mankind is inherently sinful and in need of a Savior and God's governing Word, globalists believe more man-created unity, sustainability, and equity can solve problems *independent of God*. But because their worldview is faulty, they can't properly diagnose the causes of the world's problems, much less know how to solve them. They tragically underestimate the evil of the human heart, and its need of a Savior.

Second, there are four forms of governance:

1. self-governance (personal responsibility over one's self);
2. family governance;
3. church or congregational governance;
4. and civil governance.

God defined the proper spheres of influence for the family, government, and yes—the church. For globalists to succeed, they know they need authority over all four of these realms. And, to have "unity" there will either need to be willing compliance or forced conformity. This means fewer personal freedoms for people, and the inevitable imposition of universal, everchanging values that are sinful nature-centered and not God-centered.

For example, politicians sound the alarm regarding climate change and environmentalism. They often claim climate change is the most serious threat facing humanity. Yet, if you were to ask people in Sri Lanka what the most serious threat to humanity is, they will probably tell you starvation due to massive food shortages caused by a government so focused on fighting climate change that they created a food crisis.[8] And what is true of Sri Lanka can or will be repeated in nation after nation. The coerced use of exclusively wind and solar energy at the expense of fossil fuels and nuclear power is about to bring greater poverty than the world has known in a very long time.

Again, does this mean we can just blithely mow down the rainforests and pollute our rivers and oceans at will? Definitely not. Balance and biblical stewardship are necessary. Radical environmentalism, however, is not in any way biblical.

The heart of globalism—and secular environmentalism—is not about grand initiatives or world connectedness. It is about control. Mankind's prideful nature wants to be like God, or even claim to be God—not submissive to God or the Bible. Gathering together the world's power elites and giving them the authority to make decisions on behalf of the entire world is not only risky, it threatens God-given human rights and our ability to live in conformity to God's design for our lives and our witness for Christ.

---

8 https://fee.org/articles/sri-lanka-s-food-crisis-is-man-made-and-demonstrates-the-danger-of-faux-environmentalism/?gclid=CjwKCAjwkeqkBhAnEiwA5U-uM9C8nptL1I-fYZ2BbF2Ed35_aKwaWN79xrL2yFuAxJvo1Ze1hZ07KuRoCVrQQAvD_BwE

CONTROL REQUIRES CENTRALIZED POWER

What happens when an elite few force uniformity on the masses? It never results in more freedom or prosperity. To put it succinctly: "Since the scattering and confusion at Babylon, man has been gradually working his way toward global domination in order to assert his dominion and leadership in place of God's leadership."[9]

America's Founding Fathers certainly understood the grave threat that centralized power poses to individual liberty. They believed government was a necessary evil, as Thomas Paine put it,[10] that people are inherently sinful, and that the stronger and more centralized a government becomes, the more rights people will lose. Thomas Jefferson said it this way, "The natural progress of things is for liberty to yield and government to gain ground."[11]

Since Jefferson penned those words a bit more than two centuries ago, we've seen this progression toward iron-fisted government control take place in the USSR, Maoist China, Castro's Cuba, and many other places around the world. And today we also see it growing through globalist organizations like WHO and the WEF.

BOTTOM LINE

While the messaging of globalism—always under the guise of health and environmental safety—may sound reasonable, the underlying result leads to fewer God-given individual freedoms and a greater concentration of power for a few elites who are often anti-God. The

9 William H. Bishop, PhD, in Regent University's *Leadership Advance Journal* Issue 25, 2014. https://www.regent.edu/journal/leadership-advance-online/necessity-of-unification-in-globalization-a-christian-perspective/
10 https://www.ruhr-uni-bochum.de/gna/Quellensammlung/02/02_commonsense_1776.htm
11 https://fee.org/articles/a-theme-for-the-bicentennial-the-founding-fathers-fear-of-power/

only good "globalism" is when the Messiah comes back to rule the whole earth (Revelation 20:4).

CHAPTER 35

AUTHORITARIANISM AND TOTALITARIANISM

ow many lives have been lost to oppressive regimes? Political scientist R.J. Rummel estimates there have been more than 262 million "deaths by government" ("democide") in the 20th century alone. He notes, "This democide murdered six times more people than died in combat in all the foreign and international wars of the century."[1]

The worst mass murderers include Stalin, Hitler, Mao, Amin, Hussein, and Pol Pot—and the list goes on. While Stalin is said to have been responsible for the deaths of 40-62 million people, and Hitler 17-20 million, Mao was the worst: estimates put the death toll under his regime between 45 and 75 million.[2]

---

1 https://www.hawaii.edu/powerkills/20TH.HTM
2 https://www.historydegree.net/worst-dictators-20th-century/

AUTHORITARIANISM AND TOTALITARIANISM DEFINED

The terms totalitarian and authoritarian are nearly interchangeable today, but they do differ. Authoritarian governments are characterized by a strong central government exercising control without any accountability, usually without a driving ideological objective, and are more likely to allow some freedom as long as it is not a threat to the regime's power. Totalitarian regimes are usually driven by a central ideology or national goal, striving to replace all political, legal, and social institutions with new ones.

To quote Rummel again: "Power is a continuum, with limited and responsible power at one end, and absolute power, or totalitarian governments, at the other end. Somewhat lesser extreme are authoritarian governments, that is, monarchies or dictatorships that leave social, economic, and cultural affairs and institutions largely free, but squash political opponents or critics."[3]

GOD'S STANDARD FOR EVERY NATION

God instructed Israel to obey His moral law in Exodus 20:1-17 and in many other portions of Scripture. Other nations were to look to Israel to see how God's design for government would be a blessing to those served by it (Deuteronomy 4:6-8; 28:1-68). In Romans 13:1-4, God further defined the limited role of government to punish evil and commend good for the common blessing of its citizens.

But not only did Israel fail to obey God's design for government, but so did the rest of the world. Historically, we agree with British historian Lord Acton's words that absolute power corrupts absolutely. Christians shouldn't be surprised then when ungodly dictators and corrupt political leaders oppress and even kill those they govern. Jeremiah 17:9 (NKJV) reminds us that "the heart is deceitful above all

---

3 https://www.hawaii.edu/powerkills/CHARNY.CHAP.HTM

things, and desperately wicked." Ungodly people in authority are capable of unspeakable atrocities if they have no fear of God and refuse to submit to His moral laws.

AMERICA STARTED OUT WELL

It's worth noting that America's founding was unique because its guiding principles and governmental structure were drawn from Scripture. It's far from a perfect nation, and it has been governed by imperfect leaders. But, even with its faults, personal freedom has flourished more than any other nation in history. Why? Because the bedrock of our nation's blessings (and by extension, blessings to the world) are rooted in the morality of Christianity.

This was well captured by American Supreme Court Justice Joseph Story (1779-1845), the "Father of American Jurisprudence," when he said, "One of the beautiful boasts of our municipal jurisprudence is that Christianity is a part of the Common Law. ... There never has been a period in which the Common Law did not recognize Christianity as lying at its foundations. ... I verily believe Christianity necessary to the support of civil society."[4]

Even in relatively recent times, this fact was still recognized. Supreme Court Justice Earl Warren (1891-1974) said: "I believe the entire Bill of Rights came into being because of the knowledge our forefathers had of the Bible and their belief in it: freedom of belief, of expression, of assembly, of petition, the dignity of the individual, the sanctity of the home, equal justice under law, and the reservation of powers to the people... I like to believe we are living today in the spirit of the Christian religion. I like also to believe that as long as we do so, no great harm can come to our country."[5]

---

4 https://christianheritagefellowship.com/christian-quotes-from-the-founding-fathers-2/
5 https://christianheritagefellowship.com/supreme-court-declares-america-christian/

WORLDWIDE DRIFT TOWARD CHRISTIAN PERSECUTION

Because Christians "give to Caesar what is Caesar's and to God what is God's" (Mark 12:17), believers choose obedience to God over obedience to the state. Not surprisingly then, persecution of Christians inevitably increases under authoritarian and totalitarian regimes because Christians acknowledge absolute truth is given by God, not by a dictator.

As noted elsewhere in the book, the very notion of "the Lordship of Christ" implies a limit on the role of government. As Christ followers, our *ultimate* allegiance is not to any government. It is to God, and God alone.

According to Open Doors International, globally today more than 360 million Christians suffer high levels of persecution and discrimination for their faith. In the last 30 years, the number of countries where believers experience extreme levels of persecution has almost doubled to 76 countries, with China near the top of the list. Eighty percent of the earth's population suffer religious persecution, and 80% of those are Christian. (This was the premise of the 2nd International Conference on Christian Persecution, held November 26-28, 2019 in Budapest, Hungary, which I attended with my wife, Rosemary.)

But even with persecution, Scripture tells us that God's proclaimed Word will not return void (Isaiah 55:11). In Acts 4:3-4, Peter and John were imprisoned for preaching the Gospel, but "many of those who heard them believed; and the number of the men came to be about five thousand." In fact, the Apostle Paul wrote much of the New Testament while imprisoned for preaching the Gospel. In Acts 8, the first Christian killed for their faith was Stephen. But after his death the people scattered and "preached the word wherever they went" (Acts 8:4).

This pattern is happening in our day also. Christianity has grown in China faster than anywhere else in the world. It's estimated that in the past four decades Christianity in China has risen from 1 million to more than 100 million people.

AMERICA AND CHRISTIAN PERSECUTION

It's easy to point to regimes such as China, Iran, or Russia as examples of authoritarian-totalitarian governments. But what about here in the US? Where are we headed? Consider:

1. The COVID "public health" crisis showed how elected officials can quickly exercise a massive power grab. They shut down businesses and schools, prohibited free movement/travel, and actually mandated medical decisions for people—even going so far as to declare "church" non-essential!

2. Conservatives (Christians) who are willing to be vocal about their rejection of bankrupt worldviews are now routinely discriminated against by institutions such as corporations, the media, universities, social media, and financial institutions for not holding to progressive-woke ideologies.

3. As discussed in Chapter 9, financial institutions are implementing "environmental, social, governance" (ESG) metrics and scores to be "environmentally responsible" and support social justice causes such as abortion, the LGBTQ agenda, and "equitable" standards. They close bank accounts of politicians and activists that they disagree with, and impose restrictions on industries such as gas and oil producers, and gun manufacturers.

4. In recent years, senior US government officials have colluded with social media company giants such as Facebook, Twitter, and YouTube to censor free speech by prohibiting the distribution and sharing of information they deem "misinformation" surrounding critical issues of COVID, elections, and criticism of the government.

5. At the time of this writing, the CEOs of the nation's social media giants—Meta, which owns Facebook, X (formerly

Twitter), etc.—were summoned to Capitol Hill and grilled in Senate hearings regarding their seeming inability—or unwillingness—to crack down on material deemed harmful to children. How ironic that a child with access to X or Facebook can find pornographic images and videos, yet if Christians speak out on critical issues they can be censored.

The result? People begin to "self-censor" due to the social consequences if they speak out against the values government and big corporations promote. We haven't reached the point of being physically locked up (or maybe we have), or placed in concentration camps like in North Korea, Iran, Russia, and China, but the trends are unmistakable. As free speech is silenced, so other freedoms quickly follow.

San Jose, California Calvary Chapel Pastor Mike McClure is facing millions of dollars in fines, and at one point possibly even jail time, for staying open during the early part of the pandemic, even though authorities admit that not one single case of COVID came from his church services. Pastor Che Ahn, from Pasadena, California, was informed that he—and possibly his church members—would be arrested. By any other name, this is persecution.

I have pastoral friends in Canada who paid an exorbitant price to continue preaching the Gospel during the heat of the pandemic. Artur Pawlowski was arrested and imprisoned countless times, including severe abuse in prison and solitary confinement. Pastor Henry Hildebrandt faced $52,000,000 in fines for offering in-person worship services (while also offering online services), even though not one single COVID case came from those in-person meetings.

RESIST ANY AND ALL TOTALITARIANISM TRENDS

If Jefferson is correct and the natural progression of things is for liberty to yield and government to gain ground, how do we stop the path to totalitarianism? Rod Dreher, author of *Live Not By Lies*, explains the best way to fight back is to "refuse to affirm what you do NOT believe." Want a biblical example?

When the 12 men came back from spying out the promised land (Numbers 134-5, 7, 9-15), only two (Joshua and Caleb) had the courage to see things from God's perspective and stand for truth. The other 10 were cowards who reported seeing giants who would easily defeat the Israelites. For their lack of faith, these 10 were never mentioned again in Scripture. In fact, God cursed them, and they all died of plagues!

We need to be like Caleb and Joshua: courageous in the face of "giants," standing for what is right, and condemning what is evil (Ephesians 5:11). Then, entrust the results to God.

OUR *ALMOST* NATIONAL MOTTO

There was a particular phrase that was loved by both Benjamin Franklin and Thomas Jefferson. Franklin wanted it to be our national motto, while Jefferson wanted it to be the motto for Virginia, and ended up using it on his own seal. That phrase provides the perfect close to this chapter:

"Rebellion to tyrants is obedience to God."

CHAPTER 36

THE CONSENT OF THE GOVERNED AND THE RULE OF LAW

T he phrase "consent of the governed" refers to the concept that "a government's legitimacy and moral right to use state power is justified and lawful only when consented to by the people or society over which that political power is exercised."[1]

THE GOVERNED'S SAY IN BEING GOVERNED

Historically, people were subjects of the state, with little ability to influence—much less direct—how governmental power was to be exercised. One of the many remarkable truths about the birth of the United States was the recognition that God's law was the ultimate standard that ruled over our nation, institutions (family or church), and individuals. In other words, everyone was accountable to an almighty God for their lives and how they responded to authority.

---

1 https://en.wikipedia.org/wiki/Consent of the governed

The Declaration of Independence makes this accountability explicit:

> We hold these truths to be self-evident, that all men are created equal, that they are
> endowed by their Creator with certain unalienable Rights, that among these are Life,
> Liberty, and the Pursuit of Happiness—That to secure these Rights, Governments are
> instituted among Men, deriving their just powers from the consent of the governed, ...

We all have universal God-given rights because everyone is made with value and dignity in the image of God (Genesis 1:27). However, our Constitution specifically restrains our national government by only giving it enumerated—highly specified (not unlimited)—powers. Has this understanding served us well? Yes, it has for most of our nation's existence. In fact, a quick read of Deuteronomy 28:1-14 depicts what a nation blessed by the Lord can expect. That doesn't mean we are exempt from racial difficulties, wars, economic catastrophes, crime, and every other manner of problems expected in a fallen world, but God has continued to bless and prosper us as a nation through our troubles—at least until recent times. Before I address that, however, let's review some basics.

THE LESSER MAGISTRATE

A key to understanding the power of consent of the governed is the idea of "the lesser magistrate." This doctrine has roots reaching all the way back to biblical times and is best illustrated by Peter and John's refusal to obey Jewish religious authorities that commanded them not to speak or teach in the name of Jesus (Acts 4:1-18). The Apostles chose to obey God—the higher power, or more specifically, the *highest* power—rather than the ungodly religious leaders of the day (Acts 4:19, 5:29).

For the next 1500 years, Christian influence on nations increasingly led to conflicts between the sacred and the political realms. One such conflict culminated in the city of Magdeburg, Germany in 1550. Nine pastors of that city signed the Magdeburg Confession, refusing to obey the imposition of Roman Catholicism on the city. This was one of the first formalized rejections of what was seen as tyrannical action by higher political and religious authorities to impose their unjust will on subordinate authority to the harm of "true religion." This Confession used religious arguments not only to justify the resistance of tyranny, but also to justify the right of self-defense.

The principle of the lesser magistrate is very closely related to the principle of interposition, where a person or group puts themselves between an oppressor and their intended victim. This also has biblical roots. Consider the time when King Saul made a rash vow demanding his troops fast until evening or be executed, but his son Jonathan was unaware of this command and ate honey. Saul's troops protected Jonathan from harm, thus "interposing" themselves for him so he would not be unjustly punished (1 Samuel 14:24-46).

Marvelous modern-day examples of interposition are found across our nation. For example, many are interposing on behalf of the unborn and the health of the mother: pro-life vigils at abortion clinics; the work of pro-life pregnancy care clinics; shutting down today's killing centers by legal means; and ending the work of the abortion mills. Proverbs 24:11-12 encapsulates the essence of interposition when it says we are to rescue those who are being taken away to death. Interposition is taking place not only for the unborn, but for the sick, the disabled, and the elderly (against the scourge of euthanasia).

Some of history's most dramatic interposition occurred in Europe in the late 1930s and 1940s. During the Holocaust, Christians such as Corrie Ten Boom, Irena Sendler, Chiune Sugihara, and Raoul Wallenberg risked their lives placing themselves between Hitler's death camps and the innocent Jewish people. They took Isaiah 62:1 seriously: "For Zion's sake I will not keep silent, and for Jerusalem's sake I will not be quiet..."

NULLIFICATION

Another way consent is withheld is when states nullify or render a federal law null and void within their state jurisdictions. This action can be the result of deeming the federal law unconstitutional and hence illegal, or by implementing laws that countermand federal laws. An example is when states legalize the use of marijuana while federal laws make its use illegal. (In this case, the federal law is right.) It should be noted that courts at the state, federal, and even the United States Supreme Court level have repeatedly rejected the validity of a state's nullification action by reasoning that the Supremacy Clause of the US Constitution provides that federal law is superior to state law.

At the citizens' level, nullification has occurred when juries in criminal trials refuse to find a defendant guilty when they believe the law is unjust and should never have existed to begin with. Historically, this happened before the Civil War, when in 1850 the Fugitive Slave Law was passed to return runaway slaves to their masters in slave states. Because the law was unjust, citizens repeatedly refused to enforce it. There have been other, more isolated instances of citizen jury nullification of existing laws believed to be profoundly unjust, but these actions are rarely heard of in our day. The principle, however, is timeless and goes to the heart of what is just.

So, let's define "just." The rule of law is just if evil doers are punished (Romans 13:4) according to a standard that is not capricious, tyrannical, or malicious, but is in conformance to God's standards of right and wrong.

MORE BIBLICAL EXAMPLES

Scripture also gives us examples of civil disobedience when no other means are available to prevent or circumvent evil actions and ungodly demands by the government. Remember the Egyptian midwives (Exodus 1:17,21), the hiding of Joshua's spies by Rahab (Joshua 2), Obadiah hiding the prophets of God (1 Kings 18), Moses leading the Jews out of captivity in Egypt (Exodus 14), Daniel (Daniel 6:13), and Shadrach, Meshach, and Abednego (Daniel 3:13-27) refusing to deny their faith.

These saints answered to the ultimate authority—God Almighty! They refused to bow down to evil, ungodly demands being made on them by those exercising power over them. Please note, however, that in making these decisions, they were willing to suffer whatever consequences may happen to them as a result. We know the Lord may miraculously protect His people, or He may allow them to suffer, but either way, the Lord is glorified by their faithfulness (Hebrews 11:29-38).

LAYERS OF MAGISTRATES

In our system of governance, every magistrate (a civil officer or lay judge who administers the law) at the federal level takes an oath to obey the Constitution, while magistrates at the state, county, and city levels take an oath to obey both their state's Constitution and the national Constitution. When the federal government oversteps its authority and exercises power it does not have, or legislates unjust laws, or makes ungodly judicial decisions that promote evil, states have the responsibility to take whatever legal action they can to resist those decisions. Likewise, when states act wickedly, lower magistrates are faced with the same decision—comply or resist.

But make no mistake, the government is a gift from God for our good (Romans 13:1-4), and the vast amount of its governing actions are intended to be of benefit to the citizens it represents. With that perspective, it should be a rare and egregious situation that would demand our outright disobedience. The conditions warranting these actions must be clear and compelling, grounded in God's Word, and not just a matter of preference or personal inconvenience. This requires wisdom and discernment, the very qualities God promises to provide to us when we ask for them (James 1:5).

WHAT ARE WE TO DO?

The rule of law and the enforcement of just laws are foundational pillars in maintaining a civil society and the prevention of anarchy. That is one of the primary responsibilities of government: to protect its citizens and maintain order (1 Timothy 2:1-2; 1 Peter 2:13-14).

We shouldn't be surprised, however, when we see secular and/or anti-biblical governments abusing their authority and forcing compliance on or taking advantage of its citizens. It was true in Solomon's time (Ecclesiastes 5:8), and it is true in our day. That doesn't mean we don't continue to fight to elect godly leadership into office or challenge ungodly laws with every means available to us—whether it be by legal processes, peaceful demonstrations, ballot initiatives, public exposure, exposing the evil of egregious laws, and yes, at times, disobedience when our conscience does not allow us to conform to anything that is offensive to God.

Our times of blessing by the Lord have gradually given way to times of ideological wickedness in high places of power. We see the consequences of secular worldviews that deny justice to whom it is owed while justifying evil as somehow compassionate (Isaiah 5:20-21). We are seeing God removing His protective hand on this nation as we begin to experience more and more the curses promised in Deuteronomy 28:15-68 when a nation turns its back on the God of justice.

God's people must walk in obedience to His ways, resist ungodly laws and policies, and reassert Christian influence in the public square with and through the means that are available to us, not to bring attention to ourselves but to bring attention to the almighty God we serve.

CHAPTER 37

THE BORDER

I n my book *Well Versed: Biblical Answers to Today's Tough Issues,*
I outlined what I felt was both a legal and compassionate handling
of the many who were living illegally within US borders. It was not
amnesty or a "pathway to citizenship" as such, but a "pathway to
legality."[1]

In a book I later co-authored with David Barton, we laid out a
forty-page overview of immigration, analyzing the brokenness of current
enforcement, what the Bible says about immigration, what our
Founders wrote, our early immigration laws, the reason we have
borders, and a three-step proposal for solving the current problem of
people who are in the country illegally.[2]

---

1 James L. Garlow, *Well Versed: Biblical Answers to Today's Tough Issues*, Salem Books
an imprint of Regnery Publishing, 2016, pp. 209-10.
2 James L. Garlow and David Barton, *This Precarious Moment, 6 Urgent Steps that Will
Save You, Your Family and Our Country*, Salem Books an imprint of Regnery Publishing,
2018, pp. 47-87; especially see the Three-Step Solution on pp. 82-83.

I assumed—I should say, wrongly *presumed*—that the US government would get its act together and stop further *illegal* immigration, and then proceed with appropriate *legal* immigration, and thus be able to deal with those who were illegal or "undocumented"—the preferred term—in our nation. The US both needs and values those who come to our shores *legally*, assuming they follow the biblical understanding of the Hebrew word *ger*, meaning stranger or foreigner, outlined in the previous book.[3]

THE OBSERVATION: CHINA

I have attended two "border school" training events, one in El Paso, Texas[4] and one in McAllen, Texas, both designed to make us aware of what was happening along the shared 1,954-mile boundary between the US and Mexico.[5]

The one in McAllen allowed us to go into the Central Processing Center, designed with many climate-controlled rooms full of arriving immigrants divided based on sex, age, or condition: pregnant women, young women, young men, and other groupings. People were very well cared for. No one that we observed was deported back to their home country. One's information was entered into a computer and, assuming they did not have a previous record, they were processed through the center and released in less than 72 hours. Most were out in only two days after being given a free cell phone.

What stunned us most was the presence of Chinese immigrants. At the time, we were told that the top three countries from which people came at that time were 1) Guatemala, 2) El Salvador, and 3) China. How is that possible? Guatemala is only 1,300 miles from the

---

3 James L. Garlow, *Well Versed: Biblical Answers to Today's Tough Issues*, op cit, p. 209-10; see explanation of ger.
4 Ibid, p. 205.
5 For that reason, this chapter will be written from a more personal experience standpoint.

US border. El Salvador is approximately 1,400 miles away. But China? It's about 7,500 miles away. There are more Chinese coming across the border than those from Mexico, which is next door. What is happening?

In fact, the day we were there, every single person we saw standing in a line of people who had been apprehended the night before was Chinese. As well, every single one in the line was male, specifically young, military-age males. When our tour ended in the Central Processing Center in McAllen, we saw the group of people who were being given their free cell phones and then processed out and released. Once again, every single one in this group was Chinese. All of them except two were males, and all the males were military age.

In the previous year before our visit, around 450 Chinese migrants had crossed the border. But when we were there, nearly 4,400 Chinese had crossed the border illegally in the first five months of the fiscal year, and the number has risen dramatically since we were there. Why? What is happening at our southern border?

Are the young, military age Chinese males flocking here—paying the approximate $30,000 each to the cartel, as we were told—because they love America? Or were they sent here by the Chinese Communist Party with nefarious plans? Tragically, I suspect it is the latter.

MASSIVE GLOBAL INFLUX

And it is certainly not merely Chinese. It is not just Mexicans or those from Central America and South America. People from 160 nations, including Iran, are illegally crossing the border.[6] In our trip to the border in 2023, we were told that 70% of those crossing are males. At the time we were there, 5,000 to 6,000 per day were being

---

6 https://www.nytimes.com/2021/10/22/us/politics/border-crossings-immigration-record-high.html

processed in only three Texas counties. It has skyrocketed since we were there and is now at 12,000 per day (at the time of this writing).

While writing this book, my wife and I have been on numerous flights where illegal aliens—quite identifiable by their distinctive identical backpacks and paperwork, are boarded on the plane *before* first class passengers. We have arrived at luggage carousels to see people with United Nations markings on their bags, meeting people, handing them cash and cards and giving them instructions. This is *not* legal. It is in violation of US law.

AGENTS OVERRUN

Agents are used to protecting the border. That is their task. That means not allowing non-citizens to illegally enter the country. But something has dramatically changed in recent years. Those in uniform who formerly would have been used to stop illegal entry are now "processing" people, sitting at computers.

It was explained to us that when Trump was elected, *even before the inauguration*, the numbers of illegals plummeted. In the transition from President Trump to President Biden, *even before the inauguration*, the numbers skyrocketed. When asked why people are not being stopped and turned back, the response was that "no law has changed, but policy has changed." Allow me to translate that: *the law is not being enforced.* One of them told us, "Rhetoric matters. Operation matters."

The pressure on border agents is unbearable. In a recent conversation with a close friend whose son is a border agent, my friend—who is in his 70s—began to openly weep over the conditions his son is facing. The pressures on our nation's border agents are intense.

While at the border we learned border agents are stressed beyond their capacity. We were told at that time that fourteen of them had recently committed suicide. Like underappreciated police in America's troubled urban areas, many of these border agents are taking retirement as early as they can. They stated openly, "We did not sign up for this."

For what did they sign up? To protect our nation at the border. But they are not allowed to do that.

MOTHERS AND CHILDREN

It was pointed out that these border agents have families. They have children. When they see children coming across the border who are being or have been abused—sexually and otherwise—by adults, it breaks their hearts. We were told of them finding dead babies along the border. When one agent asked a woman, "Why did you leave this baby to die?" the woman answered, "It's not my baby." Since she was merely paid to get the baby across the border, she did not care.

The agents, many or most of whom are former military, stated, "We have seen more death at the border than we ever did in battle." At one point in the river, they pointed to the place where they had picked up bodies. They explained it was not because of drownings. The people had been decapitated when the migrants lacked funds to pay the cartel. This takes an emotional toll on our border agents.

In a relatively short time, over 2,000 pregnant women had crossed the border. When we toured the Central Processing Center, there were special rooms designated just for pregnant women. In one of the prior months, border agents had helped deliver twelve babies. On the night before we arrived, "291 unaccompanied minors" had crossed the border. It was reported that they had found three dead bodies that day. Can you imagine being an agent and having to deal with such tragedy day in and day out?

In the earlier "border school" I attended in El Paso, I was told one story of what the cartel had done to the young daughter of a member of law enforcement. It was so gross, so torturous, that I have not been able to get it out of my mind. I wish I had never heard the story. I am not even able to repeat it to anyone. One person said, "There is nothing humanitarian or Christian about the current border policy."

THE PROBLEM: LEADERSHIP

I have studied political/governmental issues since I was a child. Part of my focus has been knowing a little bit about cabinet officials. I can still name a few of the cabinet officials from the time of Dwight Eisenhower and most certainly from the time of John Kennedy. However, I have never seen a person deceive the American public with the skill of Department of Homeland Security Secretary Alejandro Mayorkas. When members of Congress asked why the border was not secure, he would respond with a stunning, "The border *is* secure," while some networks ran a split screen showing people pouring across the border at that very moment.

What did "secure" mean to Mayorkas? Simply that people were processed and set free in America. The only outrage he expressed was at the cartel. He had no regret that so many—actually 2.76 million known migrants,[7] in addition to a potential 1.2 million to 1.3 million known "got-aways," were entering our nation illegally each year. And the numbers continue to skyrocket. When I inquired about the "got-aways" we were told, "We don't know who they are or where they are or what they might do."

When I asked the question regarding the young Chinese males coming across the border, the officially approved response was, "Oh, we interview them, so we know who they are." When I asked that same question one hour later, a *former* high-level border official openly admitted, "We have no idea who they are." The fact is, if they don't

---

7 https://www.nbcnews.com/politics/immigration/migrant-border-crossings-fiscal-year-2022-topped-276-million-breaking-rcna53517

show up in the computer; that is, if they have no previously known criminal activity in the US, they are set free in the US.

The result, according to those at the border? Outbound from the US are dollars, going to Mexico, paying the cartel, along with weapons. Inbound are migrants, terrorists, and drugs.

FENCES

Do border fences work? Yes, we were told. But only 700 of the 1,954-mile border has a fence. President Trump had built much of it. The US Army Corp of Engineers purchased the easement. Preliminary work had been done, and the expensive fencing had been paid for, but the Biden Administration stopped it. In fact, the fencing was left to lay in lots, with taxpayers paying for the costly rental space for what could have been miles of fencing.

To this heavy and painful topic, allow me to add a bit of an "inside story." One of the members of President Trump's cabinet told this story to a group of us after his presidency ended in 2021. When those charged with building the fence came to meet with President Trump in the White House regarding the specifications of the fence, he immediately asked about the type of rebar they were using. Remember, Trump has spent his entire career erecting buildings.

Trump informed the builders that the rebar they were using would not last, and told them to switch to another type. When the President asked about the nature of the concrete, he recommended specific changes. When he heard the depth of the footing, he insisted they go to a certain depth. When he heard of the height of the fence, he asked it to be taller, but the officials told him it could not be done. So Trump called one of his former construction men, who explained how to do it. When he asked about paint, they said they were not going to paint it. He said, "No, paint it black."

When President Trump then visited the border, they took him to the middle of an area of the fence that had been painted black for two miles. When he saw it, he immediately pointed out that the paint—for various reasons—was the wrong type and told them the specific type of paint that would last. The designers of the fence had forgotten that they were dealing with Donald Trump, the construction man. When President Trump campaigned by saying, "I am going to build a big, beautiful fence," he was not joking. In his mind, he knew how to build it and how it would look.

The fence—though ready to go up—was stopped the moment Biden came into office.

MORE THAN FENCES

It is obvious that the border agents needed much more than fences. Fences certainly help in the deterrence of illegal migration, but the agents need so much more. Currently, they are outmaneuvered and outgunned.

Drones are badly needed. At the time of our visit, the agents in that particular area had 20 drones. They needed 70 to 90 drones. The drug cartel had between 360 and 400 drones, watching every move of the border agents. They even had drones flying *above* the Border Patrol helicopters.

Those crossing illegally often hide from agents in the tall grass. There is a simple solution: mow the grass. Our US government regulations would not allow it.

In addition to drones, they need all-weather roads along the border, plus sensors. That is, cables five feet underground, in addition to cameras. This is a winnable war. But the Biden Administration has demonstrated no desire to win it. Thus, Americans are suffering. And so are the innocent people who attempt to illegally enter the US, who are being deceived, physically and sexually abused, and sometimes killed by the cartels, who have become emboldened due to the lack of good and clear immigration policies.

PAIN, SUFFERING, AND DEATH

The stories surrounding trips to, across, and beyond our border read like a "trail of tears." So many women are being raped. Thousands of people have died coming to and across the border. Tens of thousands of children have disappeared into human trafficking, with no tracking by our federal government. The current anti-humanitarian immigration policy of the Biden Administration is a horrific violation of biblical standards. The human pain and suffering defy description. It breaks the heart of God. And ours, too.

WHAT YOU CAN DO

It's critical that you let your voice be heard at the ballot box regarding our borders. As well, advocate for sane border policies in your state. As noted earlier, in *Well Versed*, written in 2016, I advocated for dealing with the problem by creating a path to legality. I did not advocate amnesty nor citizenship, as those who enter illegally are, in fact, lawbreakers. Yet, at that time, I felt some kind of a pathway to non-citizen legality could be the answer.

However, things have changed dramatically since the presidency of Joe Biden in 2021. A few points to consider as we gain context for our current situation. Consider these stark facts:

1. While amnesty was given during the Reagan administration, it was with the caveat that a massive influx of illegals would never be permitted.
2. During the Biden administration the US has had the largest invasion of illegals ever.
3. Many nefarious people, sometimes referred to as "Special Interest Aliens" (SIAs) and "Known and Suspected Terrorists" (KSTs) have entered the country.

4. Many children have entered the nation via sex trafficking, totally unaccounted for.
5. Large numbers of military-age Chinese men have come illegally.
6. Large numbers of young males are coming from nations which sponsor terrorism or host terrorist organizations.

The US has no choice but to identify who is here, where they are, and why they are here. And we must begin the painful and complex task of deportation.

It did not have to be this way. With proper leadership, the US would not have had millions coming into the country in an unmanageable and illegal manner. If America is to survive this onslaught, millions—perhaps as many as 10 or 20 million illegal people—are going to have to be found, discerning who they are.

UNDERSTAND TRUE COMPASSION

Some falsely claim that "compassion" dictates we welcome all who have come. However, it is not "compassionate" to let anyone come in, or to enter illegally. It is compassionate to protect the citizenry from undo harm. It was a lack of compassion by American leadership—Biden and Mayorkas and others—that allowed 22-year-old nursing student Laken Riley to be murdered on February 22, 2024 at the University of Georgia (UGA) by illegal alien Jose Antonio Ibarra.

On March 7, 2024, the US Congress passed the Laken Riley Act. While that is a good thing, it comes too late for Laken Riley. She is dead. And it comes too late for the many others who have suffered crimes at the hands of people who were allowed to enter the nation illegally.

And on that same day, March 7, 2024, at the State of the Union address, when Congresswoman Marjorie Taylor Greene apparently yelled out Laken Riley's name, Joe Biden decided to—for the first time—publicly acknowledge the death of Ms. Riley. But to add insult to injury, he pronounced her name as "Lincoln" Riley, once again dishonoring her (and confusing her with the head football coach of the USC Trojans). Ms. Riley's death—and the deaths of many other citizens—is demonstration of a lack of compassion on the part of the nation's highest leadership.

For compassion's sake, let all of us become informed. Activate. Vote. Educate others. Help place people in office who will follow the number one mandate for the purpose of government: to protect the citizenry.

That means stopping this untenable invasion of America.

CHAPTER 38

ELECTION FRAUD

"**T**he 2020 presidential election was STOLEN!"

Few statements can make an immediate enemy ("You are an election denier!") or a quick friend ("Yes, I agree!"). The opening six-word line to this chapter is one of them. Like the rest of the nation, I was shocked at the outcome. And I have no doubt that the details of that election will be scrutinized, researched, rehashed, theorized about, and written about for many decades into the future.

Was the presidential election stolen? Did it really defy all previous precedents? Were statistical norms really violated? Were more than 80 lawsuits filed against 12 states and Washington, DC ineffective in making any substantive changes in results,[1] or was the 2020 election the "most secure in American history?"[2] Was ballot harvesting the reason for the lopsided results? Were voting machines tampered with?

---

1 82 Post-Election Lawsuits Challenging the 2020 Presidential Election—2020Election.org
2 2020 election "most secure in history," security officials say (cbsnews.com)

Was every recount (and there were lots of them) credible and conclusive? Did lots of "dead people" vote?

These and a myriad of other questions and claims have been made. The report given to the American people: The Democrat presidential candidate received more than 81 million votes (51.34%, 306 Electoral Votes), and the Republican presidential candidate received more than 74 million votes (46.84%, 232 Electoral Votes).[3]

Sincere believers can differ. I will say it again. Sincere believers can differ as to whether the election was fraudulent or legitimate, or something in between, based on their own convictions and study. But for now, knowing that the proverbial dust will never settle, what are we as Christians to do?

A LITTLE SILVER LINING

For starters, we can be thankful that the 2020 presidential election created an enormous increase in public awareness regarding the complexity and importance of election integrity. Without confidence that elections will *accurately* record and count *only* legitimate votes, every outcome will be questioned by the losing side, and people of faith will be reticent to participate in something they see as corrupt. As a result, since 2020, there have been many positive changes to state election laws,[4] with many more changes in the works.

But changing election laws is one thing. The most important thing is whether there is a direct linkage between the change and an improvement in election *integrity* (i.e., accurately counting only those votes that are cast *lawfully*). How much these changes will affect future elections remains to be seen. There is one thing, however, I'm sure of: depending on which side of the political aisle you are on, you are either

---

3 2020 United States presidential election—Wikipedia
4 30+ states have made these voting changes since the 2020 election—USAFacts

pleased or upset with each change, depending upon the political party that pushed it through.

One more thing. Attempts on the national level to "federalize" all federal elections with massive, bureaucratic, convoluted requirements were defeated in 2021, leaving the conduct of elections under the purview of each individual state, where it belongs. For that, we can be thankful and continue to push against any effort by the federal government to assume this role.

BIBLICAL PRINCIPLES RELATING TO VOTING

We know God is a God of order (1 Corinthians 14:33), so it stands to reason that

the more complicated an election process becomes ...
the more lax the voter identification process becomes, which leads to ...
more people handling, processing, and counting a ballot, which then allows for ...
more discretion in "curing" a ballot with errors, which then causes ...
Election Day to turn into Election Season, thus opening the door to ...
more chances for unscrupulous cheating and "gaming" the system.

But who should be allowed to vote? Biblically, a person is an adult when they: think like an adult (1 Corinthians 13:11); turn 20; go to war (Numbers 1:3); bring offerings to the Temple (Exodus 30:14); have accountability for major sins (Numbers 14:29-30; 32:11). As a nation, we have decided 18 and above is best. For sure, any lowering of the age limit would be very unwise.

Also, citizenship (native-born or naturalized) is important. Just as Old Testament Israel treated everyone equally under the law (Exodus 12:49), they reserved special obligations for only those who:

- were committed to the nation formally (Exodus 12:48);
- observed national remembrance (Exodus 12:1-28);
- and recognized the reality of a transcendent God (Ezekiel 44:6-7).

The equivalent today is citizenship.

Clearly, safeguards must be put in place to prevent someone from impersonating someone else (whether they are alive or dead), from voting more than once, or from voting in different jurisdictions during the same election.

But should anyone be restrained from voting? Obviously, non-citizens. But also those convicted of serious felonies since they've shown a callous disregard for the community. Wisdom would dictate that once they've become responsible, law-abiding citizens again, then voting privileges should be reinstated.

Also, those who are mentally incapacitated—in other words, severely mentally or emotionally disabled or otherwise incapable of making informed, adult decisions. (I am not talking about mild to moderate challenges or disabilities.) Of course, clear safeguards need to be in place to prevent bad actors from taking advantage of those with mental or emotional challenges who are capable of making an informed decision.

TWO COMPETING VIEWS OF VOTING

Elections have consequences, and voting is a major citizenship responsibility for Christians. And now is the time for all believers to become even more involved and to weigh in on such critical questions as who should represent us, and what laws are just (Proverbs 11:14).

But when it comes to the implementation of voting rules, there are two divergent views.

One side claims voter fraud is extremely rare and that cleaning up voter registration rolls disenfranchises certain voter demographics, believing anyone "contributing" to our nation should be allowed to vote while pushing for ballot harvesting to "help" marginalized people, and finally wanting all voting to be by mail.

The other side believes voter fraud is far more prevalent than is being reported, wants direct evidence of personal identification and citizenship status, wants clean voter registration rolls, and has no "third-party" intervention to assist voters. This view is driven by simple principles: honesty and transparency.

WHY VOTER RIGHTS ARE SO DIVISIVE

Given the sinfulness of mankind (Jeremiah 17:9), wisdom says that extreme care should dictate the regulation of something as important as elevating governmental leaders to positions of immense power. Stated another way, a vote is so precious, and the consequences of elections are so important (Proverbs 29:2), that high accountability and minimal process confusion is crucial.

The key point: The shorter the distance between a qualified voter casting a valid (secret) ballot, and then that vote being accurately tabulated, the better the process. The more steps, the more people, the more complex the process, and the more third-party "assistance" given, the greater the opportunity for fraud. It is as simple as that.

WHAT CHRISTIANS MUST DO

First, instead of re-litigating the presidential election of 2020 or whatever election, proactively get involved in each election cycle. First and foremost, you can do this by voting biblically. As best as you are able, support a viable candidate that is closest to embracing God's biblical values with your time, treasure, and talent. Speak out on the issues of the day and encourage your elected leaders to do the right thing.

Next, find out if there is a group in your state concerned about election integrity that supports personal accountability, cleaned-up voter registration rolls, and high transparency of the election processes. In fact, by volunteering to be a poll watcher, you could have a significant impact on identifying needed changes and also preventing fraud from occurring.

Some advocate returning to paper ballots to increase the chances of election integrity. Others contend that blockchain technology is the only way to assure honesty in voting.[5]

Lastly, pray fervently (1 Thessalonians 5:17) for our nation, for its leaders, and for elections. Pray that we can have confidence that the results accurately reflect the will of the people being served and that—by the grace of God—true biblical values will again be influential across our land.

---

5 https://www.youtube.com/watch?v=MWqseNZpAIE

CHAPTER 39

THE LOSS OF MEDICAL FREEDOM

At the onset of the COVID-19 pandemic in early 2020, New York Governor Andrew Cuomo imposed a broad executive emergency order upon his state. This was followed in rapid succession by California Governor Gavin Newsom and Illinois Governor J.B. Pritzker. Within days, these three states established some of the most restrictive measures ever seen in the United States and set a precedent that many other states would follow.

PHASE ONE: COVID SHUTDOWNS

Governors enumerated activities they considered "essential." Activities not deemed essential were suddenly outlawed—such as here in San Diego (and I kid you not): prohibiting walking on an empty beach, even if no one else was in sight. Restaurants were shut down, as were public and private schools, hair salons, gyms, and public parks. Gatherings were restricted to a few people. Church services, Bible studies, small group meetings, and even prayer meetings did not make the "essential" list. Paradoxically, recreational marijuana dispensaries (illegal until recently) and strip clubs were deemed essential.

In less than a month, church attendance across the continent plummeted to nearly zero. Weddings were postponed, and funerals were not public. Taking communion and holding baptisms became clandestine affairs.

Governors enacted emergency orders for up to 30 days. However, as time ran out, new overlapping orders were issued. It became apparent that the executive restrictions on businesses, daily life, and religious liberties would not end soon.

In Illinois, a few churches openly defied the governor, such as Elim Romanian Pentecostal Church and Logos Baptist Ministries. They challenged Gov. Pritzker on constitutional and statutory grounds,[1] and a practical victory was won. The governor transformed his executive order from a mandate to 'advisory only.'

In New York, the Roman Catholic Diocese of Brooklyn and a Jewish synagogue, Agudath Israel of America, challenged the gathering limit of 25 people imposed by Governor Cuomo.[2] The Supreme Court of the United States ruled, "We hold that enforcement of the Governor's severe restrictions on the applicants' religious services must be enjoined."[3]

In California, churches challenged Governor Newsom. Among these was John MacArthur and Grace Community Church, as documented in *The Essential Church*.[4] In Canada, Pastor Artur Pawlowski, who—ironically enough—emigrated from Soviet-era Poland seeking

1 "ELIM ROMANIAN PENTECOSTAL CHURCH & LOGOS BAPTIST MINISTRIES Plaintiffs, v. JAY ROBERT PRITZKER" Elim Romanian Pentecostal Church v. Pritzker, 20 C 2782, (N.D. Ill. Jul. 26, 2021)
https://casetext.com/case/elim-romanian-pentecostal-church-v-pritzker-3
2 "ROMAN CATHOLIC DIOCESE OF BROOKLYN, New York v. Andrew M. CUOMO, Governor of New York" Roman Catholic Diocese of Brooklyn v. Cuomo, 141 S. Ct. 63, (2020)
https://casetext.com/case/roman-catholic-diocese-of-brooklyn-v-cuomo-1
3 Justice GORSUCH, final sentence.
4 2023 Grace Community Church of the Valley and Grace Productions.

religious freedom, scolded the Royal Mounties, who disrupted his church service without a warrant. Later confrontations led to record fines and extended solitary confinement.[5] Pastor Henry Hildebrant, from Aylmer, Ontario, was fined $52,000,000 for being open during COVID, even though no one contracted COVID at the church services.

PHASE TWO: MANDATORY VACCINATION

As COVID testing and vaccines became available, a new front was opened concerning government authority: should medical screening or vaccination be required as a condition of participation in public activities (e.g., grocery shopping, doctor's visits)?

In Chicago, Mayor Lightfoot enacted a quarantine executive order.[6] Everyone entering the city during the pandemic from outside the city was "subject to mandatory self-quarantine for 14 days;" only "essential workers" were excluded. Church members living in the suburbs could not travel into the city to attend church, lead a Bible study, visit members, or bring communion to shut-ins. Government actions included arrest,[7] closure of buildings, and forcible vaccination.

The Illinois governor also required all "teachers" in Illinois to be vaccinated. "Teaching" was broadly defined to include volunteers for non-degree-issuing instruction, such as teaching a Sunday school class, Bible study, or small group. But the order went further: every worker in the building and every attendee at a teaching session required vaccination.

---

5 An entire series of stories are on Rebel News. https://www.rebelnews.com/tags/pastor_artur_pawlowski
6 ORDER OF THE COMMISSIONER OF HEALTH OF THE CITY OF CHICAGO No. 2020-10 (QUARANTINE RESTRICTIONS ON PERSONS ENTERING CHICAGO FROM HIGH INCIDENCE STATES) Issued: July 2, 2020
7 May 2, 2020 "We will shut you down, we will cite you, and if we need to, we will arrest you, and we will take you to jail. Period. There should be nothing unambiguous about that. Don't make us treat you like a criminal; but if you act like a criminal, and you violate the law, and you refuse to do what is necessary to save lives in this city in the middle of a pandemic, we will take you to jail. Period."

But there's more. These so-called "novel vaccines" did not operate in the classic manner of an injected antigen to provoke an immune response. Instead, the injection was incorporated into the cell structure, causing the body to synthesize these proteins itself. Objectively, these mRNA shots were medically controversial and lacked a proven track record for safety and efficacy.

MORAL AND CONSENT ISSUES

There were moral implications as well. In the vaccine development, it was believed that cells taken from aborted children had been used to either test or cultivate products. This led to strong opposition by those who value the life of the unborn child.

When the vaccines became publicly available, they were experimental and given FDA Emergency Use Authorization (EUA). The formal notice made clear that the administration required voluntary consent. Since the FDA had only permitted release as experimental, this was an obvious impediment to mandatory vaccination since long-standing federal law barred the use of experimental drugs without consent.

This principle of consent became crucial during the Nuremberg Trials when Nazis abused prisoners under the cloak of scientific experimentation. What followed was the Nuremberg Code, which begins "1. The voluntary consent of the human subject is absolutely essential."

LIABILITY

Eventually, the FDA approved mRNA vaccines as non-experimental—but the problem was not resolved. The manufacturers enjoyed legal protection from liability for distributing the experimental vaccines but not for the approved, non-experimental vaccine. Thus, there was little incentive for the manufacturer to produce and distribute the approved form. Some believe that the experimental vaccine continued to be distributed for some time in order to reduce liability issues.

COERCION

In several states, various workers were required to be vaccinated in order to retain their jobs. Dr. May Talley Bowden was only one of many who lost their jobs. She was fired by Houston Methodist after she refused vaccination and suggested ivermectin as a treatment.[8]

Although pro forma exceptions were offered for medical or religious reasons, applications for exceptions were routinely denied. Existing state law in Illinois barred coercion of medical care "contrary to their conscience."[9] Nevertheless, hundreds of workers lost their jobs despite documented religious objections.

Federal coercion of the vaccine was ratcheted up when an OSHA emergency rule mandated organizations with 100 employees to require COVID vaccination or periodic testing of all employees. Noncomplying employees would lose their jobs. Noncomplying companies would be fined around $13,600 per violation and up to $136,000. The states of Texas, Missouri, Florida, along with the Daily Wire and Answers in Genesis, among others, sued. Issues included the privacy of employees' medical records and decisions, improper discrimination, and the free exercise of religion. Ultimately, the cases were consolidated, and SCOTUS struck down the mandate.

---

8 The court would later rule that the FDA overstepped its authority by recommending that patients avoid ivermectin. Houston Methodist dropped its policy Dec 1, 2023, after Texas forbade COVID vaccine requirements.

9 (745 ILCS 70/) Health Care Right of Conscience Act. https://www.ilga.gov/legislation/ilcs/ilcs3.asp?ActID=2082&ChapterID=58

WHO AND THE LOSS OF MEDICAL FREEDOM

However, the COVID controversies were not merely national. They were global. And that is where the story turns to the World Health Organization (WHO). It has a noble-sounding name, and one would think it has noble goals. But such is not the case.

The United Nations was founded in 1945. The following year, member nations signed off on the constitution for WHO. With a name like "health organization," what is not to like, correct? The answer: lots.

Until COVID, most people never thought much about the alphabet organizations like the CDC, NIH or WHO. Forced lockdowns, required masks, and coerced "vaccines" changed all that. They changed America. And much of the world.

As noted in another chapter, the biggest casualty of the 2020-2022 COVID pandemic era was trust. But it is the actions *after* that era that are causing the greatest consternation. WHO, at its Geneva World Health Assembly of 2023, presented a "pandemic preparedness accord." The use of the term "accord," or sometimes referred to as an "agreement," may seem innocent. However, if America is involved in a "treaty," it has to be approved by the US Senate. But if, by sleight of hand, it is called an "accord," then no such approval is needed, or so it seems. But make no mistake about it: it is a treaty.

MEDICAL TOTALITARIANISM

Previous language of WHO protected "human rights" (except, of course, for WHO "human rights" does not mean protecting the rights of the unborn due to their pro-abortion bent). The new "accord" will result in the loss of human rights and individual freedom. Dr. David Bell, a clinical and public health physician with a PhD in population health, and former WHO scientific and medical officer, wrote these jolting words in the *American Journal of Economics and Sociology*:

The COVID-19 response has demonstrated how these ideals have been undone. Decades of increasing funding within public-private partnerships have corroded the basis of global public health. The COVID-19 response, intended for a virus that overwhelmingly targeted the elderly, ignored norms of epidemic management and human rights to institute a regime of suppression, censorship, and coercion reminiscent of the power systems and governance that were previously condemned. Without pausing to examine the costs, the public health industry is developing international instruments and processes that will entrench these destructive practices in international law. Public health, presented as a series of health emergencies, is being used once again to facilitate a fascist approach to societal management. The beneficiaries will be the corporations and investors whom the COVID-19 response served well. Human rights and individual freedom, as under previous fascist regimes, will lose.[10]

Assuming the globalist so-called "health" organization gets what it wants, WHO would have a monopoly over global health governance, and that includes you. With the new proposed sweeping and coercive powers, they would have the ability to order coerced medical examinations and vaccinations, lockdowns, and travel restrictions. Having achieved the desired controls, WHO would declare a "public health emergency" of its own choosing; that is, a Public Health Emergencies of International Concern (PHEIC). WHO would decide whether medical substances could be imposed on the public without informed consent.

What is a pandemic? Whatever WHO decides it is. "Climate change" is now a pandemic. Guns are a pandemic. Some have reported

---

10 David Bell, Pandemic preparedness and the road to international fascism American Journal of Economics and Sociology, 2023, vol. 82, issue 5, pp. 395-409.

that an "infodemic," that is, "misinformation" or "disinformation," presumably based on—you guessed it!—how WHO would define it.

And there is more. WHO could officially censor information, including your free speech, if it deems you are expressing views opposing their official narrative. As if that is not enough, WHO is not accountable to any national congress or parliament, nor is the organization limited by any constitutional safeguards.[11]

CONGRESSIONAL RESPONSES

Can WHO's seemingly inexorable power monopoly be stopped? Some members of the US Congress are trying. Two US Senators—Jim Risch of Idaho and Kevin Cramer of North Dakota—introduced a resolution to prevent the President from ceding US sovereignty to WHO through the pandemic agreement unless there is—like all treaties require—Senate approval.[12] Congressman Chip Roy of Texas introduced HR6645, "to terminate membership by the United States in the United Nations…"[13] and Senator Mike Lee of Utah introduced the same bill as S3428.[14]

BIBLICAL PRINCIPLES

A pandemic provokes fear and uncertainty. This confusion was exacerbated by inconsistent admonitions of how a believer is to respond to governmental authority. Some claimed that to act in love, believers should be at the head of the line to get vaccinated (Matthew 22:39). Others claimed that being vaccinated was required to be in obedience

---

11 https://countercurrents.org/2023/12/letter-from-india-stop-world-health-organizations-pandemic-preparedness-treaty/
12 https://www.cramer.senate.gov/news/press-releases/sen-cramer-colleagues-introduce-resolution-to-help-prevent-president-biden-from-ceding-us-sovereignty-to-world-health-organization
13 https://www.congress.gov/bill/118th-congress/house-bill/6645
14 https://www.congress.gov/bill/118th-congress/senate-bill/3428/all-actions

to authority as Romans 13:1-2 commands. I have friends who embraced both these positions, and I respect their views.

But consider that Romans 13:1 expresses a complex principle in just five Greek words. Literally translated: Πᾶσα ψυχὴ ἐξουσίαις ὑπερεχούσαις ὑποτασσέσθω. "Let every soul to the authority's hyper-authority be subject."

Ultimate authority rests with Christ. Lesser authorities include a chain of human authority. This verse clarifies that it is not sufficient to just be subject to the words of a government leader. We must look to that authority's authority. In the United States, authority is subject to state and federal laws. The supreme of these laws is the US Constitution.[15] If the Constitution contradicts Christ, we must obey Christ. But if not, and an executive order or law contradicts the Constitution, then we must obey the Constitution. This is not discretionary. Rather it is our obligation as followers of Christ to follow what He commands through His Word (Acts 5:29).

Fortunately, in the US, our First Amendment guarantees us the right to peaceably assemble and exercise our religion.[16] Any order that violates that law is itself invalid. The Constitution is the earthly authority's hyper-authority, while the Word of God is the ultimate authority.

Scripture commands us not to neglect gathering together as has been the habit of some (Hebrews 10:23). Since Scripture is clear, then, we owe no deference to a mayor or governor who would dissuade us from obeying God.

---

15 Article VI "This Constitution ... shall be the supreme law of the land ..."
16 Amendment 1 Congress shall make no law respecting an establishment of religion, or prohibiting the free exercise thereof; or abridging the freedom of speech, or of the press; or the right of the people peaceably to assemble, and to petition the Government for a redress of grievances.

CHAPTER 40

"NON-ESSENTIAL" CHURCHES: KNOWING WHAT IS ESSENTIAL

In 2003 and again in 2007, the San Diego area was devastated by two major wildfires. Both times, tens of thousands of people were evacuated from their residences, not knowing if they would return to a home that was still intact or not. With little warning, people in many cases had to decide within minutes what was "essential" to take with them.

In the 2003 Cedar Fire, which eventually burned 2,800 homes, our family was one of those who was told to evacuate. What does one take in the few moments you have to prepare to leave? The most precious was family, then pets, then official documents, then prescription drugs, then family photos, then anything that was so precious that we couldn't bear leaving them to possibly burn up. Although anything left behind could end up being lost, whatever it was, it could hopefully be replaced.

KNOWING WHAT IS ESSENTIAL

I tell you about that harrowing event because it relates to what is "essential" and "non-essential."[1] Whatever was essential had high value: it was something dear, it had meaning, or was an essential part of life. Non-essentials would be missed, but they could also be replaced.

THE GOVERNMENT'S VIEW OF "ESSENTIAL"

COVID-19 was not a fire, but it swept through our communities with a different type of destructive impact. We cannot—and do not—take lightly the fact that many people became ill with the virus and its various strains, and that many people died. (I lost a handful of friends and acquaintances myself.) We are not insensitive to that very painful reality. Within these pages, however, my focus is on the human rights side of the pandemic discussion, rather than on the effects it had on friends and loved ones and their health.

On the civic/personal freedoms side of the coin, businesses were closed, as were schools, outdoor activities, restaurants, malls, parks, and a myriad of other activities. Groupings or meetings of people were forbidden, with neighbors encouraged to turn other neighbors in if there were too many people visiting at one time. Not only were the restrictions draconian (including personal requirements to socially distance, wear face masks, and limit leaving our homes), but the *government* defined what was either "essential" or "non-essential" in order to maintain a minimal level of needed services to its citizens.

Businesses that were essential were allowed to conduct business (although with restrictions), while non-essential ones had to shut

---

1 Significant portions of this chapter are excerpts from an unpublished biblical politics article entitled "Enough is Enough!" by Frank Kacer (who is the assisting author on this book), August 20, 2020; used with permission of the author.

down. Not to belabor the point, but: marijuana dispensaries, liquor stores, abortion providers, hospitals, and even golf courses and mass protests (of the "politically correct" type) were called essential.

But here is the kicker: *Churches fell into the "non-essential" category and were prohibited from gathering for worship or any other activity.*

If there was any nonconformance, churches could be subjected to contact tracing, fines, loss of power and water, forced closure, and possibly even prison time. Many of my pastor friends were threatened with fines and prison time. When churches were eventually allowed to gather, it was only if very strict protocols were followed (outdoors, social distancing, face masks, no singing, etc.).

OUR MOST PRECIOUS FREEDOM

The First Amendment to the US Constitution says, "Congress shall make no law respecting an establishment of religion, or prohibiting the free exercise thereof." "Free exercise" includes all matters of faith (doctrine), ecclesiology (organization), and practice (worship, ministry in and to our community, etc.). With such a clear protection of religious freedoms, it would seem any curtailing of religious "free exercise" must be exceptionally rare, limited in scope, only temporary, and with overwhelming justification.

Government and the church are subject to the God that created them (Colossians 1:15-17). Each is to benefit the other (Matthew 5:13-16; Romans 13:1-5), and neither has dictatorial powers over the other. However, constitutionally, government cannot dictate spiritual matters and is not allowed to control churches like they do secular businesses. When they do shut down churches, government is effectively relegating spiritual health to the status of a hobby that can wait until a more convenient time. This attitude belies a worldview that is at its core profoundly ignorant of spiritual matters (1 Corinthians 2:14).

OBEDIENCE TO GOVERNMENT

Christians are not to disobey government (Romans 13:1-5; 1 Peter 2:13), unless. ... What is the "unless?" Unless specifically ordered by government to disobey God, i.e., to stop proclaiming the Gospel (Acts 4:19-20, 5:29).

Biblically, government is intended for our good. But there is a problem: The government is always good. Therefore, when its actions run counter to that purpose, the legitimacy of governmental actions can and must be challenged.

Consider the Gospel specifically. It is proclaimed in more ways than preaching. It is proclaimed in the Lord's Supper as God's people gather together to receive it. The bread and cup are a visual and participatory reminder of the Gospel and Christ's redemptive work on the cross (1 Corinthians 11:26). Prohibiting people from gathering together for this ordinance is a direct prohibition of one of God's clearest means of grace to His people.

Consider weddings, funerals, baptisms, and gathering to study God's Word. Each is an intimate, profoundly spiritual event with the body of Christ assembled together with the Gospel central to everything. Any government-imposed limitation on the number present (even with social distancing) only serves to limit the blessings that God intends for us all, and denies the opportunity of the Gospel being preached to those who are most in need of hearing it.

And, the clearest command we have is to routinely gather together in worship (Hebrews 10:24-25). Emergencies—severe natural and manmade disasters—may override this obligation for a very short time, but God commands the entire assembly to meet together to be edified and encouraged (1 Thessalonians 5:11), to hear the Word of God and the Gospel proclaimed (Acts 2:42), and to spiritually minister to each other and comfort each other through prayer (Matthew 18:19-20) and fellowship.

Physical health is important, but spiritual health is just as—or even more—important. If COVID-19 closures taught us anything, it was that physical and emotional harm comes when people's social and spiritual needs are not met. Pastors, not the government, should be in the role of determining how to best minister to the physical, emotional, and spiritual needs of the flock, using the best information available.

STAND FIRM

By seeing churches as nonessential, government is the one that is disobeying the law of the land when it prohibits the faith community from freely exercising their constitutionally protected rights to worship and pursue ministry together. When government requires the people of God to forsake biblical imperatives to worship together, participation in the Lord's Supper together, and to freely fulfill all the other spiritual disciplines meant to build up the body of Christ while living out the Gospel, who is really the disobedient one?

If we value the religious freedoms our nation was literally created to protect, unnecessary government overreach must be resisted with all the moral, ethical, and legal means available to us. When government reserves the right to shut down churches by treating them as nonessential during any declared emergency (except in extreme and temporary cases, as mentioned above), then government is the one that is disobeying the law of the land (our Constitution).

Any non-trivial impact on the Gospel must be rejected (1 Peter 5:8-9), whether someone thinks that rejection amounts to civil disobedience or not. If government is blindly obeyed, it will only make government more emboldened to do more damage to our spiritual health and Gospel proclamation when the next government-defined emergency comes along.

CHAPTER 41

BIG PHARMA

The focus of this chapter is not to examine Big Pharma in the present tense until a few statements are made at the end. Instead, the focus will be on the events of 100 years ago, which moved the world away from what were called "natural remedies" and an emphasis on working with the human body to help it heal itself.

MODERN MEDICINE

All of us are thankful we live in communities with doctors and hospitals. Many of us have experienced successful surgeries, which made us exceptionally thankful we live after the time of the discovery of anesthesia. That is the good news.

But a look at the medical establishment today is not all positive. There are problems. As stated elsewhere, the rise of COVID resulted in an enormous loss of trust, with one of the targets of mistrust being doctors who insisted on treatment that people did not want. However, far more distrust developed toward pharmaceutical companies, which cannot be held liable for any negative impact of their so-called "vaccines."

DISCLAIMER

What follows is not a "hit piece" on all medicines or on all medical practices. I have benefitted and will continue to benefit from the wonderful doctors I visit, as well as medicines that have helped me. In addition, my family has been involved in the medical community. My sister is a nurse, and my brother is a medical doctor. Two of my late cousins in our small rural town were doctors, as well as another young cousin who is now in that town. They, along with the many doctors I have gone to over the years, are and have been models of compassion and competence. I praise God for them.

However, there is an unpleasant "dark side" to the medical industry.

UNHEALTHY

Our national medical "report card" is not good. The United States is the least healthy major country in the world.[1] We are the most heavily medicated, most chronically ill,[2] and among the most heavily vaccinated[3] and expensively treated country[4] in the world. We are 47th in life expectancy.

The trend is global: the more "conventional" medicine (also known as "allopathic medicine") a country uses, the worse its health and life expectancy. Although it is shocking to ask this question, we must do so: Could it be possible that the correlation is by design? And if so, how

---

1 Chart: The Healthiest (& Unhealthiest) Countries in the World I Statista
2 Chronic Diseases in America I CDC
3 Understanding Vaccination Progress by Country—Johns Hopkins Coronavirus Resource Center (jhu.edu)
4 Current health expenditure (% of GDP) I Data (worldbank.org)

should we view Big Pharma? Put another way, if a large piece of conventional medicine is the prescription and use of pharmaceutical drugs, doesn't it seem logical that Big Pharma benefits from our conventional medical approach?

THE KEY FIGURE: ROCKEFELLER

Dr. Rima Laibow, a graduate of the Albert Einstein School of Medicine in New York City, has practiced natural medicine for 54 years. I asked Dr. Laibow to give me a historical overview of the pharmaceutical industry to help me understand why the phrase "Big Pharma" has come to be such a negative phrase in our culture. What you are reading below is an overview from her. (Ordinarily, I would probably paraphrase such a long passage, but in this case, I decided to allow her forceful words to stand for themselves.) Allow me to warn you: the next few paragraphs are terse and aphoristic. Fasten your seat belt. Here are her unvarnished words:

> Conventional medicine, a marketing term employed to normalize chemical interventions in health profiting the owners of the chemical (i.e., pharmaceutical) companies and their distributors (aka, "doctors") was a minor branch of medicine until John D. Rockefeller, Sr., the richest man in the world, became the controlling partner in most of the world's pharmaceutical companies and set out to create a global distribution system.
>
> Using the same ruthless techniques with which he drove almost all competitors out of the oil business (e.g., buying up the entire barrel supply so competitors could not ship their oil to market, monopolizing railroad cars for the same purpose, setting fire to the tents of striking workers in Ludlow, CO, and killing their families in the night to break the

strike,[5] etc.), Rockefeller determined to destroy all competitors in the medical industry as well.

A staunch and active eugenics visionary, he brought together the globally toxic mixture of totally unprincipled business practices, a totally unscrupulous disregard for the well-being of his customers, an absolute dedication to profit generation, a keen sense of the power of relentless marketing, a firm conviction in the absolute moral justification of elimination of the unfit, the unwanted, the unproductive, and the excess members of society, and a futurist's visionary capacity to imagine an alternative world with the largest fortune ever amassed in human history.[6]

He set himself the challenge of totally remaking the world to his liking. And his liking included a world consisting of masters, then called "Fabian Socialists,"[7] now called globalists[8] and the necessary number of compliant serfs.[9]

Strong words. But Rockefeller's impact on the pharmaceutical industry was profound.

Dr. Laibow explained that the industrialist was not alone. He recruited a sort of "Who's Who" of wealthy people: Andrew Carnegie, Cornelius Vanderbilt, and others (much like Bill Gates' billionaire's "Good Club").[10] And there were others of questionable reputation: Alfred Kinsey, Margaret Sanger, and John Dewey, just to name a few.[11]

---

5 The Ludlow Massacre | American Experience | Official Site | PBS

6 In 1913, John D. Rockefeller's personal wealth was equal to 10% of US GDP. He is widely recognized as the first billionaire in human history.

7 Fabian Society | British Socialist Society | Britannica

8 Understanding The Tactics of Subversive Globalism & The Fabian Agenda—Europe Reloaded

9 Document sent to me, written by Dr. Rima Laibow, on December 27, 2023, which forms the basis for the first portion of this chapter.

10 "Billionaires Try to Shrink World's Population": Secret Gathering Sponsored by Bill Gates, 2009 Meeting of "The Good Club"—Global ResearchGlobal Research—Centre for Research on Globalization

11 Much of the early portions of the chapter come from the Laibow document.

At the same time, an organic chemistry revolution was taking place in Germany which resulted in the creation of new compounds marketed as pharmaceuticals. Residue from the massive amount of oil processing that Rockefeller controlled provided a rich source of hydrocarbon mixtures that could be used in the synthesis of these new compounds. Not surprisingly, Rockefeller bought the controlling interest in the entire German pharmaceutical industry. He then turned his attention to marketing and selling these new drugs.

THE SEISMIC SHIFT IN MEDICINE

It may seem strange to us now that at the dawn of the 20th century, most of the licensed medical practitioners avoided using pharmaceuticals. They instead used natural means of treatment. Dr. Laibow pointed out that ironically, Rockefeller himself avoided these drugs, preferring homeopathy and herbal remedies. Perhaps they worked well for him, given the fact that he lived to be 97.[12]

It is at this point that—to borrow a phrase—things start to go south. In order to sell his new drugs, Rockefeller needed to discredit all medical practitioners who did not use these new discoveries. It was important that he get the public to dismiss them as quacks and scam artists.

FOLLOW THE MONEY

It is quite amazing what dollars can do. Rockefeller set up institutes and institutions to promote his products. Here is a partial list of organizations where his "thumbprint" was felt: Eugenics Research Institute, Cold Spring Harbor Institute, the Kaiser Wilhelm Institutes (Munich, Berlin), Planned Parenthood,

12 Rima Laibow, MD, Medical Director, Natural Solutions Foundation, emailed document, December 27, 2023, titled "How – and Why - Rockefeller, Carnegie and Flexner Poisoned Humanity," page 3.

Rockefeller Institute, the Council on Foreign Relations, and other organizations, including the precursor organizations to the World Health Organization and the UN.

At this point, let's allow Dr. Rima Laibow's forceful and blunt words tell the story of Rockefeller's massive funding capabilities:

> Driving all non-pharmaceutical doctors out of the market was an essential task to clear the way for marketing drugs. To do so Rockefeller donated $1 Million US to each state in the union to encourage it to criminalize any sort of medical practice but allopathic, another $1M to each state to set up a medical board to license only allopathic doctors, an additional $1M to each state's land grant college to set up an allopathic medical school and another $1M each to Harvard, Yale, Johns Hopkins and Stanford universities to establish an elite tier of physicians. The small and previously unimportant American Medical Association also received $1Million to build up their power, prestige and visibility.

But there was more. Biologist Abraham Flexner went to every one of the 155 medical schools in the US and proclaimed all to be unnecessary, unscientific, and dangerous—except for those schools that embraced the allopathic model of medicine.

The Flexner Report[13] became the definitive guide to modern health and science. Non-conforming schools were closed. Licenses for non-allopathic doctors were revoked, and practitioners who continued to ply their arts came under threat of jail terms.

---

13 Flexner A. Medical Education in the United States and Canada: A Report To the Carnegie Foundation For the Advancement of Teaching. New York, NY, USA: The Carnegie Foundation for the Advancement of Teaching; 1910.

THE RESULT

Naturopaths, homeopaths, herbalists (known as "eclectics"), osteopaths, chiropractors, energy healers, electromedicine practitioners, acupuncturists, and the manufacturers of their tools and devices were systematically, ruthlessly, and unscientifically silenced.

Those who have battled cancer know all too well the number of options that are not allowed in this country. While unscrupulous scams should not be allowed—and scams most certainly do exist—it is unfortunate that more "natural healing" means have been so frowned upon for far too long.

Thankfully, the efficacy and excellence of many of these natural-based forms of medicine are being re-discovered and re-embraced—more than a century after being subjected to a historic smear campaign.

THE FDA

Entering into the fray was the "long arm" of the government through bureaucratic agencies such as the Food and Drug Administration. Rockefeller supported this, and it now brought a regulatory structure to reinforce the products he offered. Originally it was called the Division of Chemistry, but after 1906 was known as the Food, Drug, and Insecticide Administration. In July 1930, the name was shortened to its present form.[14]

ALLIANCE

It is at this point that an alliance was established between the regulators and the supposedly regulated pharmaceutical industry. In reality, this relationship was then, and is now, much too cozy. And that provides us with the opportunity to jump from then to now.

---

14 https://www.fda.gov/about-fda/changes-science-law-and-regulatory-authorities/fdas-origin

PRESENT TENSE

Fast-forward from the days of Rockefeller's titanic influence on the pharmaceutical industry to today, as many fresh questions continue to arise. The government-Big Pharma alliance proved to be a disaster in the outbreak of COVID. Here are only a few of the many horrific policies of that era:

- The government gave pharmaceutical companies immunity. *They were not and still are not held responsible for inferior or toxic products.* That is shocking. They made billions of dollars, and yet they are not held responsible for harm done.
- The vaccine was pushed through the process rapidly.
- The vaccine was mandated and forced on people who could not afford to lose their jobs. Most offensive was the fact that military personnel who did not want "the jab" were discharged, losing their pensions.
- When people wrote religious objections, they were almost always declined.
- Dr. Tony Fauci's dictatorial lockdowns, coercive mask mandates, and jabs did not set well with people who had enjoyed medical freedom. In fact, medical freedom was lost in America.
- The most offensive policy was the rule stating that hospitalized COVID patients could not have visitors. I know. I was one of them. Before having COVID, I had jokingly said to my children, "If I get COVID and go the hospital, do what you have to do—break in, if needed—and come see me!" Well, I did get COVID, wound up in the hospital and, sure enough, they could not come see me. But it is not about me. There were thousands and thousands of elderly people who were forced into solitary confinement as they lay dying, at the

moment they most needed their family. This medical policy was inexcusable and cruel.

- Ivermectin and hydroxychloroquine were considered anathema. Doctors who prescribed these drugs were punished. Patients who tried to get them were shamed. Not until long after COVID was over did authorities admit that Ivermectin could, in fact, help patients.

- Doctors who dared challenge the government-Big Pharma cabal paid dearly. They were shunned, shamed, fined, and at times fired. Their lives and their livelihoods were, in some cases, destroyed.

- The government-medical cabal (Fauci included) encouraged people to "report" their neighbors if anyone tried to gather for a holiday, birthday, or any family gathering.

In addition, there are some key issues that must be pursued.

First, almost no reporting is being done of the fact that actuarial tables have changed radically in the last couple years, with an inexplicable spike in deaths, particularly among those ages 18-29, especially young males. Could these mysterious deaths be linked to the vaccines these young men received?

Second, full disclosure needs to be made of the total amount of Big Pharma dollars that are flowing to any and all elected or governmental officials. We would be better served by preventative measures, which would help the American public not need the drugs which Big Pharma manufactures.

PERSONAL STORY

This chapter is not something abstract with me. It is deeply personal. In 2007 when my wife Carol was diagnosed with a form of cancer for which there is no known cure, I searched far and wide. We did not reject standard Western medicine (conventional treatment), but we also sought advice from a strong follower of Jesus originally from China, who practices Eastern medicine. (I am not referring here to New Age practices.) He was very helpful for us.

When a family member is diagnosed with cancer, one's inbox is flooded with suggestions from well-meaning people. I received and saved in my computer some 500 or so alleged "cures" for cancer, most of them totally bogus. However, I found a treatment in Mexico, which was not allowed in the US. My method for discerning what was good from bad was to first know the integrity of the doctors. The doctors in this Tijuana clinic were godly and trustworthy friends, in whom I had 100% confidence. After the issue of integrity is the issue of competence. The Oasis of Hope Hospital in Mexico had a survivability rate almost double the American treatment protocols.

My wife's oncologist strongly urged us not to go there. I asked him, "Why?" to which he responded, "The unknown." I responded, "Their unknown is not any worse than your 'known,'" based on what he had told me. We went to the Tijuana clinic.

Months later, our American oncologist saw my wife and was shocked at her improvement. Years later, when my wife's body finally did succumb to the cancer, one of her oncologists said, "With no scientific background, you somehow landed on a protocol that likely turned two years into six." In other words, her life had been extended by another four very precious years. Carol died in 2013.

THE BIBLE AND OUR HEALTH

I tell this story with an awareness of all the wonderful things about American hospitals, doctors, and medicines—and there are many, for which I am so grateful. But there are problems. The very fact that we had to go to Mexico for this well-researched treatment is not only because of the hyper protectionism of our government, but is also, in part, due to the massive lobbying power of Big Pharma. To solve the problem, we must take the scales off our eyes, hold Big Pharma accountable in the courts of both man and God and cast down the idols they have erected for us in the temples of our bodies and our minds, returning to, as much as is possible, natural, wholesome foods and healing arts to routinely keep the body as healthy as possible and prevent disease to begin with. Although our bodies are temporary on this earth, they are, according to the Apostle Paul, "temples of the Holy Spirit" (1 Corinthians 6:19). They need to be treated with respect.

And God has stated that the "leaves of the trees provide healing" (Ezekiel 47:12; Revelation 22:2). Had I not been exposed to Eastern medicine through my Christian friend from China, I would have had no idea what verses like this could possibly mean. One might legitimately wonder if access to the Tree of Life (Genesis 2:9) in the Garden of Eden wasn't some veiled reference to healing by herbs and leaves. Clearly that and the other trees mentioned in Genesis 2:9 provided healthy nutrition.

Substances that impact a person's health positively can be used as legitimate medicines, given that things were created by God for good (1 Timothy 4:4). 1 Timothy 5:23 also addresses the validity and occasional need of medicinal items. Most interesting, however, is the word *pharmakeia*, the Greek word for "pharmacy" which appears several times in the New Testament (Galatians 5:20 and Revelation 9:21; 18:23; 21:8 and 22:15). It is not a positive term as it refers to "sorcery" or "witchcraft."[15] While recognizing the value of some or much of modern-day medicine, it is absolutely imperative to be spiritually alert to the great harm that can be done to one's body by so-called modern medicine or pharmaceuticals.

While there are many altruistic and compassionate people within the pharmaceutical industry, as a general rule Big Pharma is not always your friend and does not care about you. In the New Testament is a story of a woman who had been sick for 12 years. Matthew (9:20-22) barely mentions it. The most reliable manuscripts of the Gospel of

---

15 https://www.gotquestions.org/pharmakeia-in-the-Bible.html

Luke (8:43-48), a physician himself, indicate he likely omitted the fact that she had spent so much money on physicians. In contrast, Mark (5:25-32) mentions that she had spent everything she had on doctors. Tragically, the doctors of the day were often unscrupulous, taking advantage of those who were ill. It happened then, and it can happen now. I have been blessed that my family members and I have had compassionate and competent physicians. I thank God for them. But one does need to be extremely discerning.

Given the fact that you were "fearfully and wonderfully made,"[16] seek the guidance of the Holy Spirit on how God wants to bring healing to your body. "If any of you lacks wisdom, you should ask God, who gives generously to all without finding fault, and it will be given to you" (James 1:5).

---

16 Psalm 139:14.

CHAPTER 42

BIG TECH

I used a particular social media platform for years. I never had one single disagreement with them. Then they notified me that our group calls were using too much bandwidth for their free service. We entered into an elongated time of negotiations.

Just before I was ready to sign the contract to continue our service with them, which had extended over many years in the past, I said, "I believe that marriage is between one man and one woman. You won't cancel me, will you?" The salesman said, "So long as there is no misinformation." I stated, "But who determines what misinformation is?" The conversation continued with me saying, "I don't want any vaccine forced on me. Will you block or cancel me?" "No," he replied, "so long as there is no misinformation." Again, I asked, "But who determines what 'misinformation' is?"

That question was never answered. I did not press the issue because I had not experienced one single disagreement in the many years my videos had been hosted by their company. Thus, I signed the contract.

CANCELLED

The next day—the very next day!—they pulled down three of my video interviews, one of them stretching back to nine months prior. Their "fact-checkers" wrote that I was not stating the truth. I wrote back, "Let's get on a call together. You bring your 'fact-checkers' and I will bring my experts, and let's see who is telling the truth." They never responded except with threats to sue when we balked at making payment because of their immediate cancelling of my material as soon as we had a formal contract.

This story is only one of tens of thousands across America, whether it is something as simple as a 30-day "jail time" with Facebook or entire ministries being unceremoniously dumped by some Big Tech social media platform. Cueing off of President Eisenhower's warning regarding the "military-industrial complex," Dr. Robert Malone refers to it as the "censorship-industrial complex."[1]

THE SPEED AND BREADTH OF COMMUNICATION

Whether it's good or bad, social media has become a global public square. Gigantic communication technology companies allow virtually anyone, anywhere, to communicate with anyone, anywhere. Not only that, but in a matter of seconds, influencers can charm millions of people, make people laugh, organize a mob, or spread lies. Anyone at any time can fall prey to 15 minutes of fame or have their reputation mercilessly attacked with little to no ability to correct the record.

Ecclesiastes 1:9-10 says that there is nothing new under the sun. As far as matters of the heart and the mouth (or rather text or You-Tube or whatever) are concerned, this has always been true. In the book of James, the tongue is said to be incredibly destructive, just like a small spark can set an entire forest ablaze (James 3:5). Social

---

1 Robert Malone "Who Is Robert Malone" emailed newsletter, "Citizen Journalism as Disruptive Technology," March 20, 2024,   https://substack.com.

media is the same, with the only difference being a matter of speed and the size of the audience. With communication technology, the reverse can also happen: a message or an idea or an opinion can be prevented from getting out to others, and often in ways that are not easily identified.

BIAS

Communication technology companies claim that they only enforce well-accepted content policies and that they do so impartially. If that's true, why has there been such a huge number of documented incidents that suggest a bias against Conservative political thought and Christian viewpoints? "Content moderation" sounds like a reasonable, balanced process to maybe ensure some level of civility between people or groups, but it really comes down to a communication company deciding what messages (and whose messages) they are willing to allow on their platforms.

If there really was an "impartial" judgment being made, why are virtually no progressive organizations screaming to be reinstated?

THE BIG GUYS

Big Tech companies such as Facebook, Amazon, Netflix, X (formerly Twitter), and Google have justified content moderation policies to maintain a "safe and inclusive" online environment. These policies claim to be absolutely necessary to curb hate speech, misinformation, and incitements of violence.

However, every one of those descriptive terms is "subject" to "subjective" implementation. One person's definition of inclusiveness is another person's example of perversion. One person's statement of fact is another person's trigger to becoming emotionally distraught. One person's sincere belief that young children should be sexualized at an early age is another person's nightmare.

Just a few decades ago, before our "anything goes" cultural and sexual explosion, it would have been easier to define some wider spread level of appreciation for decency and sexual appropriateness. But as many chapters in this book discuss, the times have changed, and norms (at least biblical ones) are becoming far less influential or tolerated in the wider culture. The bottom line is that the majority belief in Judeo-Christian values has seemingly become the minority.

With most Big Tech communications companies owned or run by progressives, it shouldn't surprise anyone that ideas or facts or biblical truths that challenge and contradict current, woke ideology would not be well received. More explicitly, conservative political viewpoints and Judeo-Christian beliefs, speech, values, and traditions concerning socio-economic issues are often seen as backward, discriminatory, hateful, and even evil. Sound familiar? The prophet Isaiah had strong words for anyone who called evil good, and good evil (Isaiah 5:20).

It's one thing to turn off a TV station if you don't like the content; it's quite another when someone far from you turns your channel off if they unilaterally decide you shouldn't watch the program. And it's even more if they turn off the programming or content you have created. That is the equivalent of what is happening on social media platforms. The electronic public square is becoming an echo chamber of worldviews that are anathema to a biblical one. And with that warning from Isaiah fresh in our thoughts, such evil is being justified with noble-sounding intent to prevent others from being harmed by "wrong thinking."

This reminds me of when the Apostle Paul spoke to the Roman procurator of Judea, Antonius Felix, and told him about "righteousness and self-control and the coming judgment;" Felix became alarmed and sent him away. Simply stated, Paul was "cancelled" (Acts 24:24-25). Things haven't really changed.

THE WAYS AND MEANS

My friends Gabe Joseph and Aaron Manaigo, both from Washington, DC, have been patient teachers for me regarding what is actually happening. They noted that Big Tech doesn't make it obvious what they are doing, unless they are publicly called out for some egregious error. But some of the more common techniques that are used include:

- **Algorithmic Bias:** Algorithms play a crucial role in content curation and distribution, but they lack human nuance in application. There are widespread reports of algorithmic content recommendation systems favoring liberal/progressive, secular, or non-Christian viewpoints over conservative thought leadership and traditional religious belief systems. The result: severe limitation foisted upon conservative and/or Christian content and its visibility.
- **Deplatforming:** This refers to the removal or restriction of a user or group's access to a digital platform. Several high-profile conservative and/or Christian cases have highlighted deplatforming as their content was removed or accounts suspended for allegedly violating a respective social media platform's community guidelines. Although legal (per the terms of service of the platforms), it appears to be a biased suppression of both political and religious free speech.
- **Shadow Banning:** This technique limits or blocks the visibility of a user's content without their knowledge. When conservatives and/or Christians are shadow-banned, it leads to reduced engagement and reach for their posts. While platforms deny these practices, the lack of transparency with the algorithms used makes it difficult to prove that this isn't indeed happening.

- **Labeling and Fact-Checking:** Certain posts containing conservative and/or Christian viewpoints have been labeled as "potentially false" or accompanied by fact-checking warning labels. Concerns arise when political or religious beliefs are labeled as misleading or inaccurate or lacking context, all of which are potentially stifling to any level of open dialogue. While in theory fact-checking is crucial to keeping the very bad actors in check, it brings to mind the old saying: who is watching the watchers?
- **Inconsistent Enforcement:** Critics argue that content moderation policies are not applied consistently across different political and religious viewpoints. Some claim that while platforms swiftly respond to reports about conservative and/or Christian content, they might be less proactive in addressing similar concerns with non-conservative groups or secular content.

THE NEED FOR EXAMINATION

Big Tech companies see themselves as tasked with an immense challenge—maintaining a platform where diverse voices coexist while adhering to evolving standards of content moderation. This makes it challenging to develop algorithms that consistently distinguish between genuine expression, deep beliefs, and what some may perceive as harmful rhetoric or "triggering."

Big Tech is trying to regulate something that is impossible for it to understand: biblical spirituality. In fact, 1 Corinthians 2:14 tells us the natural man (or woman) cannot understand spiritual matters, so it's no wonder there is a natural tendency to reject what Christians stand for and the values Christians espouse. Big Tech has made it very difficult for us to exercise our constitutional right to express ourselves without fear of persecution.

So, how does a tech company safeguard its platforms against hate speech and balance a user's rights to express their political and religious beliefs? There's no easy answer. Look at the triggering promised in 2 Corinthians 2:15-16 when the Gospel is presented: "For we are to God the pleasing aroma of Christ among those who are being saved and those who are perishing. To the one we are an aroma that brings death; to the other, an aroma that brings life." What does a social media platform do with those who hold to distinctively Christian values? Whose values morally contradict those of the media platform?

Part of an answer is demanding that social media companies recognize that they are incapable of being objective and that they need to openly seek the advice of those with opposing political and spiritual views, as well as legal scholars to provide insights into constitutional rights. Some practical steps would also include:

- **Transparency:** How do content moderation algorithms actually work? Transparency can help users understand how their content is treated and reduce misconceptions about censorship.
- **User Consultation:** Platforms can engage in open conversations with political and religious communities to better understand their concerns and generate more accurate policies that respect a diversity of beliefs.
- **Appeals Process:** Establishing a robust and transparent appeals process for content removal or reestablishment with a redress mechanism to contest platform utilization decisions.
- **Algorithmic Improvements:** Continuous refinement of algorithms to demonstrably reduce biases and improve context detection.

COMPETITION NEEDED

Unless and until people who write and implement decision algorithms (or corporate platform policy) recognize their conscious and unconscious biases, nothing will change. But in our capitalist nation, the option still remains to create competing platforms and support their use. Without rigorous competition, the incentive for existing companies to reform themselves may never happen.

CHAPTER 43

BIG AG, AGRARIANISM, FOOD SECURITY, AND THE FOOD CHAIN

S hould we be concerned about the food chain? While sources vary, it is generally believed that the average distance food travels from farm to table is around 1,500 miles. Thus, you need to not only thank the farmer who grew your food, but you need to thank the trucker who gets the food to you, thus keeping you from starvation. But considering that distance, ponder how little disruption it would take to cause grocery store shelves to go empty.

SO MUCH, YET SO LITTLE

When one looks around at the abundance of food in our supermarkets, it's disheartening to realize how much of it is lacking in basic nutritional value. We've advanced a long way in food production, but what have we given up by allowing agribusiness to become so huge, and government control so extensive?

Joel Salatin, who is "America's most celebrated pioneer of chemical-free farming," according to the *Guardian*,[1] weighed in on modern farming, asking the question whether or not God cares if soil erodes. Salatin noted that the land is God's. He continued his questioning, asking how you would feel if you were God and someone trashed the land that you had made, as humans have.

THE BEGINNING OF FARMING

Think back to Genesis. God's entire creation was "very good" in the beginning (Genesis 1:31). God created this world and commanded Adam and Eve to care for it, saying, "Be fruitful and multiply and fill the earth and subdue it and have dominion" (Genesis 1:28, ESV). The word "subdue" in Hebrew carries the thought of firmness rather than harshness, like a shepherd traveling with his flock.[2] Like when parents give their children responsibilities so that they can mature, God gave Adam and Eve and their descendants stewardship responsibility to care for, cultivate, and develop the land that provides for our food and a place of shelter, for the benefit of future generations. Land stewardship, and specifically ownership by families, was the pattern implied from the very beginning.

VALUING THE SOIL

The biblical narrative reinforces the concept that the soil was to be valued and cared for by families. Israelite families were given charge over the land, to care for it and pass it on to the next generation. When King Ahab of Samaria (1 Kings 21:2) treated Naboth's land as simply something for the taking, he violated Naboth's covenantal heritage and responsibilities to the next generation (1 Kings 21:3).

---

1 https://www.theguardian.com/lifeandstyle/2010/jan/31/food-industry-environment
2 Ludwig Koehler and Walter Baumgarner, "The Hebrew and Aramaic Lexicon of the Old Testament," vol 2 (Leiden: Brill, 2001), p. 1190.

Have you ever considered the number of times the Bible refers to "the land?" God loves the land. He created it. He designated His People to have from the Euphrates River to the Nile River, some 300,000 square miles, although Israel only has about 8,000 square miles presently. (See Chapter 32 for more about Israel and the land.) The Father values the land so much that He even declares on what piece of Earth to which His Son Jesus is returning. God has a special place in his heart for "the land." He made it, and someday He is making a "new Earth." One graduate student studied Virginia farmer Joel Salatin's passion for the soil and wrote a master's thesis with one section titled "Christianizing the Land."[3]

However, the passion for the land long predates Christianity. We have the Jews to thank for giving us a broader understanding of the value of the land, as is taught in the Tanakh (Old Testament). To be clear, this is not simply a love of creation. This is a reverence for creation because it was made by a divine Creator. It is an extension of one's love of God Himself. If you love Him, you will love what He made, and steward it carefully—meaning we are charged to watch over that which is not ours, on behalf of another. It might be well to remember that *adam* in Hebrew means "red earth," from which humankind was made.

The growth of the political and social philosophy referred to as agrarianism reflects the historical link between stewardship of land being tied to heritage with an emphasis on promoting subsistence agriculture, small holdings, and supporting the rights and sustainability of small farmers against the wealthy in society.[4] This movement takes seriously the words of Isaiah 5:8 (ESV) where God warns the people of Israel: "Woe to those who join house to house, who add field to field, until there is no more room, and you are made to dwell alone in the midst of the land." What is being described here is the

---

3 https://citeseerx.ist.psu.edu/document?repid=rep1&type=pdf&doi=56bed24200b0b556 460aebc6ef20d9020cb32a43—Pages 24-27
4 https://en.wikipedia.org/wiki/Agrarianism

accumulation of land and wealth to the detriment of the people who should be owning and working that land.

Wendell Berry, an agrarian and poet, aptly summarized the link between stewardship of land and heritage by saying, "Agrarians value land ... If you have no land, you have nothing: no food, no shelter, no warmth, no freedom, no life. ... People who have been landless know that the land is invaluable; it is worth everything."[5]

CONTROL OF THE LAND

Today land is often viewed simply as a commodity, with large agribusiness factory farming replacing small, family farms. These large-scale operations—at least in those cases where they lack the deeply embedded, multigenerational love for the farmland—deplete the soil of her most valuable natural commodities: minerals, trace nutrients, and mycorrhizae fungus activity, and replace these essentials with chemical supplementation.

In the three-plus years I have been co-hosting interviews on the World Prayer Network, one of the most amazing discussions was with a farmer in the Netherlands where the government is demanding to take the land from the farmers. In fact, the Dutch government has insisted that due to greenhouse gases, cowherds must be dramatically reduced. The government of the Netherlands has demonstrated egregious overreach, destroying the livelihoods of those in agriculture, not respecting their deep attachment to the land.

But what started in the Netherlands did not stay in the Netherlands. A massive farmers' protest swept across all of Europe, impacting many nations, including Germany, Belgium, France, Italy, Greece, Poland, Romania, Lithuania,[6] as well as to Canada.[7] Although issues vary from

---

5 Wendell Berry, "The Agrarian Standard" in Wirzba, Essential Agrarian Reader, 28-29.
6 https://www.politico.eu/article/farmer-protest-europe-map-france-siege-paris-germany-poland/
7 https://ca.news.yahoo.com/quebec-farmers-protest-block-roads-022851945.html

country to country, government overregulation, imports, prices, taxes, nitrogen regulations, and general governmental incompetence and mismanagement would be causative factors in most countries.

Almost 100 years ago, in 1932-1933, a man-made famine was created by Josef Stalin when he insisted on the collectivization and control of agriculture. The Ukrainian word is *Holodomor,* meaning "murder by starvation."[8] This loss of private ownership and imposition of direct governmental oversight to pursue ideological dreams eventually led to the deaths of 3.9 million Ukrainians.

Is what is happening in the Netherlands just an anomaly? No. As noted, it is occurring in many countries. In Ireland, for example, the government wants to reduce methane from belching cows, thus farmers have to vastly reduce their herds.[9] Behind the word "climate" is another "c" word: control.

Currently, the push to centralize control over farmland worldwide is being led by the World Economic Forum (WEF) and the United Nations (UN). The goal is to aggregate ownership of farming as much as possible to combat supposed global warming.[10] Former US Secretary of State John Kerry, President Biden's "climate czar," believes farms are significant emitters of greenhouse gases (carbon dioxide) and is pushing for the US federal government to crack down on farming in America in order to achieve net-zero emissions.[11]

Bill Gates has just bought up $1 billion worth of farmland.[12] There is no reason why Midwesterners should trust his motives, or those of other billionaires doing the same thing. China has bought up strategic

---

8 https://www.britannica.com/event/Holodomor

9 https://www.theguardian.com/world/2022/aug/29/irish-farmers-cull-cows-meet-climate-targets

10 https://thewashingtonstandard.com/un-world-economic-forum-behind-global-war-on-farmers/

11 https://www.msn.com/en-us/news/us/john-kerry-targets-agriculture-as-part-of-climate-crusade/ar-AA1b15ct?ocid=msedgntp&cvid=bf4cef0e55e94c7d8c5a6aabfc508b5c&ei=311

12 https://nypost.com/2023/11/14/news/bill-gates-buying-up-land-threatening-small-farms-under-guise-of-saving-planet-author-claims/

farmland, thus some states are attempting to prohibit yet more foreign ownership of America's farms.[13]

We all know that private property owners are best suited to protect and care for their own land. Not so, say the radical globalists. The 30 x 30 program is the name of a massive land grab, "an international agenda advanced by radical environmental activists to permanently protect (editor's read: "confiscate") 30 percent of the world's land and oceans in their natural state by 2030. The program in America was initiated by the Biden Administration through Executive Order 14008, 'Tackling the Climate Crisis at Home and Abroad' (86 Fed. Reg. 7,619), signed January 27, 2021."[14] To be clear, these globalists do not want just *any 30 percent* of the land. They want *the most productive* 30 percent of the land.

SMALL PRACTICAL STEPS

Given these realities, what can we do?

Return to Scripture. My friend, Doug Tjaden, says the key is understanding Genesis 2:15: "God established food production and stewardship of creation as the foundation of His economy, because without food, there is no Kingdom." Doug founded Regeneco to restore God's economy in local communities by first properly "cultivating and keeping" the land.[15]

We can all start by using our own home in agrarian ways. Warning: This is not easy, but it is fulfilling. Many of you can become your own mini-farmers. If you have a balcony, patio or even a tiny back yard you can personally be part of the creation mandate God gave us all to work and keep the land, or at least grow fruits or vegetables in

---

13 https://www.cnn.com/2023/06/19/politics/chinese-land-purchases/index.html

14 https://rwmalonemd.substack.com/p/from-sea-to-shining-sea-federal-land?utm_source=post-email-title&publication_id=583200&post_id=143429156&utm_campaign=email-post-title&isFreemail=true&r=2phskn&triedRedirect=true&utm_medium=email

15 Doug Tjaden, https://regeneco.org

a container of dirt. Yes, even that helps you fulfill Scripture: "And God said to them, '...fill the earth and subdue it and have dominion'" (Genesis 1:28).

It starts with simply planting a seed and nurturing it. Sprouting, micro greens, kitchen herbs on a windowsill, tomatoes in a pot or even the three sisters (squash, beans, and corn) planted in harmony[16] can all be done at home. Some can become creative with their limited space and learn to use lit or unlit tower gardens, or even planter boxes. The more adventuresome can learn to raise chickens in their backyards, using kitchen scraps for feed and then enjoying fresh eggs.

Second, you can even adopt your local small truck farm and patronize them. Eating their fresh produce at the *farm*acy will likely reduce your trips to the *pharm*acy.

Third, become sufficiently aware of what is happening in agriculture so you can add your voice to defend the family farm. I grew up on a wheat and corn farm in north central Kansas, where we also raised Yorkshire hogs and White-Faced Hereford steers. Farming is extremely hard work, but it is profoundly fulfilling. My father loved God deeply and was passionate about reading the Bible and worship. Yet he also understood the divine calling on his life to farm. He "romanced" farming. He farmed unto the glory of God.

My father taught me to love and respect the soil. We treated the soil with great respect by fallowing, crop rotation, building terraces and waterways, providing ground cover, and planting shelterbelts. Do not be concerned if you do not know what those terms mean. Just know that what I have expressed is how a farmer properly treats the earth, knowing that by wind and water erosion he can lose the precious topsoil.

To illustrate this, it is said that for centuries the Arab inhabitants of Israel abused the land in such a way that as much as fifteen feet of

---

16 https://www.almanac.com/content/three-sisters-corn-bean-and-squash

topsoil was washed away. That is a tragic loss, and it wasn't until the 1880s to 1930s[17] that the Jews were able to buy back large tracts of it.

The number of farmers is decreasing, particularly as farms grow larger, and as corporation farms take over massive swaths of land. During my lifetime, in the rural area where I grew up, many—actually most—of the farmsteads (houses and barns) have been bulldozed down as the remaining farmers had considerably larger acreages.

In addition, the average age of a farmer in America is 57.5.[18] This does not bode well for the future of America's family-based farms. Learn to defend the small family farm, which gives you the greatest food security possible.

As biblical stewards in our communities, we owe it to our local farmers and ranchers (land shepherds) to learn about their challenges in trying to grow and provide food. In many regions across the United States, laws designed to "protect" people actually crush small- to medium-sized farmers and promote large agribusiness.

LEGISLATION

There are, however, some encouraging pieces of legislation. Public Law 90-492 for poultry is a good example of agrarianism (Wholesome Poultry Products Act of 1957). This Act allows exemptions from USDA inspections for small farmers and has an impeccable record that has literally built the pastured poultry industry for thousands of farmers and their city patrons. Expanding this type of inspection exemption would help many other such small ranchers.

The PRIME Act (H.R. 2859/ S. 1620) is another piece of well-thought-out legislation that would allow ranchers and farmers to slaughter their livestock at local slaughterhouses instead of driving hours away to USDA-approved slaughterhouses, many of which were

---

17 https://en.wikipedia.org/wiki/Jewish_land_purchase_in_Palestine#:~:text=From%20 the%201880s%20to%20the,these%20areas%20were%20sparsely%20populated
18 https://fortune.com/2023/10/12/how-old-american-farmer-average-age-boomer-gen-x/

closed during the COVID-19 pandemic. If passed, the PRIME Act would relieve our nation's meat shortages, help small ranchers and farmers, and allow consumers to buy locally while maintaining a safe food supply.[19]

YOUR BODY: THE TEMPLE OF THE LORD

Healthy food is fundamental to how we care for our bodies and honor the Lord (1 Corinthians 6:19-20). Physically, we really are what we eat! One tangible way to support the continuation of healthy farming is to become knowledgeable about organic foods and the implications of consuming GMO and modified RNA foods, and then making purchases accordingly.

Be informed, take your own small steps at home and in what you purchase, and be vocal about supporting small farms as they fight to continue to fulfill God's design for land use.

---

19 https://ij.org/initiatives/food-freedom/prime-act/

CHAPTER 44

THE NATIONAL DEBT

n a sermon preached on July 4, 1794, pastor Joseph Lathrop of Massachusetts said:

> With a free people, the first object should be, to prevent a
> public debt. When one is incurred from necessity, the next
> object should be to extinguish it as soon as the abilities of
> the people will permit. Complete liberty and an immense
> debt are incompatible. A system that perpetuates the latter
> annihilates the former. Hence it follows, not only economy
> in government, but frugality among private citizens, is nec-
> essary to public liberty and happiness.[1]

That advice was followed for the first 150 years as the US balanced
its federal budget and only borrowed during times of war or national

---

1 https://wallbuilders.com/sermon-july-4th-1794/

emergency. And, when debt was unavoidable, the government would pay that debt down as quickly as possible.[2]

THE SEISMIC SHIFT

But then, a seismic shift occurred in our nation's finances, and our government adopted debt as an economic stimulus.

Hans F. Sennholz, former economics professor and president of the Foundation for Economic Education, explains, "The debacle of the Great Depression together with the sway of Keynesian economics gave rise to a new belief that, in periods of economic decline and stagnation, budgetary deficits could serve to stimulate economic activity." Nice in theory, if the debt is paid back. But Sennholz goes on to explain: "Instead, it invited politicians and government officials to engage in wasteful and self-interested expenditures; it not only sanctioned executive and bureaucratic profligacy but also encouraged congressional 'pork barreling.' In short, it bred huge budgetary deficits not only during recessions but also at other times."

This new Keynesian economic philosophy ignored the biblical principle that "the borrower is servant to the lender" (Proverbs 22:7, NLT). Today, America's debt has enslaved her.

EXCESSIVE DEBT

The United States' national debt is currently more than 34 trillion dollars, higher than America's gross domestic product.[3] America has more debt than the next four highly indebted countries combined (China 14 trillion, Japan 10 trillion, France 3 trillion, and Italy 2 trillion).[4]

---

2 https://fee.org/articles/the-politics-of-deficit-spending/?gclid=Cj0KCQjw5f2lBhCkARIsAHe TvljdKC7AGQeqXNHIyk3rHEZkRN5pfjfbxneGjhycaHmcj7zLKhAzv6gaAgCgEALw_wcB
3 https://www.pewresearch.org/short-reads/2023/02/14/facts-about-the-us-national-debt/
4 https://www.aljazeera.com/economy/2023/5/31/infographic-how-does-us-debt-rank-compared-world

Let me try to put it in perspective. If we were to divide the national debt by the number of people in America, it would be a staggering $101,964 for every person, and rising (at the time of this writing).[5]

Each year, rather than cutting spending to balance the budget, Congress votes to raise the debt ceiling limit and increase America's overall debt. Each new election cycle, candidates claim they will cut spending to balance the budget, but no Congress or president in recent history has made any positive progress.

DANGER AHEAD

Have politicians (and even some economists) cried wolf so long that nobody really cares?

The economy hasn't crashed, and the dollar still has value. Although things are more expensive, life has carried on for most people. But, if you ever ran up credit card debt, you know consequences, like interest, eventually catch up with you. Nationally:

- Interest payments alone were more than $663 billion in 2023, more than what was spent on veterans' benefits, transportation, and education.
- By 2028, the government will spend more on interest payments than defense.
- By fiscal year 2031, the US will spend more on interest than on non-defense discretionary spending (transportation, veterans, education, health, international affairs, natural resources and environment, general science and technology, general government, and more).[6]

---

5 https://www.pgpf.org/national-debt-clock
6 https://www.pgpf.org/blog/2023/05/what-is-the-national-debt-costing-s#:~:text=The%20Congressional%20Budget%20Office%20(CBO,to%20%241.4%20trillion%20in%202033

Politicians are essentially "buying" our votes with the things they promise us. The reason why our debt towers so high is actually quite simple. Politicians bribe the American people—with their own tax money—to expand government programs. In 1835, Alexis De Tocqueville correctly said, "The American Republic will endure until the day Congress discovers that it can bribe the public with the public's money."[7] Unfortunately, that day is now.

THE CITIZENS AND PERSONAL DEBT

It's easy to point fingers at politicians and blame them for America's dark financial future, but we would be doing ourselves a disservice if we didn't look in a mirror. After all, we elected our leaders, and somewhere along the way we ignored God's warnings and believed that debt was, in fact, a good—or at least neutral—thing.

In America today materialism is king, and consumer debt is a normal way of life. It's hard to believe, but the average American has more than $96,000 in consumer debt, the biggest contributors being mortgages, home equity lines of credit, and student loan balances.[8]

Instant gratification is the name of the game, particularly when we want the newest car or latest iPhone or to remodel our homes if we have one. And it's not as though Americans have a strong compulsion to balance their personal budgets and live within their means. It's not a big shocker that we then elect politicians who, in turn, fail to balance the federal budget and spend us into oblivion.

Here's a statement I wrote in my book *Well Versed*: "What if we first saved the money, then made a purchase? Whatever happened to earning the money to pay for something ahead of time, being patient, being appreciative of what has been worked for?"[9]

---

7 https://www.pleasantonweekly.com/square/2010/08/15/the-american-republic-will-en-dure-until-the-day-congress-discovers-that-it-can-bribe-the-public-with-the-publics-money
8 https://www.firstrepublic.com/insights-education/average-american-debt
9 James L. Garlow, *Well Versed: Biblical Answers to Today's Tough Issues*, Salem Books, an imprint of Regnery Publishing, 2016, p. 141.

A MORAL ISSUE

1 Timothy 6:6-9 says, "But godliness with contentment is great gain." But that's just the tip of the biblical iceberg about money. There are more than 2,350 scriptures that talk about money and our use of it. For some perspective, there are only about 500 verses about faith and prayer. And of Jesus' 38 parables, 16 relate to the subject of money and possessions.[10] Even two of the Ten Commandments deal with possessions: Don't covet, and don't steal.

Jesus pointed out the core issue in Matthew 6:19-21: "For where your treasure is, there your heart will be also." He knew earthly possessions could potentially pull us away from the things of His Kingdom.

Here's a question: How many sermons have you heard preached about the moral implications of personal or national debt? We get fired up about the sanctity of life and God's design for marriage, and about religious freedoms—as we certainly should—but when did you hear a sermon about the morality—and sin—of piling up unjustified debt? As one who pastored for decades, I experienced a blank stare from pastors when I tried to make the case that the national debt was a moral, biblical, and theological issue.

We know that the national debt will not be paid back in our lifetime. To whom will that debt go? To our children and grandchildren. That is wrong, and unfair to our future generations.

What's even worse, there's no real concern or intention to pay it back. Psalms 37:21 captures the issue, and it says, "The wicked borrow and do not repay." Did you catch that: "the wicked." Strong term, but accurate concerning much of our leadership.

Our nation is presuming upon future generations, our children and grandchildren. We are stealing from their wealth without their having any say, while we don't even know what next year will bring (James 4:14).

---

10 https://churchleaders.com/outreach-missions/outreach-missions-articles/314227-2350-bible-verses-money.html; https://www.envoyfinancial.com/participantresources/bible-verses-about-money-and-stewardship#:~:text=Did%20you%20know%20that%20there,related%20to%20money%20and%20possessions

Excessive spending diminishes America's wealth and is the exact opposite of wise investing (Matthew 25:14-30). We are throwing away our current financial resources more every year just to service the debt, and this is foolishness (Proverbs 21:20).

In a nutshell, our leaders are not governing and spending righteously. As a result, our groanings as a nation will only increase until we have leaders who submit to God's principles for the good of us all (Proverbs 29:2).

The national debt is, and always has been, a moral issue as our government steals from future generations, presumes upon future prosperity, and threatens the economic stability and freedom of our country.

A good place to begin making changes is with your own finances, and to refuse to be silent about our national leaders—or government leaders at any level—who continue to be irresponsible with debt and the use of our tax money.

CANCEL CULTURE

Freedom of speech, properly understood, is among the most important rights guaranteed in the US Constitution (1st Amendment). Speech can inspire, encourage, or even rally a nation in war, as Churchill's words did for Britain in its darkest hour in 1939. It can also perpetuate lies and harmful stereotypes, manipulate, and even incite violence or death.

WORDS CAN CHANGE HISTORY

An example of the power of words to change history is seen in Shakespeare's *Julius Caesar*, when Mark Antony addresses a crowd after Caesar's assassination. In short order, he turns a crowd friendly to Caesar's assassins into a howling mob looking to kill them. With a short, strategic speech—a few hundred words—Antony changed the course of history. It is arguably why Julius Caesar is remembered today more as a brilliant military commander than he is as a power-thirsty usurper who marched on Rome.

A far more profound example is when the chief priests and elders turned a crowd against Jesus (and saved Barabbas), ultimately leading to Jesus' crucifixion in the greatest miscarriage of justice—the assigning of guilt on an innocent person—in all of history (Matthew 27:15-23).

THE POWER OF THE SPOKEN WORD

The use of words has special meaning for Christians. God spoke the Creation into existence (Genesis 1:3-27). The very first sentence of the New Testament says, "In the beginning was the Word, and the Word was with God, and the Word was God" (John 1:1). Jesus is described as "the Word made flesh." The Gospel is communicated with words—"faith comes by hearing, and hearing by the Word of God" (Romans 10:17, NKJV).

For Christians, censoring speech is rightfully a major concern. So important in fact, that when the Apostles Peter and John were arrested and threatened with death for preaching the Gospel, they responded that they had to *speak*, even if it cost them their lives (Acts 5:17-32).

WHAT IS CANCEL CULTURE?

How does this apply to so-called cancel culture? The "cancellation" of someone's voice (and therefore influence) is an attempt to prevent alternative views from being expressed that are contrary to a ruling orthodoxy. *New York Times* columnist Russ Douthat gave this succinct definition of cancel culture: "Cancellation, properly understood, refers to an attack on someone's employment and reputation by a determined collective of critics, based on an opinion or an action that is alleged to be disgraceful and disqualifying."[1]

Perceptions of cancel culture differ depending on one's political leanings. A Pew Research study found that people on the Left tend to

---

1 Cancel Culture Is a Threat to Everyone | Institute for Free Speech (ifs.org)

see cancelling speech as a means to hold others accountable.[2] Conservatives, however, are more likely to see such actions as censorship, mean-spirited, or an effort to silence others who disagree with them.

ACADEMIA

Censorship is particularly notorious on university campuses against professors and students who hold disfavored views. With a progressive worldview dominating academia, it is no surprise that conservative teachers are targeted and are more likely to self-censor over fear of losing a position or being denied tenure.[3]

Consistent with the Pew Research findings, in conservative states that ban teachings like CRT or DEI, teachers on the Left are more likely to believe their own views are correct and that they are holding others accountable for their perceived "racism" or "transphobia." Conservative professors in liberal college environments often experience a school's demand that teachers affirm progressive orthodoxy, such as publicly agreeing with CRT, or using a student's preferred pronouns. In the former case, the professor is on a mission to advance leftist orthodoxy, while in the latter case the conservative professor is defending against forced speech, or demands to espouse views that defy one's religious or political beliefs. This is a critical difference; the Left's examples of cancellation are restraints against advancing their *agenda*, while conservatives are more likely defending their *personal integrity*.

Sometimes cancellation efforts are ironic. In March 2022, Yale Law School held a forum for opposing attorneys in a lawsuit dealing with cultural values. One of the speakers was from the conservative legal group Alliance Defending Freedom. Because of ADF's participation, about 120 Yale Law students conducted a loud protest in an effort to frustrate the

---

2 https://www.pewresearch.org/internet/2021/05/19/americans-and-cancel-culture-where-some-see-calls-for-accountability-others-see-censorship-punishment/

3 https://www.aei.org/articles/conservative-faculty-are-outliers-on-campus-today/

event. Ironically, both speakers—opponents in a case—were dedicated to civil discourse. The meeting was to promote civility and professionalism, and demonstrate how philosophical opponents could get along respectfully. This admirable goal was apparently too much for these offended students to bear; civility and professionalism had to yield to censoring (cancelling) someone with disfavored views. If the speaker does not affirm leftist orthodoxy, they cannot be allowed to speak.[4]

THE BUSINESS WORLD

Large corporate interests now live in dread of falling on the wrong side of diversity and inclusion "ratings." Most Americans living outside of large corporate environments do not understand the significance of these ratings, and how they advance a leftist agenda. The word "inclusion" might superficially suggest a commendable goal of allowing multiple views, respecting differences, and everyone getting along. But that is not the case. High D and I ratings demand something like quotas, donations to approved organizations, and abiding by standards on what should be allowed. For example, the traditional, religiously informed belief that gender is biological, rather than how one perceives oneself, is considered impermissible bigotry and may not be expressed. And mandatory training on D and I requires acceptance of the approved cultural orthodoxy in all respects.

Are conservatives rebelling in the business world against such demands? Oftentimes, no. The fear of losing a job (or being banned from an industry or profession) often brings self-censure. This is fine for the ruling orthodoxy: one may hold a contrary belief, so long as it is not spoken and no effort is made to persuade others of its truth. The governing orthodoxy is then able to mandate all its actions and policies with few or zero consequences.

---

4 https://www.campusreform.org/article/heres-why-david-horowitz-didnt-speak-at-berkeley/9064

CANCEL CULTURE IS NOT A GAME

The cancel culture mentality is not just inimical to the essential free speech liberties of a free nation, it tramples over the right to associate and assemble, the pursuit of happiness, and the right to live according to one's faith and moral beliefs.

An old truism reminds us that those who forget history are destined to repeat its errors. The totalitarian leaders of the 20th Century in nations like China, Russia, Germany, and Italy (among others) were notable for "cancelling" dissent—the same animating spirit we see in the cancel culture of our day. National policies that silenced speech in the prior century ultimately led to beatings, prison, and eventually even executions.

When no contrary opinion or policy is permissible, there is no restraint against an aggressive political orthodoxy. When that happens, any legal protections we thought we had may turn out to be far more fragile than we thought. As we see violence becoming a more frequent part of political opinion and dissent, sheer might may very well determine what is "right."

The solution to combat unjust or oppressive government is not only speech—it is truth. One of the simplest sayings of Jesus remains one of the most powerful: you shall know the truth, and the truth shall set you free (John 8:32, NKJV). But truth must be communicated. That's why conscience, truth, and speech must travel together. Whether symbolic, written, or spoken, there is no more powerful weapon against evil and injustice than speaking truth. Those who would cancel others will eventually end up opposing truth itself. When that happens, those that cancel others will find themselves trying to "cancel" God Himself, and not just His people. And we know who will win that battle.

CHAPTER 46

POPULATION GROWTH

magine government leaders declaring an all-out war against an existential threat! And, if they don't, the world will cease to exist in ten to fifteen years. What is that dire threat? Too many people! Now imagine what steps government will take to defeat this threat. To "save civilization" strict rules must be imposed on everyone. These mandates include involuntary sterilization and other "necessary" restrictions in order to have access to basic necessities such as housing, water, electricity, medical care, and even opportunities for education or employment.[1] Ironically, to live, you must never reproduce. Everyone must comply, or else!

---

1 https://www.smithsonianmag.com/innovation/book-incited-worldwide-fear-overpopulation-180967499/

FARFETCHED OR NOT?

The scenario above isn't all that surprising, or new. Back in 1968, Paul Ehrlich's book *The Population Bomb* helped normalize and popularize the idea of radical population control, asserting that a growing population was not just unsustainable, but dangerous to society. Ideas have consequences, and in 1975 eight million men and women were forcibly sterilized in India.[2] Now, almost 50 years later, India's leaders are again debating the resurrection of population control[3] practices. One of India's ministers even tweeted[4] that people should consider not having children for the sake of a more "sustainable future," and encouraged others to join the single's movement like him.

Since the publication of *The Population Bomb,* the world has *not* ceased to exist, despite the world's population more than doubling.[5] In fact, the world has arguably flourished because of medical, scientific, agricultural, and economic advances since then. Nevertheless, attempts to control and curb population growth are still keenly on the minds of government officials and policy influencers around the world.[6]

Not surprisingly, numerous organizations exist that singularly focus on population, including: the Population Council, Population Services International, Population Matters, and the more widely known United Nations Population Fund (UNFPA) which was founded in 1969, one year after *The Population Bomb* was published. And what do all these organizations have in common? They promote and

---

2 https://www.smithsonianmag.com/innovation/book-incited-worldwide-fear-overpopulation-180967499/

3 https://foreignpolicy.com/2023/04/28/population-control-is-back-in-india/

4 https://twitter.com/AlongImna/status/1546370828866318336?ref_src=twsrc%5Etfw%7Ctwcamp%5Etweetembed%7Ctwterm%5E1546370828866318336%7Ctwgr%5E0cd3412e0c8120e82bbd3a5fed3fde0b16daac03%7Ctwcon%5Es1_&ref_url=https://indianexpress.com/article/political-pulse/hashtag-politics-bjp-asantulan-control-opp-ponder-8024946/

5 https://www.un.org/en/dayof8billion

6 https://press.un.org/en/commission-population-and-development

support abortion all around the world in the name of health care. It is such a priority that UNFPA openly describes unintended pregnancies as having "devastating global consequences that affect almost every aspect of human [life]."[7]

CHILD OR NO CHILD

How ironic that, according to the United Nations, new life breeds the devastation of humanity instead of breeding vitality into the human race. Sadly, many young adults have taken to heart the doom and gloom message about the unsustainability of life as supposedly limited natural resources are devoured, and the world's population explodes. As a result, many have decided not to have children, choosing to believe the lie that a growing population will lead to the catastrophic end of civilization. For those who purport to be climate conscious but still want to be parents, one proposed solution—are you ready for this—is to have virtual children. What is a "virtual child?" This concept was discussed in a recent article; basically, it involves having virtual children in the metaverse by making use of the rapid advancements in artificial intelligence.[8]

THERE ARE CONSEQUENCES TO CURBING POPULATION GROWTH

In August 2023, an advisor for the World Economic Forum boldly stated that "population collapse is good for the planet."[9] But with much of the world focused on slowing population growth, the detrimental economic and societal effects have started to become apparent. Interestingly, the populations in some countries, including Japan and

7 https://www.unfpa.org/news/8-myths-about-unintended-pregnancy-debunked Myth 7
8 https://www.theguardian.com/technology/2022/may/31/tamagotchi-kids-future-parent-hood-virutal-children-metaverse
9 https://web.archive.org/web/20230817195336/https://www.telegraph.co.uk/business/2023/08/17/20-year-low-for-baby-born-in-england-good-news-for-planet/

the United States, are declining at such an alarming rate that some officials in those governments are starting to rethink their policies. Even some leaders in China are beginning to realize the adverse economic and societal impacts as their population has declined for seven years running beginning in 2016.

In 2019, my wife and I attended the Budapest Demographic Summit in Hungary, which has been held every other year since 2015. Hungarian Prime Minister Viktor Orban is one of the few world leaders to understand the critical nature of declining birth rates.

THIS IS NOT A DIRE SITUATION

Why do many on the Left believe that population growth is such a devastating problem? And why do they characterize the miracle of new life with such negative terminology as *the population problem,*[10] *population pressure,*[11] *exploding population,*[12] *overpopulation,*[13] *population disaster,*[14] *population challenges,*[15] *population explosion,*[16] and even calling for *population planning*?[17] They earnestly but erroneously believe that there are not enough natural resources, including water and food, for the amount of people that are living today, let alone for any increase in the years ahead. According to a 2023 United Nations report,[18] the situation is so dire that the UN warns there is an

10 https://pubmed.ncbi.nlm.nih.gov/635085/
11 https://www.biologicaldiversity.org/programs/population_and_sustainability/population/
12 https://pubmed.ncbi.nlm.nih.gov/14161264/
13 https://hir.harvard.edu/public-health-and-overpopulation/amp/
14 https://www.rsu.edu/rsu-public-television-to-present-population-disaster/
15 https://www.npr.org/transcripts/1151362111
16 https://www.ncbi.nlm.nih.gov/pmc/articles/PMC3987379/
17 https://pdf.usaid.gov/pdf_docs/PNAAH494.pdf
18 https://www.unesco.org/en/articles/imminent-risk-global-water-crisis-warns-un-world-water-development-report-2023

"imminent risk of a global water crisis." Headlines also warn that "the future of life on Earth depends on curbing overpopulation."[19]

But is it so dire that we as Christians ought to follow these baseless warnings, stay single, and not reproduce? Have we reached a tipping point whereby if we don't do our part, the world as we know it will end? By no means!

In 2023 my wife and I attended a conference in London called the Alliance for Responsible Citizenship, organized primarily by Jordan Peterson, with more than 90 speakers attended by approximately 1,500 invited international delegates from 73 countries. The entire thrust of this exceptional conference was diametrically opposed to the "permacrisis" and "declinist" (actual words from the ARC program) language of the doomsday leftists. In Jordan Peterson's words, "The catastrophizing must stop."[20] The conference presented expert after expert outlining the staggering and profoundly adequate resources of this wonderful Earth that God has given us.

WHAT GOD WANTS US TO DO

Having and living a biblical worldview, one centered on God's design and will for us, will help us identify the lies and propaganda that the enemy would have us believe and follow. Satan is the master of deception (John 8:44) and wants us to do exactly the opposite of what God has called us to do. God's creation mandate in Genesis 1:28 calls us to "be fruitful and multiply, fill the earth and subdue it." Curbing population growth strikes against the very first command God gave to humanity. So, have we reached the point that "filling the earth" has been fulfilled? Apparently not.

Even in a sin-filled world, even with all the mistakes that mankind makes, God's common grace (Matthew 6:24-34) has allowed humans

---

19 https://www.theguardian.com/world/2022/oct/19/the-future-of-life-on-earth-depends-on-curbing-overpopulation
20 ARC Conference 2023, A Better Story, October 20—November 1, 2023, pages 6, 9.

to multiply and adapt and even thrive. This doesn't mean mankind can shirk its responsibility to be a good steward of the resources God has provided in the created order around us. We are all responsible for being careful with those resources.

NOT TOO MANY PEOPLE

One question you may have is how many people can the earth comfortably sustain? If we were to believe secularists, the answer can range anywhere from a low of 500 million people up to 2-3 billion and even up to 8 billion (the current population!). But those estimates assume the future is known, and a belief that mankind is already ravaging and wasting limited resources that will soon be gone. The real answer is that we don't know. God has not revealed that to us. But we do know that God loves life, and where He gives life, He also gives the means to responsibly provide for it. Can the Earth sustain 10 billion people? Twenty billion people? We don't know. But one thing we do know is that God is able to provide abundantly more than we could ever imagine (Ephesians 3:20-21).

Allow me to be very practical. Is our earth overcrowded? No, it is not. But we are not distributed well. Anyone who has flown from Kansas City to Los Angeles can see the massive amounts of uninhabited land in the western half of the US. The further west one goes, the more the land is owned by the federal government. And therein lies the problem. If the federal government were to sell most of that land, we could not only pay off much of our national debt, but that land could be developed, become productive, and make room for millions of people.

But that is not true only for America. Go to many of the nations of the world. The problem is not lack of space. The problem is how humanity has "clustered," with millions crowded into tiny areas, the cities. The fact is, properly distributed, this great globe has the capacity to supply what a growing population would need.

GOVERNANCE

Allow me to cut to the chase: The problem is not too many people. It is poor governance. As noted in a previous chapter, when a nation follows the biblical principles of governance,[21] human pain, suffering, and poverty decrease. Conversely, when a nation violates biblical principles of governance, human pain, suffering, and poverty increase. Show me a nation with starving people and I will show you a nation that is violating God's principles of governance.

WHAT ARE WE TO DO?

Too often, Christians are labeled as extremists when we oppose ideologies like population control. Yet, the real war is with Satan. It's a spiritual war that attacks the biblical mandate to be fruitful and multiply with lies about abortion, climate change, transgenderism, euthanasia, and multiple other perversions that counter God's plan for human flourishing. 1 Peter 3:15 says, "Always be prepared to give an answer to everyone who asks you to give the reason for the hope that you have."

So, what can you do as a follower of Christ to combat Satan's thirst for the death and destruction of humanity? First, simply follow God's command in Genesis 1:28, but with wisdom, knowing we are to be responsible stewards of the creation around us. We don't have to be defensive about having children. We know they are a gift from God; we also know we need to be knowledgeable about Satan's schemes and be able to counter them biblically, which is what most of this book is focused on doing.

Second, remember that after God created human beings, He *blessed* them. God's blessing for us is to have children, to work hard,

---

21 For more biblical principles of governance, see the prequel to this book, James L. Garlow, *Well Versed: Biblical Answers to Today's Tough Issues*, Salem Books, an imprint of Regnery Publishing, 2016.

and to take care of His beautiful creation. This is the exact opposite of what Satan desires when he promotes population control or tries to convince leaders that we are already overpopulated. God's plan is for man to have dominion over the world. Satan wants the environment to have dominion over man. Cries to "save the environment" rather than the lives of human beings made in God's image distort His plan.

Finally, life is precious. Although God does not call everyone to marry, many of us are called to wed and procreate. While the size of a family can be a sensitive matter, Psalm 127:3-5 says, "Children are a gift from the Lord; they are a reward from him. Children born to a young man are like arrows in a warrior's hands. How joyful is the man whose quiver is full of them!" So marry, and don't unnecessarily delay having or adopting children.

"Be fertile ... and fill the earth."

CHAPTER 47

SOCIAL CREDIT SCORES AND ESG

W e're all familiar with credit scores, those pesky ratings that affect our ability to get loans. We also know (or hear stories) about how hard it is to get wrong information removed from the three main credit tracking systems.

Now think of a scoring system that measures how much of a patriot, conservative, or Bible believer you are, or even how "trustworthy" you are based on your internet searches, "associations," buying habits, or what you post online. And then, that "score" determines whether you can buy or sell anything, whether you can open a savings account, or use a credit card, or be admitted to a college, or whether your income tax will be audited every year. Maybe you will end up on a "watch list" that prevents you from flying or using public transportation. Sounds like science fiction? Sounds ludicrous? Sounds like the end times described in Revelation (13:16-18)? Well, we know it *isn't* science fiction!

BIG BROTHER IS WATCHING

China has been implementing a social credit score (SCS) system for years.[1] It is specifically intended to grade companies and individuals' "trustworthiness." Sounds scary, right? Write and post the right things, listen to the right information, support the right government actions and you're rewarded with a high score. Don't do the right things, and you're downgraded in trustworthiness and limited in job opportunities, travel options, schools, credit, and maybe even shamed publicly.

Similar assessment systems are being looked at throughout Western countries. How much and how fast is the real question? It's not just about targeting people with ads based on their internet searches. We're talking about "Big Data" collection of any electronic footprint you have: online purchases and searches, how long you spend looking at a website, public records, bank transactions, what's delivered to your door, subscriptions, energy usage, all social media access and posts, tracking of movements with your phone or car or through facial recognition algorithms processing public recordings. What about health problems, medications, doctor's visits, vaccination status, marriage counseling, gun purchases?

What about—now wait for it—your conversations? I'll just say, yes, your iPhone is listening to you.[2]

You may think, hmm, I'll just go off the grid. Well, the lack of an electronic footprint is also saying something about a person, which could invite a different type of scrutiny. Even using cash for purchases may work for a while, but how far away is a true, cashless society?[3]

ESG

And then there is the rise of Environmental, Social, and Governance (ESG) systems. These ESG programs track a company's

---

1 China Social Credit System Explained—How It Works [2023] (nhglobalpartners.com)

2 https://us.norton.com/blog/how-to/is-my-phone-listening-to-me

3 https://www.ramseysolutions.com/budgeting/cashless-society

behavior relating to its commitment to the so-called "greater good" of society and the world, not the normal business measures such as profit and loss, debt, customer satisfaction, and market share.

Factors for "Environment" can include a commitment to addressing climate change and environmental sustainability. "Social" factors range from a commitment to human rights (including abortion rights), workplace gender and diversity inclusion, privacy protection, safety, health, the servicing of underprivileged social groups, and even supply chain accountability (who supplies them). "Governance" covers a wide range of topics that can include corporate behavior, political donations, board diversity, and even lobbying efforts.

When reduced to specifics, ESG might possibly be coercive language as follows:

E—You better buy into the present-day "Environment" religion of climate change.

S—You better be "Socially" woke and make donations to BLM or some other charity with a DEI agenda.

G—You better pursue appropriate "Governance" and have some Black or Native American lesbians on your governing board.

It's clear that ESG can quickly become a measure of a company's conformance to societal and environmental issues of the day. Just like SCSs for individuals, these measures are intended to impact decisions and actions according to an "accepted" narrative for the supposed greater good. Conform, and your business prospects are improved. But if you diverge from this political correctness (or "wokeness"), you will find yourself less competitive for contracts securing business loans, or you may even be de-platformed from advertising.

ESG is not just for big business. In 2020, 88% of publicly traded companies had ESG initiatives in place, while 67% of all privately owned companies did.[4]

We've seen what happens when institutions and businesses deviate from governmental pandemic edicts. It's not a big leap to see how conformance to and promotion of the party line will be instrumental in a company's survival. This is especially disconcerting as we observe the incredible power that social media companies have over what can be posted.

THE ISSUE: CONTROL

Conform to the broken worldview and ideologies that permeate much of the public school system, academia, main-stream media, progressives in Congress and the White House, and you will thrive. Buck the progressive system and for all intents and purposes, you will most likely be deplatformed, censored, defunded, draw greater scrutiny, and, when possible, financially crippled.

ESG AND THE BIBLE

First off, whether SCS and ESG are definitive signs of the end of the age or not is difficult to say. The Lord knows what lies ahead and the timing of it (Matthew 24:36). We know that for sure.

In our information-rich lives, the government doesn't have to use its sword to force compliance (Romans 13:4). It has willing accomplices in the major institutions of society to do its bidding if you disagree with destructive, progressive goals. Just like the ungodly chief priests stirred up the crowd against Jesus (Mark 15:6-15), SCS and ESG can become weapons to silence any dissent.

---

4 https://www.navex.com/blog/article/environmental-social-governance-esg-global-survey-findings/

Proverbs says that one seems right until someone else comes forward and questions them (Proverbs 18:17). So it is in a free society that open discourse on controversial subjects is critical to ensure a well-informed public. The consistent trend by social media giants and a hostile government is to prevent that from occurring. Not only do such controls willfully neglect needed "counsel" (Proverbs 12:15; 13:18; 15:22), but they paint any alternative view (i.e., a biblical view) as something evil that should be punished.

Remember, the prophets of old were ignored and persecuted, even though they spoke the truth (Matthew 5:11-12), so we are still called to speak for righteousness even when there may be pushback and consequences (1 Peter 3:13-14).

WHAT CAN WE DO, IF ANYTHING?

In the era of Big Data, destroying a business or a person's life is extraordinarily easy and quick to do. The use of false information, deep fake videos, selective filtering, or just plain mistakes can damage a reputation and cripple one's ability to engage in the economy. Because the toll can be so high, there needs to be significant financial (if not criminal) damages brought against those who defame, harm, or effectively "blacklist" a person or business because of their beliefs, values, or opinions.

Positive change may take time, but just as the widow in Luke 18:1-5 was successful against an unjust judge, so persistence with good legal backing can punish wrongful behaviors. Even forcing prominent and public correction of the record is not unprecedented. Remember Haman's shame in having to honor Mordecai (Esther 6:1-13)?

Class action suits are also an option if a widespread pattern can be detected and documented.

Although not the best option, federal legislation that specifically prohibits organizations from discriminating against businesses or people because of their political beliefs or affiliations may be necessary to provide more consistent protection. Many states currently provide some level of protection, but it's generally very tailored.[5]

Is this the stuff of conspiracy theories? Hardly. Is it the end times? Time will tell. In the meantime, the trend is for a government hostile to our values to set the "agenda" and for Big Data and its manipulators to carry out the program.

---

5 Can You Be Fired for Political Beliefs or Affiliations? | Nolo) (Is Political Discrimination In The Workplace Legal? (forbes.com)

CHAPTER 48

THE RELIGION OF GLOBAL WARMING

Wait, shouldn't the title of this chapter be "The *Science* of Global Warming?" Initially, one would suspect a typo.

Unfortunately, however, global warming has become a tenant of faith, an all-consuming secular religion for many radical environmentalists. And make no mistake, this religion has a distinct worldview with specific beliefs and teachings. It has ritual acts focused on sacred objects, places, and times. It involves a universal moral code that transcends everyday life and applies to both believers and society in general. And, like an authoritative, cult-like religion, it has developed a social group that bonds together like-minded practitioners who attack and persecute all unbelievers.

SCIENCE, POLITICS, RELIGION—OR ALL THREE?

You may think this is hyperbole. But has any scientific topic elicited as much vitriol, as much demand to change our way of life, and as much personal attack on those who would deny the supposed scientific "consensus on the facts" than global warming (oops, sorry—climate change)? Objective scientific research on important (global) issues should be encouraging open and vigorous debate. But when it comes to global warming, the knives come out, and anything that goes against the current orthodoxy is quickly branded as ignorant and science-denying.

Mark Twain said, "Never discuss politics or religion in polite company." You can add global warming to that list, noting that it is particularly taboo since it embraces both!

GLOBAL WARMING AS A RELIGION

As Eric Hoffer wrote in *The True Believer*, "Hatred is the most accessible and comprehensive of all the unifying agents. Mass movements can rise and spread without belief in a god, but never without a belief in a devil."[1] In the global warming movement, the devils are greenhouse gases—carbon dioxide, methane, and nitrous oxide—but not the most important greenhouse gas, water vapor. Why? Because water vapor cannot be regulated; but conveniently, the other three can. The result: the *real* devils are not the gases themselves but the humans who use energy that produces them as a byproduct.

This hatred of human activity blended nicely with a decades-old hatred of humans in general. As we touched on in Chapter 46, Paul Erlich warned of the coming population bomb where hundreds of millions of people would starve to death[2] as a result of overpopulation and depleted resources. When this didn't materialize, a new *cause celebre* was needed to substantially reduce mankind's impact on the Earth, and in particular, the environment.

Enter the dire threat of global warming. With this imminent catastrophe, humans are now a double threat to the Earth: they not only

---

1 https://taylorpearson.me/bookreview/the-true-believer-summary-by-eric-hoffer/
2 https://www.smithsonianmag.com/innovation/book-incited-worldwide-fear-overpopulation-180967499/

produce Earth-destroying gases, but at the same time, they are consuming all available resources. For climate change zealots, humans are worse than a plague of locusts. Although locusts leave behind complete devastation, farmers can return to farming. But when humans destroy things, so the story goes, there is no opportunity for recovery.

For true believers of global warming, there is a god. It's the planet. This turns the Creator-creature distinction on its head. The goal of creating a pristine Earth not damaged by mankind's actions is to bring back Eden. Humans are no longer to be "fruitful and multiply, to subdue the Earth, and have dominion over every living thing" (Genesis 1:28, NKJV). No, humans are just evil producers and consumers, and their existence has signaled the ultimate demise of the planet. As Dr. James F. Bonner, a molecular biologist at Caltech proclaimed at the first Earth Day in 1970, "The whole world would be better off if man hadn't been invented."[3]

ENVIRONMENTALISM AS A SUBSTITUTE FOR CHRISTIANITY

Religion is ingrained into the human psyche. One can claim they are atheistic, but in reality, they have simply replaced the true God with something else. Within the religion of radical environmentalism, creation becomes the new god (Romans 1:22-25). But more than just a new, 20th-century religion, radical environmentalism seeks to replace both Christianity and its worldview. How does it do that?

As outlined by novelist and film maker Michael Crichton,[4] environmentalism parallels Genesis. In the beginning, everything is together as one with nature (Eden), but that order was disrupted by the fall into pollution as a result of industrialization (eating from the tree of knowledge), followed by nature's harmony becoming greatly flawed (the wilderness).

---

3 https://www.youtube.com/watch?v=QOkqI1ueZVU
4 https://spreadgreatideas.org/resources/speeches/michael-crichton-environmentalism-is-a-religion/

But there's more. Radical environmentalism then parallels the Gospels where a judgement is coming in which humans die as a result of their sin against nature (God), be it from mass starvation and/or a hothouse Earth (judgement by God). The only way out is to seek the salvation of sustainability, not the love and grace afforded to us by Jesus Christ. Organic food replaces the Lord's Supper while Earth Day is revered as much as Easter. Five-year reports of the Intergovernmental Panel on Climate Change and the US National Assessments become the new "Bible." And on and on.

At its core, radical environmentalism claims the planet is overpopulated and falling into abject poverty. The planet is warmer now than at any time since dinosaurs roamed the land, and extreme weather kills more people and destroys more property than ever before.

The problem is none of these claims are true. In 1820, there were just over 1 billion people on the planet, with nearly 95% living in extreme poverty.[5] By 2015, the population had grown to well over 7 billion people, but only about 10% were living in extreme poverty, thanks to the development of technology. The planet isn't warming beyond what we have experienced in the 20th century, and extreme weather is not on the rise.[6] Even global weather losses as a percentage of gross domestic product are on the decline.[7] No, global warming demands adherence not *because* of the evidence, but *despite* evidence to the contrary.

Where do the proclamations of impending doom and gloom originate? They come from modern-day prophets known as climate modelers, who use their predictive models just like the divination instruments of old.[8] But we have known for years that these models overstate the case for warming, being both too sensitive with respect

5 https://ourworldindata.org/grapher/world-population-in-extreme-poverty-absolute
6 https://www.nsstc.uah.edu/aosc/testimonials/ChristyJR_Written_160202.pdf and
7 https://rogerpielkejr.substack.com/p/dont-believe-the-hype
8 https://science.house.gov/_cache/files/5/6/56b2c90e-acc2-4cab-bb10-a510d3cb43ac/AD-54FE912F5E3094C8B391DA314D1E4C.hhrg-115-sy-wstate-jchristy-20170329.pdf

to a rise in carbon dioxide and using scenarios that provide flawed estimates.[9]

Think about it: Have these models accurately accounted for past warming trends over the last 50, 100 or a 1,000 years? If they can't consistently replicate (predict) what has already happened, why would we trust them to predict the future? To the true believer, however, being flawed is not an issue. After all, it isn't about the science.

THE APPROPRIATE ROLE OF ENVIRONMENTALISM

We are commanded by God to carefully use and protect his creation (Genesis 2:15), but we are strictly forbidden from worshiping it. Putting the Creation as God's second greatest gift to mankind[10]—the greatest gift being salvation—wrongly focuses our priorities. When Jesus was asked which commandment was most important, He replied with two: Put God first and treat others as we treat ourselves (Matthew 22:34-40). After other people, the remainder of creation has been given to us as a means to accomplish these commandments for His glory.

Novelist Michael Crichton warned:

> The greatest challenge facing mankind is the challenge of distinguishing reality from fantasy, truth from propaganda. Perceiving the truth has always been a challenge to mankind, but in the information age (or, as I think of it, the disinformation age), it takes on a special urgency and importance. We must daily decide whether the threats we face are real, whether the solutions we are offered will do

9 https://www.youtube.com/watch?v=Hs6lDsFipjM
10 https://www.christianpost.com/news/what-is-gods-second-greatest-gift-mankind-not-climate-change-or-creation.html

any good, whether the problems we're told exist are, in fact real problems or non-problems.[11]

As Jesus said, "If you abide in my word, you are truly my disciples, and you will know the truth, and the truth will set you free" (John 8:31b-32, ESV). That truth points us to Jesus Christ as our source of eternal life; it also commissions us all to be good stewards of the creation around us. In that, God will be well pleased.

Remember, God created Earth in all its beauty, and His children are to steward it wisely. Of course, Christians don't want the rainforests to be logged or burned into oblivion. Of course we want our rivers, seas, and lakes to thrive with life-giving waters and fish. But under the guise of environmentalism, the Left wants complete control of the world's natural resources. Gaia, after all, is the earth goddess … Earth Day celebrations, for the most part, are pagan. We are not to make an idol of anything, including the Earth.

11 https://spreadgreatideas.org/resources/speeches/michael-crichton-environmentalism-is-a-religion/

CHAPTER 49

THE 15-MINUTE CITY

As if there is not enough governmental coercion and control of private citizens, bureaucrats have found a way to limit your movement: a new type of city where vehicles are prohibited. You can walk or ride your bicycle for fifteen minutes in any direction. No car. Just walk or bike.

What has been termed the "15-minute city" is an urban planning concept that would provide for most daily necessities and services (work, shopping, education, healthcare, leisure, etc.) to be easily reached by either 15 minutes of walking or biking. But not just easily reached. That is your new boundary or limit of travel.

The rationale primarily revolves around the desire to reduce dependency on the use of cars, promote healthier and more sustainable living, and generally improve the quality of life for those who live in cities.[1] Restated: it is the government ripping away your rights.

---

1 https://en.wikipedia.org/wiki/15-minute_city

THE POLITICS OF CITY VS. RURAL

Historically, the larger and more densely packed urban areas are, the more leftist they become.[2] This could be because of a higher dependence on the government to provide for basic needs, the greater exposure to and acceptance of different value systems, and a propensity for politically aggressive ideologues to seek governmental power to impose minority viewpoints on the rest of the community.

In contrast, rural areas tend to be conservative. Knowing people throughout a community tends to build strong relationships around similar values. Self-dependence and personal responsibility tend to be more highly regarded than reliance on governmental institutions. Biblical (traditional) values are generally esteemed. Also, smaller neighborhoods allow a broader understanding of local issues and incentivize participation in the community.

An interesting way to characterize the progressive-to-conservative spectrum is by political association measured from a major city's center. The closer people are packed into urban areas, the higher the leftist affiliation; the farther one physically lives from urban centers, the higher the conservative presence.[3] Obviously, there's something about cities that affects one's politics.

THE BIBLE AND CENTRALIZATION

The mandate that Adam and Eve received in the Garden was to multiply (Genesis 1:28), go out and till and keep the earth (Genesis 2:15; 9:1). The implication is to expand and replicate the Garden while future generations expanded throughout the world. In contrast, the first cities began when Cain (Genesis 4:17), who left the presence of the Lord, established his own stronghold for protection against others.

---

2 https://source.wustl.edu/2020/02/the-divide-between-us-urban-rural-political-differences-rooted-in-geography/
3 Ibid.

Ever since Cain, cities have tended to become more ungodly as they have focused on man-centered power and less on transcendent moral values. The Tower of Babel—the first skyscraper—is a classic example of the centralization of power and people defying God (Genesis 11:1-4). The Lord destroyed their plans by confusing their language and dispersing them "over the face of the earth" (Genesis 11:9). Even Isaiah warned Israel that accumulation of land and power—that is, central-ization—by the very rich breeds a situation where strangers live next to each other, rather than the building of a healthy, thriving commu-nity (Isaiah 5:8). Even today, gentrification of major urban centers and excessive government control of property follows this same pattern.

Interestingly, God "dispersed" believers through persecution (Acts 8:1). He did not have them remain together in large groups—form their own massive cities—but instead sent them out to evangelize the world. Obviously, this allowed the Gospel to spread far faster, but it also prevented the temptation of building a city that would sooner rather than later begin to become man-centered instead of God-centered.

OLD TESTAMENT CITIES

Larger cities tended to be walled in Old Testament times (Numbers 13:17-19, 28) and were bastions of safety, while surrounding villages were "daughter" towns featuring farms and homes that provided for the basics of living.[4] This arrangement mirrors present-day urban centers surrounded by suburbs and rural areas with more spread-out populations, but with necessities well within driving distance.

The distinction between major cities and the "burbs" was that the city was a place to centralize security forces, execute justice, conduct much of the commerce for the area, and embrace wide cultural differ-ences. The surrounding villages produced the food for the area and

---

4 "The Illustrated Bible Dictionary" reprinted 1986; topic "Cities."

maintained a community setting that was less influenced by the cos-
mopolitan city.

UNINTENDED CONSEQUENCES

The 15-minute city may have reasonable-sounding goals, but what
real purpose is being served, and with what implications?

To a certain extent, suburbs are halfway houses between highly
populated urban centers and the surrounding rural communities
and tend to be mixed politically. One way to reduce the number
of suburbs is to plan, or rather force, a new community structure
that makes them far more city-like than rural-like. The inevitable
consequence is to make them into mini-cities—more leftist—
instead of just more efficient rural areas, which lean conservative.
Once applied to suburbs, centralized city planning can be forced
onto rural towns, consolidating the population into mini-cities
whereby easier control can be imposed from county, state, and
eventually the federal level.

By design, 15-minute cities are intended to reduce dependence on
the use of cars and other long-range vehicles. They would replace
mobility options with walking and bicycling paths as well as public
transportation for those who are older and more frail. To maintain the
economic viability of small, regional stores and services, there will be
increased pressure to stack more and more people (customers and
clients) together. The result will be mini-cities with the same downsides
as major cities that depend on a centralized government.

With a semi-confined citizenry—that is, a captive audience—the
government will be tempted to exercise further control on any number
of things it deems critical to restrain: certain types of foods, the amount
of power and water used, the amount of personal living space owned,
rent rates for protected classes of people, the number of vehicles
allowed (if any), how many miles can be driven, and on and on. Also,
the more densely packed a city becomes, the easier it is to implement

comprehensive surveillance to monitor movements and enforce social compliance in line with governmental expectations.

Once implemented, the basic infrastructure of limited roads and mobility options would become virtually impossible to expand into what was normal beforehand. Also, with limited personal options for easy mobility out-of-area, extreme economic and movement control can be enforced far quicker should there be another pandemic or government-defined emergency of any kind.

Fifteen-minute cities will ultimately make more people dependent on the government and restrict freedom of movement into and outside the local community, even reducing personal exposure and commerce with outsiders. Both these trends minimize our mandate to "live properly before outsiders and be dependent on no one" (1 Thessalonians 4:12, ESV).

Some contend that large cities provide more protection for the poor, the homeless, and immigrants. But one glance at our nation's urban areas reveals the devastation being experienced by the poor, homeless, and often immigrants. When a helping hand does come, that help is often provided by the government in a way that does not incentivize personal responsibility and the need to live by values consistent with biblical truths. Real help would be more prevalent in outlying regions where personal accountability would be much more highly valued and considerably more effective.

LACK OF MOBILITY MEANS LOSS OF FREEDOM TO ASSOCIATE

The seemingly good goals of the 15-minute city, in reality, are very corrosive to our constitutionally protected freedoms. Instead of planning for consolidation and centralization, cities, suburbs, and even rural planners should first design ways to accommodate our rights of assembly and speech—large parks and recreation areas, public speaking forums, town hall forums—access to worship in churches large and small, access to courts and government services, and even access to shooting ranges and training facilities (right to bear arms). Just as important, however, is our right to mobility/movement.

Loss of mobility—means to travel—has profound implications concerning our freedom of association with those outside the 15-minute city confines, as well as with our freedom of expression. Since retaining a variety of personal means to easily travel long distances is closely related to our constitutional rights,[5] it should be encouraged and planned for instead of denied or unnecessarily hindered.

Remember, in our world, God seems to favor dispersion to fulfill His purposes for man's dominion over the earth (Genesis 1:28), while the government favors centralization and control to accomplish its purposes. Not until God brings about a new heaven and a new earth (Revelation 21:1-3, 9-21) will the perfect combination of people and the presence of God exist. Until that time, we need to continue to be wary of plans that restrict our God-given rights and force conformance to governmental control of our lives and our legally protected freedoms.

---

5 "Freedom of movement under United States law," Wikipedia; https://en.wikipedia.org/wiki/Freedom_of_movement_under_United_States_law

CHAPTER 50

THE SECOND AMENDMENT AND SELF-DEFENSE

The vicious taking of another person's life is always a tragedy. But when a politician or celebrity uses these incidents to score ideological points or to project that they are somehow noble and caring, it only cheapens the loss of life. Sadly, we continue to see mass murders occurring in shopping malls, schools, businesses, and even among families.

Can anything be done?

Well, if the goal is to reduce the number of violent murders, then the real reasons behind them must first be identified. If it's purely a matter of a weapon's existence, then treating guns as equivalent to a flesh-eating virus needing to be eradicated at all costs makes sense. But if that's not the case, then any other supposed "remedies" may make the situation worse if we are not careful.

Not surprisingly, biblical principles provide a lot of insight to help us to understand weapons and the heart behind them.

WEAPONS AND THE BIBLE

Any casual reading of the Old Testament shows how commonplace mass killings and slaughters were. Weapons to carry out these battles were commonplace. Yet, never were weapons condemned as being intrinsically evil. They were what they were: inanimate objects incapable of independent action, just like bricks or razor blades. Weapons were never called morally good or bad, but people were!

It's pretty obvious that anything can be a weapon. Here's a partial listing from the Bible: swords (John 18:11; Matthew 26:52), spears (1 Samuel 19:10; John 19:34), bows and arrows (Genesis 27:3; 1 Samuel 20:20), daggers (2 Samuel 2:16), lions (Daniel 6:1-24), stones (Exodus 19:13; Numbers 14:10), clubs (Matthew 26:55), a tent peg and hammer (Judges 4:17-21), a sling and stone (1 Samuel 17:50), firebrands (Proverbs 26:18), a furnace (Daniel 3:16-27), poison (Mark 16:18), rope (Genesis 40:22; Esther 2:23, 5:14), a saw (Hebrews 11:37); hands (Matthew 18:28) and even an oxgoad (Judges 3:31). If lethality is the issue, remember that Samson struck down 1,000 Philistines with the jawbone of a donkey (Judges 15:14-17).

You get the picture.

NOT THE WEAPON, BUT THE HEART BEHIND IT

We know that unjustified killing by any means is consistently condemned in the Bible—it's a violation of our fundamental, God-given right to life (Exodus 20:13; 1 Timothy 1:8-10). So, where does this violence originate? Biblically, the devil (John 8:44) and man's wicked heart (Jeremiah 17:9) are the authors of evil and violence, no matter what weapons are used. When Peter shared the Gospel with the centurion (Acts 10:1-23), he didn't make laying down his weapons a condition of conversion. After all, Roman laws still had to be enforced (Romans 13:4).

But when weapons were inappropriately used, Jesus Himself denounced their use—not their existence, but their use (Matthew 26:51-54). This has been true from the beginning when Cain killed Abel. It was a heart issue (Genesis 4:8-11), not the rock, stick, or hands that were used to kill an innocent brother.

For those with mental health issues, it's critical to identify the problems early and apply as much compassionate supervision as possible to prevent unfortunate situations from happening. And there are, of course, some types of severe mental illnesses and psychoses which should bar a person from the ability to possess firearms.

But the evil in humanity's heart (Jeremiah 7:19) is much more complex to deal with, particularly when influenced by a culture that glorifies violence in the influential entertainment industry (Psalm 119:37) and teaches moral relativism as a way of life. So, knowing that evil and mentally unstable people will always be with us, is disarmament of everyone the answer?

THE RIGHT TO USE LETHAL FORCE IF NECESSARY

We clearly have the right and the duty to protect ourselves and our families, even by lethal means if necessary (Exodus 22:2-3; Luke 11:21, 22:26). This God-given right was recognized from the very beginning of our nation as our first line of defense to maintain community order and protect our loved ones from criminals, mobs, gangs (Exodus 20:13, 22:2-3), and even out-of-control government agents. This is the primary reason we have a right to bear arms—a right enshrined in the Constitution's Bill of Rights (2nd Amendment), which says: "A well-regulated Militia, being necessary to the security of a Free State, the right of the people to keep and bear Arms, shall not be infringed."

But given this reality, where do our politicians turn for a "quick fix" for gun violence? The one thing that has been proven to stop a violent crime—guns!

The issue isn't the size of an ammunition clip, or what makes an assault weapon, or whether gun safes and trigger locks work, or if a thousand new laws should be added to the thousands that already exist. The real issue is how responsible citizens protect themselves from those who want to do us harm, and how can this violence be prevented from happening in the first place?

CAUSES OF GUN VIOLENCE

Clearly, there's a valid debate over what factors contribute to gun violence, such as mental illness, drugs, abusive parenting, bullying, despair, or a "simple" callous disregard for another person's or one's own life. In our increasingly divisive society, we know guns aren't intrinsically evil, but that doesn't mean they're mere toys. A deep respect for their lethality, controlled access, and safe use must always be taught, just like the need to drive a car responsibly. Also, no one wants violent criminals or the mentally unstable to have access to guns, and every parent is concerned about their children and possible gun accidents.

But there are other plausible factors that influence gun violence: graphic video game violence, gratuitous TV, movies, and online media violence, music glorifying cruelty, and even demon possession (Matthew 8:28). And what about the long-term effects of trivializing the sanctity of life through legalizing and promoting euthanasia, physician-assisted suicide, and the abortion of innocent babies? Objectifying life instead of valuing it as made in God's image (Genesis 1:27) does nothing to restrain violence or instill a proper fear of an almighty, holy God that will judge how someone treats others.

MISPLACED COMPASSION

Unfortunately, there can be a misplaced, self-satisfying righteousness in condemning guns and trying to be understanding toward the killer. But saying the victims of gun violence would still be alive if guns were illegal ignores a major factor: Both evil people and the mentally unstable continue to exist. If all guns were removed from the public, only the government and criminals would remain armed. How would that work out for us? The most stringent gun control laws are found in highly urbanized cities. Unfortunately, when communities are disarmed and police are underfunded, these become the very environments where violent gun crime is the highest.

Even if the citizens of the entire nation were disarmed, consider our porous border, which allows tons of drugs and millions of illegals to enter every year. On what basis would we think guns could be kept away from criminals or even terrorist sleeper cells throughout our nation? To believe this is a realistic option is irresponsibly naive.

A PROBLEM OF OUR MAKING

When existing gun regulation (control) laws are not enforced, it creates a situation where the media and politicians can emotionally hype gun incidents to gain public support for new laws. But enacting more laws will only chip away at our constitutional right and biblical responsibility to protect ourselves. They won't decrease violent crimes. This cycle only leads to a disarmed public, making citizens completely dependent upon government for protection—the very thing our Founders warned us about. Is this a good situation to be in? Well, in 1 Samuel 13:19-23, we see that the Israelites were completely disarmed by the Philistines. How did that work out for them? I can tell you, not well.

THE LONG GOAL

We all grieve for the victims of violent crimes. But to diagnose the real problem incorrectly (the heart and mind of the criminal) and reject valid purposes for gun ownership is a recipe for disaster. Our constitutional right to be armed recognizes the true nature of mankind, our need to take responsible precautions for ourselves, our loved ones, and our property, and the potential threat of an out-of-control government. To ignore these truths and take away our God-given right to protect what is precious to us puts us all at lethal risk.

The longer goal, however, is to restore our nation's respect for life and for each other. Without a fundamental change in our nation's soul, our only recourse—other than prayer and fasting—is to be like Nehemiah's men when they were building the wall. His workers had one hand doing the work and the other hand on their sword (Nehemiah 4:15-23).

PART IV

A BIBLICAL RESPONSE
TO TECHNOLOGY

How God's people can educate themselves and protect their
families and loved ones from the darker sides of technology, and
how to harness new technological and digital advances for the
kingdom of God.

*Come, let us build ourselves a city and a tower with its top
in the sky. Let us make a name for ourselves; otherwise, we
will be scattered over the face of the whole earth.*

—GENESIS 11:4

CHAPTER 51

ARTIFICIAL INTELLIGENCE

During the height of the Cold War in the 1960s, two movies stoked people's fears about computers. The dark comedy *Dr. Strangelove* depicted the catastrophic consequences that a rogue person could bring about if he had authority over the use of nuclear weapons. The second film was a drama called *Fail Safe*. In this film, a computer error results in the accidental deployment of nuclear weapons that could not be recalled in time.

Fast forward to our present day. Computers and the Internet are ubiquitous, and we're almost completely dependent on them for everything. Now enters Artificial Intelligence and its explosive development and application. Are we entering another age of anxiety over something we will have little, if any, control over?

DEFINING ARTIFICIAL INTELLIGENCE

Artificial Intelligence (AI) has been defined as "intelligence (perceiving, synthesizing, and inferring information) demonstrated by machines, as opposed to intelligence displayed by humans or by other animals."[1]

In essence, AI is very sophisticated software running on extremely fast computers with access to incredibly vast amounts of data and knowledge.

The term AI was coined in 1956,[2] and the technology has grown from solving complex technical problems to influencing virtually every sector of society and industry. It does this by learning about and attempting to mimic human reasoning, analysis, and communication so it can support decisions in literally every aspect of our personal and business lives.

THE REASON FOR ARTIFICIAL INTELLIGENCE

Besides efficiencies in automating repetitive tasks, AI contributes to more accurate and reliable medical diagnostics and outcome predictions, product marketing, software development, self-driving cars, automated facial recognition, financial investments, traffic analysis and avoidance, hiring and firing recommendations, data security, and on and on.

AI applications can also generate art, poetry, video, research papers, and commentary, mimic a person's voice, translate speech as well as handwriting, and translate from one language into another. (Frankly, we could have used AI to generate this book. However, we used the old-fashioned method for writing: humans.)

The bottom line is that AI provides competitive advantages in the business, finance, marketing, and manufacturing worlds by generating process improvements, more accurate projections, and quality communication media by performing far more exhaustive analysis of

---

1 https://en.wikipedia.org/wiki/Artificial_intelligence
2 https://courses.cs.washington.edu/courses/csep590/06au/projects/history-ai.pdf

information and making it quickly available for human (or other computer) decision making.

THE DANGERS OF AI

Remember this quote: "To err is human; to really foul things up requires a computer."[3] Well, it's true.

World-renowned physicist Stephen Hawking had a more ominous warning: "The development of full artificial intelligence could spell the end of the human race."[4] As an atheist,[5] Hawking had no use for the providence of God and could only see things from an earthly perspective. But his concerns about AI do have merit.

AI is a tool, a very, very sophisticated tool, but it's dependent on data and information, whether it's good or bad. As AI continues to "learn" how humans think and act, it will continue to mature, but it will always be subject to what it's exposed to and how it has been taught to "think."

How will biases in hiring and firing decisions be prevented when so much toxic public and private information is available, particularly for someone in the public domain? Will policing decisions be based on the perceived human condition, or will criminal sentencing be based on a calculated "risk" of a person? And if so, what will be the margin of error?

Disinformation, "fake news," and political biases all feed into an AI assessment of "truth." How will reliable information be selected, and who will determine what's reliable, particularly with social media companies actively preventing alternative opinions and information from being made accessible?

AI can produce "deep fake" videos and speech to depict anyone doing literally anything. Once released into the cyber-world, how

---

3 https://listserv.linguistlist.org/pipermail/ads-l/2010-December/105077.html
4 Stephen Hawking's warnings: What he predicted for the future (bbc.com)
5 https://news.yahoo.com/stephen-hawking-atheist-said-god-151210108.html

will it be corrected, if at all? What if it happened just before a presidential election, for example, in the form of an "October surprise?"

How long will it be before the government or dubious tech giants start to create "social scores" to assess risk, political leanings, or personal secrets for people based on their writings, communications, monitored travel, associations, web searches, purchases, etc.? Or is all the above already happening?

HALLUCINATIONS

Unless specifically prevented from lying, some AI results are false since the data is only as good as its inputs, and much that exists in cyber-space is false, intentionally toxic, or pure conjecture. But get this: Did you know AI applications can have hallucinations?[6] In other words, AI can provide totally false reports or analyses that are not traceable to any specific source. Also, if one uses AI to translate a document from one language to another, human eyes have to inspect the new translation because AI can simply—for reasons unknown—totally mistranslate words, sentences, or paragraphs.

WEAPONRY

If the above isn't disconcerting enough, there's the issue of autonomous weapons that can identify, engage, and destroy targets without human intervention. Where does moral accountability reside when errors occur, or excessive destruction and collateral damage take place?

---

6 https://en.wikipedia.org/wiki/Hallucination_(artificial_intelligence)

AI AND BIBLICAL PRINCIPLES

First, God isn't concerned about AI. He knows all things from beginning to end (Psalm 90:2, 147:5), and He will fulfill His sovereign purposes (Romans 8:28) with or without AI. But like everything invented by man, AI can be used for either good (1 Corinthians 10:31)—that is, the things of God—or for evil (Jeremiah 17:9), the things of the evil one himself.

No matter how powerful or ingenious AI becomes, it can never be loving (1 Corinthians 13:2). It can learn to mimic love, but compassion and mercy are from the Lord (1 John 4:8), not software algorithms. For that matter, AI systems can never be alive, be self-conscious, attain sentience, or have common sense (wisdom), other than to give the impression that they have those traits.

Why? Because AI can never have a soul. It is not created in the image of God (Genesis 1:27) and it will never have moral agency or access to God (James 1:5). AI will only know good from evil, or emotions or empathy by extracting what humans have said about those things, but never with a human conscience (Romans 2:15). It may sound remedial to say this, but Jesus did not die on the cross for AI, to create a pathway for a relationship with God Himself. Jesus died on the cross for humanity. For you. For me. Only humans can have this unique relationship with their Creator.

The Lord is sovereign in the affairs of nations, and He raises them up or tears them down (Job 12:23). God may use various means to accomplish this, including AI, but it will be the Lord deciding the issue, not a rogue algorithm.

The danger will come when man places undue confidence in software to answer the ultimate questions of our existence, treating it like some sort of Delphic oracle, or worse yet, a modern-day idol (Exodus 20:3). If that happens, our AI will become no more than the ancient city of Ai—yes, that is the correct spelling of the city—in Joshua 8:28, where its name means "heap of ruins."

CAUTIONS

With the prevalence of misinformation and disinformation, trust in our institutions and sources of information is undermined. When the foundations of societal trust are destroyed (Psalm 11:3), we must be even more careful not to believe or forward whatever we cannot verify.

Clearly, accountability must be forced onto any use of AI, which means full disclosure when being used and prohibiting such things as targeting children or the vulnerable, or creating social scores of any kind. Whether governments can exercise this type of oversight effectively remains to be seen, particularly when rogue groups or nations refuse to agree.

When used in a proper trustworthy way, AI provides excellent opportunities for Bible translations, communicating the Gospel message while taking into account cultural mores, tailoring the truth of God's Word to the audience receiving it, and helping biblical research.

As a final warning, consider a statement from the Ethics and Religious Liberty Commission: "We deny that any part of creation, including any form of technology, should ever be used to usurp or subvert the dominion and stewardship which has been entrusted solely to humanity by God; nor should technology be assigned a level of human identity, worth, dignity, or moral agency."[7]

---

7 https://erlc.com/resource-library/statements/artificial-intelligence-an-evangelical-statement-of-principles/

CHAPTER 52

TRANSHUMANISM

Transhumanism is the use of science and technology to speed up the "evolution" of humans beyond their current physical and mental abilities to become far more advanced creatures. But, it's not just superhuman abilities that are envisioned, like the Superman and Spiderman figures we all grew up with. It includes the goal of overcoming any and all physical limitations, disease, and, most importantly, even death itself.

Trying to improve the human condition is as old as time. From eating well and exercising to cosmetic surgery and human growth hormones, people have tried to reverse the effects of aging and maintain youthfulness since antiquity. The Greek goddess Hebe, the daughter of Zeus and the wife of Hercules, served as the cupbearer for the gods and goddesses of Mount Olympus, and had the gift of restoring youth to mortals.[1] Hebe's counterpart among the Roman pantheon of gods is Juventas, from which we get our word "juvenile."

---

1 https://www.worldhistory.org/Hebe/#:~:text=Hebe%20(meaning%20
%22youth%22%20or,of%20restoring%20youth%20to%20mortals

In recent times, non-biblical worldviews have justified the use of eugenics, forced sterilizations, selective abortions, and euthanasia for those with a "lower quality of life" to cull "undesirable" people from the gene pool and prevent them from ever reproducing. The Nazis are most infamously known for sterilizing several hundred thousand people which then led to greater antisemitic horrors of euthanasia and eventually the death camps.

However, other nations were guilty as well, as eugenics blossomed in popularity around the turn of the 20th century. For example, between 1930 and 1970 the nation of Sweden sterilized some 60,000 people—mostly women—in an effort to reduce the number of children born with genetic diseases and disorders.[2] These secular, dehumanizing atrocities were an attempt to proactively perfect the human species, to supposedly make us less vulnerable to human disabilities or disease.

STRIVING FOR PERFECTION AND ETERNALITY

With the advent of genetic engineering, artificial intelligence, nanotechnology, artificial muscles and organs, genetically grown "spare" body parts, brain-computer interfaces, and even futuristic "uploading" of a person's mental state to a digital computer, the future appears unlimited in creating new forms of humans that would soon become unrecognizable. Some people have already gone as far as having their brain—or even their whole body—frozen (through cryogenics) to prevent physical decay until some hoped-for miraculous, future medical breakthrough that allows them to be "brought back" to life and cured of whatever they were suffering from.

In 1967, a clinical psychologist named James Bedford was the first person to be cryogenically frozen. His body—along with some 200 other brains and complete bodies—lies in sub-freezing temperatures

2 https://www.ncbi.nlm.nih.gov/pmc/articles/PMC1127045/

at a facility run by the Alcor Life Extension Foundation. For a cool $200,000 you too can be put in deep freeze in hopes that someday a cure or remedy will be found for whatever killed you.[3]

The lure of eternal life—read: the desire to become like a god—is, indeed, as old as humanity. Remember what the serpent said to Eve? Surely she "would not die" if she ate from the Tree of Knowledge of Good and Evil (Genesis 3:4). But after the Fall, God mandated that each man and woman shall die only once. Paul sums it up well:

> Just as people are destined to die once, and after that to face judgment, so Christ was sacrificed once to take away the sins of many; and he will appear a second time, not to bear sin, but to bring salvation to those who are waiting for him.
> —*Hebrews 9:27-28*

To be clear, there is no "medical resurrection" after being cryogenically frozen. That is because once the body dies, the spirit—that eternal part of us—departs. But transhumanism attempts to circumvent what God has neither sanctioned nor mandated: the ability to live eternally without the need for Him. Do you see the parallels today with what Eve fell prey to in the Garden? The serpent's deceptive tactics haven't changed—just the science and sophistication of technology.

Not only is this new wave of optimism gaining more attention and massive research funding, but it is being touted as a potential remedy to virtually all of mankind's current suffering. In fact, to improve on human biology is not only seen as compassionate, but virtually inevitable as scientists take on the noble role of "co-creator" in designing humans without the supposed flaws made originally by God. That's chilling!

---

3 https://www.smithsonianmag.com/smart-news/200-frozen-heads-and-bodies-await-revival-at-this-arizona-cryonics-facility-180980981/

THE ULTIMATE PROBLEM: THE "HEART" OF A PERSON

It's one thing to replace damaged arms and legs with prosthetics to recover what may have been lost in an accident or in combat. That is both wonderful and noble. It's quite another to artificially create a new human 2.0. As enticing as this is, it is ultimately fatally flawed because the heart of a person is not changed. By that, I'm not talking about the organ that pumps blood. I'm talking about the essence of our very being, our understanding, our wisdom, our basic emotional and spiritual makeup (Proverbs 27:19). Repeating, I am not referring to the physical organ, but rather the very "core," the "epicenter" of a person.

Since the Fall in the Garden of Eden (Genesis 3:1-19), the nature of every human heart is sinful and prone to wickedness (Jeremiah 17:9; Romans 3:10-18). We may be able to grow (or blend) new and exotic capabilities into our body or integrate vast amounts of information, knowledge, or even artificial intelligence into our brain with implants or wireless interfaces, but our very essence of being human will not change unless the heart is transformed. Scripture describes that level of transformation as being "born again" (John 3:1-16). Without a fundamental change in the condition of the human heart (Romans 12:2), what could possibly restrain new, superhuman abilities from being used for ungodly purposes?

THE INEVITABILITY OF DEATH

A second fatal flaw to creating a human 2.0 is the belief that mankind is physically perfectible and that the "sting of death" can be overcome by technology alone. God's curse on the Creation after Adam and Eve's sin included the inevitability of physical death for every living thing on the earth. Since this is the judgment of Almighty God on all of mankind, it cannot be reversed by man's efforts, no matter how creative he is.

It's one thing to develop modern medicines and medical technology to minimize a person's suffering and even prolong their life. But God's Word is clear (and to repeat): He has appointed man to live once, then face physical death and judgment (Hebrews 9:27). While medical advancements in history have increased the average life expectancy of a person by a few decades, they have not appreciably extended the life span (maximum age achievable) of the human species. This list of average life expectancies across the centuries illuminates the cumulative impact of variables such as science, diet, reduced infant mortality, and medicine:

> Ancient Rome – 20-33 years of age
> Middle Ages – 30-35
> 18th Century American Colonies – 28
> 1900 World Average – 31-32
> 1950 World Average – 45-48
> 2020 World Average – 72.6-73.25[4]

Can the average life expectancy keep increasing to some as-yet undetermined—and ever-increasing—number? Psalm 90:10 states that man may live 70 or 80 years if they have the strength. Perhaps with future medical discoveries our great-great grandchildren will all be able to live to the far extreme life span of 120 years that only a very rare number of people attain. But still, the unavoidable fact is that though death may be delayed for a few people by several decades—my mother passed away while I was writing this book, at age 102—it cannot be avoided. Death will eventually come.

The bottom line: 100% of all humans die. That has always been the ratio. And it will continue to be until the Lord returns. All the

---

4 https://en.wikipedia.org/wiki/Life_expectancy#:~:text=18th%2Dcentury%20male%20 life%20expectancy,42%20in%20the%2018th%20century.&text=For%20most%20 of%20the%20century,dipped%20as%20low%20as%2025

"eternally youthful advocates" who have claimed they were going to live forever have eventually died.

UNINTENDED CONSEQUENCES

It's one thing to have compassion to alleviate suffering in the world. It's quite another to replace our bodies with machines or genetically manipulated tissue, organs, muscles, etc. If "enhancements" can be made that are thought to speed up evolution to some higher, more perfect state of being, is this just a noble endeavor that only yields benefits, or is there a dark side to it?

Remember the old Star Trek nemesis called the Borg? They were cyborg organisms linked together in the form of a collective mind or hive. The fusion of technology and human components to create a super-being in that TV and film series foreshadows where transhuman concepts are leading. But because modern transhumanist thought is cloaked in noble intent, what could possibly go wrong?

First, think about super-soldiers, who would be permanently endowed military personnel with superhuman abilities in warfare, but with no practical purpose in civilian contexts. What about sports and the irresistible urge to create athletes with "features" specifically designed for each type of sporting event to maximize the opportunity to win? Or what about super-genius intellects, new gender types, or designer babies that are born in any color, shape, size, or personality desired by a parent?

Soon, different classes of humans—different species?—would begin to emerge, created either overtly for seemingly benign purposes or covertly by bad actors to accomplish nefarious purposes. Social classes would eventually come into existence based on their financial or political abilities to transform, leaving much of humanity behind. Quickly, the very concept of what it means to be human would become obscure and arbitrary, with inevitable "mistakes" during experimentation just becoming collateral, expendable waste that is discarded for the greater good.

Is this really God's intention for the human race?

THE PROVISION FOR PERFECTION

I met political strategist and media executive Steve Bannon once. I thought we might exchange some pleasantries. We did not. Without saying, "Hi, where are you from?" he plunged into a conversation about ideas and concepts. He showed me the tall stack of 800-page books he was reading and then, without warning, asked, "Do you know what all of these people (and here he inserted the names of some of the most famous transhumanism-affirming globalists) want?" Apparently, I paused a bit too long, so he answered, "They all want eternal life." I was taken aback by the aphoristic nature of his summation. But he was correct.

They want eternal life.

Why did I not see it before? What is tragic is transhumanists seem not to know that through Jesus Christ, they could have it! Isn't it a bit ironic that the very thing that technological futurists want to achieve by their creative genius—perfected human beings that will never experience death—is actually freely offered by the Gospel, and has been for two millennia? The redemptive message of faith in Jesus Christ being one's Lord and Savior is that when a person passes from this life, they will gain a glorified, perfect body (1 Corinthians 15:50-56) for eternity (John 3:16).

Again, we see how Satan's tricks never change. Is it any surprise that the devil attempts to deceive generation after generation and steer them away from the most beautiful thing God ever offered humanity: eternal life through Jesus Christ? Instead, he dangles the carrot of eternality apart from Jesus—a lie from the pit of hell.

The sinful nature of mankind is irreparable without the direct intervention of God (2 Corinthians 5:17). Mankind can dream about quickly "evolving" humanity and permanently overcoming death through scientific achievement, but this is no more than chasing fantasies (Proverbs 12:11). Alleviating suffering is noble (Matthew 25:35-36) and upholds the intrinsic dignity of the image of God in every human being (Genesis 1:27), but "perfecting" the imperfectible without relying on the hand of God is destined to create even more destruction and suffering.

VIGILANCE IS REQUIRED

With such immense implications for the future of humanity, government regulation alone can't be expected to adequately prevent irreversible and devastating consequences. Public exposure of the dehumanizing and moral consequences of many of the proposed transhuman technologies is critical to safeguarding the sanctity of life and the preservation of what it means to be human in the sight of God (Genesis 2:7; Psalm 8:4-5; Ecclesiastes 12:1-7).

Public debate and aggressive reporting on any permanent, other than remedial, changes to the nature of humans must be encouraged at every turn. Christians, specifically, have the unique opportunity to defend the intrinsic image of God that every person[5] has been given and to warn against scientists playing their perceived role of God in designing what they think will be a "new and improved" version of ourselves.

If we don't, who will?

---

5 "So God created man in his own image, in the image of God he created him; male and female he created them" (Genesis 1:27).

CHAPTER 53

CLONING

Making an exact copy of a living, or previously living, human being has been the stuff of science fiction and fantasy for a long time. But it turns out that God was the originator of cloning. How so? Well, identical twins are a genetic replica, or clone, of each other. When a fertilized egg (embryo) splits and begins to form two separate human beings, both these individuals share the same genetic material and have the same parents.

Technically, scientifically created clones are different from identical twins since they have only one source. The genetic material (DNA) is extracted from a cell of a person and used to replace the DNA in an embryo cell. This is called Somatic Cell Nuclear Transfer (SCNT). As the embryo grows and divides, its DNA is the same as the parent. Cloning isn't exact. There will always be slight differences between identical twins, and between a technologically created clone and its source, because the conditions in the uterus will have a significant impact on the development of the child.[1]

---

1 https://answersingenesis.org/sanctity-of-life/cloning/what-about-cloning-and-stem-cells/

WOULD A HUMAN CLONE HAVE A SOUL?

First, a soul is who we are as a living being made in the image of God (Genesis 1:27; 2:7). We are not just physical stuff. But would the soul of a human-created clone be any different from that created naturally by twinning? The short answer is that there's no biblical reason to believe the person created by SCNT wouldn't have a soul or that it would be any different from a person created through normal human reproduction. James 2:26 indicates that a body apart from the spirit is dead, so a "living" person created through SCNT may be a complete human just like any other person, and maybe possess an immortal soul, although there's no way to be sure.

But how God infuses an eternal soul into an individual person is not revealed to us in Scripture. We do know that God "saw" us before He physically brought us into existence (Psalm 139:16; Jeremiah 1:5). So, it seems natural that everything (life, the immortal soul, and the necessary genetic material to guide the development of the human body) is all present at the point of conception (Psalm 139:13-14), whether that conception is through SCNT or by natural twinning. Just to be clear, God is the only Creator of souls; humanity cannot create what is eternal.

ANIMAL CLONING

In 1996, biologist Ian Wilmut successfully cloned a sheep named Dolly using SCNT technology. Since that time, reproductive cloning has successfully cloned cattle, cats, deer, dogs, horses, mules, oxen, rabbits, and monkeys. Being genetically identical to the parent, these animals help the testing of new drugs or treatment therapies without having to account for variations among animal species. Cloned animals also ensure desirable characteristics are reproduced and that populations of endangered species can be increased to ensure their survival.[2]

---

2 https://www.genome.gov/about-genomics/fact-sheets/Cloning-Fact-Sheet

What is termed "therapeutic" cloning of animals is producing embryos by SCNT technology for the sole purpose of cultivating embryonic stem cells for experimental purposes only. With this process, there is no intention of allowing the embryo to develop into a whole animal.

But there are downsides. Both types of animal cloning—reproductive and therapeutic— are very failure-prone, inefficient, and costly, and also result in the destruction of many animal embryos before any success is achieved. In reproductive cloning, most clones will not develop into healthy animals, while with therapeutic cloning, there is no intent to continue growing the embryo to maturity.

With all the intrinsic difficulty and destruction of life, what may be justifiable with animals is not justifiable with humans.

HUMAN CLONING IS WRONG

Let's first ask the question: "What would be the reason to reproductively clone a human being?"

Would it be to scientifically prove that it can be done—i.e., "we can do it, so we should do it"—or simply to increase scientific knowledge? Would it be to recapture the "essence" of a relative or close friend that is dying? Is it necessary to demonstrate mankind's mastery over life itself? Does cloning create any medical advancements that cannot be accomplished some other way? Would cloning diminish the nobility of the human species by making life an arbitrary technological decision, as it is already with animals? Is it the only way to allow couples that are unable to produce offspring to have a genetically related son or daughter? Is it to grow replacement organs or tissue should the DNA donor ever need it?

None of the above reasons justify the unavoidable destruction of a large number—or any number—of human embryos that would be necessary to create a viable clone if it is actually possible to do so. The same is true for therapeutic cloning, where there is no intent to protect the embryo but only to use it to reap stem cells.

Biblically, we know that God is the determiner of the value of human life, not a person. We are made in God's image from conception (Genesis 1:27; Psalm 139:13-16), and it is God who determines the number of our days. Every life has meaning, value, and a purpose. To dispose of it for some pragmatic reason is to assume the prerogative of God while denying any personal accountability for destroying life. This directly violates Exodus 20:13, which forbids the taking of innocent life.

Moreover, tinkering with the unnatural creation of a new human life is experimentation with unknown and profound consequences. Proverbs 14:15-16 warns against carelessly doing evil and that extreme caution must be taken when there are unknown results from our actions. Not only is knowingly destroying life a wicked act, but even if reproductive cloning was successfully accomplished, the results from animal experiments indicate the cloned person would probably be subjected to harmful defects, deformities, and even a shortened life, not to mention the emotional, mental, and cultural impacts a cloned person would be subjected to (see also Proverbs 22:3).

GENERAL CONSENSUS PRESENTLY REGARDING HUMAN CLONING

The moral, ethical, and practical issues surrounding the use of SCNT to clone a person are so profound that even secular authorities have implemented restrictions, with many countries implementing strict prohibitions. The movement to ban all human cloning was given a big push in 2005 when the United Nations approved a non-binding "Declaration on Human Cloning" that called for all member states to prohibit all forms of human cloning. It states that human cloning is "incompatible with human dignity and the protection of human life."[3] Unfortunately, because the declaration is non-binding and didn't explicitly call out reproductive and therapeutic cloning, there's ambiguity in its interpretation.

To date, forty-six countries have passed legislation banning *human* reproductive cloning.[4] However, far fewer countries ban *therapeutic* cloning. Although there's no compelling evidence that human beings have ever been cloned,[5] the technology exists. And it would be naïve to think that all nations and scientists will continue to unilaterally restrain themselves from pursuing human cloning unless they are forced to.

HUMAN CLONING AND THE BIBLE

Even though the United Nations has voted against human cloning, what if they were to someday decide to vote the opposite way? We need a transcendent source—that which supersedes time, space, and culture, that which is always true, everywhere, that does not change. Where can we find that? The Bible.

For 2,700 years now, this has been a trustworthy axiom regarding human life: "But now, O LORD, you are our Father; we are the clay, and you are our potter; we are all the work of your hand" (Isaiah 64:8, ESV). In the New Testament, the "God-as-the-potter" motif is repeated (Romans 9:20-21).

Human life is something to be cherished and not treated as a commodity or a "thing" to be preserved or destroyed at will. Christians, especially, are in the best position to carry this message and to vigorously make the moral case against any form of human cloning until the day comes when there is universal revulsion against the cloning of humans, with enforceable laws that reflect that sentiment.

---

4 https://www.genome.gov/about-genomics/fact-sheets/Cloning-Fact-Sheet
5 https://www.genome.gov/about-genomics/fact-sheets/Cloning-Fact-Sheet

CHAPTER 54

GENETIC ENGINEERING

I f you hear someone say, "I wouldn't eat Frankenfood if it were given to me for free!" you might wonder if it was a new horror movie pitching some zombie dinner or a reference to a chef at a new restaurant. Turns out, this term refers to one small tip of a biotechnology explosion that's been going on for decades.

Once the genetic code of living organisms was cracked (circa 1953), and the technology developed to engineer individual pieces of DNA (i.e., CRISPR, that is, "clustered regularly interspaced short palindromic repeats"[1] and its enhancements), the opportunity to play god with new life forms was thrown wide open. Many of the early applications of genetic engineering (GE) had to do with food production, vastly increasing crop productivity, and making plants less desirable for insects to munch on.[2] Besides being a boon for feeding a growing

---

1 https://pubmed.ncbi.nlm.nih.gov/19521870/#:~:text=Abstract,may%20be%20
used%20for%20genotyping.
2 www.fda.gov "Science and History of GMOs and Other Food Modification Processes"

world population, altered texture, taste, appearance, and shelf life made fruit more appealing to consumers.

WORLDVIEWS MATTER

Not surprisingly, a person's worldview impacts their view of genetic engineering (GE). If evolution brought all life into existence over hundreds of millions (billions?) of years, then engineering life to better adapt to its environment or correct weaknesses is a logical extension of what's naturally going on already. In effect, GE is just a high-tech form of natural selection and breeding to create improved varieties of living "things" much faster.

The alternate worldview sees a God-created natural order for different plant and animal species, with potentially irreversible and catastrophic risks occurring by co-mingling genetic material and changing the very nature of life as we know it.

As intriguing as playing with life is, the bottom line is that science doesn't know, and cannot predict, what the long-term impact will be when new life forms are created. I'm not talking about a variation on a common theme like a bigger and stronger horse, I'm talking about selectively cross-blending human or plant or animal genes with any other organism to create a "living thing" that never existed before.

If you're concerned about a new strain of flu bug or COVID virus coming around each year, think what will happen if an entirely new disease, accidentally or intentionally, is created that can live indefinitely without oxygen, can kill humans within hours, and has no known antidote. Think rogue nations that want to kill as many adversaries as possible without affecting their own racial gene pool.

What about creating "designer babies" with features someone thinks are cute, like glowing in the dark or bright orange eyes? What about creating a super athlete or soldier, or the equivalent of dinosaurs again? Is this just hype? I don't think so.

NOT JUST PARTS FOR PARTS

The basic issue has to do with what we mean when we say GE. If we mean replacing genes that may be damaged in the DNA strand of a living thing with other identical genes from either the same creature or even a like creature (i.e., the same or very similar species), then that is replacing damaged parts with the same undamaged parts. But if by GE we mean splicing in genes containing unique functional and physical hereditary information from one organism into the chromosomes of a different type of organism, then we're talking about creating an entirely different living thing.

The latter process amps up the stakes on what could happen and what it will mean for all of us, whether it's a bacterium that now eats plastic or a cross between a monkey and who knows what. Visa founder Dee Hock noted how fast this could take place: "With the advent of genetic engineering, the time required for the evolution of new species may literally collapse."[3]

Interestingly, lots of controversy revolves around issues of who controls or owns the products of this technology, whether new life forms can be patented, who is liable if there's a catastrophic problem, and for what limits, if any, there are to creating "enhanced" human life forms. Even some environmentalists have concerns about the potential for new life forms to wreak havoc on the delicate natural order all around us.

Not surprisingly, the moral issues from a biblical perspective are rarely, if ever, even considered in these assessments.

---

3 https://quotefancy.com/quote/1556018/Dee-Hock-With-the-advent-of-genetic-engineering-the-time-required-for-the-evolution-of#:~:text=Dee%20Hock%20Quote%3A%20%E2%80%9CWith%20the,new%20species%20may%20literally%20collapse.%E2%80%9D

MORAL ISSUES

The first moral issue is that God created each living thing to reproduce after its own kind (Genesis 1:11-12, 21, 24-25). Genesis 1:24 (ESV) states, "And God said, 'Let the earth bring forth living creatures according to their kinds.'" The term "kind" has been loosely associated with the modern categorization called "species," but they are not identical. Biblically, "kind" implies the ability to breed with that same "kind." And what God has created to be separate is to remain separate to fulfill His purposes (i.e., not cross-bred with a different "kind"). Artificially splicing different genes from one organism into the genetic code of another organism produces a result that God never intended to occur in the natural world.

Mixing of parts (pig valves to replace diseased human heart valves) is not interbreeding. It is exchanging functionally near-identical parts. Repairing a damaged gene in a DNA strand with the identical gene sequence from some other organism is also replacing a part for the same part. It is not creating an entirely new life form. Plant hybridization, animal husbandry (Genesis 30:31-43), and other forms of breeding within "kinds" have been going on for thousands of years and don't violate God's fundamental wall of protection between "kinds." GE, however, crosses this line intentionally. And in a fallen world, the sky becomes the limit to what will be tried without knowing the eventual consequences years, decades, if not hundreds of years later.

"PERFECTING" HUMANITY

A particularly troubling aspect of unrestrained GE is to create a super, perfected human. What the Nazis were not able to accomplish with their selective breeding during World War II to create a superior human race, modern science is now on the cusp of doing by manipulating human DNA. Resistance to disease, genius intellect, superhuman strength, beautiful features, and selected aptitudes are all thought to eventually be within the sciences' grasp given enough time and willingness to dispose of embryos and "mistakes" along the way.

The drive to perfect humanity—which is unachievable since there is only One who is perfect—is a fundamentally different goal from efforts to alleviate human suffering. To perfect man is to make him into a "god," the pinnacle of evolutionary progress. In effect, man attempts to self-create himself into what he thinks is God's image. This is something warned against from the very beginning (Genesis 3:5), and will only feed man's ungodly desire to be autonomous from the One who gave him life to begin with (Psalm 53:1).

Will there be inevitably destructive consequences for "playing" with life? A casual reading of the Book of Revelation seems to give imagery to catastrophic events created by rogue viruses, bacteria, or new creatures with unusually deadly attributes (Revelation 6:8; 8:8,10; 9:3-11, 17-19). This alone should give pause to where science for science's sake may be taking us, especially when virtually no moral limits are applied.

WHAT SHOULD WE DO?

The bottom line is that man cannot anticipate the ultimate consequences of GE in a fallen, corrupt, sinful world (Ecclesiastes 3:11). In fact, Scripture tells us very clearly that the secret things belong to God alone (Deuteronomy 29:29), but the things revealed belong to us and our children forever. Going beyond God's designed limits that He created from the very beginning will not end well for anyone and will not glorify the One who created the natural order for our good.

If and when one has a choice between eating a GMO or a non-GMO food, wise is the person who chooses non-GMO. As far as creating new, exotic living things, God's warning about staying "within kinds" should be the moral marker that should not be crossed.

CHAPTER 55

SCREEN ADDICTION, VIDEO GAMES, AND CELL PHONES

T he relatively quiet pace of my life as a child would undoubtedly be alien for children in the 2020s. Life back then consisted of chores, play, study, and family time on a family farm. We walked or rode bikes to the country school, went to church three times a week (Sunday morning, Sunday night, and Wednesday night), read books (*Tom Sawyer, Huckleberry Finn,* and *The Hardy Boys*), had family devotions, and (age appropriately) worked hard. We used our imagination to entertain and challenge ourselves and each other and learned the interpersonal skills needed to survive "growing up."

FROM THE SIMPLE LIFE TO THE COMPLEX

In one generation, most of those activities would now be considered boring to the average media-savvy child of today. The question is, why? What has changed? Fewer kids growing up on farms had something to do with it, but when the television—in the 60s and

70s—became the center of "family time" and "entertainment," it paved the way for individualized electronic games—in the late 80s and 90s—that acted as convenient babysitters for overworked parents. Now, some three-plus decades after the invention of the game-changing Nintendo Game Boy in 1989, we have a galaxy of electronic options for kids.

But then in the 2000s something even more revolutionary broke on the scene. Smartphones quickly became ubiquitous. But it wasn't just smartphones, it was an entire technologically savvy industry investing billions of dollars to create *addictive* content that glued a person's attention to a tiny little screen for hours. Life became focused on a kaleidoscope of electronic color and stimulation, while close, person-to-person interaction became boring or was too risk-prone for "sensitive" personalities.

SOCIAL MEDIA IS NOT SOCIAL

So, where are children and adults spending their time? Currently, YouTube, TikTok, Instagram, Snapchat, and Facebook dominate the social media landscape for young people, with new media platforms being released all the time.[1] How can these handheld "portals" to the world hold such an attraction to so many for so long? Well, the hook is how the brain works.

The human brain is wired to seek out pleasure and comfort. With the advent of social media, technology has provided a new avenue for an instant and steady diet of entertainment gratification that is then reinforced by the brain producing dopamine (more on this below). The problem with this social media "diet" is that it is analogous to consuming fast and processed food, as opposed to eating a healthy, nutritious

---

1 https://www.pewresearch.org/short-reads/2023/04/24/teens-and-social-media-key-findings-from-pew-research-center-surveys/

diet. The result is more apt to end in a painful addiction rather than a healthy mind, body, and soul.

SCREEN TIMES ARE ASTRONOMICAL

Among the 7.91 billion people in the world (as of 2022), there were 4.62 billion active social media users (over 58% of the world's population). These users, individually, spent an average of 6 hours and 58 minutes per day using the Internet, with an average use of social media platforms of 2 hours and 27 minutes.[2] That's 11.2 billion hours a day spent on social media. To quantify this more meaningfully, that amount of social media engagement has the net effect of 280 million 40-hour work weeks that are lost each and every *day*. Think about that: most of this time is not productive in the sense of adding to the survival or well-being or improvement of our species. But is that a good thing or a bad thing?

SOCIAL MEDIA ADDICTION

The first step in assessing the value—or detriment—to society of this obsessive social media usage is to find the reasons for the extraordinary quantity of time spent on it.

A recent *Washington Post* survey suggests that many people already know they spend too much time on social media. In fact, social media and smartphone use are two of the top five activities where people feel that they have self-control problems (along with exercising, saving money and eating unhealthy food). But it's more than just a self-control problem. It turns out heavy social media usage is more akin to being "addicted."[3]

---

2 https://www.ncbi.nlm.nih.gov/pmc/articles/PMC9707397/n
3 https://www.washingtonpost.com/outlook/2021/07/19/social-media-addiction-social-science/

But how can we be addicted to something that is not from a habit-forming chemical being introduced into our bodies? The answer is our brain, and it produces a neurotransmitter called dopamine that is responsible for pleasure. The more pleasurable an event is to us, the more dopamine our brain releases into our body. So, you may not be habituated to a foreign chemical like alcohol or opiates, but you are indeed becoming addicted to the habit-forming properties that result from your own dopamine production.

In case you are wondering, social media addiction is not the first behavioral addiction that humans can have. Two quick examples are sexual addiction and addiction to gambling. Whether we ingest certain substances or engage in certain behaviors, our brain's production of dopamine either goes up or down in response to that substance or behavior. So, for example, chocolate increases dopamine above a baseline level by about 50%. Sex is about a 100% increase. Nicotine is about a 150% increase. And amphetamines are about a 1,000% increase.[4]

Not surprisingly, it is harder to measure the effects of social media addiction because of the myriad of ways that media algorithms work in, out, and around our ways of communicating. But by the sheer volume of social media participation, it is clear that there is a powerful correlation.

PROGRAMMING FOR ADDICTION

Is this phenomenon by chance, or is it a psycho-social model created by sophisticated behavioralists in coordination with Artificial Intelligence to lure people into addiction, much like the neighborhood pusher of heroin or meth. Congressional testimony in 2021 by Facebook whistleblower Frances Haugen said that the social media giant

4 https://neuroscience.stanford.edu/news/dopamine-nation-overabundance-keeps-us-craving-more

Meta (Facebook) was aware of the negative impact the platforms have on young users and that leaked documents show that the platforms had a particularly toxic effect on teenage girls, but the corporations chose profits instead.

"The defendants knew that their products and related services were dangerous to young and impressionable children and teens, yet they completely disregarded their own information," said Beasley Allen Law Firm attorney Andy Birchfield in the statement. "They implemented sophisticated algorithms designed to encourage frequent access to the platforms and prolonged exposure to harmful content."[5]

As *New York Times* reporter Max Fisher explains in his new book, *The Chaos Machine*, "Dopamine creates a positive association with whatever behaviors prompted its release, training you to repeat them. ... When that dopamine reward system gets hijacked, it can compel you to repeat self-destructive behaviors. To place one more bet, binge on alcohol—or spend hours on apps even when they make you unhappy."[6]

Kelsey Hansen notes in an article for the *Harvard Business Review*, "Fisher says that the notifications themselves aren't the problem. But they become one when social media platforms pair them with positive affirmation—those likes, follows, updates from friends, and photographs of family, pets, food, and beautiful scenery."[7]

ADDICTION ISN'T THE ONLY PROBLEM

So, what's the big problem really? If it makes people happy it must be okay, right? Here's what a recent Pew survey revealed:

---

5 https://petapixel.com/2022/06/13/meta-accused-by-lawsuits-of-using-a-deliberately-addictive-algorithm/
6 Fisher, Max, The Chaos Machine, Little, Brown and Company, NY, September 6, 2022.
7 https://hbr.org/2022/11/our-social-media-addiction

- More than a third of teens on Instagram feel peer pressure to post content that will garner likes and comments.
- Over 40% feel pressured to only post content that makes them look good.
- 13% of female teens say Instagram exacerbates suicidal thoughts.
- 17% said their eating disorders worsened due to Instagram usage. [8]

Other studies have observed links between high levels of social media use and depression or anxiety symptoms. A 2016 study of more than 450 teens found that greater social media use, nighttime social media use, and emotional investment in social media—such as feeling upset when prevented from logging on—were each linked with worse sleep quality and higher levels of anxiety and depression.[9] Compared with participants who used less than two hours per day of social media, for example, young adults who used more than five hours per day were 2.8 times more likely to become depressed within six months.[10]

Although there is a surprising lack of conclusive evidence between suicidality and social media addiction, the research clearly shows a significant surge in suicide since around 2007. The problem, of course, is correlation. According to a report from the Centers for Disease Control and Prevention (CDC), suicide rates for children and young adults have continued to rise for the last decade and a half, increasing among young people ages 10 to 24 by 62% from

8 https://www.health.harvard.edu/blog/a-conversation-about-reducing-the-harms-of-social-media-202111052632

9 https://www.mayoclinic.org/healthy-lifestyle/tween-and-teen-health/in-depth/teens-and-social-media-use/art-20474437

10 https://news.uark.edu/articles/55480/increased-social-media-use-linked-to-developing-depression-research-finds

2007 through 2021, from 6.8 deaths per 100,000 to 11.0 deaths per 100,000.[11]

EARLY HABITS ARE CRITICAL

Habits form early. Proverbs 22:6 tells us to train children well when they are young so that good habits will be with them for the rest of their lives. It is more important than ever for parents to invest themselves in their children and not rely on electronic devices (and later cell phones) to entertain and occupy their time. Instead of staring at a screen and comparing themselves to other people's lives, how much better it is to be productive with hands-on creative projects and socializing with others in play, conversation, and meaningful work. Again, Scripture captures this necessity when it says to not follow worthless pursuits but instead be productive (Proverbs 12:11; 28:19).

Scripture also says the eye is the lamp of the body (Matthew 6:22). Whatever we feed, our eyes will eventually fill our minds and our souls. Feed it addictive entertainment and social content that dampens the soul and life wastes away, much to Satan's glee. Feed the eyes good things, and healthy growth will naturally follow. May we and our children develop the self-discipline that Psalm 119:37 asks for: "Turn my eyes from looking at worthless things; and give me life in your ways." That will please God.

THE CHALLENGE

If a thief were to approach you with plans to steal either your car or your cellphone, which would you tell him to take? Likely your car. You cannot bear the thought of being without your phone. Are you addicted to your cell phone? The probable answer is, "yes." If you said

---

11 https://www.health.com/youth-suicide-rate-increase-cdc-report-7551663

"no," here is the challenge: Turn your phone off and put it away for a full 24-hour period one day a week.

Orthodox Jews turn off all modern electronics for Shabbat, from sundown Friday to sundown Saturday. Some evangelical Christians are following this example. I recently heard Charlie Kirk speak and even though he leads a very large organization, he shuts his cell phone off from Friday night to Sunday morning. He described how focused he is on his family and on relaxing and reading books. Frankly, when I hear a story like that, it convicts me.

In the spirit of the popular movie "A Christmas Story," when Schwarz dares Flick with the "triple-dog-dare-you" (a phrase from the childhoods of some of us), I challenge you to shut off your phone and put it away for a full 24-hour period one day a week.

PART V

A BIBLICAL UNDERSTANDING
OF CONSEQUENCES

How anti-biblical policies and beliefs have affected key societal sectors such as energy
and currency, and how the people of God can respond and act biblically.

When your judgments come upon the earth,
the people of the world learn righteousness.

—Isaiah 26:9

A BIBLICAL UNDERSTANDING OF CONSEQUENCES

CHAPTER 56

FIAT CURRENCY, GOLD, AND SILVER MONEY

When you hear the word "fiat," what is the first thing that comes to your mind? Is it the well-known Italian automobile wherein the letters actually stand for Fabbrica Italiana Automobili Torino? Most people have probably never thought about that word in relation to our nation's money supply. But financially, "fiat currency" refers to a government-issued currency that is not exchangeable for something of value that the government has, such as gold or silver.

DEFINING FIAT

The actual term "fiat" is Latin for "it shall be" or "let it be done." Not being made with precious metal, fiat currencies such as paper money only have value because the government maintains that value. Basically, there is no intrinsic value to fiat money in itself. It is just paper.[1] The value that paper money has is really only a reflection of how much trust people have in our government.

NOT ALL THAT GLITTERS IS GOLD

For thousands of years, gold and silver were used to reflect the wealth of a person. There was intrinsic value to precious metal that remained fairly fixed for very long periods of time. This is attested to by statements throughout the Bible. Abram was rich in livestock, along with silver and gold (Genesis 13:2). Peter said to the lame man, "I do not possess silver and gold, but what I do have I give to you: In the name of Jesus Christ the Nazarene, walk!" (Acts 3:6, NASB.)

But even in ancient times, gold and silver weren't always what they appeared to be. The government tactic of "debasement" was used to replace the precious metal content in currency with metals of less value, yet the coinage retained its same "face value," or denomination. This had the effect of multiplying the amount of currency in circulation but costing far less to produce. Even the Roman Emperor Nero debased Roman currency by reducing its silver content from 100% to 90%.[2] Not to be outdone, over the next 150 years later emperors reduced coinage silver content to 50%, and by 265 AD the amount of silver had dropped to only 5%.[3]

I have a friend who collects ancient coins, and he says the fall of the Roman Empire can be traced by a steady decline in both the worth and size of its coinage. For example, during the height of the Empire the classic Roman silver denarius was approximately 20mm wide. But by the time of Constantine's sons and onward, the coinage became increasingly smaller, with more bronze and much less silver and gold being used.

---

1 https://www.investopedia.com/terms/f/fiatmoney.asp, Accessed 11 August 2023
2 https://www.investopedia.com/terms/d/debasement.asp
3 What Is Currency Debasement With Examples (investopedia.com)

Fast forward to modern times. Prior to 1933, gold coins were legal tender in the United States, but the economics of the Depression led President Roosevelt to stop issuing gold coins and prevented their continued use as legal currency. Silver coins were eventually phased out of production from 1965 to 1969.[4] The United States isn't alone in this modern-day practice; the entire world has followed this pattern so that there is no common-use coinage now being made of precious metals, anywhere.

PAPER MONEY

For more than eighty-five years the United States printed one dollar "silver certificates" (paper currency) that could be redeemed for silver from the US government. By 1968 these certificates (as well as all other paper currency denominations) were no longer redeemable for silver.

So, what does that mean? It means that now money is only backed by the full faith and credit of the United States rather than by bullion, that is, gold or silver. Said another way, paper currency has no intrinsic value except the "paper" it is printed on, and what the government says it is worth. The "value" of our currency can fluctuate based on monetary policy, fiscal policy, the relationship between widespread supply and demand, the stability of the issuing government, and especially inflation. That is what "fiat currency" means.

Do you see a pattern here? Our coinage is made of very cheap metals instead of having any silver or gold content, and our paper money cannot be redeemed for any precious metal. The value of our money is not rooted in anything tangible, but it is legal tender—approved by the government for payment—for all debts, public and private, as long as public trust remains in it. Is that a big deal? Yes, it is a very big deal.

---

4 Debasement of Modern Circulating Coinage (pcgs.com)

THE RICH VS. THE POOR

When our government prints money without reconciling the amount of currency produced with the amount of bullion it owns to back it up, inflation eventually kicks in. As more dollars are produced and available to buy goods and services that are not being produced at as fast of a pace, prices begin to rise—basic supply and demand principles. The net result: our purchasing power begins to drop.

What happens when inflation increases? You know the result too well. The cost of everything increases, and your ability to "live within your means" becomes that much more difficult.

Nineteenth century Romantic poet Percy Bysshe Shelley said the rich get richer and the poor get poorer, and it's true today when inflation takes control of our economy. Generally, wages and personal savings lose ground since they do not generally keep up with inflation increases. Even though bank interest rates may rise, they will never keep up with inflation, so savings gradually lose buying power over time.

When so many lower-income families end up with less buying power, they end up with less money (if any) to invest in tangible wealth-growth things like real estate, or other investments that could help sustain or increase long-term financial viability. The wealthy, however, will still be able to invest in ways that provide a hedge against inflation—real estate, art, collectibles, stocks, and other areas that in the long run outgrow the effects of inflation.

One entity that benefits from creating inflationary spending is the federal government. Government accrues massive debt as it prints and spends money far beyond what it takes in from taxes. As inflation eats away at the value of money, government in the following years will be paying back its debts with inflated dollars that are worth less than when it borrowed the money. Biblically, this is stealing from those the government has borrowed from because it is paying them back with financial instruments that will be worth far less later (Exodus 20:15).

BIBLICAL THOUGHTS

So, what is the government really doing, biblically? Scripture says the Lord hates the use of unjust weights or dishonest scales (Deuteronomy 25:13-16; Proverbs 11:1). By debasing our coinage while at the same time printing paper money that is not backed by anything of substance, the government is forcing its citizens to accept currency that is cheapened year by year through inflation. And yet, the government acts like nothing is happening.

Eventually, this cycle will lead to massive economic turmoil and uncertainty that will impact everyone, especially the most vulnerable among us. The Bible reminds us that even an ant can plan ahead (Proverbs 6:6-8), so shouldn't our elected representatives at least be able to do the same and prevent the inevitable economic ruin that is coming?

Another biblical principle that is violated when government borrows from future generations by going into massive debt is that of presumption (James 4:13-17). There is no guarantee that the future will bring prosperity to our nation and that the resources will be available to pay off multiplied tens of trillions of dollars in irresponsible debt that our government is racking up today.

Debt must eventually be paid off if our government is to remain solvent. By stealing from the next generations of citizens—since they are the ones who will carry the burden of paying off our national debt, and they have no say in the matter—our generation will face a future where our offspring will not have the resources to care for us as they should (1 Timothy 5:4). Proverbs 22:7 says the borrower is slave to the lender. Our massive national debt is producing enslaved future generations.

We know that Proverbs warns us not to put our trust in money (Proverbs 11:28). Our trust is to reside in our Lord (Proverbs 3:5-6) as He promises to meet our needs (Matthew 6:25-34) day-by-day. That doesn't mean, however, that we are to ignore our responsibility to be good stewards of what we have, whether that is much or little (Matthew 25:14-23).

In times of economic uncertainty, as we are able, we need to influence our elected leaders to be good stewards of the resources they have at their disposal and not squander the prosperity of our nation and our lives by going into unjustified debt. For our part, we need to seek wisdom from above (James 1:5) and counsel from those we trust in where to put what resources we can into areas that will grow in value over time. Consider alternate types of investments as your income level allows—ones that don't rely on the vicissitudes of paper money (e.g., precious metals, real estate, art, etc.).

In light of the above, remember that even our currency reminds us where our attention needs to be focused when it says: "In God We Trust."

CHAPTER 57

CENTRAL BANK DIGITAL CURRENCY

L et us suppose that you stop your car at a convenience store and run inside to buy a bottle of water. In a hurry to make your next appointment, you pull out a $10 bill. But to your shock, the clerk refuses to use it. You must use a credit card. The days of cash are disappearing. What happened to your freedom to use cash, just as you have your whole life?

Your options now are credit cards, pre-paid debit cards, gift cards, virtual credit cards, cryptocurrency, online third-party payment services, and any manner of automatic electronic funds transfer.

Why bring all this up? Because of the explosion of ways to "spend" money, there is also a strong trend away from "handling" money (cash). A significant portion of the general public, 41%, according to Pew Research,[1] go cashless in a typical week. So, where is this headed?

---

1 Share of Americans who go 'cashless' in typical week continues to grow | Pew Research Center

DIGITAL CURRENCY IS COMING

The use of electronic, programmable money issued by a central bank is gaining a lot of traction. Specifically, Central Bank Digital Currency (CBDC) technology is already being considered by 90% of the world's governments.[2] If and when such a system becomes implemented (and it may be by the time you read this), private (individualized) bank accounts would be replaced by everyone having an account with the central bank. Cash, currency, and paper money, which allow people to conduct transactions in private, would be replaced by a cyber-based digital account. Convenient? Yes. But that also means central bankers would be able to know every transaction you make. In other words, nothing would be private.

THE CASE FOR CBDC

We live in a fallen world, so any new technological advance will come with goods and bads attached to it.

It's claimed that the CBDC approach to financial transactions is necessary to eliminate the use of cash, which in turn would dramatically disrupt human trafficking, drug smuggling, the dark economy (black market), counterfeiting, and any other illicit activity that thrives with the use of cash instruments. Paper currency would be completely replaced with a digital equivalent that would have its own unique number or even a "digital watermark" to prevent cyber counterfeiting. This is particularly important since modern copying technology is so sophisticated that cash counterfeits are very difficult to detect.

This is fundamentally different from cryptocurrencies like Bitcoin, which is decentralized without any single authority that controls it. CBDC is the exact opposite—a central bank controls everything about the electronic funds being used.

---

2 Gaining momentum—Results of the 2021 BIS survey on central bank digital currencies

CBDC MEANS CONTROL

To start with, let me ask you, do you have a lot of confidence in our government? Your answer may reflect whether you live in a conservative or progressive state, but recent history tells us that federal agencies can be "weaponized" against its citizens depending upon the political exigencies of the day.

Remember what happened in Canada when truckers protested during the pandemic? The government leaned on private banks to freeze the financial transactions of those involved in the demonstrations.[3] What do you think would happen if Canada had a central bank that everyone was required to use? Accounts could be frozen for any number of reasons at any time.

What about China's social credit score that calculates a person's or business' trustworthiness and then grants privileges or punishments accordingly?

Combine these two factors and unimaginable control can be exercised over everyone in the country at the whim of political ideology. Is your carbon footprint too large? Are you financially supporting organizations critical of the federal government? Have you been accessing websites that are deemed by somebody as "ultra-right wing" in nature? Have you been purchasing books that allegedly spread "disinformation?" Have you posted social media comments that condemn current woke ideologies that are sweeping our public school systems and businesses? Are you White and, hence, a "racist," according to the woke crowd, who doesn't deserve the same financial privileges as others?

Freezing accounts is one thing. Punishing savings accounts with decreased interest rates based on buying or contribution habits is another. Putting an expiration date on your digital dollar so that it will be "spent" prior to disappearing is not out of the realm of possibility to stimulate a sluggish economy in a state of perceived emergency.

---

3 Canada Ends Its Freeze on Hundreds of Accounts Tied to Protests—*The New York Times* (nytimes.com)

What about conformance to pandemic edicts? If a church refuses to comply with mandates, staff salary payments may be indefinitely frozen or financial penalties applied. The carrot and stick implications are endless!

But there's more. All electronic systems are subject to cyber-attack. When financial systems are centralized, it provides a big, focused target for the world of cyber-criminals to steal information or corrupt databases to create havoc. This is not a trivial concern, even for sensitive government systems.[4]

Finally, what happens when someone or some organization spreads misinformation, disinformation, or out-and-out lies about you? Government monitoring services could result in adverse actions being taken against your CBDC account until you can prove you were smeared. How long could that take? A very long time. Or maybe never.

CBDC AND THE BIBLE

While many Bible prophecies are subject to debate, one thing is clear: Oppressive, anti-Christian worldviews that despise our values would relish controlling the extent of our influence, particularly as the return of our Lord draws closer (2 Timothy 3:12). Having complete control over all financial transactions would be a huge hammer in the hands of those who want to silence followers of the God of the Bible.

It's not surprising, therefore, that economic means of control are very conspicuous in the Book of Revelation. Chapter 13:16-18 vividly describes a time when nobody will be able to buy or sell without submitting to the powers that be. Whatever the actual mechanisms are that will be used to bring this about, CBDC appears to be a significant stepping stone to bringing this level of control to fruition. If it were just a few autocratic nations who were considering this path forward, it would be one thing. But most of the world's nations are now looking

---

4 https://www.comparitech.com/blog/vpn-privacy/us-government-breaches/

at this financial transaction paradigm shift—and *that* should give us real pause as the world continues to embrace globalism.

Two more points need to be made. Any implementation of such an all-encompassing financial system is only as good as those who actually control it. Even if there are overwhelming reasons to take this path, in the hands of the unrighteous, the godly will suffer. Proverbs 29:2 summarizes it well: "when the wicked rule, the people groan"—not those that do the bidding of those in power, but those who refuse to bow the knee to wickedness.

Secondly, Proverbs 22:7 reminds us that the borrower is the lender's slave. But financial slavery can come from more than just an unpaid loan. It can come from excessive regulations and controls. When the state controls all means of buying and selling anything, when it determines how much financial wealth you actually have, or how you can use it, you become a slave to the system. You also become enslaved when the state can arbitrarily decrease the value or personal wealth or collect penalties for your "non-conformance" to the current political mantra.

The longer we can prevent this scenario from occurring, the better. But the Bible is pretty clear: The eventuality of something like this being implemented—to the exclusion of all other legitimate means to conduct financial transactions—is virtually guaranteed.

A PARALLEL UNIVERSE

We know the Lord will provide for our needs as the future continues to unfold (Matthew 6:25-34). In fact, His promise is that if and when difficulties arise and the temptation to conform becomes overwhelming, He will provide a means of escape (1 Corinthians 10:13).

Whether that means for the family of God to provide for each other's needs in a manner that doesn't require making financial purchases, time will tell. Does that mean having cash on hand to conduct personal business with others still honoring cash, basically continuing an underground black market of sorts? Time will tell. Does it mean bartering or some kind of "local currency?" Time will tell.

The Lord doesn't show us the details of the future because He is a God we can trust, and He tells us to put our trust in Him and not in the rulers of our day (Psalm 118:8-9). He will provide for our needs (Philippians 4:19), but we need to be diligent to plan for an uncertain future. I can assure you that alternatives to CBDC implementations will arise, so be looking for developments in the days ahead.

Finally, continue to pray, and know that the Lord will use these developments to strengthen the saints, the serious followers of God, and provide opportunities for the Gospel as the world becomes more desperate.

CHAPTER 58

ENERGY DEPENDENCE

My first wife, Carol, died of cancer in 2013. After a time of grief, I decided to sell about 95% of what we owned in an estate sale, to sell the large home and buy a small home, approximately one fourth the size. One of the benefits would be considerably lower utility bills. And it was. For a while. Yet after eleven years, my utility bills in the small house are now what they were in the big house a decade ago. Why? There is no way to sugarcoat this: It is due to the incompetency and mismanagement of our nation's resources by federal and state officials.

DEFINING ENERGY INDEPENDENCE

Everyone who drives or pays monthly home power bills has some appreciation for the value and cost of energy. Energy impacts our lives, every day, whether it's the volatile price of gasoline, increasing rates paid to power utility companies, or just replacing batteries in our flashlight. You can "go off the grid," but escaping the need for energy is a tough proposition.

So, energy is important. But how important? The United States Office of Energy and Efficiency and Renewable Energy states, "Together, energy independence and energy security enhance national security, American competitiveness, and economic standing."[1]

Before we go further, let's define terms. The United States Office of Energy Efficiency and Renewable Energy defines *energy independence* as "the state in which a nation does not need to import energy resources to meet its energy demand," while *energy security* is "having enough energy to meet demand and having a power system and infrastructure that are protected against physical and cyber threats."[2]

Though hard to believe, it appears that major political leaders on both sides of the aisle agree that energy independence and energy security are desirable for the United States.

How we do that, however, is another matter.

STILL ENERGY DEPENDENT

In 2019, for the first time since 1957, the United States produced more energy than it consumed, but we still import crude oil and natural gas to meet our energy needs. Why? Because the United States chooses to primarily produce "lighter crude oil" (roughly 88% of all our crude oil exports) to maximize capacity, and imports "heavy crude oil" to meet different energy needs. The bottom line: we remain "energy dependent" on foreign nations.[3]

Since we're not energy independent and secure, and we want to be both, what's keeping us from getting where we need to be? In a nutshell, foreign policy and climate change policy.

1 https://www.energy.gov/eere/energy-independence-and-security
2 https://www.energy.gov/eere/energy-independence-and-security
3 https://usafacts.org/articles/is-the-us-energy-independent/ https://www.eia.gov/today-inenergy/detail.php?id=41033

EMISSION FROM ELECTRIC CAR BATTERY PRODUCTION

The United Nations states that fossil fuels are "by far the largest contributor to global climate change, accounting for over 75 percent of global greenhouse gas emissions and nearly 90 percent of all carbon dioxide emissions," resulting in warming of the planet.[4]

The Biden Administration wants to entirely end the use of fossil fuels.[5] What's more, in their "Blueprint to Decarbonize America's Transportation Sector," they have a goal of "securing a 100% clean electrical grid by 2035 and reaching net-zero carbon emissions by 2050."[6]

Is that possible? Well, in 2022 the United States generated about 4,243 billion kilowatt hours of electricity. Roughly "60% of this electricity generation was from fossil fuels—coal, natural gas, petroleum, and other gasses. About 18% was from nuclear energy, and about 22% was from renewable energy sources."[7] This means that to end the use of fossil fuels, America would need to replace 60% of her energy supply with "renewable energy" solutions—quickly.

But it gets worse: the Environmental Protection Agency (EPA) has proposed a new rule to require 60% of all new cars sold in the United States to be electric by the year 2030. The problem, as the Heritage Foundation points out, is that China produces nearly all of the batteries used in electric cars as they source the minerals needed to create the batteries.[8]

---

4 https://www.un.org/en/climatechange/science/causes-effects-climate-change#:~:text=Fossil%20fuels%20E2%80%93%20coal%2C%20oil%20and,they%20trap%20the%20sun's%20heat
5 https://www.foxbusiness.com/politics/biden-fossil-fuel-gas-prices-promise-republican-study-comittee-memo
6 https://www.energy.gov/sites/default/files/2023-05/DOE%20-%20100%25%20Clean%20Electricity%20-%20Final.pdf
7 https://www.eia.gov/tools/faqs/faq.php?id=427&t=3
8 https://www.heritage.org/government-regulation/commentary/bidens-plan-phase-out-gas-powered-cars-all-pain-consumers-and-no

Let's ignore the China battery dependence issue for a moment, and assume electric vehicles become commonplace. In such a case, would emissions be reduced? Well, electric cars produce less emissions than gas-powered automobiles during operation, but the production of batteries—especially the mining of lithium for the batteries—produces significant amounts of emissions, not to mention all kinds of other impacts. *The Guardian* summarizes it well: "By 2050 the US alone would need triple the amount of lithium currently produced for the entire global market, which would have dire consequences for water and food supplies, biodiversity, and Indigenous rights."[9]

One more inconvenient reality check: even if it were feasible for America to replace a majority of our energy supply (more than 60%) with renewable energy solutions, "climate change" would remain a global problem since China, Russia, India, and Japan combined emit nearly three times as much CO2 as the United States.[10] Are they willing to take draconian measures to reduce their CO2 emissions?

GLOBAL TEMPERATURE UNAFFECTED

Would eliminating all fossil fuels actually help the climate? Research by Dr. Kevin Dayaratna, chief statistician and senior research fellow at the Heritage Foundation, has shown that even completely eliminating all fossil fuels from the US (while wrecking the economy) would result in less than 0.2 degrees Celsius in temperature mitigation by 2100.[11]

THE POOR

As Christians, we know God created humans to be of greater importance than animals or even the earth. Humans are the only

9 https://www.theguardian.com/us-news/2023/jan/24/us-electric-vehicles-lithium-conse-quences-research
10 https://climatetrade.com/which-countries-are-the-worlds-biggest-carbon-polluters/
11 https://www.heritage.org/sites/default/files/2022-06/BG3713_0.pdf

creatures made in the image of God (Genesis 1:27), and the only ones God instructs to "subdue" the earth and "have dominion" over it (Genesis 1:28). In effect, God commissioned the entire human race to be good stewards of the earth—not polluters, not destroyers, but benevolent users (if you will), accountable to God for the wise use and development of available resources.

Most environmentalists (and climate alarmists), however, largely reject God, refuse to trust Him with our future, and wrongly believe people are just a product of evolution in a Darwinian "survival of the fittest" process. Leftist and progressive climate voices tend to value the environment over people. Based on this reality, they generally have less concern for the weak and poor among us. So, they ignore the consequences of all-or-nothing environmental policies that will have catastrophic impacts on economies, societal stability, or even which specific economic segments of society would be impacted the hardest. Not surprisingly, when energy costs are driven (pardon the pun) through the roof, marginalized people with limited income are disproportionately harmed around the world.

All throughout Scripture, God calls us to care for the poor (Deuteronomy 15:7-8; Isaiah 58:7; Matthew 19:21; James 1:27). There are far more scriptural teachings on caring for the poor than caring for the environment. This is not by mistake. God did not simply forget to talk about the "warming of the earth" and the need to protect animals and nature. Are we called to care for the earth and steward it? Absolutely, and as we've already discussed, our biblical stewardship mandate regarding God's wonderful Creation is given to us in Genesis 1:27. But Scripture is clear that humans are of the highest value, and caring for the poor and destitute is of the utmost importance. Proverbs 14:31 says, "Whoever oppresses a poor man insults his Maker, but he who is generous to the needy honors him."

What's ignored in the energy usage debate is the remarkable improvements that have occurred worldwide in the global standard of living because of the access to abundant and inexpensive energy. Make no mistake about it, that is because of fossil fuels. Doesn't it make sense, therefore, that any major curtailing of the production of energy must be evaluated in light of the detrimental impacts that will occur on people compared to the minimal "improvement" that is claimed in "mitigating" the alleged warming of the planet.

As noted in another chapter, my wife and I attended the "Alliance for Responsible Citizenship" in 2023 in London, England, with delegates from 73 nations. Every single speaker on the topic of energy warned us that if fossil and nuclear energy usage is curtailed, and if governmental coercion for the present unrealistic quotas in solar and wind energy continues, we are going to see a staggering increase in global poverty, with an exorbitant cost that humanity would have to carry to appease the climate change alarmists.

Let's take a step back for a moment and consider what are called non-renewable energy sources—specifically, fossil fuels. Is there a finite amount of such fossil fuels present on the earth? Yes. But despite what you might hear from climate change alarmists, the supply is far from being exhausted. In fact, energy science experts and fuel companies are finding new deposits every year. The truth is, no one can accurately depict when fossil fuel deposits will be exhausted.

Do we need to find other sources of energy to power our nation—such as more efficient forms of solar and nuclear, geothermal, hydroelectrical, etc.—for the next generations? Yes. But currently our government—and globalists—want you to believe that the problem is much worse than it is.

ENERGY DEPENDENCE: A NATIONAL SECURITY THREAT

The current plan to make America achieve net-zero emissions will rely more and more heavily on Chinese products, including wind turbines, solar panels, and particularly batteries for global electric vehicles. Said another way, this is greater dependence on our greatest world rival.

If the United States capriciously and hastily eliminates use of fossil fuels, the void in the international marketplace for oil will be filled by another foreign nation—most likely a foreign adversary of the United States (China, Russia, Iran, and others). Will that bring greater or less stability to the world? You know the answer.

That's why fossil fuels should remain America's primary source of energy into the foreseeable future until other sound, practical, and biblically compatible sources are found. Eliminating them out of panic will have a negligible impact on the environment and create international instability (energy insecurity). Speaking of instability, relying too heavily on "renewable energy" sources will undoubtedly lead to inconsistent production shortages which could lead to blackouts and worse.

We need to create an energy usage plan for America that does not jeopardize our national security, and one that isn't driven by rash, leftist—and ungodly—global agendas.

REALITY CHECK

Is making America more dependent on foreign adversaries—such as China, Russia, and Iran—a wise decision that will lead to better lives for people, particularly the poor, around the world? No.

Are the proposed dramatic eliminations of fossil fuel usage, massive increase in dependence on alternative sources of energy, and the resulting unavoidable instability in economies and living standards going to improve the world's climate by any appreciable amount? No.

We trust in the Lord, but He also gives us the responsibility to be good stewards of the resources at hand to be used for the benefit of everyone. As discussed above, a viable energy policy would make balanced use of all available and emerging technologies to provide stable, cheap energy for our own use—that is, energy *in*dependence, while producing an abundance for other nations for their good as well.

CHAPTER 59

EXTRATERRESTRIALS AND UFOS

On June 14, 2012, my family and I were enjoying a backyard BBQ with our friends Jimmy and Vickie from Oklahoma City, who were visiting us in San Diego. Jimmy and I walked around the side of the house to the driveway to get something. It was around 7pm and as we walked to the driveway, we both noticed something odd in the sky to the north of our house. We conversed, trying to figure out what it was. My son Joshua joined us at that time. We were so shocked by it that it did not even occur to us to do the most obvious thing: Get our phones out and take a picture. In fact, the thought of a UFO did not really occur to us. We just thought, "Wow, that is so odd."

The object had the basic appearance of an old wooden wagon wheel, one like you would see on an old covered wagon. It had a sizeable hub with many spokes and a rim. (Sort of sounds like "Ezekiel's wheels" in Ezekiel 1:16, correct? Only, we only saw one "wheel."). It is impossible to know how far away it was, but I felt it could be about 10 miles away.

We occasionally see planes flying over, coming to land at the San Diego International Airport, and this object appeared to be a bit lower than those planes usually are. It was large—about the size of a dime held between your fingers if you hold your arm out fully extended toward the sky. When we first saw it, it was mid-sky, directly north of us. It moved slowly to the east, to our right. It was not moving fast. However, if it were 10 or more miles away, then it would have been moving at a significant speed.

As it continued east, it went out of view behind some trees. Since our house sits very low, we ran out to the street and up the hill to the right in an attempt to follow its path, where the trees were not blocking it. Unfortunately, we never saw it again. We were baffled. What was it?

By the way, my friend Jimmy from Oklahoma City is a psychiatrist. If I may inject humor, it is always nice to have a psychiatrist with you the first time you see a UFO! To be candid, I don't know if it was a UFO. It was certainly "unidentified," it was "flying," and it was an "object." But a UFO? I don't know.

I actually thought it must be some very strange version of a weather balloon, admittedly oddly shaped as a "wheel." I went online to try to find something—anything—on it. I thought Facebook would have lit up with "What was that?" comments. I saw nothing. So, we just dismissed it as, "Wow, that was strange."

Did we actually see a *bona fide* UFO? Or, to use the newer, more politically correct phrase, was it a UAP (Unidentified Aerial Phenomena)? I have no idea. And frankly, I have had little interest in the topic. However, given more recent Congressional hearings on the topic and the slow release of information on the part of our government, I am including a chapter on this most unusual topic.

AN AVALANCHE OF INTEREST

Even though my interest in UFOs has been low, there are plenty of other people who are very fascinated with the topic. With the leak of TikTok recordings made in 2004 of a Navy fighter cockpit which displayed the tracking of an unidentified flying object, a new chapter in the saga of extraterrestrials burst open. Confirmed as authentic recordings by the government, the official assessment is that these objects remain "unidentified." That's not a very satisfying explanation, but it's probably the best the government can do.

But let's go back. Years ago, a TV series captured our imagination when it opened with the line: "Look! Up in the sky! It's a bird. It's a plane. It's Superman!" The popularity of Superman (an extraterrestrial, by the way) foreshadowed an immense interest in space and space exploration—are you old enough to remember the USSR-USA space race?—and all things science-fiction (Sci-Fi). Now, we are awash in Sci-Fi movies, cartoon shows, books, toys, and even conventions that explore futuristic technology and the possibility of advanced (friend or foe) "beings" from outer space. Lovable or diabolical, the concept of aliens from outer space is now engrained in us starting from childhood.

UNANSWERED QUESTIONS

In a nutshell, besides futuristic movies, TV series like "Ancient Aliens" have captured the attention of many by re-interpreting ancient historical accounts (like Ezekiel 1:4-28) and past technological feats as the result of earthly encounters with beings from somewhere else in the universe. Credible accounts of aerial phenomena that defy physical laws have existed for a long time, but the number of documented reports of unusual aerial sightings, strange physical phenomena, alien implants, and even abductions have skyrocketed since the middle of the last century.

With "encounters" happening worldwide and little authoritative government clarity being provided, it's no wonder skepticism, paranoia, confusion, fear, and ridicule are commonplace. Did God create beings on planets throughout the universe that are superior to us? If there are extraterrestrials, do they want to wipe us out or save us from destroying ourselves? Did ETs start life on our planet eons ago? Is the government already communicating with ETs and waiting to reveal them at the right time so the shock to humanity won't be catastrophic? Are ETs covertly walking among us today, and if so, why are they here at all?

UFOS AND CONGRESS

Without conclusive evidence, speculation can run wild. Are UFOs and ETs from another dimension, creations of our own mind, from other galaxies, or from the future? Are they demons? Or angels? Could they be creatures that live inside our planet and come out periodically for unknown reasons?

Although hoaxes are very common, there are just too many credible witness accounts, both by people and by instrumentation, to rule out every encounter as being fake. So, something is going on, and our government's lack of transparency and questionable handling of UFO events for decades hasn't reduced our skepticism about what they do and don't report. Not surprisingly, then, theories of nefarious government coverups abound.

With Congress getting into the act to try and prevent public panic, you can be assured the situation will only get more confused. Why do I say that? Because there are only a few options available to explain the thousands of credible reports. Beyond the demons or angels explanations, either they are:

1. unknown aerial/atmospheric phenomena (hard to believe);
2. advanced technology possessed by "somebody" that defies the laws of physics (a serious national security risk);
3. or extraterrestrials from other planets (really a serious national security risk).

In the past, the government has been clumsy in claiming that this is simply a natural phenomenon. That doesn't sell any longer. The other two options imply we are in serious trouble if the technology possessors turn against us. So, if those are the only options the government is willing to consider, their best option is to say credible witnesses and recordings exist of "something" they cannot explain.

The bottom line is that our government—virtually all governments—are in a conundrum. The best answer for what is going on is that there is a spiritual dimension to it. But being secular, the government can't officially attribute events to a demonic or angelic origin. It's not that serious investigators and scientists are ignoring factual data. It is just that they're incapable of going against their naturalistic worldview (1 Corinthians 2:14). This is particularly disturbing since so many reports describe encounters with beings that are malevolent in nature.

LIFE ON OTHER PLANETS?

The Bible does not say whether God created living, physical beings on other worlds. The Bible does, however, focus on the centrality of Earth and mankind in God's eternal, redemptive plans. The entire universe—and that means the *entire* cosmos; that is, everything that exists, anywhere—was cursed because of man's sin (Romans 8:20-22). But God's Son came only to Earth, based on the Scriptures, to redeem His people, those made in His image here (Genesis 1:27). That atonement was once for all (Hebrews 7:27), based on all we know from God's revealed Word, and there is no biblical indication that it needs—or ever needed—to be repeated elsewhere because there is no need elsewhere.

If earthlings are the only entities made in God's image, then why are scientists spending so much time and energy trying to find life in the cosmos? With new, incredibly sophisticated observational technology, scientists are giddy over the thought of finally being able to discover evidence of any kind of "life" somewhere else. Not only would this guarantee a Nobel Prize, but the "scientists" would twist this to justify their false belief that random, purposeless, evolutionary "time and chance" brought life into existence without the need for a Creator God. However, just to be clear: wherever there is life, *God is the creator of it.*

ANGELS, DEMONS, AND THE WORLD BEYOND

We know that there is a spiritual realm and that angels and demons are real (Hebrews 1:13-14; Revelation 12:3-4). We also know that Satan can appear as an angel of light (2 Corinthians 11:14). It's not farfetched to believe that he and his demon followers could appear as "benevolent" entities from other planets to deceive people into looking to them rather than to Christ for salvation from the world's woes.

On the other hand, the more malevolent demonic encounters around the world (cattle mutilations, human abductions, bizarre medical experiments) are intended to terrify the demonic realm's victims, and destroy any hope they may have in this life of finding spiritual security.

LIFE BEYOND EARTH?

Can there be indications of life out there? Well, yes, there can.

But we need to be careful to distinguish between "indications" and "proof." Astrophysicists who are desperate to believe in a creation without a Creator will eventually find something, anything, to allow them to infer the presence of life on exoplanets (planets revolving around other stars).

I want to be very clear. Whether there are simple organic lifeforms of some kind or not in another world, my faith is not at risk. If God decided to create bacterial life or supposed "precursors" to organic life of some kind on another world, that is His prerogative. We are the only entities that God has definitively revealed to us that He has created in *His own image.* Could God have created human-like organisms somewhere else in the vastness of the universe? I doubt that He did since the Bible does not give even a hint of such a thing, and a generation of the most sophisticated scientific investigation has found zero evidence of life beyond our world.

Could other life form naturally? It could never happen. The transition from non-living material to something that is alive is such a profound leap that science has been incapable of demonstrating anything even close to it. It's far more reasonable to assume God's once-and-for-all creation of life here than to assume a spontaneous, purposeless, statistically impossible appearance of any type of life form anywhere else, no matter how simple it may be, much less the emergence of some alien superintelligence.

Another thought. If there are super-advanced beings visiting us from other planets, and they're brilliant enough technologically to figure out how to safely travel all the way here (defying current laws of physics), then why are there so many claimed extraterrestrial crash sites? I'm just asking.

THE CHRISTIAN VIEWPOINT

First off, as Christians, we can sympathize with the anxiety or skepticism of others when the question of UFOs and extraterrestrials comes up. We know the broader context and that the issue is more of a spiritual matter than a scientific matter.

If someone is anxious about the threat of the unknown, we have the words of hope that point toward the God of hope—Jesus Christ (Romans 15:13). If a person is skeptical about all the sightings and is paranoid about government secrecies, we have God's truth in our hands, which points to the "way, and the truth, and the life" that is God's Son incarnate (John 14:6). If someone is caught up in looking to extraterrestrials for help in this world, tell them how Satan deceives to destroy, and how salvation—eternal salvation—is only found through the God-man Jesus Christ (Acts 4:11-12).

Years ago, I invited Dr. Michael Heiser, a scholar of Hebrew and ancient literature to speak at Skyline Church in San Diego, where I then pastored. Among his many areas of expertise were extraterrestrial beings, who he contended were largely demonic. His knowledge caused him to be invited to speak at—of all things—UFO conferences, which tend to attract a rather unique crowd. He said to me, "You have not lived until you have given an invitation to receive Jesus Christ as Savior at a UFO conference!" My point for telling this, besides the obvious humor of it: In the midst of all this uncertainty—i.e., "who are these beings?"—we have much more important questions that can be answered: Who is Christ? And have I made Him Lord and Savior of my life?

Finally, remember, the real "extraterrestrial" will be coming to take us home. His name is Jesus Christ (1 Thessalonians 4:15-18). He visited us once to save us from ourselves, and He will return again to take us home (John 14:1-3).

SUMMARY

How we can move into the future without fear, trusting that God will guide us in our pursuit of bringing His kingdom to Earth as it is in heaven.

... and let them call out mightily to God. Let everyone turn from his evil way and from the violence that is in his hands. Who knows? God may turn and relent and turn from his fierce anger, so that we may not perish. When God saw what they did, how they turned from their evil way, God relented of the disaster that he had said he would do to them, and he did not do it.
—Jonah 3:8b-10

Lord, to whom would we go? You have the words that give eternal life...

—John 6:68

Just and true are your ways, O King of the nations!
—Revelation 15:3

CHAPTER 60

A REASON FOR HOPE

After reading through all the topics in the previous chapters, many of which are blatantly negative and discouraging, we need to ask the obvious question: Is there a reason for hope? The answer is a resounding yes. I am not being Pollyanna. Why do I have hope? Well, the short answer is because of God. Let me explain.

SEEING THROUGH THE FACADE OF WOKENESS

An uprising is happening. In the midst of woke insanity, there is an uprising of truth and sanity. There is evidence that people are coming to the end of themselves, knowing they have no place to turn. Even some leftists are questioning the wokeness of the culture.

They are beginning to say that we should not be mutilating the genitals of little boys and calling them girls. Or cutting off the breasts of little girls and calling them boys. Even secularists are cynical of calling mothers "birthing people" or saying "men can have babies." People know that is, well, just nutty.

When men don skirts and lipstick and read books to kindergart-ners in libraries, people inherently know we are experiencing national rot. When "prideful" people "parade" down the streets of our cities semi-nude simulating same-sex acts, decent people know this is wrong.

When someone declares that they are non-binary, gender non-conforming, gender fluid, transgender, bigender, omnigender, pangen-der, polygender, or any of the dozens and dozens of other preposterous labels, sane people know that they are spouting foolishness. When someone insists on telling you their "preferred pronouns"—including the bizarre "they/them"—intelligent people know it is lunacy.

People don't like hearing they can't have a gas stove or drive their car while John Kerry and Bill Gates fly around the world in private jets. Citizens don't like being told to eat bugs, while Klaus Schwab eats steaks. The population does not like being told, "You will own noth-ing and be happy." They realize that the religion of climate change worships false gods.

During the time it took me to write this book, DEI, ESG, BLM, and CRT have begun to fall out of favor. It is possible that in a few years, people who once embraced the wokeness of our culture will run from it, ashamed they ever spouted such nonsense.

People have grown weary of being called racists simply for being White. And Blacks are realizing that being told you must be a "victim" is ultimately racist in itself. Industrious Americans are done with being condemned because they are "privileged" just for working hard and keeping their marriages together.

When thinking men and women hear supposedly bright educators say, "We won't give grades anymore in school, as it might offend someone," or "2 plus 2 equals four" is racist, or learning good English grammar is inherently Eurocentric and racist, they know that irratio-nality prevails.

People are now beginning to discern that since so-called "ethicists" say that we need to have a "conversation" about whether *one can kill one's baby up to 30 days after birth*, maybe abortion and "reproductive rights" weren't such a good thing after all, and that these same ethicists paved the way for this type of evil talk.

When people watch students at elite colleges riot on behalf of Hamas terrorists, and then watch the presidents of those colleges refuse to say that calling for the genocide or slaughter of all Jews is wrong, the populace gets it. They see evil and recognize it.

People in America and many Western nations may be coming to realize that something is wrong. Very wrong. The world is on fire.

The human institutions in which they have trusted are failing them. Once highly respected institutions are now mocked, whether it is Harvard or the CDC.

What has happened?

As a nation, we are wallowing in sin. Sin is a violation of God's ways. But sin has a by-product: Wrong and harmful thinking.

Fasten your seatbelt, please. Sin causes irrationality. Sin causes one to become illogical.

Allow me to use the "Left-Right" analogy and say it succinctly: Antibiblical Left thinking is irrational and is perhaps an indication of mental issues. It is irrational for men to dress up like girls and want to compete with them in women's sports. Equally irrational is the fact that anyone could possibly defend these men by calling them girls and then supporting their competing against women. It is irrational for people to call themselves cats. It is irrational for a woman to want to marry a tree, or for a man to want to marry himself.

But that is bad news, and I promised you good news in this chapter. And here it is:

When it gets dark, the light is that much more powerful.

The darkness of this world is making people search for light. And some are finding it exactly where it has always been: In the Word of God.

I heard people at one conference in Europe—not necessarily people of faith—say that transgenderism and climate change regulations were "a bridge too far" for the general public. The citizenry is rising up and saying, "No." Even in the secular culture of Western civilization, there are enough vestiges of Judeo-Christian values left in people to cause them to want to return to biblical values, even if they don't realize that the Bible is the basis for the values they want restored.

THE FIRST REASON FOR HOPE: THE WORD

Therein is our hope: The Word of God. Follow His Word, and you will be blessed. I did not say you will be trouble free or financially wealthy, but you will walk under the blessings of God. Violate His ways, and you invite consequences upon you that are not good. There is a name for those. They are called curses (see Deuteronomy 28:15-68). Even if the general population is not stating it in the terms I am using here, there is a longing to return to saner values. And this means they are searching.

At the November 2023 Alliance for Responsible Citizenship (ARC) in London, the high-profile, internationally known organizer of the conference, Dr. Jordan Peterson, who was known to be an atheist only months or years before, spoke openly of his recent arrival at a belief in God and a personal transformation that he was undergoing. Another high-profile, internationally renowned thinker, Ayaan Hirsi Ali, shocked the crowd when she announced her newfound commitment to Judeo-Christian values and the truths contained in the Bible. Could these conversions be a harbinger of what is coming?

What is the answer for our nation? For our world? In the previous pages, I have tried to make it very clear: The Word of God. Throughout every chapter of this book, I have made the case that "God has the answer in His Word." It is stunning how relevant the Word of God is to the governmental-political realm.

I live with the understanding that God is smarter than me. And you. He knows how communities and nations are to be run. The pattern is in the biblical text, if—and this is a big "if"—you and I are willing to "dig" for it. You have done that, in part, by reading this book.

I praise God for His Word. His Word is so good for personal growth and development, for family life, and for church or congregational life. And it is also good for civil governance. My hope is not in a political party or a candidate, although we do express our citizenship by way of parties and people running for office. However, the answers for our nation and the nations of the earth are found in God's Word, the Bible.

But there is more. What makes the Word of God come to life is knowing the author. Let me illustrate. There are two types of people who will read this book: those who know me and those who don't. Those who know me as the author will have a more fine-tuned appreciation for the book than those who don't. Why? Because as they are reading these pages, they can "see" me and "hear" my voice. Don't get me wrong: People who don't know me can still appreciate the book, and I hope they do. But "knowing the author" counts.

So it is with the Bible. The way to know the author is to repent of your sins and ask Jesus to become your Savior (i.e., to save you from the sins, spiritual shortcomings, moral failings—basically the "junk"—in your life). Ask Him to take charge of your life. That means He becomes Lord. Ask Him now. You will suddenly "know the author." The Bible will come to life and be transformative in your life. Thus, become well "versed," that is, knowing the Bible *verses.*

THE SECOND REASON FOR HOPE: NATIONAL REPENTANCE

I want to shift from personal repentance to national repentance. Repentance means turning around—a 180-degree turn—and going in the opposite direction. Among other things, repentance means we become re-*versed; that* is, we once again embrace the Bible's *verses.* In so doing, we go from being *culturally woke* (in sin) to being *biblically awake* (obeying God's ways).

We are all aware that we have not, as a nation, walked in His ways. The previous pages have provided many examples of personal sins and national sins.

Even in the church, there has been disobedience, compromise, and capitulation. Some of the greatest grief I have known in recent years is seeing institutions, Christian colleges, and denominations that I once trusted, in whom I now have little to no confidence or respect. Particularly disappointing to me have been the so-called Christian universities that are now woke. (The good news is that some Christian organizations are not "going woke," but tragically, there are many who are capitulating.)

Some Christian leaders who were once willing to stand for such obvious truths as the sanctity of life in the womb and the sacredness of biblical marriage now equivocate and theologically "twist like a pretzel" in theological casuistry—excessively subtle reasoning intended to rationalize behavior—rather than straightforwardly affirming biblical orthodoxy. If this grieves me, what must it do to God?

Yet there is hope. How could that be? God is gracious. God is merciful. He is sovereign. I am not suggesting that the discipline or judgment or even wrath of God won't be released on our nation. It might be. In fact, we are already under discipline. But it would appear to me that there is a remnant rising up that "gets it," a remnant that understands that we are standing before a God who is holy, righteous, and just.

On two occasions in this book I have referred to the National Gathering for Prayer and Repentance, held in Washington, DC on February 1, 2023 and again on January 31, 2024. The reason I am mentioning it again is what I, or rather we, experienced there. Most encouraging was the fact that no one had to be convinced to repent. People saw the need for it. They understood it.

Secondly, people were willing to come faceless, nameless, without egos and logos. That is not some cute phrase. They came in real contriteness of heart. The members of Congress who were selected and asked to pray openly wept as they prayed and repented on behalf of their nation, fully aware that the secular leftist press would mock them for it. At the end of the two-and-a-half hours of prayer in 2023, one presidential candidate from a Latin American nation told her driver to go on without her, as she "did not want to leave the presence of the Lord" in the auditorium where the event was held. The 2024 event lasted five hours and included members of parliaments from Europe, members of Congress from Latin America, along with leaders from many nations, who repented of the sins of their respective nations before a Holy God.

There is good news to report. During the latter days of writing this book, I heard of several prominent organizations in which the board of directors rose up and placed a new leader in the position of authority with the directive, "Get this place back to our biblical values." We are witnessing some restorations to the things of God.

I have recently seen some denomination leaders rise up and do what they had never done: Hold an ecclesiastic trial and remove a woke pastor who began preaching heresy. One of America's larger denominations has recently had what some have called a "split." In my opinion, it wasn't a split at all. It was a division of the true church and the apostates. The faithful were simply forced out or walked out, created a healthy, spiritually vibrant new church movement, and are no longer "dragging the old dead body" of the apostates with them. These are good signs. God is moving in our midst.

DO NOT BE DISMAYED

Psalms 11:3 says, "When the foundations are destroyed, what can the righteous do?" It sounds as if when the foundations of the nation are being destroyed, the righteous people, not knowing what to do, are wringing their hands in confusion and terror. However, there is a Hebrew rendition of the verse that reads slightly differently, "When the foundations are being destroyed, what is the *Righteous One* (that is, God) doing?" In other words, when things look bleak, what is God up to? That is the question to ask. When it looks so dark, look for God's hand at work. Why? Because He *is* at work.

In addition, God shows us what to do, just like He did for the descendants of Issachar when they understood the times and knew what to do (1 Chronicles 12:32).

BLESSED NATIONS

Proverbs 29:2 states, "When the righteous thrive, the people rejoice; when the wicked rule, the people groan." Admittedly, there are many wicked people (that is, leaders violating the Word of God) in various levels of authority and rule all around the world, and thus many people groan in pain. Fortunately, however, there are some nations that have elected leaders who—knowingly or sometimes even unknowingly—choose to follow God's will. As a result, the people rejoice.

As we close this book, allow me to repeat what was stated earlier in the book: To the extent that a government *violates* biblical principles of governance, to that extent, human pain, suffering, and poverty increase.

However, to the extent that a government *follows* biblical principles of governance, to that extent, human pain, suffering, and poverty decrease. After all, "Blessed is the nation whose God is the Lord" (Psalm 33:12).

As the Word of God is released upon the civil governments of the nations of the world, human pain and suffering are decreased. This is, in part, the "discipling of the nations" (Matthew 28:19), the "Great Commission" that Christ admonished us to do.

Let's go do it.

ACKNOWLEDGMENTS

THE PEOPLE WHO HELPED MAKE THIS HAPPEN

A TEAM EFFORT

Every book is the result of a team of people working together. This book is no exception. Were it not for the people listed in this section, there would have been no book.

FRANK KACER

As I began this daunting process, there were no plans to have Frank's name on the front cover, since I was authoring the book. However, his support turned out to be much greater than I originally envisioned. There are so many things that would not have been included in this book, had Frank not been my writing and research companion. Thus, I created the title of "Assisting Author" as a way of honoring his contributions.

Frank is no stranger to partnering with me in writing projects. He helped me write what has now been labeled as the prequel to *ReVersed*; that is, *Well Versed: Biblical Answers to Today's Tough Issues*. As a board member to our ministry, which is also called Well Versed, he has assisted us in many ways. As our Research Director for Well Versed, he has helped us process so many theological-governmental concepts and has written extensively for Well Versed.

For this book, Frank helped on such topics as consent of the governed, election fraud, so-called "non-essential" churches, central bank digital currency, social credit and ESGs, the 15-minute city, Second Amendment and gun rights, transhumanism, cloning, genetic engineering, fiat currency, and gold and silver. However, his contribution went beyond merely these topics, as his "thumbprint" is all over this book.

OUR METHODOLOGY

Over an extended period of time, I selected and laid out the topics to be covered, and then submitted it for casual review to numerous people. In time, the topics were refined to what comprises this book.

We developed a large team of researchers and writers, along with some consultants. There were basically five steps in our methodology for writing the chapters of this book.

1. I wrote many original chapters, and then Frank would make his edits, suggested corrections, additions, and subtractions. Then the chapter would come back to me, and I would refine it.
2. Frank wrote many original chapters, and then I would make my edits, suggested corrections, additions, and subtractions. The chapter would then go back to Frank, and finally, once again, back to me, for tweaking or some reworking.

3. But there were many others (see list below) who helped in research and original writing. The first draft of chapters from them would initially go to Frank for his additions and subtractions, or sometimes total reworking. It then came to me for my additions and subtractions, revoicing, rewriting, or redoing, and oftentimes back and forth several more times. Sometimes the original writing had few changes. Sometimes it was totally overhauled, to keep within the scope and style of writing needed for such a book. Although there were a myriad of people who assisted, given that I did the final reworking of each chapter, I alone am responsible for all content (see more below).
4. Sometimes people were consulted who were not writers, while others did some writing and thinking on issues that eventually were not able to be included in the book due to size limitations.
5. As noted in Chapter 1, the Scripture references listed in parentheses sometimes, or often, do not specifically address the topic being covered by name. However, they are listed because they reveal distinct biblical principles that are applicable to the respective topic. This is an extremely important clarification.

RESPONSIBILITY FOR WHAT IS WRITTEN

A clarification is in order. Since I was the one to envision, launch, and execute this project, and have the final word on what was included in the book, my name is on the cover, which means I am responsible for the content. That means that if there is something incorrectly stated in the book, the fault lies not with the research and writing team, or with Frank Kacer, but with me. Simply stated, Frank cannot be blamed, nor can any members of the research-writing team. All of us have made every effort to make sure that details covered in this book are accurate. If we find anything that we perceive to be an error or misstatement (as often is the case after the first release of a book), we will do our best to correct it in future editions of the book.

There were so many highly technical topics to be covered, I needed this wonderful team to lay out the key issues, which allowed Frank, and finally me, to establish the biblical issues at stake on each governmental-political topic. Some of the topics covered are far outside my expertise, training, or full understanding, thus it was a team effort.

THE WRITING AND RESEARCH TEAM

I cannot state how significant was the contribution by this team. Without them there would have been no book. They are (in random order):

AUDREA TAYLOR DECKER, a good friend who has been involved with the Well Versed ministry from its inception, was still a teenager when she was part of a team of four that helped write *Well Versed: Biblical Answers to Today's Tough Issues*. She was assigned a number of difficult topics covered in this book, including homosexuality, transgenderism, authoritarianism, totalitarianism, globalism, the World Economic Forum, the national debt, and energy dependence/independence. It is not surprising that Glenn Beck and David Barton hired her for research and writing.

GARY CASS, a friend and colleague, a San Diego pastor, and an articulate political activist, who was part of the "team of four" on the *Well Versed* book. Gary is brilliant in the relationship of biblical truth and government, and was responsible for several chapters, covering topics such as biblical worldview, parental authority, sexual chaos, social justice vs. biblical justice, wokeness in the military, and others.

KEVIN McGARY, a brother whom I so respect, who I love to have travel and speak alongside. Kevin is a San Francisco Bay Area businessman and leads a remarkable program known as Every Black Life Matters (EveryBLM.org). He is a genius on DEI, ESGs, BLM, CRT, fatherhood (or the lack of the same), the feminization of men, reparations, and a host of other topics. He is an exceptional author and speaker in his own right.

BILL WELLS, a close friend, and the mayor of my city of 100,000 people (El Cajon, California). Bill is highly trained as a registered nurse and has a doctorate in clinical psychology, along with being a skilled musician (piano, guitar, saxophone, and vocals, and leader of his own 14-member band). He took the time from his busy schedule of running for Congress to write about homelessness, addictions (including video and cell phone addiction), the social contagion of transgenderism and other topics.

ANN GILLIES, Ph.D., is a Canadian trauma specialist, pastor, author, activist, speaker, rancher, wife, mother, and grandmother. Ann has dealt with so many topics, including pedophilia, child sex trafficking, and pornography. She spent more than 25 years in private counselling practice working extensively with trauma survivors, and now focuses on advocacy and political reform for the traumatized, those struggling with unwanted sexual attractions, and for the most vulnerable—our children. She is also an established author and speaker.

JOE INFRANCO, is an attorney and very close friend, and received his B.S. from Manhattan College in New York, and his law degree from the University of New Hampshire. He is admitted to the bars in several states, but most notably before the US Supreme Court, where he has been involved in some of the most high-profile cases involving religious liberty. Joe was able to help us understand the legal issues on such topics as infanticide, the marginalization of Christianity, along with cancel culture, and free speech. Formerly with Alliance Defending Freedom, he is also an associate pastor.

GABRIEL JOSEPH and AARON MANIAGO gave their expertise on the censorship by Big Tech. Gabe, a good friend, is a serial entrepreneur and founder of XODS Web Services (a private data center which provides safe and secure cloud hosting and services for those that do not trust Big Tech with their digital assets). Aaron is Senior Partner at Global Political Solutions based in Washington, DC, and former Bronx County District Leader 78th Assembly District. They have, among many other talents, led major public events dealing with this topic at the *Washington Times* offices in Washington, DC.

DAVID LEGATES is a former professor of geography at the University of Delaware, former Director of the Center for Climatic Research at the same university, and former Delaware state climatologist. President Trump appointed him as Deputy Assistant Secretary of Commerce for observation and prediction at the National Oceanic and Atmospheric Administration. His contribution on the religion of global warming was priceless.

BETHANY KOZMA, formerly served as Deputy Chief of Staff for the United States Agency for International Development (USAID). Having represented the United States to the United Nations, serving on multiple delegations including the United Nations Commission on the Status of Women and the Nairobi Summit (International Conference on Population and Development (ICPD+25)), she understands the complex issue of world population along with many other issues.

KURT FUQUA, computational linguist trained in linguistic analysis, semantics, and high-quality machine translation, is a graduate of Moody

Bible Institute, Illinois Institute of Technology (computer science), and the University of North Dakota (Summer Institute of Linguistics). Kurt, also a member of the board of Well Versed, contributed to the topics of pandemics, COVID restrictions, "vaccines," lockdowns, and loss of medical freedoms.

DR. RIMA LAIBOW, an M.D. specializing in Psychiatric Medicine, is a graduate of Albert Einstein College of Medicine in New York City. As one who believes passionately in the right of Americans to choose their own health paths, she has practiced drug-free, natural medicine for 54 years, and is the Medical Director for the Natural Solutions Foundation. She is also a global issues expert, who has helped us to understand Big Pharma, and who gave us two informative interviews on the World Health Organization (www.PreventGenocide2030.org). She is 80 years of age, going on 25, as she is so full of energy.

PAM HOLLOWAY, a nurse from Colorado Springs, with background experience relating to the military, particularly in Germany, is brilliant on the topics of food, famine, food supply, food chain, food security, and agrarianism. Her teachings for church congregations on farming and gardening are desperately needed.

OTHERS FROM WHOM I RECEIVED COUNSEL AND INSIGHTS

In many books, there are topics which, due to size limitations, unfortunately, have to be deleted or modified before going to print. Here are some who assisted us in the process: **DAVID STILWELL** (China), **MORSE TAN** (China, North Korea, Russia, and Iran), Greg Berg (multiple topics), **DAMIAN WILLIAMS** (wokeness in professional sports), **ROB PRICE** (wokeness in entertainment), and **SARAH SUMNER** (deconstructionism) were a few of the people who assisted us in concepts that, to our disappointment, never made it into the final product. **BENJAMIN PARRIS** (UFOs) the youngest on this team, who is actively working for American

Liberty, shared concepts on extraterrestrials, flowing out of a conversation as he drove me to the airport.

MARK NUTTLE, an attorney-friend of mine, who sometimes travels with us, and an economist who served under President Reagan, who is an expert on China, Russia, and many other countries, gave me excellent advice on many issues. **CALVIN BEISNER**, an American Christian interdisciplinary scholar and writer in the fields of theology, Christian apologetics, church history, political philosophy, and environmental ethics and stewardship, also guided me in this endeavor, and assisted me in this process.

DOUG TJADEN, was another one who helped me process things, particularly in the areas of food security and the economic reset.

THE KEY RESOURCE PERSON

PAM PRYOR, a very close friend of our family, somewhat like a younger sister, and formerly US State Department, Senior Bureau Official for International Organization Affairs, which included US engagement at the United Nations and dozens of other international organizations, received so many calls from me, while I was building the research and writing team. She was always able to help me find exactly the right specialist I needed to cover these relevant topics. She introduced me to so many, as well as prayed for me.

OTHERS BEHIND THE SCENES

DAVID HOFFMAN, who was my next-door neighbor when he was a teenager, who became an extremely brilliant technology expert, is a computer genius who is always willing to take (panicky?) calls from me early or late. He calmly and patiently handles my computer issues remotely, including when I was only three days away from my manuscript deadline. Praise God for David for reducing the anxiety I feel when my computer suddenly becomes uncooperative.

JEANETTE BRADLEY does not mind, with almost no warning, working late into the night proofreading chapters, emailing back and forth, even if the need falls on holiday weekends. When my 102-year-old mother, who could still proofread with a 100% accuracy, graduated to heaven, Jeanette, a successful businesswoman and author, picked up the "proofreading mantle" and carried on. **KURT FUQUA** (whose bio is above), with no notice, also jumped in and helped with proofreading. Given the shortness of time allowed, his wonderful wife **JANICE FUQUA** also took on a lion's share of the proofreading. How grateful I am for these three who were willing to work late nights and early morning.

TERRY BARNES, a guitarist, vocalist, and worship leader, is our remarkable web/tech guy. When I am trying to find things, I have previously written or taught, Terry is able to find them in a heartbeat, even when that means working until 11pm at night.

ALLEN INGRAM, a successful businessman, guitarist, and worship leader, and **TRISTAN TENG**, a college student and speech/debate competitor, are the behind-the-scenes tech guys on the World Prayer Network calls which I have hosted or co-hosted, many of them with **MARIO BRAMNICK**—about 350 of them thus far, interviewing almost 1,000 guests over a more than three-year period —who have helped me understand so many of the topics covered in this book. To Allen, Tristan, Mario, and those many guests, I say "thank you" for educating me.

WELL VERSED

JUDY GARLOW WADE, my sister, a trained psychiatric nurse, skilled pianist, who lost both her husband—Keat Wade—and her mother—Winifred Jane McHenry Garlow (mentioned on the dedication page) during the writing of this book, oversaw countless details while managing the World Prayer Network calls which, as noted above, helped educate me on many issues for which I have had no formal training. Judy has been my protective "big sister" and intercessor since the day I was born.

HOLLY SORELL, the busy wife of a doctor at one of America's most prestigious hospitals, and mother (including a special needs child), brilliantly and thoroughly assisted in so many of these calls from which I received my "crash" education.

TRACY BURGER has been my executive administrative assistant since 2007. She has had to effectively "manage my life," from the time we received the word that my (now late) wife Carol was informed she had cancer (only a couple weeks after Tracy began employment in 2007), and who walked with us through the six-year battle with cancer, the painful goodbye to Carol, my deep grief as a widower, the "restabilizing" of my life, my meeting Rosemary, the marriage to Rosemary, and the launch of the Well Versed ministry. Tracy is a "rock" to our family. And during that time, Tracy has gone from a newlywed to the mother of four beautiful little girls.

GIULIA GIAMPA, a skilled musician, equestrian, and marksman, even at a very young age of 20, has managed so many details of the Well Versed ministry, not the least of which is taking my material on so many of these topics and then formatting it and sending it out as newsletters.

TIMOTHY PETERSON and KYLE DUNCAN, best friends with each other, have been in the book business with high profile publishing firms for decades. They are the two, along with their team, who took the manuscript, edited it, typeset it, and turned hundreds of manuscript pages into a bound book. As an author, I have partnered with them for many years at various publishers for whom they have worked. Now it was my privilege to work directly with Tim in this process, with Kyle assisting him. Words cannot express the depth of my appreciation for them.

ENCOURAGERS

I had wanted to write this book for some time. However, the Lord put certain people in my pathway to serve as "cheerleaders," of sorts, to say, "Yes, do this." These wonderful people include:

GLENN CLARY, Liberty University Vice President of Strategic Partnership and Alliances, came to me and said, in effect, "You have to write this! We will help you!" He brought a team together to brainstorm, then sent me a check to help this project "get going." I am so grateful to Glenn!

RYAN HELFENBEIN, Executive Director of Standing for Freedom Center, and Vice President of Communications and Public Engagement at Liberty University, was always in the background, cheering me on.

PAULA WHITE and TODD LAMPHERE so encouraged me, saying, "Pastors need this!"

And finally, and most importantly, ROSEMARY SCHINDLER GARLOW, my wife, was the greatest encourager. She took care of so many things to which I should have attended, so that I could stay focused on writing.

She is my friend, my comforter, my counselor, my advisor, my lover, and my confidante.

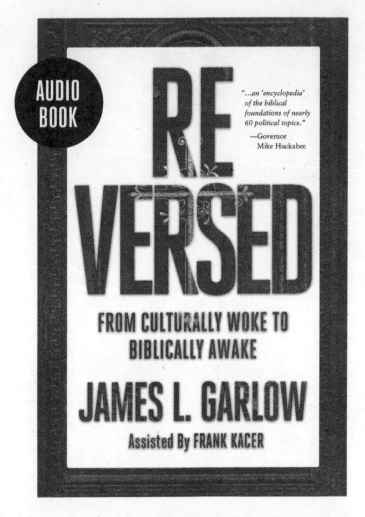

ReVERSED: From Culturally Woke to Biblically Awake
Audio Version
Like the book, it covers the Bibical foundations for nearly
60 political-governmental topics.

AVAILABLE AT
www.wellversedworld.org/store

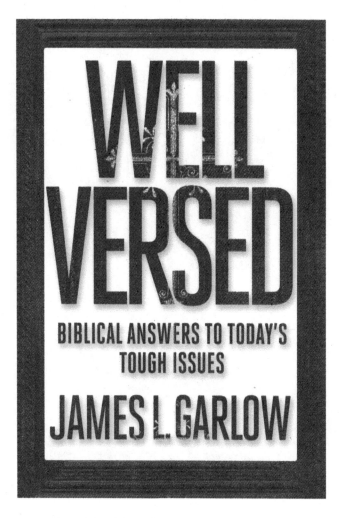

WELL VERSED

BIBLICAL ANSWERS TO TODAY'S TOUGH ISSUES

JAMES L. GARLOW

Covering the Biblical foundations to 30 political-governmental topics, including minimum wage, social security, healthcare, welfare, taxes and many other topics.

Complete with 30 short videos, one for each chapter, along with discussion questions at www.WellVersedBook.com

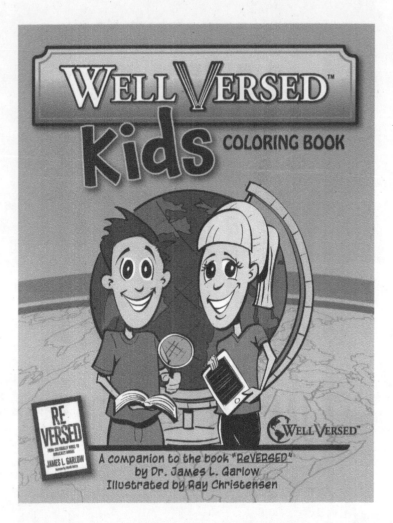

Along with ReVERSED: From Culturally Woke to Biblically Awake, there is special book for children. It is the Well Versed Kids Coloring Book. Each page of the coloring book corresponds with the chapter in the ReVERSED book.

AVAILABLE AT
www.wellversedworld.org/store

In addition, there is a special book for junior high students, titled Well Versed Students. Once again, the page numbers of this book correspond with the chapters in the ReVERSED book.

AVAILABLE AT
www.wellversedworld.org/store